The Future of Post-Human Religion

The Future of Post-Human Religion

A Preface to a New Theory of Spirituality

Peter Baofu

Viva Books

New Delhi | Mumbai | Chennai | Kolkata | Bengaluru | Hyderabad | Kochi | Guwahati

First Indian Edition 2012

VIVA BOOKS PRIVATE LIMITED

- 4737/23 Ansari Road, Daryaganj, New Delhi 110 002
  E-mail: vivadelhi@vivagroupindia.net, Tel. 42242200
- 76, Service Industries, Shirvane, Sector 1, Nerul, Navi Mumbai 400 706
  E-mail: vivamumbai@vivagroupindia.net, Tel. 27721273, 27721274
- Jamals Fazal Chambers, 26 Greams Road, Chennai 600 006
  E-mail: vivachennai@vivagroupindia.net, Tel. 28290304, 28294241
- B-103, Jindal Towers, 21/1A/3 Darga Road, Kolkata 700 017
  E-mail: vivakolkata@vivagroupindia.net, Tel. 22836381, 22816713
- 7, Sovereign Park Apartments, 56-58, K. R. Road, Basavanagudi, Bangalore 560 004
  E-mail: vivabangalore@vivagroupindia.net, Tel. 26607409, 26607410
- 101-102 Mughal Marc Apartments, 3-4-637 to 641, Narayanguda, Hyderabad 500 029
  E-mail: vivahyderabad@vivagroupindia.net, Tel. 27564481, 27564482
- Beevi Towers, First Floor, SRM Road, Kaloor, Kochi 682 018, Kerala
  E-mail: vivakochi@vivagroupindia.net, Tel: 0484-2403055, 2403056
- 232, GNB Road, Beside UCO Bank, Silpukhuri, Guwahati 781 003
  E-mail: vivaguwahati@vivagroupindia.net, Tel: 0361-2666386

www.vivagroupindia.com

Published by arrangement with
Cambridge International Science Publishing
7, Meadow Walk, Great Abington
Cambridge CB1 6AZ, UK

ISBN : 978-81-309-1997-3

Published by Vinod Vasishtha for Viva Books Private Limited, 4737/23, Ansari Road, Daryaganj, New Delhi-110 002. Printed and bound by Syndicate Binders, Noida.

To Those in the Future World Beyond Sacredness and Secularness

BOOKS ALSO BY PETER BAOFU

Category I: Social Sciences and Related Fields

- 35. *The Future of Post-Human War and Peace* (2010)
- 34. *The Future of Post-Human Law* (2010)
- 33. *The Future of Post-Human Organization* (2009)
- 32. *The Future of Post-Human Mass Media* (2009)
- 31. *The Rise of Authoritarian Liberal Democracy* (2007)
- 30. *Beyond the World of Titans, and the Remaking of World Order* (2007)
- 29. *Beyond Capitalism to Post-Capitalism* (2005)
- 28. Volume 1: *Beyond Democracy to Post-Democracy* (2004)
- 27. Volume 2: *Beyond Democracy to Post-Democracy* (2004)
- 26. *The Future of Capitalism and Democracy* (2002)

Category II: Natural Sciences and Related Fields

- 25. *The Future of Post-Human Geology* (2010)
- 24. *Beyond Cosmology to Post-Cosmology* (2010)
- 23. *The Future of Post-Human Personality* (2010)
- 22. *The Future of Post-Human Sexuality* (2010)
- 21. *The Future of Post-Human Urban Planning* (2009)
- 20. *The Future of Post-Human Engineering* (2009)
- 19. *The Future of Post-Human Unconsciousness* (2008)
- 18. *The Future of Complexity* (2007)
- 17. *Beyond Nature and Nurture* (2006)
- 16. *The Future of Post-Human Space-Time* (2006)
- 15. *The Future of Post-Human Consciousness* (2004)

Category III: Formal Sciences and Related Fields

- 14. *The Future of Post-Human Formal Science* (2010)
- 13. *The Future of Post-Human Language* (2009)
- 12. *The Future of Post-Human Geometry* (2009)
- 11. *The Future of Post-Human Mathematical Logic* (2008)
- 10. *The Future of Information Architecture* (2008)

Category IV: The Humanities and Related Fields

- 9. *The Future of Post-Human Chess* (2010)
- 8. *Beyond Ethics to Post-Ethics* (2010)
- 7. *The Future of Post-Human Martial Arts* (2009)
- 6. *The Future of Post-Human Creative Thinking* (2009)
- 5. *The Future of Post-Human Knowledge* (2008)
- 4. *The Future of Aesthetic Experience* (2007)
- 3. *Beyond Civilization to Post-Civilization* (2006)
- 2. Volume 1: *The Future of Human Civilization* (2000)
- 1. Volume 2: *The Future of Human Civilization* (2000)

CONTENTS

Part Three: Secularness

Part Four: Conclusion

TABLES

Category III: Visions on the Mind

Category IV: Visions on History

Category VII. Visions on Society (Socio-Political)

Category VIII. Visions on Society (Socio-Economic)

Category IX: Visions on Culture

FOREWORD

Religion is admittedly one of the most contentious topics in the history of humankind. The contention can range from mild disagreements between friends to persecutions and full-scale wars that continue unabatedly to the present day, and humanity has been unsuccessful in resolving its religious battles.

Dr. Peter Baofu brings a ray of understanding to this contentious topic by examining the elements that make it so. He also posits a fascinating way to make it less contentious and offers a vision of its future direction. His research represents a significant step forward in addressing a hot topic.

It is hoped that other researchers will be motivated by this book, to take this exploration further.

Sylvan Von Burg
School of Business
George Washington University

ACKNOWLEDGMENTS

Like all other previous books of mine, this one is written to challenge conventional wisdom and to replace it with an original way of thinking—or more specifically in the current context, a new theory to understand the future fate of religion.

Consequently, this book receives no external funding nor help from any formal organization or institution, because of its political incorrectness—as this is something that I often emphasized in all my previous books.

My only reward is that joyful wonder of something new not thought of before in history.

In addition, I greatly appreciate the foreword by Sylvan von Burg at George Washington University School of Business.

In any event, and as always, I bear the sole responsibility for the ideas presented in this book.

ABBREVIATIONS

ALD = Peter Baofu. 2007. *The Rise of Authoritarian Liberal Democracy: A Preface to a New Theory of Comparative Political Systems*. Cambridge, England: Cambridge Scholars Publishing, Ltd.

BCIV = Peter Baofu. 2006. *Beyond Civilization to Post-Civilization: Conceiving a Better Model of Life Settlement to Supersede Civilization*. NY: Peter Lang Publishing, Inc.

BCPC = Peter Baofu. 2005. *Beyond Capitalism to Post-Capitalism: Conceiving a Better Model of Wealth Acquisition to Supersede Capitalism*. NY: The Edwin Mellen Press.

BCOS = Peter Baofu. 2010. *Beyond Cosmology to Post-Cosmology: A Preface to a New Theory of Different Worlds*. Cambridge, England: Cambridge International Science Publishing, Ltd.

BDPD1 = Peter Baofu. 2004. Volume 1. *Beyond Democracy to Post-Democracy: Conceiving a Better Model of Governance to Supersede Democracy*. NY: The Edwin Mellen Press.

BDPD2 = Peter Baofu. 2004. Volume 2. *Beyond Democracy to Post-Democracy: Conceiving a Better Model of Governance to Supersede Democracy*. NY: The Edwin Mellen Press.

BEPE = Peter Baofu. 2010. *Beyond Ethics to Post-Ethics: A Preface to a New Theory of Morality and Immorality*. Charlotte, NC: Infomration Age Publishing.

BNN = Peter Baofu. 2006. *Beyond Nature and Nurture: Conceivng a Better Way to Understand Genes and Memes*. Cambridge, England: Cambridge Scholars Publishing, Ltd.

BWT = Peter Baofu. 2007. *Beyond the World of Titans, and the Renaking of World Order: A Preface to a New Logic of Empire-Building*. Cambridge, England: Cambridge Scholars Publishing, Ltd.

FAE = Peter Baofu. 2007. *The Future of Aesthetic Experience: Conceiving a Better Way to Understand Beauty, Ugliness and the Rest*. Cambridge, England: Cambridge Scholars Publishing, Ltd.

FC = Peter Baofu. 2007. *The Future of Complexity: Conceiving a Better Way to Understand Order and Chaos.* London, United Kingdom: World Scientific Publishing Co.

FCD = Peter Baofu. 2002. *The Future of Capitalism and Democracy.* MD: The University Press of America.

FHC1 = Peter Baofu. 2000. Volume 1. *The Future of Human Civilization.* NY: The Edwin Mellen Press.

FHC2 = Peter Baofu. 2000. Volume 2. *The Future of Human Civilization.* NY: The Edwin Mellen Press.

FIA = Peter Baofu. 2008. *The Future of Information Architecture: Conceiving a Better Way to Understand Taxonomy, Network, and Intelligence.* Oxford, England: Chandos Publishing (Oxford) Limited.

FPHC = Peter Baofu. 2004. *The Future of Post-Human Consciousness.* NY: The Edwin Mellen Press.

FPHCHESS = Peter Baofu. 2010. *The Future of Post-Human Chess: A Preface to a New Theory of Tactics and Strategy.* Cambridge, England: Cambridge International Science Publishing, Ltd.

FPHCT = Peter Baofu. 2009. *The Future of Post-Human Creative Thinking: A Preface to a New Theory of Invention and Innovation.* Cambridge, England: Cambridge Scholars Publishing, Ltd.

FPHE = Peter Baofu. 2009. *The Future of Post-Human Engineering: A Preface to a New Theory of Technology.* Cambridge, England: Cambridge Scholars Publishing, Ltd.

FPHFS = Peter Baofu. 2010. *The Future of Post-Human Formal Science: A Preface to a New Theory of Abstraction and Application.* Cambridge, England: Cambridge Scholars Publishing, Ltd.

FPHG = Peter Baofu. 2009. *The Future of Post-Human Geometry: A Preface to a New Theory of Infinity, Symmetry, and Dimensionality.* Cambridge, England: Cambridge Scholars Publishing, Ltd.

FPHGEOL = Peter Baofu. 2010. *The Future of Post-Human Geology: A Preface to a New Theory of Statics and Dynamics.* Cambridge, England: Cambridge International Science Publishing, Ltd.

FPHK = Peter Baofu. 2008. *The Future of Post-Human Knowledge: A Preface to a New Theory of Methodology and Ontology.* Oxford, England: Chandos Publishing (Oxford) Limited.

FPHL = Peter Baofu. 2009. *The Future of Post-Human Language: A Preface to a New Theory of Structure, Context, and Learning.* Cambridge, England: Cambridge Scholars Publishing, Ltd.

FPHLAW = Peter Baofu. 2010. *The Future of Post-Human Law: A Preface to a New Theory of Necessity, Contingency, and Justice.* Cambridge, England: Cambridge Scholars Publishing, Ltd.

FPHMA = Peter Baofu. 2009. *The Future of Post-Human Martial Arts: A Preface to a New Theory of the Body and Spirit of Warriors.* Cambridge, England: Cambridge Scholars Publishing, Ltd.

FPHML = Peter Baofu. 2008. *The Future of Post-Human Mathematical Logic: A Preface to a New Theory of Rationality.* Cambridge, England: Cambridge Scholars Publishing, Ltd.

FPHMM = Peter Baofu. 2009. *The Future of Post-Human Mass Media: A Preface to a New Theory of Technology.* Cambridge, England: Cambridge Scholars Publishing, Ltd.

FPHO = Peter Baofu. 2009. *The Future of Post-Human Organization: A Preface to a New Theory of Communication, Decision-Making, and Leadership.*.Cambridge, England: Cambridge Scholars Publishing, Ltd.

FPHP = Peter Baofu. 2010. *The Future of Post-Human Personality: A Preface to a New Theory of Normality and Abnormality.* Cambridge, England: Cambridge International Science Publishing, Ltd.

FPHR = Peter Baofu. 2010. *The Future of Post-Human Religion: A Preface to a New Theory of Spirituality.* Cambridge, England: Cambridge International Science Publishing, Ltd.

FPHS = Peter Baofu. 2010. *The Future of Post-Human Sexuality: A Preface to a New Theory of the Body and Spirit of Love-Makers.* Cambridge, England: Cambridge Scholars Publishing, Ltd.

FPHST = Peter Baofu. 2006. *The Future of Post-Human Space-Time: Conceivng a Better Way to Understand Space and Time.* New York: Peter Lang Publishing, Inc.

FPHU = Peter Baofu. 2008. *The Future of Post-Human Unconsciousness: A Preface to a New Theory of Anomalous Experience.* Cambridge, England: Cambridge Scholars Publishing, Ltd.

FPHUP = Peter Baofu. 2009. *The Future of Post-Human Urban Planning: A Preface to a New Theory of Density, Void, and Sustainability.* Cambridge, England: Cambridge Scholars Publishing, Ltd.

FPHWP = Peter Baofu. 2010. *The Future of Post-Human War and Peace: A Preface to a New Theory of Aggression and Pacificity.* Cambridge, England: Cambridge Scholars Publishing, Ltd.

• Part One •

Introduction

CHAPTER 1
INTRODUCTION—THE AWE OF RELIGION

> I expect to live to see the evaporation of the powerful mystique of religion. I think that in about twenty-five years almost all religions will have evolved into very different phenomena, so much so that in most quarters religion will no longer command the awe it does today.
> —Daniel Dennett (2007)

The Secular Underestimation of Religion

Is the awe of religion really so declining that, in this day and age of ours, there is even this premature prediction by a known scholar in 2007 that "in about twenty-five years almost all religions will have evolved into very different phenomena, so much so that in most quarters religion will no longer command the awe it does today"?

The secular underestimation of religion in this premature prediction can be contrasted with an opposing idea back in the old days, when Francois-Marie Arouet Voltaire once sarcastically said that "[i]f God did not exist, it would be necessary to invent Him." (A. Rocco 2007)

Contrary to the two opposing sides of this debate on the future of religion (and other views as will be discussed in the book), the promise of secularness (on one side of the fence) and the importance of sacredness (on the other side of the fence) are neither possible nor desirable to the extent that their respective ideologues would like us to believe.

But one should not misconstrue this challenge to the two contrastive versions of the conventional wisdom on the future of religion (and other views as will be clear later) as a suggestion that religion is an useless field of study, or that other fields of study (related to religion) like philosophy, psychology, biology, or even cosmology are to be dismissed. Surely, neither of these two extreme views is plausible either.

Instead, this book provides an alternative (better) way to understand the future of religion, especially in the dialectic context of sacredness and secularness—while learning from different approaches in the literature but without favoring any one of them (nor integrating them, since they are not necessarily compatible with each other). Thus, this book offers a new theory to go beyond the existing approaches in the literature on religion in a new way not thought of before.

If successful, this seminal project is to fundamentally change the way that we think about religion, from the combined perspectives of the mind, nature, society, and culture, with enormous implications for the human future and what I originally called its "post-human" fate.

Religious Studies vs. Theology

A good point of departure is to distinguish, at the outset, two often confused terms like "religious studies" and "theology" in popular usage.

Religious Studies

The term "religious studies" (also known as "religious education") refers to "the academic field of multi-disciplinary, secular study of religious beliefs, behaviors, and institutions." (WK 2010)

Religious studies (or religious education) thus "describes, compares, interprets, and explains religion, emphasizing systematic, historically-based, and cross-cultural perspectives….Religious studies draws upon multiple disciplines and their methodologies including anthropology, sociology, psychology, philosophy, and history of religion." (WK 2010)

Some well-known sub-fields of religious studies include, for example, "psychology of religion," "anthropology of religion," "sociology of religion," "history of religion," "philosophy of religion," and the like. (WK 2010 & 2010a)

The history of religious studies can be traced back to "the nineteenth century, when scholarly and historical analysis of the Bible had flourished, and Hindu and Buddhist texts were first being translated into European languages. Early influential scholars included Friedrich Max Müller, in England, and Cornelius P. Tiele, in the Netherlands." (WK 2010)

Nowadays, "religious studies is practiced by scholars worldwide. In its early years, it was known as Comparative Religion or the Science of Religion and, in the U.S…., there are those who today also know the field as the History of religion (associated with methodological traditions traced to the University of Chicago in general, and in particular Mircea Eliade, from the late 1950's through to the late 1980's). The field is known as *Religionswissenschaft* in Germany and Italy and *Sciences de la religion* in the French-speaking world." (WK 2010)

Theology

By contrast, the term "theology" refers to "the study of a god or, more generally, the study of religious faith, practice, and experience, or of spirituality"—but, unlike religious studies, is not generally "written from a third party perspective." (WK 2010 & 2010a)

In fact, "theology stands in contrast to the philosophy of religion and religious studies in that, generally, the scholar is first and foremost a believer employing both logic and scripture as evidence"—whereas "religious studies tries to study human religious behavior and belief from outside any particular religious viewpoint." (WK 2010)

Therefore, "a distinction is made between theology, which is seen as involving some level of commitment to the truth of the religious tradition being studied, and religious studies, which is not. If contrasted with theology in this way, religious studies is normally seen as requiring the bracketing of the question of the truth of the religious traditions studied, and as involving the study of the historical or contemporary practices or ideas those traditions using intellectual tools and frameworks that are not themselves specifically tied to any religious tradition, and that are normally understood to be neutral or secular." (WK 2010a; D. Wiebe 2000)

This distinction between "theology" and "religious studies" is also a point of contention among different scholars in the literature on religion.

For instance, one group of scholars consider theology and religious studies as "being in tension." (WK 2010a; K. Knoll 2009)

A second group of scholars think that they can "coexist without serious tension." (WK 2010a; D. Ford 2009)

And the third group of scholars even reject the idea that "there is as clear a boundary between them as the brief description here suggests." (WK 2010a & T. Fitzgerald 2000) For instance, "a group of scholars have criticized religious studies beginning in the 1990s as a theological project which actually imposes views onto the people it aims to survey. Prominent voices in this critical view include Robert A. Orsi, Timothy Fitzgerald, Talal Asad, Tomoko Masuzawa, G.A. Oddie, Richard King, Russell T.

McCutcheon, and Daniel Dubuisson. Their areas of research overlap heavily with postcolonial studies." (WK 2010; D. Dubuisson 2007)

Religion vs. Spirituality

Another distinction to be clarified at the outset concerns the two terms like "religion" and "spirituality" often used in the literature on religion (as summarized in *Table 1.1*).

Religion

The term "religion" is "from the Latin *religiō*, the ultimate origins of which are obscure. One possibility is derivation from a reduplicated *le-ligare*, an interpretation traced to Cicero connecting *lego* 'read,' i.e. *re* (again) + *lego* in the sense of 'choose,' 'go over again' or 'consider carefully.'" (WK 2010b)

An alternative interpretation of the term "religion" was suggested by Tom Harpur (2004) and Joseph Campbell (1991), who "favor the derivation from *ligare* 'bind, connect,' probably from a prefixed *re-ligare*, i.e. *re* (again) + *ligare* or 'to reconnect,' which was made prominent by St. Augustine, following the interpretation of Lactantius." (WK 2010b)

But the critics like Daniel Dubuisson (2003) argue that "relying on this etymology 'tends to minimize or cancel out the role of history'" and that "Augustine gave a lengthy definition of *religio* that sets it quite apart from the modern word 'religion.'" (WK 2010b)

This hermeneutic dispute aside—the term "religion" in general refers to "a set of beliefs concerning the cause, nature, and purpose of the universe, especially when considered as the creation of a supernatural agency or agencies, usually involving devotional and ritual observances, and often containing a moral code governing the conduct of human affairs." (WK 2010b)

This set of beliefs in religion is "to give meaning to the practitioner's experiences of life," so as to "consider carefully" his life again or to "reconnect" his life in a deeper way. (WK 2010b)

And "the meaning centers on a deity or deities" and/or, alternatively, on "an ultimate truth." (WK 2010b)

Spirituality

By contrast, the term "spirituality" refers to "an ultimate reality or transcendent dimension of the world; an inner path enabling a person to discover the essence of his or her being, or the 'deepest values and meanings by which people live.'" (WK 2010c; E. Cousins 1992; P. Sheldrake 2007)

Spirituality often relies on "meditation, prayer and contemplation" to "develop an individual's inner life; such practices often lead to an experience of connectedness with a larger reality: a more comprehensive self; other individuals or the human community; nature or the cosmos; or the divine realm." (WK 2010c; M. Burkhardt 2002)

On the one hand, the terms "religion" and "spirituality" have much in common, insofar as both are concerned with "an ultimate reality," the practices of "meditation, prayer and contemplation," and so on.

On the other hand, the terms "religion" and "spirituality" have much to differ from each other, in two major ways.

Firstly, spirituality differs from religion, because "some individuals...see spirituality as a belief in ideas of religious significance (such as God, the Soul, or Heaven), but not feel bound to the bureaucratic structure and creeds of a particular organized religion." (WK 2010b)

Thus, these individuals "choose the term spirituality rather than religion to describe their form of belief, perhaps reflecting a disillusionment with organized religion...and a movement towards a more 'modern'—more tolerant, and more intuitive—form of religion. These individuals may reject organized religion because of historical acts by religious organizations, such as Christian Crusades and Islamic Jihad, the marginalisation and persecution of various minorities, or the Spanish Inquisition." (WK 2010b)

These individuals seeking spirituality in this more "tolerant" way tend to be relatively less "extreme" (or "radical") than their counterparts in mainstream organized religions, especially those who are fundamentalist in orientation.

And secondly, spirituality differs from religion in another way, in that religion is also concerned with the understanding of "the intentions of a supernatural force (such as deities)"—but spirituality, for some individuals, is not necessarily concerned with supernatural force. (WK 2010) This then leads us to the third distinction (in what follows).

Religion and Supernatural Reality

The third distinction to be clarified at the outset concerns the two terms "religion" and "supernatural reality," because the term "religion" often goes side by side with the term "supernatural reality" (or something equivalent).

Since different religions differ from each other in regard to the understanding of supernatural reality, there are different interpretations of what it refers to, as summarized in *Table 1.2*.

Monotheism vs. Polytheism

A common disagreement among different religions in regard to supernatural reality concerns the "monotheistic" and "polytheistic" definitions of supernatural reality.

In regard to "monotheism"—some religions (like Christianity, Judaism, and Islam) accept the view that "only one God exists (as opposed to multiple gods). In Western thought, God is traditionally described as a being that possesses at least three necessary properties: omniscience (all-knowing), omnipotence (all-powerful), and omnipresence (present every where). In other words, God knows everything, has the power to do anything, and is present where He wishes. Many other properties (e.g., omnibenevolence) have been alleged to be necessary properties of a god; however, these are the three most uncontroversial and dominant in Christian tradition." (WK 2010d)

And in regard to "polytheism"—other religions hold the opposite view that there are "more than one god(dess). There can be as few as two (such as a classical Western understanding of Zoroastrian dualism) or an innumerably large amount, as in Hinduism (as the Western world perceives it)." (WK 2010d)

However, even in polythesism, not all gods or goddesses are created equal, because, although "many varieties of polytheism…all accept that many gods exist," they "differ in their responses to that belief. Henotheists for example, worship only one of the many gods, either because it is held to be more powerful or worthy of worship than the others (some pseudo-Christian sects take this view of the Trinity, holding that only God the Father should be worshipped, Jesus and the Holy Spirit being distinct and lesser gods), or because it is associated with their own group, culture, state, etc. The distinction isn't a clear one, of course, as most people consider their own culture superior to others, and this will also apply to their culture's God. Kathenotheists have similar beliefs, but worship a different god at different times or places." (WK 2010d)

Pantheism vs. Deism vs. Panentheism

Another common disagreement among different religions in regard to supernatural reality concerns the distinction between "Pantheism" (for the immanence of God), "Deism" (for the transcendence of God), and "Panentheism" (for both the immanence and transcendence of God), as explained below. (WK 2010d)

- "Pantheism"—This term refers to "the belief that God exists as all things of the cosmos, that God is one and all is God; God is immanent." (WK 2010d) Spinoza in the West—and many Taoists as well as Hindus in the East—hold this position. (WK 2010d & 2010e)
- "Deism" —This term refers to "the belief that God does exist but does not interfere with human life and the laws of the universe; God is transcendent." (WK 2010d) And this "can be determined using reason and observation of the natural world alone, without the need for either faith or organized religion"; Matthew Tindal, Thomas Jefferson, and others hold this position. (WK 2010g)
- "Panentheism"—This term refers to "the belief that God encompasses all things of the cosmos but that God is greater than the cosmos; God is both immanent and transcendent." (WK 2010d) Many Eastern and Oriental Orthodox Christians hold this position. (WK 2010f)

Surely, there can be other disagreements, but the two examples above suffice for the present purpose at hand.

The Theoretical Debate

This introduction to the three distinctions in the study of religion (in the previous three sections) reveals some fundamental disagreements in the literature on religion, which have been much debated in the history of religion.

For a more systematic analysis of the fundamental disagreements among different religions, there are four main theoretical approaches in the debate to be summarized hereafter, and they can be called, in the absence of better words, namely, (a) the *theistic* argument, (b) the *skeptical* argument, (c) the *critical* argument, and (d) the *comparative-substitutive* argument (which is my original contribution to the debate)—to be elabroated hereafter, respectively.

Lest misunderstanding occurs, two clarifications should be made here, as this is something that I regularly emphasize in my previous books, whenever a theoretical debate is summarized for a topic, *almost verbatim*.

Firstly, there can be other arguments (and theories within each) besides the first three here, that is, the "theistic," the "skeptical," and the "critical" arguments (as indicated above). The advantage to select these three here has to do with their illustrative representation of the diverse theories in the literature (which are deemed sufficient for the purpose at hand in this book).

And secondly, the three arguments are not necessarily mutually exclusive. For instance, those who advocate the "skeptical" argument can also consider the "critical" (or the "theistic") argument, although they do not focus on the latter.

And the reverse is also true, in that those who make the "critical" (or the "theistic") argument can also consider the "skeptical" argument, although they do not focus on the latter.

For instance, a version of the "skeptical" argument concerns "agnosticism," which, however, overlaps with the scientific critique of religion in the "critical" argument, although it does not focus on the latter (as will be clear later).

In other words, their disagreement is often one in degree, not in kind.

The Theistic Argument

With these two clarifications in mind—the first major theoretical approach is called, in the absence of better words, the *theistic* argument, which focuses, relatively speaking of course, more on "the belief in the existence of one or more divinities or deities." (WK 2010d)

Therefore, the word "theistic" in the title of the argument is suggestive, because it refers to the existence of "God," whether there is only one or more than one—with the caution that the word "God" here is used in a broad sense, such that it does not discriminate against certain definitions of "God" in favor of others (as will be clear later). (WK 2010h)

Yet, the theistic argument has different issues of concern, and different defenders of the argument offer their own distinctive stands on the issues, depending on their own interests.

For illustration, consider three main positions in the theistic argument, namely, (a) "Pantheism", (b) "Deism," and (c) "Panentheism," in what follows, respectively.

Although these three positions were already mentioned in the previous section, they will be elaborated in the context of the theoretical debate on religion in what follows.

Pantheism

The term "Pantheism" is "from the Ancient Greek: πᾶν (pan) meaning 'All' and θεός (theos) meaning 'God'—literally 'All is God.' As such Pantheism promotes the idea that 'God' is better understood as a way of relating to nature and the Universe as a whole—all that was, is and shall be—rather than as a transcendent, mental, personal or creator entity." (WK 2010e; H. Owen 1971)

In other words, "Pantheism is the view that the Universe (Nature) and God are identical, or that the Universe (including Nature on Earth) is the only thing deserving the deepest kind of reverence." (WK 2010e) God is thus immanent.

In this sense, "Pantheists…do not believe in a personal, anthropomorphic or creator god. Although there are divergences within Pantheism, the central ideas found in almost all versions are the Cosmos as an all-encompassing unity and the 'sacredness' of Nature." (WK 2010e)

The term "Pantheism" was probably first intorduced "in English by Irish writer John Toland in his 1705 work, *Socinianism Truly Stated, by a pantheist*. He clarified the idea in a 1710 letter to Leibniz when he referred to 'the pantheistic opinion of those who believe in no other eternal being but the universe.'" (WK 2010e; P. Harrison 1999)

However, "many earlier writers, schools of philosophy, and religious movements expressed pantheistic ideas. They include some of the Presocratics such as Heraclitus and Anaximander. The Stoics were Pantheists, beginning with Zeno of Citium and culminating in the emperor-philosopher Marcus Aurelius….The early Taoism of Laozi and Zhuangzi is also pantheistic." (WK 2010e; P. Harrison 1999)

But for the critics, there are major problems with Pantheism in relation to the claim that God is immanent; consider two of them below for illustration.

Firstly, one criticism of Pantheism is that "Pantheism is little more than a redefinition of the word 'God' to mean 'Nature,' 'Universe,' or 'reality.'" (WK 2010e)

And secondly, another criticism of Pantheism is that "there are disagreements as to whether Pantheism is atheistic or not." (WK 2010e) For instance, for the atheists, "the…god of pantheism is not a god (according to the traditional definition)." (WK 2010e; R. Dawkins 2006)

But for the Pantheists, "a deity is not necessarily transcendent" (in that it is a "'personal' God that transcends…the world" or "is separate from" it), because "Pantheists deny the existence of a personal God. They deny the existence of a 'minded' Being that has intentional states and associated capacities like the ability to make decisions." (WK 2010e; SEP 2007)

Deism

Unlike the Pantheist claim that God is immanent—the Deists make the opposite claim that God is transcendent. Matthew Tindal, Thomas Jefferson, and others hold this position. (WK 2010g)

More specifically, there are two major beliefs in "Deism."

The first major belief in Deism is that "a supreme being created the universe," but without the belief that "God intervenes in human affairs, for example through miracles and revelations. These views contrast with the dependence on revelations, miracles, and faith found in many Jewish, Christian, Islamic and other theistic teachings." (WK 2010g)

In other words, "Deists typically reject most supernatural events (prophecy, miracles) and tend to assert that God (or 'The Supreme Architect') has a plan for the universe that is not altered either by God intervening in the affairs of human life or by suspending the natural laws of the universe. What organized religions see as divine revelation and holy books, most deists see as interpretations made by other humans, rather than as authoritative sources." (WK 2010g)

And the second major belief in Deism is that "this (and religious truth in general) can be determined using reason and observation of the natural world alone, without the need for either faith or organized religion." (WK 2010g)

As an alternative position to Pantheism—"Deism became prominent in the 17th and 18th centuries during the Age of Enlightenment, especially in what is now the United Kingdom, France, United States and Ireland, mostly among those raised as Christians who found they could not believe in either a triune God, the divinity of Jesus, miracles, or the inerrancy of scriptures, but who did believe in one god. Initially it did not form any congregations, but in time deism strongly influenced other religious groups, such as Unitarianism and Universalism, which developed from it. It continues to this day in the forms of classical deism and modern deism." (WK 2010g)

But for the critics, there are major problems with Deism in relation to the claim that God is transcendent; consider two of them below for illustration.

Firstly, one criticism of Deism is that the rise of science in modern times "increased doubt about the first cause argument and the argument from design, turning many (though not all) potential deists towards atheism instead." (WK 2010g; IEP 2006; E. Mossner 1967)

And secondly, another criticism of Deism is that the "excesses of the French Revolution" as criticized by "writers such as Joseph-Marie de Maistre and Edmund Burke" had raised serious "doubts that reason and rationalism [as championed by the Deists] could solve all problems." (WK 2010g; E. Mossner 1967)

Panentheism

Unlike the Pantheist claim (that God is immanent) and the Deist claim (that God is transcendent)—the Panentheists offer a different claim, in that God is both transcendent and immanent.

The term "Panentheism"—which is "from Greek πᾶν (pân) 'all,' ἐν (en) 'in,' and θεός (theós) 'God,'" to mean "all-in-God"—thus refers to "a belief system which posits that God exists and interpenetrates every part of nature, and timelessly extends beyond as well." (WK 2010f)

In this sense, "God is not necessarily viewed as the creator or demiurge, but the eternal animating force behind the universe, with the universe as nothing more than the manifest part of God. The cosmos exists within God, who in turn 'pervades' or is 'in' the cosmos....[P]anentheism claims that God is greater than the universe and that the universe is contained within God." (WK 2010f; E. Fahlbusch 1999)

Panentheism is influential in Eastern and Oriental Orthodox Christianity, where "creation is not considered to be a literal 'part of" God, and the Godhead is distinct from creation. There is, in other words, an eternal difference between the uncreated (i.e., God) and the created (i.e., everything else). This does not mean, however, that the creation is wholly separated from God, because the creation exists by and in the Divine energies. These energies are the operations of God and are God, but the created is not God in the Divine essence." (WK 2010f)

In addition, "in the theology of the Eastern and Oriental Orthodox Churches, God is not merely creator of the universe; his active presence is necessary in some way for every bit of creation, from smallest to greatest, to continue to exist at all. That is, God's energies (that is, activities) maintain all things and all beings....His love of creation is such that he will not withdraw his presence...." (WK 2010f)

Panentheism is also influential in Hinduism, where "Brahman is the transcendent and immanent Ultimate Reality....Many schools of Hinduism are panentheistic and the first and most ancient ideas of panentheism originate in the Vedas, Upanishads, as well as the Bhagavad Gita. The Purusha Sukta and Hiranyagarbha Sukta of Rig Veda and verses from the Bhagavad Gita and Shri Rudram support this viewpoint." (WK 2010f)

But for the critics, there are major problems with Panentheism; consider two of them below for illustration.

Firstly, one criticism of Panentheism is that it is contradictory (or incoherent) to claim that God is both transcendent and immanent. (N. Geisler 1999)

And secondly, another criticism of Panentheism is that, as pointed out by H. P. Owen, "there seems to be no real distinction between the two divine poles" of God in the transcendent and immanent realms. (N. Geisler 1999)

The Skeptical Argument

The second theoretical approach is called, in the absence of better words, the *skeptical* argument, which focuses, relatively speaking of course, more on the extent to which there are no solid evidences on the basis of which religious beliefs can be verified among people who disagree with each other.

In this sense, the word "skeptical" in the title of the argument is suggestive, because it refers to the extent of the lack of solid evidences in religious beliefs.

Like the theist argument—the skeptical one also has different issues of concern, and different defenders of the argument offer their own distinctive stands on the issues, depending on their own interests.

For illustration, consider the skeptical argument in relation to (a) agnosticsm and (b) atheism, as shown below, respectively.

Agnosticism

The term "agnosticism" is derived from "agnostic (Greek: ἀ- a-, without + γνῶσις gnōsis, knowledge"), which thus means "without knowledge" (or something which is a mere "belief"). (WK 2010i)

Thomas Henry Huxley first used the term "in a speech at a meeting of the Metaphysical Society in 1876 to describe his philosophy which rejects all claims of spiritual or mystical knowledge....Agnosticism is not to be confused with religious views opposing the ancient religious movement of Gnosticism in particular; Huxley used the term in a broader, more abstract sense. Huxley identified agnosticism not as a creed but rather as a method of skeptical, evidence-based inquiry." (WK 2010i; A. Cline 2010)

In this sense, "agnosticism is the view that the truth value of certain claims—especially claims about the existence or non-existence of any deity, but also other religious and metaphysical claims—is unknown or unknowable. Agnosticism can be defined in various ways, and is sometimes used to indicate doubt or a skeptical approach to questions. In some senses, agnosticism is a stance about the differences between belief and knowledge, rather than about any specific claim or belief." (WK 2010i; R. Carroll 2009)

Even before Huxley—"earlier thinkers and written works have promoted agnostic points of view. They include Protagoras, a 5th-century BCE Greek philosopher, and the Nasadiya Sukta creation myth in the Rig Veda, an ancient Hindu religious text," for instance. (WK 2010i; U. Patri 1990; C. Poster 2005)

There are two most often cited variants of agnosticism, as shown below:

- "Strong Agnosticism"—This is "the view that the question of the existence or nonexistence of a deity or deities and the nature of ultimate reality is unknowable by reason of our natural inability to verify any experience with anything but another subjective experience. A strong agnostic would say, 'I cannot know whether a deity exists or not, and neither can you.'" (WK 2010i)
- "Weak Agnosticism"—This is "the view that the existence or nonexistence of any deities is currently unknown but is not necessarily unknowable, therefore one will withhold judgment until/if any evidence is available. A weak agnostic would say, 'I don't know whether any deities exist or not, but maybe one day when there is evidence we can find something out.'" (WK 2010i)

Surely, there are other variants of agnosticism too, but these two suffice for illustration.

But for the critics, there are major problems with agnosticism, regardless of which variant it belongs to; consider two of them below for illustration.

Firstly, one criticism of agnosticism is that "some religious thinkers see agnosticism as a limitation of the mind's capacity to know reality other than material objects." (WK 2010i) This limitation, for them, does not prove that God does not exist.

And secondly, another criticism of agnosticism is that "some atheists [like Richard Dawkins (2006)]...criticize the use of the term agnosticism as functionally indistinguishable from atheism." (WK 2010i)

Atheism

Unlike agnosticism—the degree of skepticism is more intense in atheism, such that "atheism is commonly described as the position that there are no deities. It can also mean the rejection of belief in the existence of deities. A broader meaning is simply the absence of belief that any deities exist." (WK 2010j; W. Rowe 1998; K. Nielsen 2010; P. Edwards 2005)

In general, "atheists tend to lean towards skepticism regarding supernatural claims, citing a lack of empirical evidence. Common rationales for not believing in any deity include the problem of evil, the argument from inconsistent revelations, and the argument from nonbelief. Other arguments for atheism range from the philosophical to the social to the historical. Although some atheists tend toward secular philosophies such as humanism, rationalism, and naturalism, there is no one ideology or set of behaviors to which all atheists adhere." (WK 2010j; OCP 1995; E. Fales 2007; J. Baggini 2003)

However, things get complicated when there are also different variants of atheism, because different scholars "disagree how best to define and classify atheism, contesting what supernatural entities it applies to, whether it is an assertion in its own right or merely the absence of one, and whether it requires a conscious, explicit rejection. A variety of categories have been proposed to try to distinguish the different forms of atheism," like "range," "explict vs. implicit," "strong vs. weak," and so on. (WK 2010j; EB 2007)

But for the critics, there are major problems with atheism; consider three of them below for illustration.

Firstly, one criticism of atheism is that there is no sufficient ground for the atheists to reject the existence of God. For instance, "criticism of atheism in its strong form…comes from agnostics, who contend that there are insufficient grounds to assert authoritatively that any supreme being does not exist, and from ignostics, who take the theological noncognitivist position that the question of the existence of God (per that definition) is meaningless or not properly defined to allow one to take a meaningful position on." (WK 2010k; A. Kenny 2006)

Secondly, another criticism of atheism is that it has a negative effect on some individuals and societies leading to destructive consequences. For instance, some critics remind us about the oppressive state atheism in the former Soviet Union, with "an ideological creed which professed that all religion would atrophy." (WK 2010k)

Others, however, like "some philosophers and world religions," have repeated time and again that the "acknowledgment of God or the gods is a major factor in motivating people towards moral behavior....The French philosopher Voltaire stated 'If God did not exist, it would be necessary to invent him.' Speaking for the Catholic Church in 2009, Cardinal Cormac Murphy-O'Connor...expressed this position" and "blamed atheism for war and destruction." (WK 2010k; R. Gledhill 2009)

And thirdly, still another criticism of atheism is that it has been used by some of its ideologues as a new form of intolerant ideology and politics, this time, against faith. For instance, "R. J. Eskow [2005 & 2006] has accused him [Sam Harris] of fostering an intolerance towards faith, potentially as damaging as the religious fanaticism which he opposes." (WK 2010k)

And "Madeleine Bunting [2007] wrote in *The Guardian* that the purpose of recent books by Richard Dawkins, Daniel Dennett, Sam Harris and Christopher Hitchens 'is to pour scorn on religious belief—they want it eradicated,' and argues that the books are 'deeply political,' sharing a 'loathing' of the role of religion in U.S. politics." (WK 2010k)

The Critical Argument

The third theoretical approach is called, in the absence of better words, the *critical* argument, which focuses, relatively speaking of course, more on the extent to which science is used as the basis to question religious beliefs, but without necessarily (and explicitly) committing to agnosticism or atheism.

In this sense, the word "critical" in the title of the argument is suggestive, because it refers to the extent of the use of the critical spirit in science to examine religious beliefs.

Like the skeptical argument, however—the critical one also has different issues of concern, and different defenders of the argument offer their own distinctive stands on the issues, depending on their own interests.

For illustration, consider the critical argument in relation to (a) the appeal of science and (b) the rise of secularism, as shown below, respectively.

The Appeal of Science

Science has a major role to play in the theoretical debate on the existence and nature of God, because "statements about the world made by science and religion rely on different methodologies. Religions rely on revelation and faith, while science relies on observable, repeatable experiences," and others. (WK 2010l)

In general, there are four main positions in regard to the relationship between science and religion, namely, (a) "conflict," (b) "independence," (c) "dialogue," and (d) "integration," to be summarized hereafter, in that order. (WK 2010l; J. Polkinghorne 1998)

(a) Conflict

This position on the relationship between science and religion refers to the view that "either discipline threatens to take over the legitimate concerns of the other," as argued by its proponents like John William Draper and Andrew Dickson White. (WK 2010l)

Some good examples of "historical, philosophical, and scientific arguments…in favor of the idea that science and religion are in conflict" include "creationism, the Roman Catholic Church's opposition to heliocentrism from 1616 to 1757 including the Galileo affair, and more recently, Pope Benedict XVI's 2009 statements claiming that the use of condoms to combat the AIDS epidemic in Africa was ineffective and counterproductive." (WK 2010l; R. Owen 2009; P. Dimond 2010)

But for the critics, this view of conflict has been much criticized as exaggerated or even inaccurate. For instance, "the claim that people of the Middle Ages widely believed that the Earth was flat…is mistaken, as the contemporary historians of science David C. Lindberg and Ronald L. Numbers write: 'there was scarcely a Christian scholar of the Middle Ages who did not acknowledge [earth's] sphericity and even know its approximate circumference.'" (WK 2010l; J. Russell 1997; D. Lindberg 2010)

In fact, "Oxford historian Peter Harrison [1998] has further developed the idea that the Protestant Reformation had a significant and positive influence on the development of modern science." (WK 2010l)

(b) Independence

This position on the relationship between science and religion refers to the view that it is important to "treat…each as quite separate realms of enquiry," as proposed by "Stephen Jay Gould's Non-Overlapping Magisteria (NOMA)." (WK 2010l)

For instance, "science and religion represent distinct ways of approaching experience and these differences are sources of debate. Science is closely tied to mathematics—a very abstract experience, while religion is more closely tied to the ordinary experience of life. As interpretations of experience, science is descriptive and religion is prescriptive." (WK 2010l; J. Habgood 1964)

Therefore, both of them should not be mixed: "For science and mathematics to concentrate on what the world ought to be like in the way that religion does can be inappropriate and may lead to improperly ascribing properties to the natural world as happened among the followers of Pythagoras in the sixth century B.C. The reverse situation where religion attempts to be descriptive can also lead to inappropriately assigning properties to the natural world. A notable example is the now defunct belief in the Ptolemy planetary model that held sway until changes in scientific and religious thinking were brought about by Galileo and proponents of his views." (WK 2010l; J. Habgood 1964)

But for the critics, this view of independence does not give justice to the similarities that science and religion have with each other. For instance, "Thomas S. Kuhn asserted that science is made up of paradigms that arise from cultural traditions, which is similar to the secular perspective on religion." (WK 2010l; I. Barbour 1968)

(c) Dialogue

This position on the relationship between science and religion refers to the view that "each field has things to say to each other about phenomena in which their interests overlap," as suggested by scholars like William G. Pollard (1961). (WK 2010l)

For instance, "in the early 20th century with the decline of Logical Empiricism and the rise of linguistic and sociological understandings of science...[m]odern scientists are less concerned with establishing universal or ontological truth (which is seen, and dismissed, as the pursuit of philosophy), and more inclined towards the creation of pragmatic, functional models of physical systems. Christian Theology—excluding those fundamentalist churches whose aim is to reassert doctrinal truths—has likewise softened many of its ontological claims, due to increased exposure to both scientific insights and the contrasting theological claims of other faiths." (WK 2010l)

Therefore, "[s]cientific and theological perspectives often coexist peacefully. Non-Christian faiths have historically integrated well with scientific ideas, as in the ancient Egyptian technological mastery applied to monotheistic ends, the flourishing of logic and mathematics under Hinduism and Buddhism, and the scientific advances made by Muslim scholars during the Ottoman empire. Even many 19th century Christian communities welcomed scientists who claimed that science was not at all concerned with discovering the ultimate nature of reality." (WK 2010l; J. Habgood 1964)

But for the critics, this view of dialogue is limited, because science and religion differ from each other in some fundamental ways. For instance, "science in the Enlightenment...was conceived as ontological investigation which uncovered 'facts' about physical nature. This was often explicitly opposed to Christian Theology and the latter's assertions of truth based on doctrine," especially for "those fundamentalist churches whose aim is to reassert doctrinal truths." (WK 2010l)

(d) Integration

This position on the relationship between science and religion refers to the view that it is better "to unify both fields into a single discourse," as suggested by Pierre Teilhard de Chardin and Ian Barbour. (WK 2010l; S. Bonting 2005)

A good illustration of possible integration between science and religion concerns Buddhism and science, because "some philosophic and psychological teachings within Buddhism share commonalities with modern Western scientific and philosophic thought. For example, Buddhism encourages the impartial investigation of nature (an activity referred to as Dhamma-Vicaya in the Pali Canon)—the principal object of study being oneself. A reliance on causality and empiricism are common philosophical principles shared between Buddhism and science." (WK 2010l; A. Yong 2005)

But for the critics, the talk of integration is more a popular myth than a substantive achievement. For instance, in the case concerning Buddhism and science, "Buddhism doesn't focus on materialism," even when it talks about the scientific method. (WK 2010l; D. Kalupahana 1975; B. Wallace 2003)

The same is true for the historical attempt to integrate science and other religions like Christianity: "The reconciliation of Christianity with science has had at least three attempted solutions that have proven themselves quite problematic. These three problematic solutions are biblical literalism, religious experience, and the evolving consensus of scientific truth. Each of these methods of reconciliation have various historical and present-day examples. Respective examples include creationism, liberal Christianity, and scientific imperialism." (WK 2010l)

The Rise of Secularism

Secularism, especially since modern times, has had a major influence on the theoretical debate in regard to the existence and nature of God, since it advocates that "government or other entities should exist separately from religion and/or religious beliefs." (WK 2010m)

Influential scholars on secularism include "Greek and Roman philosophers such as Marcus Aurelius and Epicurus; medieval Muslim polymaths such as Ibn Rushd; Enlightenment thinkers like Denis Diderot, Voltaire, John Locke, James Madison, Thomas Jefferson, and Thomas

Paine; and modern freethinkers, agnostics and atheists such as Bertrand Russell and Robert Ingersoll." (WK 2010m)

A good illustration of secularism in action in the modern West is that, "as religion became a more personal matter" (away from the public realm in the separation of church and state), "discussions of society found a new focus on political and scientific meaning, and religious attitudes were increasingly seen as irrelevant for the needs of the European world." (WK 2010b)

In this modern secular environment, "Ludwig Feuerbach recast Christian beliefs in light of humanism, paving the way for Karl Marx's famous characterization of religion as 'the opiate of the masses'....Later, Bertrand Russell told the world *Why I Am Not a Christian.*" (WK 2010b)

For "many modern-day critics..., religion lacks utility in human society," and they "assert that religion is irrational. Some assert that dogmatic religions are in effect morally deficient, elevating to moral status ancient, arbitrary, and ill-informed rules—taboos on eating pork, for example, as well as dress codes and sexual practices—possibly designed for reasons of hygiene or even mere politics in a bygone era." (WK 2010b; B. Caplan 2010)

But for the critics, the problem with secularism is that it can also degenerate into a militant form with destructive consequences, as shown by "the hostile model of militant secularism" in "the French Revolution," "the Mexican Revolution and the Spanish Constitution of 1931. The hostile model exhibited during these events can be seen as approaching the type of political religion seen in totalitarian states." (WK 2010n; J. Martinez-Torron 2001; H. Maier 2004)

The Comparative-Substitutive Argument

And fourthly, unlike the previous three arguments (viz., the theistic, the skeptical, and the critical)—the fourth one to be introduced here can be called, in the absence of better words again, the *comparative-substitutive* argument, which learns from all other theoretical approaches (which include the three previous arguments and also other examples as will be introduced in the rest of this book), without, however, favoring any of them, nor trying to integrate them (as they are not necessarily compatible with each other, as the introduction of the theoretical debate in the previous sub-sections has shown).

The Comparative-Substitutive Theory of Religion

My *comparative-substitutive* argument can be more precisely called *the comparative-substitutive theory of religion*, since it is to propose a new theory of religion.

This theory was first proposed in a preliminary way in Ch.9 of *The Future of Capitalism and Democracy* (or *FCD*) and in Ch.3 of the 2 volumes titled *The Future of Human* Civilization (*FHC*), especially with the conclusion in Ch.3 of *FHC*, where I wrote: "The idea of a post-secular society is a postmodern myth, just as the vision of a liberating secular society was a modern myth."

This view was then known as "the comparative theory of religion" in Ch.1 of *The Future of Post-Human Knowledge* (or *FPHK*). And this book (*FPHR*) provides a solid foundation for the *comparative-substitutive* argument here.

There are two words here, *comparative* and *substitutive*, in the title of the argument.

My argument is "comparative" because it provides a comparative analysis of different theoretical approaches in the literature by learning from them but without favoring any of them nor trying to integrate them (as they are not necessarily compatible with each other).

And my argument is also "substitutive," because it offers a visionary prediction of the different forms of religion that the post-humans will use as substitutes for the human ones (hitherto existing in human history) which will no longer be much useful in the post-human future.

With this clarification in mind—the comparative-substitutive theory of religion has four distinctive features to remember.

Firstly, my theory makes good use of all theoretical approaches in the literature on religion, be they about the theist argument, the skeptical argument, or the critical argument—especially from the most comprehensive combined perspectives of the mind, nature, society, and culture (as will be clear in Chapter Two and Chapter Three).

Secondly, just like many other theories of mine in my previous books, my theory here does not heavily favor any specific theory over others in the literature, nor trying to integrate them (as they are not necessarily compatible with each other).

Thirdly, my theory treats the issue of religion in the distinctive dialectic context of sacredness and secularness—especially in the larger dialectic context of no sacredness without secularness, and vice versa, together with the subsequent transcendence of both.

And fourthly, it contains sixteen major theses, namely, (a) the first thesis: the absoluteness-relativeness principle, (b) the second thesis: the predictability-unpredictability principle, (c) the third thesis: the explicability-inexplicability principle, (d) the fourth thesis: the preciseness-vagueness principle, (e) the fifth thesis: the simpleness-complicatedness principle, (f) the sixth thesis: the openness-hiddenness principle, (g) the seventh thesis: the denseness-emptiness principle, (h) the eighth thesis: the slowness-quickness principle, (i) the nineth thesis: the expansion-contraction principle, (j) the tenth thesis: the convention-novelty principle, (k) the eleventh thesis: the evolution-transformation principle, (l) the twelveth thesis: the symmetry-asymmetry principle, (m) the thirteenth thesis: the softness-hardness principle, (n) the fourteenth thesis: the regression-progression principle, (o) the fifteenth thesis: the sameness-difference principle, and (p) the sixteenth thesis: the post-human substitution—to be elaborated in the rest of the book, with a summary in the concluding chapter.

Of course, as this is something that I often emphasized in my previous books, other principles (besides the 15 as cited above) are also relevant, but these 15 are the most relevant in the current case study (in terms of the number of citations of each principle in the book).

Even then, in some cases, the difference between any two given principles, for instance, in terms of the number of citations in a book, is rather small, so the reason in those cases is more aesthetic (than otherwise), because it looks nicer to list only 15 theses for 15 principles (than 21 theses for all of the 21 principles) in the Table of Contents.

This is true, even if different studies of the same kind can yield different views about the degree of relevance for each principle, depending on the specific nature of a research in question, needless to say. So, if a different author analyzes the same subject matter in a different way, the relevance of the principles will be different.

With this clarification in mind—the seminal project here, if successful, will fundamentally change the way that we think about religion, from the combined perspectives of the mind, nature, society, and culture, with enormous implications for the human future and what I originally called its "post-human" fate.

Theory and Meta-Theory

The *comparative-substitutive* argument, or *the comparative-substitutive theory of religion*, presupposes some kind of meta-theory, in special relation to methodology and ontology—just as all theories, either explicitly or implicitly, require their own versions of meta-theory.

In my case, I already proposed (in my previous books) my distinctive approach to methodology (known as "sophisticated methodological holism") and ontology (known as "existential dialectics").

The next two sections are to introduce my meta-theory—that is, existential dialectics and sophisticated methodological holism, respectively—to be repeated, *often verbatim* (with only a few updated revisions), from my previous works, as this is something that I often do in each new book of mine as an introduction to some background information for the convenience of the readers.

A Unified Theory of Everything

In the end, my distinctive approach to meta-theory serves as a foundation to unify all domains of knowledge for an overarching understanding of all forms of reality (by way of some ontological principles at the meta-theoretical level and the comprehensive perspectives of the mind, nature, society, and culture at the theoretical level—as will be explained in the next two sections).

This is so, without commiting the sins of reductionism and reverse-reductionism (as often seen in many holistic approaches, with the fad of systems approach as a most recent notorious example, as already critically explained in *The Future of Post-Human Formal Science*, or *FPHFS*), since my distinctive approach makes good use of different schools of thought without favoring any of them nor trying to integrate them (as they are not necessarily compatible with each other), so as to include (or adjust for) heterogeneity, conflict, subjectivity, and complexity, for example.

In this sense, the word "unified" does not have to mean an integrative approach, in a narrow sense, nor a systems approach, in a broad one, both of which I have critically rebuked (in my previous books), while learning from them.

This overarching project (consisting of numerous theories of mine, as will be summarized in the next section), thus, constitutes my grand unifed theory of everything in the world and beyond.

The Logic of Existential Dialectics

To start, the ontology of existential dialectics can be summarized in this section—*often verbatim* (with only a few updated revisions), from my previous works, as this is something that I regularly do in each new book of mine as an introduction to some background information for the convenience of the readers.

After all, this book, like all others of mine, is in conversation with all previous ones of mine, for the final aim to converge all of them into a larger grand project on the future of intelligent life, both here on earth and there in deep space unto multiverses.

The summary can be organized in relation to (a) the conception of existential dialectics (or its ontics), (b) the syntax of existential dialectics (or its ontomethodology and ontologic), (c) the semantics of existential dialectics (or its ontosemantics), and (d) the pragmatics of existential dialectics (or its ontopragmatics), respectively hereafter—again *often verbatim*.

This means that, for those readers who had read some of my previous books, the summary below is really not much new (*almost verbatim*, with only some updated revisions).

But for those who have never read my previous books, it is a good review of them.

The Conception of Existential Dialectics (or Its Ontics)

This ontology was originally designated as "existential dialectics" in *Beyond Capitalism to Post-Capitalism* (herein abbreviated as *BCPC*), although it was already analyzed in other books of mine like the 2 volumes of *The Future of Human Civilization* (*FHC*), *The Future of Capitalism and Democracy* (*FCD*), *The Future of Post-Human Consciousness* (*FPHC*), and the 2 volumes of *Beyond Democracy to Post-Democracy* (*BDPD*).

Lest any confusion occurs, it is important to stress at the outset that the word 'existential' in "existential dialectics" has nothing to do with Existentialism, which I rebuked in *FHC*, *FCD*, and also *FPHC*. Instead, the word here merely refers to the existence of intelligent life (both primitive and advanced) in a broad sense.

Some Basic Concepts

The conception of existential dialectics (or its ontics) makes use of different concepts (like "sets," "elements," "relations," "operations," "functions," "truth values," "axioms," "postulates," and "principles"—as shown in *Table 4.3*), which are important for the understanding of any logic of ontology.

That clarified—existential dialectics, as a language of ontology, can be analyzed in different ways that a language, as an analogy, is often analyzed, namely, in relation to phonology ("the study of patterns of a language's sounds"), phonetics ("the study of the physical aspects of sounds of human language"), morphonology ("the study of the internal structure of words"), syntax ("the study of how words combine to form grammatical sentences"), semantics ("the study of the meaning of words [lexical semantics] and fixed word combinations [phraseology]"), and pragmatics ("the study of how utterances are used…literally, figuratively, or otherwise…in communicative acts"). (WK 2007)

But since my theory of existential dialectics makes use of the English language for communication here, it does not propose a new way to make the patterns of a language's sounds (as in phonology), to study the physical aspects of sounds (as in phonetics), or even to strive for a new organization of the internal structure of words for the English language (as in morphonology).

For this reason, the language of existential dialectics to be analyzed hereafter is not concerned with the phonological, phonetic, and morphonological aspects of the English language. Instead, the analysis will explore the syntax, semantics, and pragmatics of existential dialectics as a language of ontology to improve our understanding of reality.

The Ontic Dispute

But first, there is an ontic dispute to be addressed, which is related to what I called "the dilemma of ontology" as introduced earlier in *Sec. 1.4* of *The Future of Post-Human Knowledge* (*FPHK*).

A good point of departure concerns what I want to call *the ontic dispute*, on how to understand the very nature of ontology.

Traditionally, scholars in the field used to study the conception of ontology in terms of its entities (e.g., material objects, abstract numbers), properties (e.g., duration, plurality), and relationships (e.g., causation).

This is a good starting point, but it suffers from different problems. Consider three examples of bias below, which are quite common in the literature, and the recent version (of treating concepts and principles in ontology on the basis of "plurality," "dynamism," "duration," "interaction," "life," "consciousness," and "volition") by Reginald Firehammer (2005) only constitutes a latest addition to this old (impoverishing) tradition.

Firstly, the classification of entities, properties, and relationships is too material-centric, in often focusing more on the existence of material entities than on non-material ones.

Secondly, the classification is too anthropo-centric, in often favoring the factor of human agency in depicting reality.

And lastly, the classification is too confused among the three categories relating to each other, in often lumping them together without adequate consideration of their intricated interrelationships (both in relation to each and in relation to all).

A good alternative is precisely what I want to offer in this debate, that is, a new classification of ontological entities, properties, and their relationships in terms of *method*, *structure*, *process*, *agency*, and *outcome* instead. Let me explicate what these words mean below.

In relation to "method"—it concerns how ontology is to be studied. In this sense, the word 'method' here should not be confused with the different usage of the same term 'method' as a technique of investigation in the context of methodology (as already introduced in *Sec. 1.2* of *FPHK*).

In relation to "structure"—it concerns what the general patterns of entities, properties, and relationships are.

In relation to "process"—it concerns how these general patterns change over time.

In relation to "agency"—it concerns how agency affects any change of these general patterns over time (without putting, however, too much emphasis on the role of human agency).

And in relation to "outcome"—it concerns what the outputs of this change over time are.

The Syntax of Existential Dialectics (or Its Ontomethodology and Ontologic)

The syntax of existential dialectics, analogously speaking, refers here to the structure of an ontology which can be studied by way of combining ideas into complex relationships like ontological principles to depict reality in the world—and can be analyzed in seven sub-sections, namely, (a) the selection criteria, (b) further clarifications on classification, (c) ontomethodology, (d) ontologic, (e) the principles as short cuts, (f) the principles as family resemblances, and (g) the dialectic constraints imposed by the principles, respectively hereafter.

The Selection Criteria

To start, not any pair of relationship can be chosen as an ontological principle in existential dialectics; otherwise, there could be billions of them under the sky.

Four illustrations below suffice to clarify this point.

(a) Firstly, an ontological principle cannot *overlap* with other principles, in that it is too closely related with other ones.

Of course, one cannot totally rule out any relationship between two entities, especially in a complex world of everything being linked to everything else—but the comparison here is relative, not absolute.

In this sense, the flexibility-inflexibility pair cannot be an ontological principle, since it has something closely in common with other ones (like the simpleness-complicatedness principle, for instance).

As an illustration, something which is flexible in interpretation is more likely to allow multiple viewpoints and thus makes the overall picture more complicated than otherwise (simple).

(b) Secondly, an ontological principle cannot be *redundant* in relation to other principles, in that it somehow duplicates other principles.

In this sense, for instance, the directness-indirectness pair cannot be an ontological principle, because it somehow duplicates other ontological principles (like the preciseness-vagueness principle, for instance).

As an illustration, something which is direct means to be right to the point and does not need to go to an unnecessarily long loop—so it is less vague, in being clearer about the thing in question.

(c) Thirdly, an ontological principle cannot be *derived* from other ones—as if it is a child-parent relationship.

In this sense, the convenience-inconvenience pair cannot be an ontological principle, because it can be derived from other ones (like the slowness-quickness principle, for instance).

For instance, something which is convenient already implies that it can be obtained quickly (rather than slowly)—all things considered.

(d) And fourthly, an ontological principle cannot be *trivial* (or *parochial*)—as if it is only one component competing with other ones for inclusion in a set.

In this sense, the consistency-inconsistency pair cannot be an ontological principle, because its validity is limited (or parochial), as it can be easily challenged and replaced by opposing major (not minor) theories (e.g., the correspondence theory of truth, the pragmatic theory of truth, the semantic theory of truth, and whatnot), not just in accordance to the consistency theory of truth (for consistency).

In this sense, the consistency argument is only one among different opposing arguments in relation to the logic of what constitutes "truth."

Although these examples are not exhaustive, they illustrative the selectiveness of any ontological principle to be existentially dialectic.

Further Clarifications on Classification

Lest any misunderstanding carelessly occurs, some further clarifications on classification should be made here (and summarized in *Table 4.8*).

(a) Firstly, the total number of ontological principles is unknown, to be discovered later, as our knowledge of the world becomes more advanced.

Consequently, the principles as introduced in my books are not exhaustive, with new ones being added, whenever more of them are discovered in later research.

At least, future generations can pick up where I leave off and continue the discovery.

In this sense, my work should be treated as a pioneering effort for the development of a systematic, comprehensive analysis of a new general ontology for the future of knowledge.

(b) Secondly, the principles are not rigidly classified, as they can be reclassified in a different way.

For instance, the preciseness-vagueness principle is classified under the category of "structure" but can be reclassified under the category of "method," although in so doing, it has a different meaning in the context of method.

The same logic applies to the same-difference principle under the category of "outcome," which can be reclassified under the category of "structure," although in so doing, once more, it has a different meaning in the context of structure.

(c) Thirdly, the principles are to be understood together, not that each prinicple is to be treated independently of others. After all, the principles are mutually constraining, in that they work together as a whole.

(d) Fourthly, the principles are relevant to all subject matters, but some principles are, relatively speaking of course, more useful to some subject matters than others under certain conditions—as implied in the symmetry-asymmetry principle.

(e) And fifthly, the principles constitute only two levels of analysis, this time, at the ontological and methodological levels—while other levels of analysis (from the perspectives of the mind, nature, society, and culture) are also needed, in order to understand reality in its totality (as explained in the section on "sophisticated methodological holism," so as to avoid the dual dangers of reductionism and reverse-reductionism).

Ontomethodology

With these selection criteria and clarifications in mind—the syntax of existential dialectics can be divided into two main smaller sections for analysis, since they are related to each other in the context of some fundamental principles, that is, (a) ontomethodology and (b) ontologic, to be addressed hereafter, respectively.

In the context of ontomethodology, some ontological principles are proposed here in relation to the nature of methodology, which however is tied up with the general issue of ontology in the context of knowledge.

In this sense, ontomethodology (in the context of these ontological principles in the category of method) are related with ontologic in general (in the context of ontological principles in general).

Some good instances of ontological principles involving ontomethodology include the formalness-informalness principle, the predictability-unpredictability principle, the explicability-inexplicability principle, the partiality-totality principle, and the absoluteness-relativeness principle, which will be introduced in conjunction with ontological principles in the ontologic of existential dialectics in general hereafter.

Ontologic

With this clarification of the relationship between ontomethodology and ontologic in mind (which is comparable to the relationship between methodology and ontology as described in *Sec. 1.3* of *FPHK*)—the first three principles in existential dialectics were introduced in *BCPC*. And more principles were later added to the logic in my subsequent books (like *FC*, *FAE*, and others).

More specifically, in *BCPC*, I proposed three principles (based on previous works of mine, not just something out of the blue) for the ontological logic, namely, (a) the regression-progression principle on the direction of history, (b) the symmetry-asymmetry principle on the relationships among existents, and (c) the change-constancy principle on the alteration of things—or in a more elegant term, the dynamics of space-time (in *FC*).

In *The Future of Complexity* (*FC*), I added three more principles, on top of the three aforementioned, namely, (d) the partiality-totality principle on the relationships between the parts and the whole, (e) the order-chaos principle on the pattern of things, and (f) the predictability-unpredictability principle on the occurrence of things—as part of the ontological logic of existential dialectics.

In *The Future of Aesthetic Experience* (or simply *FAE*), another principle is added, namely, (g) the evolution-transformation principle (on the multiple kinds of agency).

Also in *FAE*, I then reclassified the 7 principles into four categories, namely, (i) in relation to method, for the partiality-totality principle and the predictability-unpredictability principle, (ii) in relation to process, for the change-constancy principle and the order-chaos principle, (iii) in relation to agency, for the symmetry-asymmetry principle and the evolution-transformation principle, and (iv) in relation to outcome, for the regression-progression principle.

In *The Rise of Authoritarian Liberal Democracy* (*ALD*), I added two more principles, namely, (h) the softness-hardness principle on the force of agency (which is to be classified under the category about agency) and (i) the same-difference principle on the metamorphosis of change (which is to be classified under the category about outcome).

In *The Future of Information Architecture* (*FIA*), I introduce three additional principles, that is, (j) the simpleness-complicadness principle on the interconnection among things, (k) the preciseness-vagueness principle on the refinement of things, and (l) the slowness-quickness principle on the speed of change—with the first two in relation to structure and the third in relation to process.

In *The Future of Post-Human Unconsciousness* (*FPHU*), I added three more principles, that is, (m) the openness-hidden principle on the detection of things, in relation to structure, (n) the explicability-inexplicability principle on the underlying mechanisms of things, in relation to method, and (o) the expansion-contraction principle on the growth of things, in relation to process.

In *The Future of Post-Human Knowledge* (*FPHK*), I added one more principle, that is, (p) the absoluteness-relativeness principle on the multiplicity of entities, in relation to method.

In *The Future of Post-Human Mathematical Logic* (*FPHML*), I added one more principle, that is, (q) the formalness-informalness principle on the formal requirements of systems, in relation to method.

In *The Future of Post-Human Engineering* (*FPHE*), I added one more principle, that is, (r) the theory-praxis principle on the duality of knowledge, in relation to agency.

In *The Future of Post-Human Creative Thinking* (*FPHCT*), I added one more principle, that is, (s) the convention-novelty principle on the nature of creative thinking, in relation to agency.

In *The Future of Post-Human Geometry* (*FPHG*) here, I added one more principle, that is, (t) the finiteness-transfiniteness principle on the nature of numbers, in relation to structure.

And in *The Future of Post-Human Urban Planning* (*FPHUP*), I added one more principle, that is, (u) the denseness-emptiness principle on the distribution of entities in space, in relation to structure.

With this update, there are twenty-one principles so far in existential dialectics, that is, five principles for the category in relation to method (viz., the formalness-informalness principle, the partiality-totality principle, the predictability-unpredictability principle, the explicability-inexplicability principle, and the absoluteness-relativeness principle), five principles for the category in relation to structure (viz., the finiteness-transfiniteness principle, the simpleness-complicatedness principle, the preciseness-vagueness principle, the openness-hiddenness principle, and the denseness-emptiness principle), four principles for the category in relation to process (viz., the change-constancy principle, the slowness-quickness principle, the order-chaos principle, and the expansion-contraction principle), five principles for the category in relation to agency (viz., the theory-praxis principle, the convention-novelty principle, the symmetry-asymmetry principle, the evolution-transformation principle, and the softness-hardness principle), and two principles for the category in relation to outcome (viz., the regression-progression principle and the same-difference principle).

There are thus twenty-one principles in existential dialectics—so far (as summarized in *Table 4.4*).

The Principles as Short Cuts

Yet, these principles should be treated with caution, lest misunderstanding occurs, since they do not constitute rigid dualities (or dichotomies).

The reason is that each pair in an ontological principle consists of two opposites, which are, however, merely short cuts both for multiple variations and degrees, as well as for different interactions with multiple other entities unlike them.

In this light, each pair can end up having hundred (or even thousand, if not more) different versions, which interact with hundred (or even thousand, if not more) other entities—as summarized in *Table 4.5*.

There are two clarifications here.

Firstly, this conception of shortcuts is not mutually exclusive nor absolute, in that the opposites can come in all shapes and sizes, with different degrees. For instance, by analogy, just as there are different degrees of the two colors "white" and "black"—there are likewise different degrees of the opposites in each ontological pair, to the extent that there can be multiple entities (not only two) interacting with each other in each pair.

And secondly, this conception of shortcuts do not ignore other possible entities in interacting with the two opposites (with their different versions) in each pair. For instance, by analogy, there are not only the two colors "white" and "black" as opposites, since there are other colors too besides them like "yellow," "green," "purple," or else. The same logic can be applied to each ontological pair, in that they also interact with other entities, not with only two of them (with their different versions).

Therefore, with these two clarifications in mind—each pair in an ontological principle serves only as an abbreviation for something more complicated and, therefore, although it contains two opposites, it should not be confused as a duality (dualism).

Existential dialectics rejects any dualism (or dichotomy) as too rigid and instead allows the multiplicity of entities, to the extent that between the two opposites in each pair exist many other alternatives to choose from. They are named in that short form for aesthetic elegance only, instead of listing all possible entities between the two opposites in the title (which would be too cumbersome and sound extremely awkward).

To be dialectic is to go beyond any rigid dichotomy and transcend into something different altogether in the long haul. One may be tempted to call the dialectic logic here with a different name like existential "multilectics" (instead of "dialectics"), but this naming is incorrect (or even misleading), for the two reasons aforestated.

After all, all the possible entities between any two opposites in an ontological pair are still about the two opposites, although each ontological pair come in all shapes and sizes (with different degrees) and do not exist by themselves but also interact with other entities unlike them. The virtue of revealing an ontological pair is to show how they relate within themselves (in multiple versions) and also interact with others unlike them (also in multiple versions).

This will be clear in a later sub-section titled "the dialectic constraints imposed by the principles."

The Principles as Family Resemblances

In addition, each ontological principle is generic, with some other comparable ontological pairs to be put in the same family (like a *family resemblance*)—as summarized in *Table 4.6*.

Ludwig Wittgenstein (1953) once suggested the idea of "family resemblance" in explaining different games classified under the same family called *games*.

Why should, for instance, playing football and chess as playing "games," when it is well understood that football is not the same as chess? The answer is that, although each game is different and has different rules, many of them (though not all) share, more or less, some commonalites (e.g., scoring as necessary for winning).

And this is so, even though some games share more than some others in any given selection of critieria, and no two games are exactly identical. So, Wittgenstein's point here is that there is no essential core which is common to all games, and the best that one can look for is some characteristics which are common to many (but not all) games. (A. Biletzki 2006)

(a) Appropriate Family Resemblances

In the context of existential dialectics, I want to distinguish two types of family resemblances, and, in the absence of better words, let me call them (a) *appropriate* family resemblances and (b) *inappropriate* family resemblances.

In regard to appropriate family resemblances—good examples include some of the pairs as already explained in an earlier section on selection criteria, like the flexibility-inflexibility pair, which can be put in the family resemblance of the simpleness-complicatedness principle, although the two pairs are not exactly identical. Likewise, the directness-indirectness pair can be put in the family resemblance of the preciseness-vagueness principle, although, again, the two pairs are not exactly identical.

In this sense, which specific pair in a family should be used to designate the name of the family can be at times a bit arbitrary, but with good reason.

For illustration, in the context of method, the partiality-totality principle can take the different form like individualisticness-holisticness, just as the explicability-inexplicability principle can take the different form like underlyingness-regularness—although each two pairs are not exactly identical and have slightly different meanings and usages.

A more comprehensive listing of this family resemblance for all other principles is shown in *Table 4.6* on the syntax of existential dialectics.

In fact, this section on family resemblances overlaps with the semantics of existential dialectics, which will be introduced later in the next section (and summarized in *Table 4.11*).

(b) Inappropriate Family Resemblances

However, there are some family resemblances which are not appropriate, and let me distinugish two of them by calling them, in the absence of better words, (b1) *inadequate* family resemblances and (b2) *compound* family resemblances (as summarized in *Table 4.10*).

(b1) In regard to "inadequate" family resemblances—there are some pairs which are not adequate, because they fail the test of selection criteria (as already pointed out in an earlier section), especially in relation to the criterion of not being *trivial* (or *parochial*)—as if it is only one component competing with other ones for inclusion in a set.

For instance, the *consistency-inconsistency* pair is inadequate, because it is only one component competing with other ones for inclusion in the larger set of the formalness-informalenss principle (like the *completeness-incompleteness* pair and the *soundness-unsoundness* pair, as discussed in my book titled *The Future of Post-Human Mathematical Logic*, or *FPHML* in short).

The same is true for the *cognition-noncognition* pair, which overlaps with both the completeness-incompleteness pair and the soundness-unsoundness pair in the larger set of the formalness-informalenss principle.

(b2) In regard to "compound" (or non-atomic) family resemblances—there are some pairs which are not appropriate for a different reason, because they fail the test of selection criteria (as already pointed out in an earlier section), especially in relation to the criterion of not *overlapping* with other principles, in that it is too closely related with other ones.

For instance, the *normality-abnormality* pair is compound (and thus inappropriate), because it overlaps with several other principles, like the symmetry-asymmetry principle, the density-emptiness principle, the convention-novelty principle, and the same-difference principle, for instance (as already discussed in *FPHP*).

The normality-abnormality pair overlaps with the symmetry-asymmetry principle, because being "abnormal" (say, for those with mental illnesses) is often treated not equally by others who are "normal." So, the relationship reveals the symmetry-asymmetry principle.

The normality-abnormality pair also overlaps with the density-emptiness principle, because being "abnormal" (say, for those with mental illnesses) is often not as dense in the overall (not local) distribution of a population as those who are "normal." So, the relationship reveals the density-emptiness principle.

The normality-abnormality pair also overlaps with the convention-novelty principle, because being "abnormal" (say, for those with mental illnesses) often exhibits non-conventional (non-conformist) ideas and behaviors when contrasted with those who are "normal." So, the relationship reveals the convention-novelty principle.

The normality-abnormality pair also overlaps with the same-difference principle, because being "abnormal" (say, for those with mental illnesses) shares some similarities in outcome when compared with those who are "normal" (in that both contribute to the control and regulation of human thoughts and behaviors in society, albeit in different ways). Yet, being "abnormal" also has something different from being "normal," in that abnormal thoughts and behaviors follow a different pattern when contrasted with those which are normal. So, the relationship reveals the same-difference principle.

These illustrations of indequate and compound family resemblances show how difficult it is to come up with an ontological principle in existential dialectics out of the blue, because many of them violate the selection criteria in one way or the other. It is all too easy to join two opposing words and simply make them into a pair, but it is all too difficult to pass the test of the selection criteria to be qualified as an ontological principle in existential dialectics.

Other examples of compound (and inadequate) family resemblances are shown in *Table 4.10* on "The Syntax of Existential Dialectics VII: Types of Inappropriate Family Resemblances."

The Dialectic Constraints Imposed by the Principles

The principles, as they constitute the syntax of existential dialectics, are dialectic in character, such that, when they are applied, they impose dialectic constraints on how reality is to be understood.

Consider, say, the symmetry-asymmetry principle as an illustration here, in order to summarize two main characters of the dialectic constraints in question (as summarized in *Table 4.7*).

Firstly, to be dialectic here is to go beyond the narrow dichotomies (and, for that matter, any rigid multi-dimensional classificatory scheme), be they about "self" vs. "world," "freedom" vs. "unfreedom," "barbarity" vs. "civilization," "individuality" vs. "communality," and so on.

One way to do so (to go beyond) is to consider them all in terms of co-existence (without favoring one over the rest). For instance, my theory of "post-civilization" (to be summarized later in the section on the pragmatics of existential dialectics) is to go beyond barbarity and civilization in terms of understanding barbarity and civilization as being co-existent.

And the same logic can be said in relation to my theories of "post-democracy," "post-capitalsm," and others (also to be introduced later in the section on the pragmatics of existential dialectics), in regard to freedom vs. unfreedom, equality vs. inequality, communality vs. individuality, spirituality vs. materiality, and so on.

But to consider them all (in the dichotomies—and, for that matter, in any rigid multi-dimensional classifactory scheme) as co-existent is not the same as to imply that the opposing categories in any classificatory scheme are all equal, since, in accordance to the symmetry-asymmetry principle (as an illustration here), if they are equal in terms of being considered as co-existent, they are asymmetric in terms of being unequal in dialectic interaction (e.g., X can be more dominant than Y in case A, or Y is more dominant than X in case B), although in some special cases, they can be relatively equal (e.g., X and Y are relatively equal in case C).

For this reason, there are different versions of "post-democracy" and "post-capitalism" in my theories. As an illustration, in version I of the theory of post-democracy, freedom is more dominant than equality, whereas in version II of the theory of post-democracy, equality is more so than freedom.

But this "X more than Y" has to be understood in the context of dialectic logic (not in symbolic logic, as conventionally understood), in that both "X" and "Y" are important in post-democracy (in the context of dialectic logic), but in an asymmetry way.

By contrast, in symbolic logic, it often favors one over the other—be it in regard to privileging freedom over equality (in Fascism), favoring freedom relatively more than equality (in Liberal Democracy), or favoring equality relatively more than freedom (in Socialist Democracy). In regard to the latter two cases (about Liberal Democracy and Socialist Democracy), the difference between dialectic logic and symbolic logic can be one in degree, not in kind—in this sense, albeit not in other senses.

The same reasoning can be said about the relatonships between individuality and communality, between spirituality and materiality, and between formal legalism and informal legalism in the different versions of my theory of "post-capitalism."

Secondly, to be dialectic is to go beyond the narrow dichotomies (and, for that matter, any rigid multi-dimensional classificatory scheme) in another way, this time, in a transcendent way, that is, in exploring other possibilities or even other issues not considered within the narrow confines of narrow dichotomies (and, for that matter, any rigid multi-dimensional classificatory scheme).

As an analogy, in this second meaning, to go beyond the narrow dichotomy of "black" vs. "white" is not just to choose both "black" and "white" (as in the first meaning) but also to explore other options (e.g., "green," "purple," "blue," etc.—and, alternatively, "shade," "line," "curve," etc.).

By the same reasoning, to go beyond "democracy" is to transcend democracy (as in version III of my theory of "post-democracy") and to explore other possibilties of lifeforms (e.g., "floating consciousness," "hyper-spatial consciousness," etc., to live beyond the narrow obsession with freedom and equality).

This dialectic character of the principles in existential dialectics has important implications for the pragmatics of existential dialectics (as will be clear shortly, in the section on the pragmatics of existential dialectics).

The Semantics of Existential Dialectics (or Its Ontosemantics)

The syntax of existential dialectics so understood in terms of ontological principles only gives us the structure of ontology in the world, in an abstract (general) sense. These principles by themselves do not tell us the specific meanings in a given context.

In order to grasp the specific meanings of the principles in a given context, it is necessary to study the semantics of existential dialectics (as summarized in *Table 4.11*).

And the analysis of the ontological principles as family resemblances in the previous section on syntax is only a starting point (and thus overlaps a bit with the semantics of existential dialectics here).

For this reason, I have often gone to great lengths in my previous books on different subjects to explain the specific meanings of the principles when applied in different contexts.

Consider two examples below for illustration, which are not exhaustive.

In *FPHST*, for instance, I used the first three principles (i.e., the change-constancy principle, the regression-progression principle, and the symmetry-asymmetry principle) to propose "the perspectival theory of space-time," for a better way to understand space and time—especially, though not exclusively, in relation to future post-human history (as summarized in *Table 1.3*, *Table 1.4*, *Table 1.5*, and *Table 1.6*).

In so doing, I had to introduce concepts and theories specific to the field of physics and other related fields (e.g., "absolute space" and "absolute time" in "classical mechanics" and "relative space-time" in "the theory of relativity").

And in *BNN*, I also exploited the three principles to propose the "transcendent" approach to the study of genes and memes as a new way to understand the interaction between nature and nurture.

In so doing, I had to explore concepts and theories in the world of evolutionary biology (e.g., "mutation," "variation," "adaptation," "selection," and "inheritance" in classical evolutionary theory) and neural biology (e.g., "chromosome," "gene," "DNA," "RNA," "protein," "neuron," "neural network," and "behavior").

Other examples, besdies these two here, are given in other books of mine on different topics.

Therefore, this semantic dimension of existential dialectics is important, since, in each of my books when the ontological principles are used, each principle becomes relevant in a different meaning when contextualized within a given case study in question.

In this book, for instance, the principles are relevant in relation to the subject matter of cosmology (as summarized in the concluding chapter), and they can be shown in all shapes and sizes (since they are also to be treated as "short cuts," as indicated before), without, however, being reduced to "specific ontology" (as opposed to "general ontology"), as explained in *Table 4.9*.

The Pragmatics of Existential Dialectics (or Its Ontopragmatics)

Even the semantics of existential dialectics is not enough to understand reality, since semantics by itself does not tell us the nature of intentionality and interests in relation to the matrix of power formations and conflicting interests when existential dialectics as an ontology is applied.

Surely, one cannot completely separate the pragmatics of existential dialectics from its semantics (and for that matter, its syntax), but the point here is to give each a more elaborated analysis.

For this reason, the pragmatics of existential dialectics needs to be studied too, in special relation to the inclusion of power formation and conflicting interests in the application of the principles of existential dialectics (as summarized in *Table 4.12*).

It is thus no wonder that all my previous books have shown in different ways how and why these ontological principles and their theoretical applications can reveal the future world to come in a way that humans have never known, in a totally different battleground for competing human (and later post-human) interests by myriad groups fighting for their own versions of hegemony.

Perhaps a summary of my previous works in relation to existential dialectics and their contributions to my new theories as proposed over the years is deemed revealing here, for the further understanding of the pragmatics of existential dialectics (in close relation to the semantics of existential dialectics too).

That stressed—the following summary in four sub-sections is something that I often do in my previous books too, as a way to introduce the intellectual background of my ideas.

So, for those readers who had read my previous works, the following sub-sections serve as a reminder, as they are repeated hereafter *often verbatim* (with only some updated changes, with the rest kept intact).

These sub-sections are, namely, (a) the two-way street connecting theory with meta-theory, (b) the theoretical application of existential dialectics, (c) direct and indirect applications of existential dialectics, and (d) multiple applications of existential dialectics—to be summaried herefafter, respectively.

The Two-Way Street Connecting Theory and Meta-Theory

However, lest any misunderstanding occurs, it is important to remember that the pragmatics of existential dialectics is not a one-way street (that is, using the ontological principles for theoretical insights in praxis) but a two-way one, namely, (a) from meta-theory to theory, and (b) from theory to meta-theory.

(a) On one side of the street, the ontological principles can inspire some theoretical insights in praxis, that is, in relation to some specific fields.

(b) On the other (opposing) side of the street, however, the study of a subject matter in the specific fields in turn reveals some more hitherto unknown ontological principles to be discovered and identified.

For this reason, three new principles were added in *FC*, one in *FAE*, two in *ALD*, and three in *FIA*, on top of the original three in *BCPC*, for example (as there are more)—after some research on the specific subject matters.

Both theory and meta-theory enrich each other in all my works over the years.

The Theoretical Application of Existential Dialectics

This two-way street connecting theory and meta-theory has contributed to my original construction of 45 specific theories in 35 books (including this one here, up to now, in mid-2010) on numerous fields in all domains of knowledge, which can be classified in terms of specific "meta-theories" (about epistemology, methodology, logic, ontology, etc.) and specific "theories" (about the mind, nature, culture, society, and the rest—as will be further explained later in the sub-section on "the holistic organization of an inquiry" in the section about "sophisticated methodological holism").

The final aim of my numerous new specific theories (on both theory and meta-theory) is to converge all of them (as proposed in my numerous books) into a grand project about the future of intelligent life, both here on earth and in deep space.

In fact, all these theories of mine serve as a foundation to unify all domains of knowledge for an overarching understanding of all forms of reality (by way of some ontological principles and the comprehensive perspectives of the mind, nature, society, and culture), while allowing for heterogeneity, conflict, subjectivity, and complexity, for example.

With this grand project in mind—the summary of my specific theories on meta-theory are given in this section (on "existential dialectics") and the next (on "sophisticated methodological holism"), whereas the specific theories on theory will be summarized in the following categories of (a) society, (b) culture, (c) the mind, (d) nature, and (e) the rest, as shown below, in that order.

(a) Society

The category of "society" here can be divided into four sub-categories, i.e., (a1) social organizations, (a2) social institutions, (a3) social structure, and (a4) social systems.

(a1) Social Organizations

In relation to social organizations, I proposed a new thesis on the ambivalent nature of virtual organizations in the future, known as "the theory of e-civic alienation" in *FCD* (and summarized in *Table 4.19*).

And in *FPHO*, another theory called "the combinational theory of organization" is worked out, although it was first proposed in Ch.6 of *ALD*.

(a2) Social Institutions

There are different social institutions, be they about (a2.1) politics, (a2.2) economics, (a2.3) military affairs, and (a2.4) mass media, for instance.

(a2.1) In relation to politics, I offered different visions on (a2.1.1) political theory, (a2.1.2) comparative politics, and (a2.1.3) international relations, to cite three main ones.

(a2.1.1) In the context of political theory, my vision of a path-breaking political system in future times concerns the different forms of "post-democracy" to supersede democracy unto the post-human age.

My vision of post-democracy was called "the theory of post-democracy" (as summarized in *Table 4.22*, *Table 4.23*, and *Table 4.24*), whereas *Table 4.25* explains the distinctions among democracy, non-democracy, and post-democracy.

And *Table 4.26* stresses the multiple causes of the emergence of post-democracy, while *Table 4.27* clarifies some possible misunderstandings in regard to post-capitalism and post-democracy.

(a2.1.2) In the context of comparative politics, I also showed, in *ALD*, how and why authoritarianism can be an advanced form of liberal democracy (just as it has its own counterpart in non-liberal democracy), or what I originally called "authoritarian liberal democracy" (as summarized in *Table 4.21*), before it is to be superceded by "post-democracy."

(a2.1.3) In the context of international relations (both at the institutional and structural levels), I provided, in *BWT*, "the theory of cyclical progression of empire-building," for a better way to understand the logic of empire-building on earth and beyond—with the rise of what I originally envisioned as "hyper-empires" (like "the Chinese Union" and "the Indian Union"), "meso-empires" (like "the European Union" and "the North American Union") and "micro-empires" (like "the Middle Eastern Union" and "the Latin American Union") in the coming "post-post-Cold War era" as a visionary illustration, as summarized in *Table 4.20*.

In addition, in *FPHWP*, I proposed "the multifaceted theory of war and peace" to understand war and peace, in a small sense—or aggression and pacificity, in a broad sense.

(a2.2) In relation to economics, I also offered another vision, this time to understand the future forms of economic systems, that is, the different forms of "post-capitalism" to supersede capitalism unto the post-human age.

My vision of post-capitalism was referred to (in *FCD*, *BDPD* and *BCPC*) as "the theory of post-capitalism" (as summarized in *Table 4.28*, *Table 4.29*, *Table 4.30*, *Table 4.31*, and *Table 4.32*). And *Table 4.33* clarifies the differences among capitalism, non-capitalism, and post-capitalism, whereas *Table 4.34* shows multiple causes of the emergence of post-capitalism.

This vision on "post-capitalism" constitutes the third theoretical application of existential dialectics, this time, in that there is no wealth without poverty (or the wealth/poverty dialectics).

(a2.3) In relation to military affairs, I also proposed "the multifaceted theory of war and peace" (in *FCD*, although it was first so labeled in *FPHK*) for a new way to understand the causes of war—and, for that matter, the rise and fall of different forms of warfare over time.

This theory was further expanded in *FPHWP*, where I suggested a new way to understand war and peace, in a small sense—or aggression and pacificity, in a broad sense.

(a2.4) In relation to mass media, I also proposed "the totalistic theory of communication" in *The Future of Post-Human Mass Media* (or in short, *FPHMM*).

(a3) Social Structure

In relation to social structure, I proposed two additional theories, that is, "the theory of the cyclical progression of hegemony" in *FCD* (and also in *FPHC* and *BDPD*), and "the theory of the cyclical progression of empire-building" (in *BWT*, as already indicated above)—with important implications for the symmetry-asymmetry princple in existential dialectics, just to cite one example.

Also, in *BNN*, I also proposed "the theory of contrastive advantages" to understand the persistence of social structure by gender, race, ethnicity, or any other groupings.

(a4) Social Systems

In relation to social systems, there are several sub-categories for illustration, which can be about (a4.1) urbanization, (a4.2) technology, (a4.3) demography, (a4.4) the environment, and (a4.5) social trends as a whole.

(a4.1) In relation to urbanization, I proposed "the contingent theory of urban planning" in *FPHUP* for a new way to understand density and void.

(a4.2) In relation to technology, I worked out "the ambivalent theory of technology" in *FPHE* for a new way to understand the nature of technology.

Some other books (like *FPHMM*, *FAE*, *FCD*, and *FHC*) also deal with technology, and a good example concerns "the synthetic theory of information architecture" in *FIA* on taxonomy, network, and intelligence, in conjunction with the rise of technology.

(a4.3) In relation to demography, I proposed, first in *FHC* (and later in other books like *FCD*, *FPHC*, *FPHU*, etc.), "the theory of post-humanity," in relation to the "post-human" age at some distant point of "after-postmodernity," long after human extinction, to be eventually superseded by "post-humans" of various forms.

Some good candidates of the post-human lifeforms include, for instance, "thinking robots," "thinking machines," "cyborgs," "genetically altered superior beings," "floating consciousness," "hyper-spatial consciousness," "unfolding unconsciousness," "the hyper-sexual body," and "the hyper-martial body." This post-human vision of mine was first originally worked out in *FHC* and further elaborated in both *FCD*, *FPHC*, *FPHU*, *FPHS*, and *FPHMA*, for instance.

Lest any confusion occurs, I need to emphasize two clarifications here about the term "post-human" as a neologism in my works.

Firstly, the word "post-human" here should *not* be confused with another term which looks similar but has a totally different meaning in the literature of postmodernism, namely, "post-humanism"—which constitutes a critique of "humanism" as tradionally understood (especially, though not exclusively, in relation to the idea of progress in science and reason in the Enlightenment project). (WK 2008)

And secondly, the word "post-human" here should also *not* be confused with a similar term which is used to champion the ideology of technology for the future co-existence between humans and cyborgs in "trans-humanism." (WK 2008a)

Instead, my term "post-human" in relation to "posthuman-ism" also rejects "transhumanism" (especially, though not exclusively, in relation to the promises of technology) and refers to something else altogether, that is, the future extinction of humans and its post-human successors in deep space and beyond unto multiverses.

Later, in *BEPE*, I went further and provided a more comprehensive critique of "transhumanism," together with other issues.

With these two clarifications in mind (as summarized in *Table 1.31*)—in the end, a most fundamental question about intelligent life now has an answer, in that, if asked, "What is the future of human civilization?"—my answer in *FCD* (89) is thus: "As addressed in Ch.7 of *FHC*, a later epoch of the age of after-postmodernity (that is, at some point further away from after-postmodernity) will begin, as what I called the 'post-human' history (with the term 'post-human' originally used in my doctoral dissertation at M.I.T., which was finished in November 1995, under the title *After Postmodernity*, still available at M.I.T. library, and was later revised and published as *FHC*). The post-human history will be such that humans are nothing in the end, other than what culture, society, and nature (with some luck) have shaped them into, to be eventually superseded by post-humans (e.g., cyborgs, thinking machines, genetically altered superior beings, and others), if humans are not destroyed long before then."

(a4.4) In relation to the environment, I also addressed the issue of sustainability, especially in *FHC*, *FCD*, and *FPHUP*. For instance, in *FPHUP*, I specifically proposed a new theory, "the contingent theory of urban planning," on the need to go beyond the contemporoary obsession with sustainability, in the context of not only the environment but also other issues.

(a4.5) In relation to social trends as a whole, I proposed in Ch.9 of *FCD* (367-8), that "civilizational history will continue into the following cyclical progression of expansion, before it is to be superseded (solely as a high probability, since humans might be destroyed sooner either by themselves or in a gigantic natural calamity) by posthumans at some distant point in after-postmodernity (which I already discussed in *FHC*)" unto multiverses (different constellations of universes):

Local → Regional → Global →Solar →
Galactic → Clustery…→ Multiversal

In *BDPD*, this thesis of mine was referred to as "the theory of the cyclical progression of system integration and fragmentation," at the systemic level—in close relation to another thesis analyzed in Ch.9 of *FCD*, which was called, in the absence of better words, "the multifaceted theory of war and peace" in *FPHK* (as already indicated above).

In *FC*, I also proposed "the dialectic theory of complexity" to account for the factor of uncertainty, which can have a major role to play in the world.

(b) Culture

The category of "culture" here can also be divided into different sub-categories like (b1) aesthetics, (b2) religion, (b3) popular (mass) culture, (b4), logic, (b5) civilization as a whole, (b6) ethics, (b7) epistemology (methodology), (b8) metaphysics (ontology), and (b9) ideology.

However, (b7) epistemology (methodology), (b8) metaphysics (ontology), and (b9) ideology are already discussed elsewhere, be they about "meta-theory" (e.g., methodology and ontology under the categories of "existential dialectics" here and "sophisticated methodological holism" in the next section) or "theory" (e.g., ideology under the categories of "social institutions," as described earlier, and also of "civilization as a whole," as will be addressed shortly).

(b1) Aesthetics

In relation to aesthetics, I proposed "the transformative theory of aesthetic experience" in *FAE* about some great transformations of aesthetic experience in future history.

(b2) Religion

In relation to religion, I proposed "the comparative theory of religion" in *FHC* (and also in *FCD*, although it was first so labeled in *FPHK*).

And in *FPHR*, I provide a solid foundation of this theory with a better name, that is, "the comparative-substitutive theory of religion" for a new way to understand spirituality.

(b3) Popular (Mass) Culture

In relation to popular (mass) culture, there are some sub-categories for illustration, which can be, for example, (b3.1) mass culture in general and (b3.2) sports (like chess).

(b3.1) In relation to mass culture in general, I proposed, in *FHC*, a new way to understand mass culture in terms of some fundamental dilemmas, which is called, in the absence of better words, "the dualistic theory of mass culture" in *FPHO*.

(b3.2) In relation to sports (like chess), I proposed, in *FPHCHESS*, "the mediative-variative theory of chess" for a new way to understand tactics and strategy (in different traditions).

(b4) Logic

In relation to logic, I also worked out, in *FPHML*, "the contrastive theory of rationality" for a new way to understand rationality and knowledge (in the context of mathematical logic).

(b5) Civilization as a Whole

In relation to civilization as a whole, I also argued, in *FHC*, no freedom without unfreedom (as shown in *Table 4.13*) and no equality without inequality (as shown in *Table 4.14*), especially in relation to the seven dimensions of life existence first worked out in *FHC* (i.e., the technological, the everyday, the true, the holy, the sublime/beautiful, the good, and the just).

Even more interestingly, in *BDPD* and later in *BCIV*, I further revealed a theoretical refinement of existential dialectics, this time, in arguing that there is no civilization without barbarity, with human civilization to be eventually superseded by what I originally analyzed as "post-human post-civilization" (which should not be confused with "post-human civilization"), in the context of the freedom/unfreedom and equality/inequality dialectics.

In the final analysis, civilization cannot live without barbarity and has to learn to co-exist with it in ever new ways. Preposteorus as this may seem to many contemporaries—it is no more imperative to preserve civilization than necessary to destroy barbarity, and the ideal of civilization is essentially bankrupt, to be eventually superseded by "post-civilization" (as summarized in *Tables 4.35-4.43*).

This freedom/unfreedom and equality/inequality dialectics holds in pre-moderny, modernity, postmodernity, and what I orignally called "after-postmodernity" in *FHC* and *FCD*—especially, though not exclusively, in the context of the emergence of "post-humans."

There are two specific theories about "after-postmodernity" here. The first theory about "after-postmodernity" is about the trinity of pre-modernity, modernity, postmodernity, and after-postmodernity at the cultural level—and was called, in *BDPD*, "the theory of the trinity of modernity to its after-postmodern counterpart," although it was first analyzed in *FHC* and later in *FCD* and also *BCIV* (as summarized in *Table 1.34*, *Table 1.35*, *Table 1.36*, and *Table 1.37* and will be elaborated further in the later sub-section on "the rest" about future history).

The second theory about "after-postmodernity" is about pre-modernity, modernity, postmodernity, and after-postmodernity at the historical level. For instance, a conclusion in *FHC*, which is shocking indeed for many contemporaries, is none other than that "[t]he post-human history will therefore mark the end of human history as we know it and, for that matter, the end of human dominance and, practically speaking, the end of humans as well. The entire history of human civilization, from its beginning to the end, can be summarized by four words, linked by three arrows (as already discussed in *FHC*)":

Pre-Modernity → Modernity →
Post-Modernity → After-Postmodernity

In *BDPD*, this thesis of mine was specifically called "the theory of the evolution from pre-modernity to after-postmodernity," at the historical level—as shown in *Table 1.34*, *Table 1.35*, *Table 1.36*, and *Table 1.37* (and will be elaborated further in the later sub-section on "the rest" about future history).

Therefore, "[t]he end of humanity in the coming human extinction is the beginning of post-humanity. To say an untimely farewell to humanity is to foretell the future welcome of post-humanity." (P. Baofu 2002: 89) This thesis of mine was known in *BDPD* as "the theory of post-humanity," at the systemic level—as already indicated in (a4.3) above.

(b6) Ethics

In relation to ethics, I proposed, in *BEPE*, "the theory of post-ethics" for a new way to understand morality and immorality.

(c) The Mind

This important vision about "post-humans" (as summarized above) brings us to the category of "the mind" here, which, as is often understood in everyday's usage, refers to the "brain" and the "body" (together with their interactions) and has different levels of consciousness which can be both "spiritual" and non-spiritual.

Therefore, the "mind" already presupposes the "brain," "body," and "spirit" (or "soul"), so that one does not fall into the intellectual trap of the "mind-body dualism" as debunked in modern (and especially, postmodern) philosophy (which I already went to great lengths to explain in *The Future of Human Civilization*).

That said—the category of "the mind" can be divided into two sub-categories, namely, in relation to (c1) biology and (c2) psychology.

(c1) Biology

In relation to biology, there are two concerns here, namely, (c1.1) genes and intelligence and (c1.2) the human body.

(c1.1) In relation to genes and intelligence, I worked out "the theory of contrastive advantages" (which was originally proposed in *FCD* and further worked out in *BNN*, as summarized in *Table 1.24*), to show the nature-nurture interactions of multiple levels in action (e.g., the biological, the psychological, the structural, the systemic, the cultural, and others) for humans and post-humans on earth and beyond, to the extent that different groups, be they on the basis of race, gender, ethnicity, class, age, or else, are not equal, on average, and have never been, nor will they be, even if there can be exceptions.

(c1.2) In relation to the human body, for instance, in *FPHMA*, I suggested "the expansive-contractive theory of martial arts," in which two great future transformations of the martial body were envisioned, that is, both "with the hyper-martial body" and "without the body" (as summarized in *Table 1.32*)—although this issue can also be classified under the category of "culture."

And in *FPHS*, I proposed "the theory of virtual sexuality," in which three great future transformations of the sexual body were envisioned, that is, "virtual pleasure," "the hyper-sexual body," and "the post-sexual floating mind" (as summarized in *Table 1.33*).

(c2) Psychology

In relation to psypchology (which also overlaps with biology too, however), I also proposed some greater transformations of the mind to come in the future, especially though not exclusively in the post-human age.

These greater transformations of the mind in psychology can be further sub-divided into different categories, namely, (c2.1) consciousness, (c2.2) unconsciousness (together with subconsciousness), (c2.3) creativity, (c2.4) learning, (c2.5) aggression (and pacificity), and (c2.6) personality.

(c2.1) In relation to consciousness, I analyzed, in *FPHC*, the nature of consciousness in relation to the conceptual dimensions of consciousness (as shown in *Table 1.12*), the theoretical levels of consciousness (as shown in *Table 1.13*), the thematic issues of consciousness (as shown in *Table 1.14*), the different dimensions of human existence (viz., having-ness, belonging-ness, and being-ness) in relation to consciousness (as shown in *Table 1.15*, *Table 1.16*, *Table 1.17*, and *Table 1.18*).

In *BCPC*, the nature of consciousness was further explored in relation to cognition, emotion, and behavior, which can be in consciousness and other mental states (e.g., subconsciousness and unconsciousness), in the context of existential dialectics, as shown in *Table 1.19*, *Table 1.20*, *Table 1.21*, *Table 1.22,* and *Table 1.23*.

In fact, in *FCD*, I already proposed three different theories in relation to the limits of cognition, emotion, and behavior, namely, "the theory of cognitive partiality," "the theory of emotional non-neutrality," and "the theory of behavioral alteration."

Then, I argued that the existence of human consciousness will be superseded one day with "floating consciousness" (as first proposed in *FCD*) and "hyper-spatial consciousness" (as first proposed in *FPHC*) as a climax of evolution in consciousness, after the future extinction of human consciousness (as shown below):

Primordial consciousness → Human consciousness →
Post-human consciousness (with floating consciousness and hyper-spatial consciousness as a climax in the evolution of consciousness)

In *BDPD*, these latest theses of mine were called "the theory of floating consciousness" and "the theory of hyper-spatial consciousness," both at the cosmological and psychological levels (as summarized in *Table 1.26* and *Table 1.25*).

(c2.2) In relation to unconsciousness, for instance, in *FPHU*, the unconsious mind will undergo tremendous change, to the rise of what I originally called "unfolding unconsciousess" in relation to anomalous experience, as a climax of evolution in unconsciousness, in conjunction with the conscious mind (both human now and post-human later), especially at the psychological level, as shown below:

Primordial unconsciousness → Human unconsciousness → Post-human unconsciousness (with unfolding unconsciousness as a climax in the evolution of unconsciousness)

In *FPHU*, this thesis of mine is called "the theory of unfolding unconsciousness" in a small sense, or "the unfolding theory of anomalous experience," in a larger one, as shown in *Table 1.27* and *Table 1.28.*

(c2.3) In relation to creativity, for instance, in *FPHCT*, I also proposed "the comprehensive theory of creative thinking" to explore the role of creative thinking, in relation to technology and other factors, together with my original proposal of important creative techniques and traits (as shown in *Table 1.29*) and its double nature of desirability and undesirability (as shown in *Table 1.30*).

(c2.4) In relation to learning, for instance, in *FPHL*, I worked out "the multilogical theory of learning" for a new way to understand the nature of structure and context in language, in relation to learning and its future development in the context of the mind.

(c2.5) In relation to aggression (and pacificity), I proposed "the multifaceted theory of war and peace" in *FPHWP* (as mentioned above).

(c2.6) And in relation to personality, I worked out "the contrarian theory of personality" in *FPHP* for a new way to understand normality and abnormality.

(d) Nature

The category of "nature" here refers to the state of nature, which can be divided into some sub-categories like (d1) physics, (d2) cosmology, (d3) biology, (d4) geography, and (d5) geology.

But since biology in (d3) overlaps with biology in (c1)—only phyiscs, cosmology, geography, and geology are addressed hereafter.

(d1) Physics

In relation to physics, I also proposed "the perspectival theory of space-time" in *FPHST* (based on *FPHC*) for a new way to understand space and time, as shown in *Table 1.3*, *Table 1.4*, *Table 1.5*, and *Table 1.7.*

In *FPHG* (based on *FPHC* and *FPHST*), I proposed "the selective theory of geometry" for a new way to understand geometry, with implications for the understanding of space-time in the context of infinity, symmetry, and dimensionality for future lifeforms that our world has never known (as shown in *Table 1.6*, *Table 1.7*, *Table 1.8; Table 1.9*, *Table 1.10,* and *Table 1.11*).

And in *FC*, I proposed "the dialectic theory of complexity" for a new way to understand order and chaos in the state of nature and beyond.

(d2) Cosmology

In relation to cosmology, my theories on physics (as indicated above) already have important implications for understanding the nature and the future of the universe (which was also addressed in *FHC*, among other works aforcited).

I also proposed "the theory of hyper-spatial consciousness" in *FPHC* (and also in *FPHG*) for a new way to understand the future evolution of the mind to enter into different dimensions of space-time that our current world has never known.

In addition, in *BCOS*, I proposed "the theory of post-cosmology" for a new way to understand the beginnings and ends of the cosmos and beyond.

(d4) Geography

In relation to geography, I proposed "the theory of the geopower of nature" in *ALD* for a different way to understand the relationships between geography and other entities (like the mind, culture, and society).

(d5) Geology

And in relation to geology, I proposed "the resettlement theory of geology" in *FPHGEOL* for a different way to understand the relationships between statics and dynamics.

(e) The Rest

The category of "the rest" here refers to what cannot be strictly classified in any of the previous categories (i.e., society, culture, the mind, and nature). A good illustration of "the rest" refers to that which is, namely, (e1) historical.

(e1) Historical

Precisely here, I proposed "the theory of the evolution from pre-modernity to after-postmodernity" (as first worked out in *FHC* and later in *FCD* and *FPHC*), which overlaps—as a reminder from (b5)—with the issue concerning "civilization as a whole" in (b5).

For instance, in both *FCD* and *FPHC*, I worked out the structure of "post-human civilization" in terms of the trinity of after-postmodernity (i.e., "free-spirited after-postmodernity," "post-capitalist after-postmodernity," and "hegemonic after-postmodernity").

Both conceptually and theoretically, the trinity of after-postmodernity is a sequential extension to the trinity of modernity (i.e., "free-spirited modernity," "capitalist modernity,"and "hegemonic modernity") and the trinity of postmodernity (i.e., "free-spirited postmodernity," "capitalist postmodernity," and "hegemonic postmodernity") as first proposed in *FHC*.

And the trinity of pre-modernity (i.e., "pre-free-spirited pre-modernity," "pre-capitalist pre-modernity" and "hegemonic pre-modernity") was later conceived in *BCIV* to complete the historical set from pre-modernity to after-postmodernity.

In *BDPD*, this thesis about the trinity of pre-modernity, modernity, postmodernity, and after-postmodernity was collectively known as "the theory of the trinity of modernity to its after-postmodern counterpart," at the cultural level—as already so mentioned in (b5) earlier, and summarized in *Table 1.34*, *Table 1.35*, *Table 1.36*, and *Table 1.37*.

At the structural level, all these trinities are subject to the existential constraints (e.g., the freedom/unfreedom and equality/inequality dialectics in the context of "the cyclical progression of hegemony"), be the historical epoch in pre-modernity, modernity, postmodernity, or after-postmodernity in future times. Each of the historical epochs has its ever new ways of coming to terms with the ever new (different) mixtures of freedom/unfreedom and equality/inequality.

This is importantly so, not because, as is falsely assumed in conventional wisdom, one certain way is superior (or better) than another in terms of achieving more freedom and less unfreedom, or more equality with less inequality.

On the contrary, indeed, in each of the historical epochs, each increase of unfreedom greets each freedom achieved, just as each increase of inequality welcomes each equality achieved, albeit in ever new (different) ways. In *BDPD*, this thesis of mine was labeled as "the theory of the cyclical progression of hegemony," at the structural level, though it was first analyzed in *FCD*.

In *BDPD*, more theoretical applications of existential dialectics were further examined, in relation to five main features, in the context of the duality of oppression, namely, (a) that each freedom/equality achieved is also each unfreedom/inequality created, (b) that the subsequent oppressiveness is dualistic, both by the Same against the Others and itself and by the Others against the Same and themselves, (c) that both oppression and self-oppression can be achieved by way of downgrading differences (between the Same and the Others) and of accentuating them, (d) that the relationships are relatively asymmetric among them but relatively symmetric within them, even when the Same can be relatively asymmetric towards itself in self-oppression, and the Others can be likewise towards themselves, and (e) that symmetry and asymmetry change over time, with ever new players, new causes, and new forms, be the locality here on Earth or in deep space unto multiverses—as summarized in *Table.4.13*, *Table 4.14*, *Table 4.15*, and *Table 4.16*.

The same logic also holds both in relation to wealth and poverty (as addressed in *BCPC* and summarized in *Table 4.17* on the wealth/poverty dialectics) and in relation to civilization and barbarity (as addressed in *BCIV* and summarized in *Table 4.18* on the civilization/barbarity dialectics).

In *BDPD*, this thesis on existential dialectics was labeled as "the theory of existential dialectics."

Direct and Indirect Applications of Existential Dialectics

A different way to appreciate the usefulness of existential dialectics is by way of the analysis of its (a) direct and (b) indirect applications.

(a) In direct applications, on the one hand, the logic of existential dialectics can shed some theoretical insights on diverse phenomena in the world, and good instances are the usage of the principles of existential dialectics for the theoretical insights on the freedom/unfreedom dialectics, the equality/inequality dialectics, and the wealth/poverty dialectics—as introduced earlier in (b5) and (e) in the previous sub-section.

For instance, my books like *FPHST*, *BNN*, *FAE*, *FC*, *FIA*, *FPHU*, *FPHK*, *FPHML*, *FPHE*, *FPHMM*, *FPHCT*, *FPHG*, *FPHUP*, *FPHL*, *FPHO*, *FPHMA*, *FPHS*, *FPHLAW*, *FPHFS*, *FPHWP*, *FPHP*, *BEPE*, *BCOS*, *FPHGEOL*, *FPHCHESS*, and *FPHR* use the principles to reveal some theoretical insights on the perspectives of space and time (as in *FPHST*), of nature and nurture (as in *BNN*), of beauty and ugliness (as in *FAE*), of order and chaos (as in *FC*), of taxonomy and network (as in *FIA*), of the unconscious mind (as in *FPHU*), of the nature of knowledge (as in *FPHK*), of mathematical logic (as in *FPHML*), of engineering (as in *FPHE*), of mass media (as in *FPHMM*), of creative thinking (as in *FPHCT*), of geometry (as in *FPHG*), of urban planning (as in *FPHUP*), of language (as in *FPHL*), of organization (as in *FPHO*), of martial arts (as in *FPHMA*), of sexuality (as in *FPHS*), of law (as in *FPHLAW*), of formal science (as in *FPHFS*), of aggression and pacificity (as in *FPHWP*), of normality and abnormality (as in *FPHP*). of morality and immorality (as in *BEPE*), of the beginnings and ends of the universe (as in *BOCS*), of statics and dynamics (as in *FPHGEOL*), of tactics and strategy (as in *FPHCHESS*), and of secularness and sacredness (as in *FPHR*).

(b) In indirect applications, on the other hand, the theoretical insights can further be used to reveal other phenomena directly from them (viz., the theoretical insights) and therefore indirectly from the principles themselves.

A good illustration is of course the use of the theoretical insights on the freedom/unfreedom and equality/inequality dialectics for the understanding of the civilization/barbarity dialectics.

This distinction between direct and indirect applications may sound a bit academic, since even in indirect applications, the phenomena under study can still be directly related back to the principles themselves.

In the previous example, as an illustration, the civilization/barbarity dialectics can be directly related to the principles of existential dialectics without the intermediate role of the freedom/unfreedom and equality/inequality dialectics.

Multiple Levels of Application

There is another issue to be clarified, however. In other words, the theoretical insights can be applied to multiple levels of analysis—even though, in a given example, it may refer to one level or a few only.

For instance, in the example concerning the freedom/unfreedom dialectics, it can be used at the structural level (e.g., in relation to the theory of the cyclical progression of hegemony), but it can also be exploited for other levels (e.g., the theory of post-capitalism at the institutional level).

All these levels of application should not be misleadingly construed, as I stress this before, as a one-way street (that is, to use the ontological principles for theoretical application at multiple levels of specific analysis) but a two-way one, in which theoretical insights in praxis, when studied in more specific contexts, can in turn refine the nature of existential dialectics (for example, with the addition of new principles).

Sophisticated Methodological Holism

The summary of my original meta-theory on methodology is provided below, again, to be repeated *often verbatim* from my previous works—as this is something I regularly do in each new book to introduce my past works, which are in conversation with this current one.

This means that, for those readers who had read some of my previous books, the summary below is really not much new (*almost verbatim*, with only some updated revisions).

That clarified—this original contribution of mine to the study of methodology takes the form of an approach known as "the theory of methodological holism" or "methodological holism" in short, as already worked out in *FPHC* (2004).

I have made good use of this methodological approach of mine for all of my previous works.

The Confusion of Holism with Systems Approach

Yet, it is imperative to stress at the outset, as I often emphasized this in all my previous books, that my approach of "methodological holism" does not oppose or exclude "methodological individualism" (as some readers may be tempted to assume, as is conventionally understood) but actually includes it.

The confusion here has to do with equating holism with systems approach in general (be it about systems theory, chaos theory, complexity theory, or else), which I debunked, while learning something from it, as already elaborated in *The Future of Complexity* (2007)—and *The Future of Post-Human Formal Science* (2010) is another addition to this critique of the intellectual fad of systems approach.

In other words, my meta-theory of holism, or sophisticated methodological holism in short, makes a distinction between doing holistic work and doing systems work, for two reasons.

The first reason is that holism, in my theory, does not imply systems approach, since it rejects systems approach because of the myriad problems that the literature on systems approach has been unable to resolve, while learning something from it.

And the second reason is that my theory is related to the other theory of mine, that is, existential dialectics, which does not exclude methodological individualism (but includes it, because it simply goes beyond both reductionism and reverse-reductionism in a dialectic way).

For these reasons (and others too, as summarized in *Table 4.1*), my version of methodological holism is *sophisticated*—not *vulgar* as sometimes used by inapt scholars employing the same term.

The Ontological Constraints

Sophisticated methodological holism is subject to some ontological constraints, and five good examples include "the partiality-totality principle," "the predictability-unpredictability principle," "the explicability-inexplicability principle," "the absoluteness-relativeness principle," and "the formalness-informalness principle" in existential dialectics.

Of course, there can be more than five ontological principles in relation to method, but the five examples here are sufficient to illustrate the point in question.

With this caveat in mind—the first two were already analyzed in previous books of mine like *FC* and *FAE*, whereas the third one was addressed in *FPHU*, and the last two were accounted for in *FPHK* and *FPHML*, respectively.

For now, it suffices to show that sophisticted methodological holism, because of these ontological constraints on methodology, targets two major sins of methodology, namely, what I call, in the absence of better words, (a) *reductionism* and (b) *reverse-reductionism*—both of which come in all shapes and sizes, to be summarized below (and also shown in *Table 4.2*).

Against the Varieties of Reductionism

There are four versions of reductionism to be summarized here, which sophisticated methodological holism rejects, namely, (a1) conceptual, (a2) theoretical, (a3) methodological, and (a4) ontological forms of reductionism.

(a1) In conceptual reductionism, a good case in point concerns myriad dualities like mind vs. body, self vs. world, democracy vs non-democracy, and the like (as already addressed in *FHC*, *FPHC*, and *BDPD*, for instance).

(a2) In theoretical reductionism, an illuminating case study is best exemplified by what I originally called "the foundation fallacy" in *FPHST*, in any attempt to naively understand space-time from the physical perspective as the foundation and, consequently, to dangerously dismiss (or belittle) other perspectives.

In *FAE*, I elaborated further these versions of reductionism in the literature on aesthetics (e.g., form vs. content, representation vs. expression, critics vs. artists, and externalism vs. internalism).

In *FIA*, I revealed other forms of reductionism in the literature on information architecture (e.g., the constructivist argument and the representational argument).

In *FPHU*, I showed the persistent legacy of reductionism, this time, in the literature on anomalous experience (e.g., the obsession with physics, chemistry, and biology for explaining anomalous experience).

In *FPHE*, I examined another case of reductionism in action, in the context of engineering (e.g., technical constraints vs. normative constraints).

In *FPHMM*, I elaborated one more version of reductionism, in relation to the three domains of communication (e.g., the competing views on sending, connecting, and receiving).

In *FPHCT*, I explored another version of reductionism, in relation to invention and innovation (e.g., the bio-psychological argument vs. the socio-cultural arguments).

In *FPHG*, I identified another version of reductionism, in relation to infinity, symmetry, and dimensionality (e.g., the Euclidean argument vs. the non-Euclidean arguments).

In *FPHUP*, I analyzed another version of reductionism, in relation to density and void (e.g., the engineering argument and the ecology argument).

In *PFHL*, I examined another version of reductionism, in relation to structure and context (e.g., the structuralist argument and the contextualist argument).

In *PFHO*, I explored another version of reductionism, in relation to communcation, decision-making, and leadership (e.g., the rational-system argument vs. the natural-system argument vs. the open-system argument).

In *PFHMA*, I revealed another version of reductionism, in relation to the martial body and spirit (e.g., the spiritual argument vs. the materialist argument vs. the defensive argument).

In *PFHS*, I analyzed another version of reductionism, in relation to the sexual body and spirit (e.g., the naturalist argument vs. the constructivist argument).

In *PFHLAW*, I examined another version of reductionism, in relation to law (e.g., the necessity argument vs. the contengency argument).

In *FPHWP*, I show another version of reductionism, in relation to war and peace (e.g., the aggressivist argument vs. the pacifist argument).

In *BEPE*, I analyzed another version of reductionism, in relation to morality and immorality (e.g., the objectivist argument vs. the non-objectivist argument vs. the skeptical argument).

In *BCOS*, I examined another version of reductionism, in relation to the contested beginnings and speculative ends of the universe (e.g., the scientific argument vs. the religious argument vs. the esoteric argument vs. the metaphysical argument).

In *FPHP*, I showed another version of reductionism, in relation to normality and abnormality (e.g., the natural argument vs. the social argument vs. the cultural argument vs. the mental argument).

In *FPHGEOL*, I scrutinized another version of reductionism, in relation to statics and dynamics (e.g., the catastrophe argument vs. the uniformity argument vs. the revision argument).

In *FPHCHESS*, I showed another version of reductionism, in relation to tactics and strategy (e.g., the natural argument vs. the social argument vs. the cultural argument vs. the mental argument).

And in *FPHR* here, I reveal another version of reductionism, in relation to secularness and sacredness (e.g., the critical argument vs. the skeptical argument vs. the theist argument).

(a3) In methodological reductionism, a good illustration can be the debate between different versions of qualitative and quantitative methods (as already analyzed in *FC* and also *FHC*).

In *FPHML*, I examined similar reductionism, this time, in the literature on mathematical logic (e.g., the obsession with consistency, soundness, and completeness).

And in *FPHFS*, I explored the problems of reductionism in the context of formal science (e.g., the analytical argument, as opposed to the synthetic argument).

(a4) In ontological reductionism, an excellent instance involves another debate, this time between emergentism and reductionism in complexity theory (as addressed in *FC*) and also in psychology (as elaborated in *FPHC*, in the context of Being and Belonging).

But to target against the varieties of reductionism constitutes only a side of the same coin, and the other side concerns the varieties of reverse-reductionism.

Against the Varieties of Reverse-Reductionism

The other side of the same coin is the reverse version of reductionism, which is what I want to call, in the absence of better words, *reverse-reductionism.*

My sophisticated version of methodological holism targets against the varieties of reverse-reductionism (just as it also rejects the ones of reductionism).

Perhaps nothing expresses better the popularity of reverse-reductionim than the "anything-goes" mentality in postmodernism of our time, as shown in the following four versions.

(b1) In conceptual reverse-reductionism, any concept of "art" (e.g., fine art, applied art, outsider art, junk art) is welcome in postmodernism (as already analyzed in Ch.4 of *FHC*—and also in *FAE*).

(b2) In theoretical reverse-reductionism, a variety of art and literary theories co-exist. Take the case of literary studies, as there are now Literary Structuralism, Marxist Literary Criticism, New Criticism, Phenomenology, Hermeneutics, Language-Game Literary Criticism, Feminist Literary Criticism, Reception Theory, Reader Response Criticism, Poststructuralism, Semiotics, Pyschoanalytic Literary Criticism, just to cite some well-known ones, with no one being said to be better than any others (as detailedly analyzed in Ch.4 of *FHC*). (S. Raman 1997)

In *BNN*, I even introduced "the compromise fallacy" as another good illustration of theoretical reverse-reductionism, in misleadingly treating both genetic and environmental approaches as equally valid.

(b3) In methodological reverse-reductionism, multiple methodologies are deemed as acceptable in postmodernism (e.g., doing art without praxis, doing art with praxis, and doing art by sublation), as analyzed in Ch.4 of *FHC*.

And in *FPHFS*, I exposed the problems of reverse-reductionism in the context of formal science in relation to systems theory (e.g., the synthetic argument).

(b4) In ontological reverse-reductionism, no privileged ontology is allowed, and the door is open practically for anything in postmodernism (e.g., the equal status of the ontology of Being vs. that of Becoming, as already addressed in Ch.4 of *FHC*—and also in *FPHC*).

In *FAE*, I also introduced another version of reverse-reductionism, that is, "the pluralist fallacy," in the context of understanding aesthetic experience, for instance—although this fallacy has been committed not exclusively in relation to the ontological level (but also at the conceptual, theoretical, and methodological ones).

These dual dangers against reverse-reductionism (in this sub-section) and reductionism (in the previous sub-section) are something that sophisticated methodological holism rejects. And in *FPHFS*, I addressed these two problems further.

This point about the dual dangers is important enough, since many scholars often favor one against the other, but it is vital to target both.

The Holistic Organization of an Inquiry

With these dual dangers against reductionism and reverse-reductionism in mind—sophisticated methodological holism suggests that an inquiry of any given phenomenon is more complete, if treated in the context of a comprehensive analysis at all relevant levels, which challengingly encompass all the fields of human knowledge, ranging from the natural sciences and formal sciences through the social sciences to the humanities.

This section is something that I had already stressed in all my previous books and repeat (*often verbatim*) hereafter. But, for those readers who had read my previous books, this serves as a reminder.

With this reminder in mind—there are multiple ways to engage in a holistic inquiry with all relevent levels of analysis. Over the years, I have proposed different ways to fulfill this holistic methodological requirement, as repeated in my previous books.

Hereafter is a summary of four major ways, namely, (a) by discipline, (b) by domain, (c) by subject, and (d) by meta-analysis—all of which fulfill the holistic requirement of sophisticated methodological holism on a given issue.

(a) In a holistic organization by discipline, a good illustration is the multiple levels of analysis, namely, (a1) the micro-physical, (a2) the chemical, (a3) the biological, (a4) the psychological, (a5) the organizational, (a6) the institutional, (a7) the structural, (a8) the systemic, (a9) the cultural, (a10) the macro-physical (cosmological), and (a11) other relevant levels, which are either a combination of all these levels or the practical applications with a combination of them.

This holistic organization by discipline is used in *FCD* and *BCPC*, for instance.

(b) In a holistic organization by domain, some good candidates include the classification of different perspectives of analysis in relation to (b1) nature, (b2) the mind, (b3) society, and (b4) culture, as already worked out in *BCIV*, *FPHST*, *FC*, *FAE*, *FPHU*, *FPHK*, *FPHE*, and *FPHFS*.

Culture in (b4), in this re-classification, is the same as culture in (a9) and can be further divided into different sub-categories, with good examples like (a9i) epistemology (methodology), (a9ii) aesthetics, (a9iii) ethics, (a9iv) metaphysics (ontology), and (a9v) religion. For clarification, epistemology (methodology) in (a9i) and metaphysics (ontology) in (a9iv) overlap with the category of "meta-theory."

Society in (b3) includes the organizational in (a5), the institutional in (a6), the structural in (a7), and the systemic in (a8).

The mind (b2) has more to do with the chemical in (a2), the biological in (a3), and the psychological in (a4), although it can overlap with (a1), (b3) and (b4), for instance.

It should be stressed that the "mind" here also includes the categories like the "brain," "body," and the "spirit" (or the "soul")—whenever needed in a given context, so that one does not fall into the intellectual trap of the "mind-body dualism" in the history of modern (and especially, postmodern) philosophy, which I already went to great lengths to explain in *The Future of Human Civilization.* After all, in everyday's usage, the "mind" already implies the "brain" and the "body" (together with their interactions) and has different levels of consciousness which can be both "spiritual" and non-spiritual.

And nature in (b1) refers to the micro-physical in (a1) and the macro-physical (cosmological) in (a10), although it can also overlap with (a2), (a3) and (a4).

(c) In a holistic organization by subject, some excellent examples concern the analysis of consciousness in *FPHC* (i.e., on Having, Belonging, and Being); of civilization in *FHC* (i.e., the True, the Holy, the Everyday, the Technological, the Beautiful/Sublime, the Good, and the Just); of international politics in *BWT* (i.e., Hyper-Empires, Meso-Empires, and Micro-Empires); of nature and nurture in *BNN* (i.e., genes and memes); of information architecture in *FIA* (i.e., taxonomy and network); of mathematical logic in *FPHML* (i.e., consistency, soundness, and completeness); of communication in *FPHMM* (i.e., sending, connecting, and receiving); of creative thinking in *FPHCT* (i.e., invention and innovation); of geometry in *FPHG* (i.e., infinity, symmetry, and dimensionality); of urban planning in *FPHUP* (i.e., density and void), of language in *FPHL* (i.e., structure and context), and of organization in *FPHO* (i.e., communication, decision-making, and leadership), in *FPHMA* (i.e., the martial body and the martial spirit), in *FPHS* (i.e., the sexual body and the sexual spirit), in *FPHLAW* (i.e., necessity and contingency), in *FPHWP* (i.e., aggression and pacificity), in *FPHP* (i.e., normality and abnormality), in *BEPE* (i.e., morality and immorality), in *BCOS* (i.e., the beginnings and ends of the universe), in *FPHGEOL* (i.e., statics and dynamics), in *FPHCHESS* (i.e., tactics and strategy), and in *FPHR* (i.e., secularness and sacredness—by incorporating all the relevent levels of analysis as cited above in each.

(d) And in a holistic organization by meta-analysis, two good cases in point involve the works on post-capitalism in *BCPC* and on authoritarian liberal democracy in *ALD*, with the classification of analysis in theory and meta-theory.

The essential point to remember here, as I thus stress in all my previous books, is that the multiple levels of analysis can be reorganized in many different ways, insofar as none of the levels (if relevant to an inquiry in question) is ignored or dismissed, to avoid the danger of reductionism (and for that matter, the one of reverse-reductionism, in the opposite direction).

Three Clarifications

Three clarifications are needed here, however, to avoid any hasty misunderstanding.

Firstly, the entities in each classification are not mutually exclusive. For instance, in the holisitc organization by domain, nature in (b1) can also be linked to the chemical in (a2), the biological in (a3), and the systemic in (a8). And the mind (b3) can alternatively be related to the micro-physical in (a1) and the chemical in (a2), for example.

Secondly, there is also the important factor of luck (or uncertainty in conventional usage), but it is already implied or allowed in each of the organizations of an inquiry—especially in relation to the predictability-unpredictability principle and the order-chaos principle in existential dialectics. This topic about uncertainty was already addressed in *FHC*—and more extensively, in *FC*, in the context of order and chaos.

And lastly, the comparison in a classification is not absolute, but relative, as there are often some shades of gray, not exactly black or white (figuratively speaking).

Some further clarifications and qualifications of sophisticated methodological holism are shown in *Table 4.2*.

Some Distinctive Usefulness

In the end, sophisticated methodological holism—when applied, especially though not exclusively, as illustrated in my numerous works—can enrich the understanding of reality in some distinctive ways. Here are four examples (as revealed in each of my books).

Firstly, it provides a comprehensive analysis of a subject matter, from which much can be learned about reality, both in relation to the perspectives of the mind, nature, society, and culture.

Secondly, it offers a new classification of the subject matter.

Thirdly, it suggests some visions of the future in relation to the subject matter in question.

And fourthly, it proposes some insights on meta-theory (e.g., methodology and ontology) in general—with the clear understanding, however, of the dilemma of specific vs. general ontology (as shown in *Table 4.9* on the syntax of existential dialectics in the context of the dilemma of ontology).

For this very reason, all of these ways are important, without reducing one into the analysis of another. (*FPHCT*)

Chapter Outline

With this summary of my two original meta-theories (on methodology and ontology, *almost verbatim* from my previous works) in mind—this book is organized in four main parts, namely, (a) Part I on the introduction to this book, (b) Part II on sacredness, (c) Part III on secularness, and (d) Part IV on the conclusion of the book.

The book is thus organized in four chapters.

The introductory chapter here, that is, Chapter One titled "Introduction—The Awe of Religion," begins by first challenging the secular underestimation of religion and then clarifying religious studies vs. theology, religion vs. spirituality, and religion and supernatural reality—together with the theoretical debate in the literature, my comparative-substitutive theory of religion, the relationship between theory and meta-theory, existential dialectics, sophisticated methodological holism, and some further clarifications.

Chapter Two titled "Sacredness and Its Limits" examines the nature of sacredness from the four perspectives of the mind, nature, society, and culture , with a constructive critique of each.

Chapter Three titled "Secularness and Its Faults" explores the nature of secularness from the four perspectives of the mind, nature, society, and culture, with a deconstructive analysis of each.

The last chapter titled "Conclusion—The Future of Religion" summarizes the analysis in the book in the dialectic context of sacredness and secularness, with sixteen major theses, namely, (a) the first thesis: the absoluteness-relativeness principle, (b) the second thesis: the predictability-unpredictability principle, (c) the third thesis: the explicability-inexplicability principle, (d) the fourth thesis: the preciseness-vagueness principle, (e) the fifth thesis: the simpleness-complicatedness principle, (f) the sixth thesis: the openness-hiddenness principle, (g) the seventh thesis: the denseness-emptiness principle, (h) the eighth thesis: the slowness-quickness principle, (i) the nineth thesis: the expansion-contraction principle, (j) the tenth thesis: the convention-novelty principle, (k) the eleventh thesis: the evolution-transformation principle, (l) the twelveth thesis: the symmetry-asymmetry principle, (m) the thirteenth thesis: the softness-hardness principle, (n) the fourteenth thesis: the regression-progression principle, (o) the fifteenth thesis: the sameness-difference principle, and (p) the sixteenth thesis: the post-human substitution—to be elaborated in the rest of the book, with a summary in the concluding chapter.

This seminal project is to fundamentally alter the way that we think about religion, from the combined perspectives of the mind, nature, society, and culture, with enormous implications for the human future and what I originally called its "post-human" fate.

Some Clarifications

But some additional clarifications are needed, before a formal analysis of the nature of religion is to begin in Chapter Two.

These clarifications, lest any potential misunderstanding by the readers occurs, refer to (a) the conversation with my previous books, (b) the illustrative selection of case studies and examples, (c) detailed analysis versus overall analysis, (d) two distinctive features of using quotations, and (e) the use of neologisms.

These clarifications are something that I also regularly repeat in my previous books too, so these points are repeated hereafter, *often verbatim*—albeit in a different context this time.

In Conversation with My Previous Books

Firstly, my theory of post-ethics is constructed on the theoretical foundation of my previous books (i.e., *FHC*, *FCD*, *FPHC*, *BDPD*, *BCPC*, *BCIV*, *FPHST*, *BNN*, *BWT*, *FC*, *FAE*, *ALD*, *FIA*, *FPHU*, *FPHK*, *FPHML*, *FPHE*, *FPHMM*, *FPHCT*, *FPHG*, *FPHUP*, *FPHL*, *FPHO*, *FPHMA*, *FPHS*, *FPHLAW*, *FPHFS*, *FPHWP*, *FPHP*, *BCOS*, *BEPE*, *FPHGEOL*, and *FPHCHESS*—as explicated in "The List of Abbreviations").

Just consider the following two illustrations, namely, (a) in relation to other related theoretical debates and (b) in relation to different visions as worked out in my previous books.

(a) The first illustration is that the theoretical debate on the nature of morality and immorality also involves a few other related theoretical issues.

These other related theoretical issues have to do with some deeply contested theoretical debates, which, however, I had already gone to great lengths to analyze in my numerous (previous) books, as summarized below. It should also be stressed, lest misunderstanding occurs, that each of the theoretical debates (as listed below) does not exhaust the issues covered in the books, as each book covers more issues than what is listed below (for illustration only).

- On Comparaive Religion
  –Ex: 2 volumes, *The Future of Human Civilization*
- On Science and Religion
  –Ex: 2 volumes, *The Future of Human Civilization*
  –Ex: *Beyond Cosmology to Post-Cosmology*
- On Religion and the Environment
  –Ex: *The Future of Capitalism and Democracy*
- On the Separation of Church and State
  –Ex: 2 volumes, *The Future of Human Civilization*

- On Spirituality
  - –Ex: 2 volumes, *The Future of Human Civilization*
  - –Ex: *The Future of Capitalism and Democracy*
  - –Ex: *Beyond Capitalism to Post-Capitalism*
  - –Ex: *The Future of Post-Human Sexuality*
  - –Ex: *The Future of Post-Human Martial Arts*
  - –Ex: *The Future of Post-Human Unconsciousness*
  - –Ex: *The Future of Post-Human Consciousness*
  - –Ex: *Beyond Ethics to Post-Ethics*
- On science
  - –Ex: 2 volumes, *The Future of Human Civilization*
  - –Ex: *The Future of Complexity*
  - –Ex: *The Future of Post-Human Knowledge*
  - –Ex: *The Future of Post-Human Geology*
- On the Cosmos
  - –Ex: 2 volumes, *The Future of Human Civilization*
  - –Ex: *The Future of Post-Human Space-Time*
  - –Ex: *Beyond Cosmology to Post-Cosmology*
  - –Ex: *The Future of Post-Human Geometry*
- On No Morality Without Immoralitiy
  - –Ex: 2 volumes, *The Future of Human Civilization*
  - –Ex: *The Future of Capitalism and Democracy*
  - –Ex: *Beyond Democracy to Post-Democracy*
  - –Ex: *Beyond Ethics to Post-Ethics*
- On No Freedom Without Unfreedom
  - –Ex: 2 volumes, *The Future of Human Civilization*
  - –Ex: *The Future of Capitalism and Democracy*
  - –Ex: *Beyond Capitalism to Post-Capitalism*
  - –Ex: *Beyond Democracy to Post-Democracy*
  - –Ex: *Beyond Civilization to Post-Civilization*
- On Being and Belonging
  - –Ex: *The Future of Post-Human Consciousness*
  - –Ex: 2 volumes, *The Future of Human Civilization*
- On Different Dimensions of Human Existence
  - –Ex: 2 volumes, *The Future of Human Civilization*
- On War
  - –Ex: *Beyond Democracy to Post-Democracy*
  - –Ex: *The Future of Capitalism and Democracy*
  - –Ex: *The Future of Post-Human War and Peace*
- On Violence
  - –Ex: *The Future of Capitalism and Democracy*

–Ex: *The Future of Post-Human Law*
–Ex: *The Future of Post-Human War and Peace*
–Ex: *The Future of Post-Human Sexuality*
–Ex: *The Future of Post-Human Martial Arts*

- On Conflict Resolution
  –Ex: *The Future of Capitalism and Democracy*
  –Ex: *The Future of Post-Human War and Peace*
- On Modernity, Post-Modernity, and After-Postmodernity
  –Ex: 2 volumes, *The Future of Human Civilization*
  –Ex: *Beyond Civilization to Post-Civilization*
- On Pre-Modernity
  –Ex: *Beyond Civilization to Post-Civilization*
- On Uncertainty
  –Ex: *The Future of Complexity*
  –Ex: 2 volumes, *The Future of Human Civilization*
- On Creativity
  –Ex: *The Future of Post-Human Creative Thinking*
  –Ex: *The Future of Aesthetic Experience*
- On Cognition
  –Ex: *The Future of Post-Human Unconsciousness*
  –Ex: *The Future of Post-Human Consciousness*
  –Ex: *The Future of Capitalism and Democracy*
  –Ex: *The Future of Post-Human Creative Thinking*
  –Ex: *The Future of Post-Human Personality*
- On Intuition
  –Ex: *The Future of Post-Human Unconsciousness*
  –Ex: *The Future of Post-Human Consciousness*
  –Ex: *Beyond Capitalism to Post-Capitalism*
  –Ex: *The Future of Capitalism and Democracy*
- On Emotion
  –Ex: *The Future of Post-Human Unconsciousness*
  –Ex: *The Future of Post-Human Consciousness*
  –Ex: *The Future of Aesthetic Experience*
  –Ex: *Beyond Capitalism to Post-Capitalism*
  –Ex: *The Future of Capitalism and Democracy*
  –Ex: *The Future of Post-Human Personality*
- On Behavior
  –Ex: *The Future of Post-Human Language*
  –Ex: *The Future of Post-Human Unconsciousness*
  –Ex: *The Future of Post-Human Consciousness*
  –Ex: *Beyond Capitalism to Post-Capitalism*

–Ex: *The Future of Capitalism and Democracy*
–Ex: *The Future of Post-Human Sexuality*
–Ex: *The Future of Post-Human Personality*

Therefore, those who are interested in these other theoretical issues (and debates) which are related to the current context can consult these other books of mine for more details.

(b) And the second illustration is that one of the major theses of this book concerns the future, be it human and later post-human, which is closely linked with the different visions that I had worked out in my previous books, in relation to the mind, nature, society, and culture.

Of course, for the convenience of the readers, a summary of some of these visions will be provided whenever necessary, as shown in the two sections on meta-theory above (*often verbatim*) and in different tables at the end of this chapter and the concluding chapter, for instance.

Yet, I still expect the readers to read my previous books directly for more details—as this book is written in conversation with my previous ones.

Case Studies and Examples

Secondly, the case studies and examples in the chapters are not exhaustive but solely illustrative. Nor are they necessarily mutually exclusive, as they can be reclassified in a different way. And exceptions are allowed.

One is tempted to assume, however, that, since the case studies and their examples are not exhaustive, more case studies and examples are needed. But the problem here is that just adding more of them does not necessarily change the conclusions to be drawn and may even lead to redundancy.

After all, the case studies and examples used in this book are chosen with care and deemed sufficient for the purpose at hand, even though they are solely illustrative.

Detailed Analysis versus Overall Synthesis

Thirdly, there is a distinction between detailed analysis and overall synthesis, in that the former is, especially though not exclusively, more for the specialized viewpoint of a specific discipline, whereas the latter is, especially though not exclusively, more for the broad horizon of an interdisciplinary approach—relatively speaking, of course.

Or, by analogy, there is a distinction between depicting a "tree" (with tiny details) in a "forest" and viewing the entire "forest" itself (with the broader horizon).

This book, like all previous ones of mine, tries to strike a balance between the two forms of understanding, although this does not imply that the two forms should be exactly equally offered, in an exact 50-50 balance.

Instead, the book, more often than not, does not allow the tiny details to obscure the larger picture in a given case study, because the entire book is inter-disciplinary in nature and tries to look at the entire "forest," not being bogged down with the detailed analysis of an individual "tree" in the forest, by analogy.

In this sense, although detailed analysis can be provided whenever needed for a given case study, the important point to remember is the overall horizon with its broadness of scope.

Two Distinctive Features of Using Quotations

Fourthly, the way that quotes are used in this book (and others of mine) has two distinctive features, as explained below.

The first distinctive feature is that, at the end of each quotation, sometimes there are more than one reference—in which case the first reference is for the original citation, and the rest of the references are for the convenience of the reader for more information about the issue under quotation.

And the second feature is that quotations are used as often as possible, so as to let others speak for themselves, without the nuisance of putting my own words into their mouths. Even more importantly, this allows me to use the original text as an evidence for critical analysis at the end of each section.

The Use of Neologisms

And finally, I use different neologisms in my books, mostly to introduce my original concepts and theories, and good instances include those here or elsewhere in my previous books (e.g., "the comparative-substitutive theory of religion," "post-democracy," "hyper-spatial consciousness," "post-capitalism," and whatnot). Needless to say, they are used here solely for our current intellectual convenience, as they will be renamed differently in different ways in future history.

As I thus wrote in *FCD* (508-9), "all these terms 'post-capitalism,' 'post-democracy'...and other ones as introduced in...[the] project (e.g.,...'posthuman elitists,' and 'posthuman counter-elitists,' just to cite a few of them) are more for our current intellectual convenience than to the liking of future humans and post-humans, who will surely invent more tasteful neologisms to call their own eras, entities, and everything else, for that matter. But the didactic point here is to use the terms to foretell what the future might be like, not that its eras and entities must be called so exactly and permanently. After all, William Shakespeare (1995: Act II, Scene II, Line 47) well said long ago: 'What is in a name? That which we call a rose by any other name would smell as sweet.'"

As I had also stressed time and again before, each of the neologisms can be re-written as a different "X," only to be re-named differently by the powers that be in different eras of future history.

With these clarifications for thought in mind—I now proceed to Chapter Two on sacredness and its limits.

Table 1.1. Religion vs. Spirituality (Part I)

- **Religion**
  - —The term "religion" in general refers to "a set of beliefs concerning the cause, nature, and purpose of the universe, especially when considered as the creation of a supernatural agency or agencies, usually involving devotional and ritual observances, and often containing a moral code governing the conduct of human affairs." (WK 2010b)
  - —This set of beliefs in religion is "to give meaning to the practitioner's experiences of life," so as to "consider carefully" his life again or to "reconnect" his life in a deeper way. (WK 2010b)
  - —And "the meaning centers on a deity or deities" and/or, alternatively, on "an ultimate truth." (WK 2010b)

- **Spirituality**
  - —The term "spirituality" refers to "an ultimate reality or transcendent dimension of the world; an inner path enabling a person to discover the essence of his or her being, or the 'deepest values and meanings by which people live.'" (WK 2010c; E. Cousins 1992; P. Sheldrake 2007)
  - —Spirituality often relies on "meditation, prayer and contemplation" to "develop an individual's inner life; such practices often lead to an experience of connectedness with a larger reality: a more comprehensive self; other individuals or the human community; nature or the cosmos; or the divine realm." (WK 2010c; M. Burkhardt 2002)
  - —On the one hand, the terms "religion" and "spirituality" have much in common, insofar as both are concerned with "an ultimate reality," the practices of "meditation, prayer and contemplation," and so on.
  - —On the other hand, the terms "religion" and "spirituality" have much to differ from each other, in two major ways.

(continued on next page)

Table 1.1. Religion vs. Spirituality
(Part II)

- **Spirituality** ***(cont'd)***
  —Firstly, spirituality differs from religion, because "some individuals…see spirituality as a belief in ideas of religious significance (such as God, the Soul, or Heaven), but not feel bound to the bureaucratic structure and creeds of a particular organized religion." (WK 2010b)
  —And secondly, spirituality differs from religion in another way, in that religion is also concerned with the understanding of "the intentions of a supernatural force (such as deities)"—but spirituality, for some individuals, is not necessarily concerned with supernatural force. (WK 2010) This then leads us to the third distinction (in what follows).

Notes: The examples in the categories are solely illustrative (not exhaustive), and the comparison is relative (not absolute), nor are they necessarily mutually exclusive. And some can be easily re-classified elsewhere. As generalities, they allow exceptions.
Source: From *Sec. 1.3* of *FPHR*. See book for citations.

Table 1.2. The Varieties of Supernatural Reality (Part I)

- **Monotheism vs. Polytheism**
  —A common disagreement among different religions in regard to supernatural reality concerns the "monotheistic" and "polytheistic" definitions of supernatural reality.
  —In regard to "monotheism"—some religions (like Christianity, Judaism, and Islam) accept the view that "only one God exists (as opposed to multiple gods). In Western thought, God is traditionally described as a being that possesses at least three necessary properties: omniscience (all-knowing), omnipotence (all-powerful), and omnipresence (present every where). In other words, God knows everything, has the power to do anything, and is present where He wishes. Many other properties (e.g., omnibenevolence) have been alleged to be necessary properties of a god; however, these are the three most uncontroversial and dominant in Christian tradition." (WK 2010d)
  —And in regard to "polytheism"—other religions hold the opposite view that there are "more than one god(dess). There can be as few as two (such as a classical Western understanding of Zoroastrian dualism) or an innumerably large amount, as in Hinduism (as the Western world perceives it)." (WK 2010d)
  —However, even in polythesism, not all gods or goddesses are created equal, because, although "many varieties of polytheism…all accept that many gods exist," they "differ in their responses to that belief. Henotheists for example, worship only one of the many gods, either because it is held to be more powerful or worthy of worship than the others (some pseudo-Christian sects take this view of the Trinity, holding that only God the Father should be worshipped, Jesus and the Holy Spirit being distinct and lesser gods), or because it is associated with their own group, culture, state, etc. The distinction isn't a clear one, of course, as most people consider their own culture superior to others, and this will also apply to their culture's God. Kathenotheists have similar beliefs, but worship a different god at different times or places." (WK 2010d)

(continued on next page)

Table 1.2. The Varieties of Supernatural Reality (Part II)

• **Pantheism vs. Deism vs. Panentheism**

—Another common disagreement among different religions in regard to supernatural reality concerns the distinction between "Pantheism" (for the immanence of God), "Deism" (for the transcendence of God), and "Panentheism" (for both the immanence and transcendence of God), as explained below. (WK 2010d)

- "Pantheism"—This term refers to "the belief that God exists as all things of the cosmos, that God is one and all is God; God is immanent." (WK 2010d) Spinoza in the West—and many Taoists as well as Hindus in the East—hold this position. (WK 2010d & 2010e)
- "Deism" —This term refers to "the belief that God does exist but does not interfere with human life and the laws of the universe; God is transcendent." (WK 2010d) And this "can be determined using reason and observation of the natural world alone, without the need for either faith or organized religion"; Matthew Tindal, Thomas Jefferson, and others hold this position. (WK 2010g)
- "Panentheism"—This term refers to "the belief that God encompasses all things of the cosmos but that God is greater than the cosmos; God is both immanent and transcendent." (WK 2010d) Many Eastern and Oriental Orthodox Christians hold this position. (WK 2010f)

Notes: The examples in the categories are solely illustrative (not exhaustive), and the comparison is relative (not absolute), nor are they necessarily mutually exclusive. And some can be easily re-classified elsewhere. As generalities, they allow exceptions.

Source: From *Sec. 1.4* of *FPHR*. See book for citations.

Table 1.3. The Theoretical Debate on Space-Time (Part I)

• **Isaac Newton's Absolutist (Substantivist) Theory of Space-Time**

—space and time are independent from each other. The structure of space-time is $E3 \times E1$ (with the structure of space, *P*, as the set of spatial locations in a three-dimensional Euclidean space, *E3*, and the structure of time as the set of temporal moments, *T*, in the one-dimensional real time, *E1*).

—space and time are also independent from the effects of matter and events. The existence of space and time is possible even in a world absent of matter (and, for that matter, even in a world absent of events), as if they were material objects but with their total unchangingness thorough time.

• **Albert Einstein's Relativist Theory of Space-Time**

—space and time are interchangeable (not absolute), just as matter and energy are equivalent (not independent) with the famous equation, $E = mc^2$ (as in the special theory of relativity in 1905).

—space-time and matter-energy are also relative in a grand union (as in the general theory of relativity in 1915). Thus, each pair affects the other pair, as "matter 'tells' spacetime how to curve [in a non-Euclidean geometry] and curved spacetime 'tells' matter how to behave….Space contracts near mass and dilates away from it. Time dilates near mass and contracts away from it. Clocks positioned farther away from the mass of the earth run faster than clocks closer to the earth." (L. Shlain 1991: 328-330)

(continued on next page)

Table 1.3. The Theoretical Debate on Space-Time (Part II)

- **Peter Baofu's Perspectival Theory of Space-Time**
  —space and time can be understood from multiple perspectives, be they in relation to culture, society, nature, and the mind, with each perspective revealing something about the nature of space-time and simultaneously delimiting its view. This is subject to "the regression-progression principle" in existential dialectics.
  —each perspective of space and time exists in society and culture with good reasons, with some being more successful and hegemonic (dominant) than others. This is subject to "the symmetry-asymmetry principle" in existential dialectics.
  —space and time will not last, to be eventually superseded (altered) by post-humans in different forms (e.g.,stretching/shrinking space-time, engineering more dimensions of space-time, and manipulating multiverses), be they here in this universe or in multiverses. Thus, even the physical existence of space-time cannot last forever, with ever more transformations in the process. This is subject to "the change-constancy principle" in existential dialectics.
  —the conventional wisdom (especially by physicists) of treating the physical perspective of space and time as the foundation of all other perspectives (of space and time) and of regarding them as much less important is a form of reductionism,committing what I call *the foundation fallacy*, in misleadingly dismissing the multiple perspectives of space and time in relation to culture, society, nature, and the mind.

Notes: The examples in each category are solely illustrative (not exhaustive), and the comparison is relative (not absolute), nor are they necessarily mutually exclusive. Some can be easily re-classified elsewhere. As generalities, they allow exceptions.
Source: A summary of *Sec.1.1*, *Sec.1.2*, and *Sec.1.3* of *FPHST*—and, for that matter, the rest of *FPHST*

Table 1.4. Main Reasons for Altering Space-Time

- **The Need to Make New Energy-Matter**
  —Ex: manipulating molecular bonds for new materials
  —Ex: creating nanotechnologies on the atomic scale
  —Ex: engineering the atomic nucleus
  —Ex: restructuring most elementary particles
  —Ex: inventing new forms of matter and energy

- **The Need to Create New Space-Time**
  —Ex: creating "warp drive" (as in science fiction) for space travel
  —Ex: creating "pocket universes"

- **The Need to Conquer the Cosmos unto Multiverses**
  —Ex: spreading floating consciousness and hyper-spatial consciousness, besides other forms that humans have never known, in the cosmos and beyond unto multiverses for ultimate conquest

Notes: The examples in each category are solely illustrative (not exhaustive) nor necessarily mutually exclusive, and the comparison is relative (not absolute). As generalities, they allow exceptions. Also, it should be stressed that the three reasons are all related, in that they all contribute to the evolution of intelligent life in the cosmos unto multiverses in the most distant future beyond our current knowledge.
Sources: A summary of *Sec.6.2* of *FPHST*. See also *FHC*, *FCD*, *FPHC*, *FC*, *FPHU*, and *FPHG*, for example.

Table 1.5. The Technological Frontiers of the Micro-World

- **Type I-Minus**
  —Ex: building structures and mining

- **Type II-Minus**
  —Ex: playing with the genetic makeups of living things

- **Type III-Minus**
  —Ex: manipulating molecular bonds for new materials

- **Type IV-Minus**
  —Ex: creating nanotechnologies on the atomic scale

- **Type V-Minus**
  —Ex: engineering the atomic nucleus

- **Type VI-Minus**
  —Ex: restructuring most elementary particles

- **Type Ω-Minus**
  —Ex: altering the structure of space-time

Notes: As already indicated in *Sec.4.4.2.2* of *FPHC*, the problem with this micro-classification (from Barrow's work) is that the civilization types (with the exception of Type Ω-Minus, for example) are not quite distinct, since many of them can be achieved more or less in a civilization, to the extent that Type II-minus and Type III-minus, just to cite two plausible types, can be historically contemporaneous, relatively speaking, unlike the vast historical distance between, say, Type O and Type I (or Type I and Type II) civilizations. In other words, the micro-classification here is not very useful to understand civilization types but is revealing to see the technological frontiers of the micro-world.
Sources: A reconstruction from J.Barrow (1998:133), as originally shown in *Table 4.7* of *FPHC*. See *FPHC* for more info.

Table 1.6. Finity, Transfinity, and Infinity (Part I)

• **Infinity**

—The term "infinity," which is "symbolically represented with ∞," derives from the Latin *infinitas* (or "unboundedness"), to refer to "several distinct concepts—usually linked to the idea of 'without end'—which arise in philosophy, mathematics, and theology." (WK 2008c)

—In the context of mathematics, "infinity" is often "treated as if it were a number (i.e., it counts or measures things: 'an infinite number of terms') but it is a different type of 'number' from the real numbers. Infinity is related to limits,...large cardinals,...projective geometry, extended real numbers and the absolute Infinite," for instance. (WK 2008c)

• **Transfinity**

—To avoid confusion, my usage of the word "transfinite" (as used here in the ontological principle) is not the same as the one which was originally coined by Georg Cantor to refer to "cardinal numbers or ordinal numbers that are larger than all finite numbers, yet not necessarily absolutely infinite" (in the mind of God), as opposed to "relative" infinity (in the mind of Man). (WK 2008d) In other words, for Cantor, there are two kinds of infinity, "absolute" and "relative"—with "relative" infinity or "transfinity" (in the mind of Man) being dependent on "absolute" infinity (in the mind of God) for its existence.

—By contrast, my usage of the word "transfinite" here differs radically from the one used by Cantor (and other mathematicians) and is more limited, in light of the problems confronting any attempt to understand the idea of infinity, be it by intuition, imagination, and conception (as already shown in the prevous three sub-sections).

—With this clarification in mind, I allow numbers which can be many times larger—or smaller, for that matter—than the finite things that we encounter in daily life, but they do not have to be related to the idea of infinity at all (which may not exist).

(continued on next page)

Table 1.6. Finity, Transfinity, and Infinity (Part II)

• **Transfinity** ***(cont'd)***

—Of course, there may be some *borderline* cases, in which it is not clear whether the number in question is transfinite (in my usage) or simply a mathematical convenience. A good example of a borderline case is the Planck unit of length for "the smallest space possibly measured in nature," which is "less than billionths of trillionths of trillionths of an inch" (or something like 1.6×10^{-35} meters). (P. Baofu 2006a; N. McAleer 1987: 219; WKV 2008; D. Corbett 2008)

—The ideas concerning symmetry and dimensions in the examples above were addressed in Chapter Three and Chapter Four of *FPHG*. For now, it suffices to further add that it is mind-boggling to even conceive or imagine extreme numbers like the Planck unit of length (or others). Does it really exist at all? Or is it merely a mathematical convenience to describe a physical situation that the human mind does not understand properly?

—In any event, "transfinity" (in my usage) can be used as a further extension (of number) to the finite numbers in daily life—albeit with some borderline cases in mind.

• **Finity**

—It refers to numbers which are bounded (that is, with an end), especially (though not exclusively) in relation to things in everyday life.

Source: From *Sec. 1.4* and *Sec. 2.2.3* of *FPHG*

Table 1.7. Theoretical Speculations of Multiverses

- **"Baby Universes" (Ex: Andre Linde and others)**
  —Ex: In a flat universe theory, "even if our part of it eventually collapses,...some spots in the cosmos would suddenly start inflating on their own, creating brand-new 'baby universes.'" (P. Baofu 2000: 623)

- **"Parallel Universes" (Ex: Stephen Hawking and others)**
  —Ex: In quantum cosmology, there allows the existence of infinite numbers of parallel universes, with tunneling among them. (M. Kaku 1994: 256) Hawking later revised his views on this.

- **"Pocket Universes" (Ex: Alan Guth)**
  —Ex: "As the pocket universes live out their lives and recollapse or dwindle away, new universes are generated to take their place....While life in our pocket universe will presumably die out, life in the universe as a whole will thrive for eternity." (A. Guth 1997: 248; P. Baofu 2002: 482)

- **"Brane Worlds" (Ex: Warren Siegel, Lisa Randall, and others)**
  —Ex: Our universe is stuck on a membrane of space-time embedded in a larger cosmos, with different brane worlds connecting and/or colliding with each other.

Notes: These examples are solely illustrative (not exhaustive), and some of the items can be reclassified somewhere else. Nor are they always mutually exclusive. Since they are generalities, exceptions are expected.
Source: From *Table 4.8* of *FPHC*

Table 1.8. The Confusion between "Many Worlds" and "Multiverse" (Part I)

• **First Problem**

—The first problem in this second confusion concerns a debate between the "many-worlds" interpretation of quantum mechanics by Hugh Everett (1957) and others, and the Copenhagen interpretation by Niels Bohr and Werner Heisenberg on the effects of quantum states after interacting with an external environment (e.g., by a measuring observer).

—On the one hand, the Copenhagen interpretation of quantum mechanics is more indeterministic in its concern with the probabilities of the outcomes of a wave function after interacting with an external environment (e.g., by a measuring observer using light to detect, for example, "an electron in a particular region around the nucleus at a particular time." (WK 2008e) Each wave function for the state of a particle refers to "a mathematical representation used to calculate the probability for it to be found in a location, or state of motion." (WK 2008f) And the "wavefunction collapse" means that "the act of measurement causes the calculated set of probabilities to 'collapse' to the value defined by the measurement." (WK 2008f)

—On the other hand, the Everett's interrpetation is more deterministic, in rejecting "the objective reality of wavefunction collapse" and "instead explaining the subjective appearance of wavefunction collapse with the mechanism of quantum decoherence." (WK 2008g) The words "quantum decoherence" here refers to "the mechanism by which quantum systems interact with their environments to exhibit probabilistically additive behavior," in such a way that "the quantum nature of the system is simply 'leaked' into the environment." (WK 2008g) For example, "[a]s a result of an interaction, the wave functions of the system and the measuring device become entangled with each other. Decoherence happens when different portions of the system's wavefunction become entangled *in different ways* [italic added] with the measuring device...." (WK 2008g) Thus, for Everett, the appearance of "wavefunction collapse" can be explained by "quantum decoherence" for quantum states to branch out in different independent worlds after interacting with an external environment.

(continued on next page)

Table 1.8. The Confusion between "Many Worlds" and "Multiverse" (Part II)

- **First Problem *(cont'd)***
  —Yet, a major criticism against Everett's interpretation is that these different independent worlds in Everett's sense "will never be accessible to us," because of the interference by the measuring observer in an external environment. (WK 2008g)
  —For illustration, "once a measurement is done, the measured system becomes entangled with both the physicist who measured it and a huge number of other particles, some of which are photons flying away towards the other end of the universe; in order to prove that the wave function did not collapse one would have to bring all these particles back and measure them again, together with the system that was measured originally. This is completely impractical, but even if one can theoretically do this, it would destroy any evidence that the original measurement took place (including the physicist's memory)." (WK 2008g)
  —But then, the critics ask, If these independent worlds in Everett's sense are inaccessible to us, how do we know much of anything really about them?

- **Second Problem**
  —What is relevant at the quantum mechanical level may not necessarily apply to the world at the physicsl level.
  —In fact, the persistent inability among contemporoary physicists to unifiy the theory of relativity for large objects at the physical level and quantum mechanics for tiny objects at the quantum mechanical level should warn us about the danger of reductionism, by reducing the understanding of different universes ("parallel universes") at the physical level from a generalization of "many worlds" at the quantum mechanical level.

- **Third Problem**
  —There is no empirical evidence to suggest that there are infinite (or extremely many) possible worlds in the cosmos as the many-worlds model by Everett would have us to believe.

Source: From *Sec.4.4.1* of *FPHG*

Table 1.9. Hyperspace and Its Challenge (Part I)

- **First Problem**

—Hyperspace for intra- and inter-universal travel is assumed to be possible, on the basis of four main assumptions; although there may be others, these are the often cited ones.

—The first assumption concerns the existence of "entry" and "exit" points in hyperspace, which is easier said than done to enter, go through, and then exit hyperspace.

—For instance, using hyperspace "requires complex calculations…of single or multiple hyperspace jumps and the control of the jump….Peturbations such as those experienced by ship in space from the gravitional field around an object such as a planet or even a star are exacerbated in hyperspatial travel, since mass in real space distorts hyperspace in an equal measure. 'Jumping' near to a gravitational mass is likely to make resulting exit from hyperspace to be highly uncertain, with the level of improbability *i* increasing with the square of the distance to the nearest gravitional 'well.'" (WK 2008h)

—Besides, "[o]nly spaceships equipped with a special force field can enter hyperspace, because exposure to hyperspace even for short period of time is hazardous to unprotected humans." (WK 2008h)

- **Second Problem**

—The second assumption concerns the faster-than-light speed. It is well known that Einstein argued for the speed of light as the ultimate limit, but nowadays phyiscists do allow the violation of this limit under certain conditions (like the hypothetical existence of tachyons, as will be explained further in a later sub-section on time travel).

—Even then, there is a challenge to explain in science fiction "why ships can travel faster than light in hyperspace," and two good arguments are that "hyperspace may be smaller than real space and therefore a star ship's propulsion seems to be greatly multiplied, or else the speed of light in hyperspace is not a barrier as it is in real space. Whatever the reasoning, the general effect is that ships traveling in hyperspace seem to have broken the speed of light, appearing at their destinations much more quickly and without the shift in time that the Theory of Relativity would suggest." (WK 2008h)

(continued on next page)

Table 1.9. Hyperspace and Its Challenge (Part II)

• **Third Problem**

—The third assumption concerns the speed of time (to be measured, say, by a clock), but this is elaborated in a different section on the related issue of "time travel" (as shown in a different table on time travel).

• **Fourth Problem**

—The fourth assumption concerns spatial shortcut, as it is possible, because of the curvature of space, in that "the manifold of ordinary three-dimensional space is curved in four or more 'higher' spacial dimensions (a 'hyperspace' in the geometric sense…). This curvature causes certain widely separated points in three-dimensional space to nonetheless be 'adjacent' to each other four-dimensionally. Creating an aperture in 4D space (a wormhole) between these locations can allow instantaneous transit between the two locations; a common comparison is that of a folded piece of paper, where a hole punched through two folded sections is more direct than a line drawn between them on the sheet. This idea probably arose out of certain popular descriptions of General Relativity and/or Riemannian manifolds, and may be the original form from which later concepts of hyperspace arose." (WK 2008h)

—But this does not mean that hyperpsace is always safe. In fact, "in some science fiction, the danger of hyperspace travel is due to the chance that the route through hyperspace may take a ship too close to a celestial body with a large gravitational field, such as a star. In such scenarios, if a starship passes too close to a large gravitational field while in hyperspace, the ship is forcibly pulled out of hyperspace and reverts to normal space. Therefore, certain hyperspace 'routes' may be mapped out that are safe, not passing too close to stars or other dangers." (WJ 2008h)

Source: From *Sec.4.4.1* of *FPHG*

Table 1.10. The Problems of Time Travel into the Future (Part I)

- **First Problem**
  —The first problem concerns "time dilation under the Theory of Special Relativity" (which separates space-time from mass-energy as special cases). Suppose you are on a moving train and an observer outside the train is watching you along the tracks. As your train moves along at the speed of light (or something close to it), "time, as measured by your watch, ticked along at a slower pace than time measured by the observer. Not only that, distance changed, too. For the observer, a one-foot ruler whizzing by on the train would have measured less than a foot." (NO 2000)
  —In fact, you may not even notice that this slower clicking of the clock; in fact, everything looks normal to you inside the train as it was before: "The weird thing is that, for you on the train, time wouldn't seem to be moving slower and your ruler wouldn't be shorter—all would appear normal." (NO 2008) By contrast, you instead think that "time on the rest of the Earth would appear to be ticking along slower and its rulers would be shorter." (NO 2000) So, both of you insist that the other clock (not his) is clicking more slowly—assuming, of course, an inertial frame of reference.
  —Now, change the story a bit, in that, this time, instead of an "inertial reference frame," acceleration is allowed, and you are on your way to board a spaceship. As an illustration, suppose "[y]ou board a spaceship and take off for deep space. The ship approaches the speed of light. Time for you seems to pass as it always has. It takes you about five seconds to tie your shoe. But to an observer on Earth (assuming he or she could watch you), you are moving at a snail's pace. It takes hours to tie your shoe." (NO 2000) In any event, "you continue on your journey. You slow down, stop, and accelerate back to Earth. You arrive home. You have aged two years during your flight. Two hundred years have passed on Earth. You have successfully travelled forward through time." (NO 2000) In this case, both the observer (if he is still alive) and you agree that you have aged less.

(continued on next page)

Table 1.10. The Problems of Time Travel into the Future (Part II)

- **First Problem *(cont'd)***
  —In other words, when you are back to Earth, a lot of things have changed since, and you may find rather strange to be in a new environment which you hardly recognize, when compared with what you used to think as your city, or the Earth (two years ago, well, in accordance to your time of measurement). This means that you are in the future (two hundred years later), even though you are still relatively young (only two years older). But, can you go back? Well, no. The reason is that "[a]ccording to relativity, you can only move through time in one direction." (NO 2000)

- **Second Problem**
  —The second problem concerns "time dilation under the Theory of General Relativity" (which unifies space-time with mass-energy in a general theory), the same result of time dilation occurs.
  —For instance, when "one clock is deeper in a gravity well than the other," a result is that "the clock deeper in the well" will "tick…more slowly; this effect must be taken into account when calibrating the clocks on the satellites of the Global Positioning System, and it could lead to significant differences in rates of aging for observers at different distances from a black hole." (WK 2008i)
  —More precisely, by way of another example, "it has been calculated that, under general relativity, a person could travel forward in time at a rate four times that of distant observers by residing inside a spherical shell with a diameter of 5 meters and the mass of Jupiter. For such a person, every one second of their 'personal' time would correspond to four seconds for distant observers. Of course, squeezing the mass of a large planet into such a structure is not expected to be within our technological capabilities in the near future." (WK 2008i; R. Gott 2002)
  —The point here, however, is that time travel into the future, in this sense, is allowed, theoretically speaking, but in a very limited way, from the theory of relativity. But one can also ask, What if the theory of relativity were wrong? Well, in that case, there would be a need to find a better theory to explain time travel into the future.

Source: From *Sec.4.4.2* of *FPHG*

Table 1.11. The Problems of Time Travel into the Past (Part I)

• **First Problem**

—The first problem concerns the faster-than-light-speed, since, in accordance to the theory of special relativity, when an object goes faster than the speed of light, something weird can happen, in that, instead of having the clock clicking more slowly, it is moving backward, in relation to some inertial frame of reference—which then raisies the issue of whether time travel into the past is possible at all.

—But the problem here is about the violation of the law of casuality. In everyday language, an excellent illustration of causality violation is that, suppose you travel back into the past and then kill your parents, this then means that you could not have been born. But this is not true, since you are alive.

—Yet, "in the case of a hypothetical signal moving faster than light, there would always be some frames in which the signal was received before it was sent, so that the signal could be said to have moved backwards in time." The violation of casuality exists in this case.

—The first part of the problem is that, in accordance to the theory of special relativity, "it would take an infinite amount of energy to accelerate a slower-than-light object to the speed of light"—let alone the energy needed to propel an object to go faster than the speed of light. (WK 2008i) Although some suggest the possibility of "negative energy," it remains to be seen to what extent this is true.

—And the second part of the problem is that, "although relativity does not forbid the theoretical possibility of tachyons which move faster than light at all times, when analyzed using quantum field theory it seems that it would not actually be possible to use them to transmit information faster than light and there is no evidence for their existence." (WK 2008i; S. Chase 1993)

(continued on next page)

Table 1.11. The Problems of Time Travel into the Past (Part II)

- **Second Problem**
  —The second problem concerns cosmic string and black holes, since it is the theory of general relativity which "extends the special theory to cover gravity, illustrating it in terms of curvature in spacetime caused by mass-energy and the flow of momentum." (WK 2008i)
  —On the other hand, "[g]eneral relativity describes the universe under a system of field equations…and there exist solutions to these equations that permit what are called 'closed time-like curves,' and hence time travel into the past….The first of these was proposed by Kurt Gödel, a solution known as the Gödel metric, but his (and many others') example requires the universe to have physical characteristics that it does not appear to have." (WK 2008i; K. Thorne 1994)
  —But then, the problem now becomes: "Whether general relativity forbids closed time-like curves for all realistic conditions is unknown." (WK 2008i)

- **Third Problem**
  —The third problem concerns wormholes and related ones, and "[w]ormholes are a hypothetical warped spacetime which are also permitted by the Einstein field equations of general relativity, although it would be impossible to travel through a wormhole unless it was what is known as a traversable wormhole." (WK 2008i; M. Visser 1995) In other words, "a wormhole is a hypothetical topological feature of spacetime that is fundamentally a 'shortcut' through space and time. Spacetime can be viewed as a 2D surface, and when 'folded' over, a wormhole bridge can be formed. A wormhole has at least two mouths which are connected to a single throat or tube. If the wormhole is traversable, matter can 'travel' from one mouth to the other by passing through the throat." (WK 2008j)
  —But the problem here is three-fold, as shown in what follows.

(continued on next page)

Table 1.11. The Problems of Time Travel into the Past (Part III)

• **Third Problem *(cont'd)***

—The first part of the problem is that "there is no observational evidence for wormholes." (WK 2008j)

—The second part of the problem is that it is not clear how exactly wormholes (and black holes, for that matter) could allow time travel into the past at all.

—And the third part of the problem is that if using wormholes (and black holes, for that matter) to travel into the past requires something to go faster than light too, then this raises another issue concerning the two problems as previously indicated in the sub-section on the faster-than-light-speed.

• **Fourth Problem**

—The fourth problem is that some physicists have argued that, even should time travel into the past be possible, by way of these three methods, the person still would not return to the same past history that he exactly experienced before, but in a different one. (WK 2008i)

—In other words, "strictly speaking," time travel into the past is not "really" possible, in light of these criticisms, so there is no need to worry that one could travel into the past and kill one's parent, as a way to violate the law of casuality.

Source: From *Sec.4.4.2* of *FPHG*

Table 1.12. The Conceptual Dimensions of Consciousness (and Other Mental States)

- **On Heredity and Time**
  —Heredity and the Environment
  —The Past and the Present

- **On Layers of Mental States and Abnormality**
  —Consciousness, Unconsciousness, and Preconsciousness
  —Normality and Paranormality

- **On Organicity and Motivation**
  —Mechanicity and Organicity
  —Primary Motivations and Multiple Motivations

- **On Other (Mostly Epistemic) Considerations**
  —Synthesis and Analysis
  —Situation and the Subject
  —Process and Outcome
  —Reasoning and Other Modes of Thinking
  —Meta-Conceptual Nominalism and Realism

Notes:: These examples are solely illustrative (not exhaustive), and some of the items can be reclassified somewhere else. Nor are they always mutually exclusive. Since they are generalities, exceptions are expected.
Sources: From *FPHC*. A re-construction, but with my own contribution, originally from G.Lindzey & C.Hall, *Introduction to Theories of Personality* (NY: John Wiley & Sons, 1985).

Table 1.13. The Theoretical Levels of Consciousness (and Other Mental States) (Part I)

- **At the Micro-Physical Theoretical Level**
  - —Quantum-Mechanics
  - —Electromagnetism

- **At the Chemical Theoretical Level**
  - —Biochemistry

- **At the Biological Theoretical Level**
  - —Evolutionary Biology
  - —Neuroscience
  - —Artificial Intelligence

- **At the Psychological Theoretical Level**
  - —Psychodynamic Psychology
    - Psychoanalytical Psychology
    - Analytical Psychology
    - Socially Oriented Psychology
  - —Experimental (Behavioral) Psychology
    - Operant Reinforcement Theory
    - Stimulus-Response Theory
    - Social Learning Theory
  - —Cognitive (Gestalt) Psychology
    - Humanist Psychology
    - Existential Psychology
    - Field Theory
  - —Psychometric Psychology
    - Idiographics
    - Constitutional Psychology
  - —Social Psychology
    - Symbolic Interactive Theory
    - Social Exchange Theory

(continued on next page)

Table 1.13. The Theoretical Levels of Consciousness (and Other Mental States) (Part II)

- **At the Organizational Theoretical Level**
  —Managerial-Bureaucratic Theory
  —Oligarchic Theory
  —Network Theory

- **At the Institutional Theoretical Level**
  —Functionalist Theory
  —Anomic Theory

- **At the Structural Theoretical Level**
  —Conflict Theory
    - Marxian Theory
    - Critical Theory
    - Weberian Theory

  —Games Theory (in Formal Theory)
  —Feminist Theory
    - Feminist Concerns
    - Feminist Hopes

- **At the Systemic Theoretical Level**
  —Equilibrium Theory
  —System Theory
  —Chaos Theory

- **At the Cosmological Theoretical Level**
  —Superluminal Model
  —The Theory of Floating Consciousness

(continued on next page)

Table 1.13. The Theoretical Levels of Consciousness (and Other Mental States) (Part III)

- **At the Cultural Theoretical Level**
  - —Substantive Theories
    - Structuralist Theory
    - Post-Structuralist Theory (in Postmodernism)
  - —Meta-Theories
    - Epistemic Objectivism vs. Epistemic Historicism
    - Epistemic Subjectivism vs. Epistemic Non-Subjectivism
      - –Phenomenology
      - –Ethnomethodology
      - –Hermeneutics
    - Epistemic Relativism vs. Epistemic Absolutism
    - Epistemic Reductionism vs. Epistemic Emergencism

- **At Other Levels**
  - —Structuration Theory
  - —Reflexive Socioanalysis

Notes: These examples are solely illustrative (not exhaustive), and some of the items can be reclassified somewhere else. Nor are they always mutually exclusive. Since they are generalities, exceptions are expected.
Source: From many different sources as indicated in *FPHC*

Table 1.14. The Thematic Issues of Consciousness (and Other Mental States)

- **The Factor of History**
  —Pre-Modernity
  —Modernity
  —Postmodernity
  —After-Postmodernity

- **The Importance of Needs**
  —Having (e.g., the everyday, the technological)
  —Belonging (e.g., the just and the good)
  —Being (e.g., the true, the holy, the sublime/beautiful, and the good)

Notes: These examples are solely illustrative (not exhaustive). Nor are they always mutually exclusive. Since they are generalities, exceptions are expected. Also, some categories overlap with others; for instance, the good is also related with being-ness, just as the everyday can be connected with belong-ness.
Sources: From *FPHC*, based on *FHC* and *FCD*

Table 1.15. Having, Belonging, and Being in Consciousness

- **Having (e.g., About the Everyday and Technological)**
  —Ex: Physiological needs (e.g., thirst, hunger, sex)
  —Ex: Safety (e.g., stability, freedom from fear and anxiety)

- **Belonging (e.g., About the Good and Just)**
  —Ex: Social interaction
  —Ex: Friendship, acquaintance
  —Ex: Love, family
  —Ex: Self-respect, respect from others

- **Being (e.g., About the True, Holy, Beautiful/Sublime, and Good)**
  —Ex: Understanding of reality about self and world
  —Ex: Spiritual quest for holiness, beauty, sublimity, and goodness

Notes: These examples are solely illustrative (not exhaustive), and some of the items can be reclassified somewhere else. Nor are they always mutually exclusive. Since they are generalities, exceptions are expected.
Sources: From *FPHC*, based on *FHC* and *FCD*

Table 1.16. The Having-Ness of Consciousness (and Other Mental States)

- **At the Micro-Physical Level**
  —Ex: The finer physics of nutrition

- **At the Chemical Level**
  —Ex: Food guide pyramid

- **At the Bio-Psychological Level**
  —Ex: The hierarchy of needs

- **At the Institutional Level**
  —Ex: The production of commodity fetishism

- **At the Organizational Level**
  —Ex: Mass standardization (and customization); bureaucratic rationality

- **At the Structural Level**
  —Ex: The divide between the haves and the have-nots

- **At the Cultural Level**
  —Ex: The bondage of greater expectations

- **At the Systemic Level**
  —Ex: The technological transformation of poverty with transvaluations

- **At the Cosmological Level**
  —Ex: Floating consciousness in deep space without the human physiological needs

Notes: These examples are solely illustrative (not exhaustive), and some of the items can be reclassified somewhere else. Nor are they always mutually exclusive. Since they are generalities, exceptions are expected.
Sources: From *FPHC*. See also *FCD* and *FHC*.

Table 1.17. The Belonging-Ness of Consciousness (and Other Mental States)

- **At the Micro-Physical Level**
  —Ex: Statistical physics and social networks

- **At the Chemical Level**
  —Ex: Olfaction and social relations

- **At the Bio-Psychological Level**
  —Ex: Dual human nature on relationships

- **At the Institutional Level**
  —Ex: Private property and social cleavage

- **At the Organizational Level**
  —Ex: Legal formalism and iron cage

- **At the Structural Level**
  —Ex: Class conflicts and social alienation

- **At the Cultural Level**
  —Ex: Ruthless society and the culture of law

- **At the Systemic Level**
  —Ex: Human extinction and post-human relations

- **At the Cosmological Level**
  —Ex: The transcendence of equality in the cosmos and beyond

Notes: These examples are solely illustrative (not exhaustive), and some of the items can be reclassified somewhere else. Nor are they always mutually exclusive. Since they are generalities, exceptions are expected.
Sources: From *FPHC*. See also *FCD* and *FHC*.

Table 1.18. The Being-Ness of Consciousness (and Other Mental States) (Part I)

- **At the Micro-Physical Level**
  —Ex: Space-time and matter-energy in classical mechanics, quantum mechanics, and the theory of relativity

- **At the Chemical Level**
  —Ex: Drugs and well being

- **At the Biological Level**
  —Ex: Neuroscience and mystical experiences

- **At the Psychological Level**
  —Ex: Reductionism and emergencism

- **At the Institutional Level**
  —Ex: The proliferation of cults and sects, and the corporate-art industry

- **At the Organizational Level**
  —Ex: The organization of ideas in the scheme of things

- **At the Structural Level**
  —Ex: Disciplinary power and control in the order of things

- **At the Systemic Level**
  —Ex: Mutualism and ecological psychology

- **At the Cultural Level**
  —Ex: The recurrence of competing spirits, and floating consciousness as a climax of evolution

(continued on next page)

Table 1.18. The Being-Ness of Consciousness (and Other Mental States) (Part II)

- **At the Cosmological Level**
  —Ex: The search for elsewherewhen, and the evolution of other consciousnesses (e.g., the hyper-spatial consciousness)

Notes: These examples are solely illustrative (not exhaustive), and some of the items can be reclassified somewhere else. Nor are they always mutually exclusive. Since they are generalities, exceptions are expected.
Sources: From *FPHC*. See also *FCD* and *FHC*.

Table 1.19. Cognitive Partiality in Different Mental States

- **The Conscious**
  - —*Biased*
    - Ex: Self-overratingness
    - Ex: Self-modesty
    - Ex: Self-fulfilling prophesy
  - —*Shallow*
    - Ex: Attribution error
    - Ex: Heuristics
    - Ex: Illusory thinking
  - —*Short-term*
    - Ex: Deindividuation
  - —*Materialistic*
    - Ex: Hierarchy of needs

- **The Subconscious**
  - Ex: mental reconstruction
  - Ex: stereotyping

- **The Unconscious**
  - Ex: automatic processing
  - Ex: cognitive intuition

Notes: These examples are solely illustrative (not exhaustive), and some of the items can be reclassified somewhere else. Nor are they always mutually exclusive. Since they are generalities, exceptions are expected. And the comparison is relative, not absolute.

Source: From *BCPC*

Table 1.20. Emotional Non-Neutrality and Behavioral Alteration in Different Mental States

- **The Emotional**
  - —*Conscious*
    - Ex: Feelings
  - —*Subconscious*
    - Ex: Moods
  - —*Unconscious*
    - Ex: Empathy
    - Ex: Instincts

- **The Behavioral**
  - —*Conscious*
    - Ex: Foot-in-the-door
    - Ex: Role playing
    - Ex: Saying-is-believing
  - —*Subconscious*
    - Ex: Discrimination
  - —*Unconscious*
    - Ex: Non-Verbal Communication

Notes: These examples are solely illustrative (not exhaustive), and some of the items can be reclassified somewhere else. Nor are they always mutually exclusive. Since they are generalities, exceptions are expected. And the comparison is relative, not absolute.
Source: From *BCPC*

Table 1.21. The Limits of Intuition in Unconsciousness

- **Cognitive Intuition (or Intuitive Thinking)**
  —*Features*
  Ex: mental schemas
  Ex: expertise
  Ex: blindsight
  —*Problems*
  Ex: inaccurate
  Ex: non-explanatory

- **Emotional Intuition**
  —*Features*
  Ex: empathy
  Ex: instincts
  —*Problems*
  Ex: over-generalized
  Ex: non-explanatory

- **Behavioral Intuition**
  —*Features*
  Ex: prosemics
  Ex: kinesics
  —*Problems*
  Ex: unreliable
  Ex: non-explanatory

Notes: These examples are solely illustrative (not exhaustive), and some of the items can be reclassified somewhere else. Nor are they always mutually exclusive. Since they are generalities, exceptions are expected. And the comparison is relative, not absolute.
Source: From *BCPC*

Table 1.22. The Wealth/Poverty Dialectics in Different Mental States: The Case of Cognition

- **The Conscious**
  - —*Biased*
    - Ex: If richer in self-serving bias, then poorer in understanding others
  - —*Shallow*
    - Ex: If richer in heuristic thinking, then poorer in comprehending reality
  - —*Short-term*
    - Ex: If richer in short-term tendency, then poorer in long-term planning
  - —*Materialistic*
    - Ex: If richer in physiological obsession, then poorer in spiritual enlightenment

- **The Subconscious**
  - Ex: If richer in mental reconstruction, then poorer in accuracy of recall
  - Ex: If richer in stereotyping, then poorer in understanding groups

- **The Unconscious**
  - Ex: If richer in automatic processing, then poorer in depth of analysis
  - Ex: If richer in cognitive intuition, then poorer in reliability of judgments

Notes: These examples are solely illustrative (not exhaustive), and some of the items can be reclassified somewhere else. Nor are they always mutually exclusive. Since they are generalities, exceptions are expected. And the comparison is relative, not absolute.
Source: From *BCPC*

Table 1.23. The Wealth/Poverty Dialectics in Different Mental States: The Case of Emotion and Behavior

- **Emotion**
  - —*Conscious*
    - Ex: If richer in relying on familiarity and similarity for social attraction, then poorer in having diverse social relations
  - —*Subconscious*
    - Ex: If richer in moodiness, then poorer in sober thinking
  - —*Unconscious*
    - Ex: If richer in empathy, then poorer in task-oriented efficiency
    - Ex: If richer in instincts, then poorer in critical thinking

- **Behavior**
  - —*Conscious*
    - Ex: If richer in foot-in-the-door technique, then poorer in instant Gratification
    - Ex: If richer in role playing, then poorer in identity stability
  - —*Subconscious*
    - Ex: If richer in discriminating, then poorer in social harmony
  - —*Unconscious*
    - Ex: If richer in kinesics and proxemics, then poorer in verbal skills, relatively speaking.

Notes: These examples are solely illustrative (not exhaustive), and some of the items can be reclassified somewhere else. Nor are they always mutually exclusive. Since they are generalities, exceptions are expected. And the comparison is relative, not absolute.
Source: From *BCPC*

Table 1.24. The Theoretical Debate on Nature vs. Nurture (Part I)

- **The Environmental Approach**
  —*Thesis*: It focuses, relatively speaking, more on the environment (culture and society) in explaining the achievement gap among individuals and for that matter, countries or regions, when contrasted with the natural factors.
  —*Discourse*: Examples include Jose Ortega y Gasset ("Man has no nature; what he has is history"), Ashley Montagu ("Man is man because he has no instincts, because everything he is and has become he has learned from his culture, from the man-made part of the environment, from other human beings"), Stephen Jay Gould ("[The] brain [is] capable of a full range of behaviors and predisposed to none"), and Jesse Jackson (who blames white racism for the failure of blacks to close the achievement gap between whites and blacks in America). The works on dependency theory in international political economy (with a Marxian influence) and on the Protestant work ethic (by Max Weber) also point to this environmental direction.

- **The Genetic Approach**
  —*Thesis*: It focuses instead, relatively speaking again, on hereditory factors (e.g., genes and evolution) in explaining the achievement gap among individuals and for that matter, countries or regions, when contrasted with the envrionmental factors.
  —*Discourse*: Examples are Hans Eysenck and William Sheldon (in constitutional psychology), Konrad Lorenz (in his work on innate aggressive human nature), Gary Marcus (on the complexities of human thought by a tiny number of genes) and Robert Plomin, together with Michael Owen and Peter McGuffin (on the genetic basis of complex human behaviors).

(continued on next page)

Table 1.24. The Theoretical Debate on Nature vs. Nurture (Part II)

- **The Compromise Approach**
  —*Thesis*: It seeks the middle-of-the-road argument in regard to nature and nurture and regards all differences among individuals and groups as the result of the mixture of both nature and nurture, more or less equally.
  —*Discourse*: Examples include C. Murray and R. Herrnstein ("It seems highly likely to us that both genes and environment have something to do with this issue") and Dan Dennett ("Surely 'everyone knows' that the nature-nurture debate was resolved long ago, and neither side wins since everything – is – a – mixture – of – both – and - it's – all – very -complicated…."

- **The Transcendent Approach**
  —*Thesis*: It goes beyond both nature and nurture (without, however, committing the compromise fallacy) in showing their closely intertwined interactions in producing the behavioral differences as often seen in individual human endeavors on the micro scale, and for that matter, in country (or regional) endeavors on the macro one—in the context of my five theses, namely, (a) the compromise fallacy, (b) no oppression without self-oppression, (c) no success without failure, (d) the factor of randomness, and (e) the post-human vision, to be elaborated in Chapter Six.
  —*Discourse*: Peter Baofu proposed this approach on the basis of his "theory of contrastive advantages" (as an original theoretical contribution to the debate, which was first proposed and analyzed in *The Future of Capitalism and Democracy*). In the end, the human genes will not last, to be eventually superseded by post-human life forms, so the debate between genes and memes has obscured something profoundly important about the future that the world has never known. And the debate is also misleading and faulty in its dichotomy.

Source: From *BNN*. See the book for citations and details.

Table 1.25. Physical Challenges to Hyper-Spatial Consciousness

- **The Understanding of a Higher-Dimensional World of Space-Time**
  —Ex: 4 for traditional aspects of space-time (e.g., length, width, breadth and time) plus 6 more new dimensions in theory of hyper-space, with profound implications for practical applications to new forms of consciousness.

- **The Mastering of Dark Matter and Dark Energy**
  —Ex: "ordinary matter" (e.g., atoms, molecules) as a mere 4.4% of the universe, with 23% made of "cold dark matter" and the rest (about 73%) of mysterious "dark energy," with fundamental significance to questions about the limit of the speed of energy (or info), the availability of energy for use, and the nature of space-time, just to cite some examples.

- **The Exploration of Multiverses**
  —Ex: theoretical speculation of other universes (e.g., "baby universes," "gateways" in black holes, "wave function of the universe," "many worlds," "brane worlds"), with potentially seminary discoveries of different physical laws in relation to matter-energy and space-time, and vital differences to the future of post-human conquest of other universes (for the emergence of new forms of consciousness).

Notes: These examples are solely illustrative (not exhaustive), and some of the items can be reclassified somewhere else. Nor are they always mutually exclusive. Since they are generalities, exceptions are expected. The point here is to give a rough picture of the evolution of consciousness to the hyper-spatial consciousness and others totally unknown to current earthlings. As a note of clarification, it makes no difference to my argument as to whether or not the hyper-spatial consciousness may emerge before, during, and after floating consciousness.
Source: From *Table 4.5* of *FPHC*

Table 1.26. The Theory of Floating Consciousness (Part I)

- **At the Micro-Physical Level**
  —Ex: intelligent life without the human physical-chemical system

- **At the Chemical Level**
  —Ex: space radiation and toxins

- **At the Bio-Psychological Level**
  —Ex: exo-biological evolution in deep space
  —Ex: genetic engineering of new beings

- **At the Institutional Level**
  —Ex: post-capitalism
  —Ex: post-democracy

- **At the Organizational Level**
  —Ex: less legal-formalistic routines

- **At the Structural Level**
  —Ex: alien forms of violence

- **At the Cultural Level**
  —Ex: transcending freedom
  —Ex: transcending equality

(continued on next page)

Table 1.26. The Theory of Floating Consciousness (Part II)

- **At the Cosmological Level**
  —Ex: parallel universes
  —Ex: pocket universes

- **At the Systemic Level**
  —Ex: space habitats (in zero-gravity)

Notes: Each example draws from the works of different scholars in the field. For instance, at the cosmological level, the idea of parallel universes is from the theoretical speculation in quantum cosmology by Stephen Hawking and others, while the one of pocket universes comes from the theoretical work of Allan Guth at MIT. And at the institutional level, I proposed post-capitalism and post-democracy in *FCD* (and later, from *BDPD* and *BCPC*). In addition, the examples are solely illustrative (not exhaustive), and some of the items can be reclassified somewhere else. Nor are they always mutually exclusive. Since they are generalities, exceptions are expected.
Sources: From *FPHC*—and, originally, from *FCD*

Table 1.27. The Potential of Unfolding Unconsciousness

- **Superior Senses**
  - —*Through space*
    - Ex: clair-sentience (in feeling)
    - Ex: clair-voyance (in seeing)
    - Ex: clair-audience (in hearing)
    - Ex: clair-austance (in tasting)
    - Ex: clair-alience (in smelling)
    - Ex: clair-cognizance (in knowing)
  - —*Through time*
    - Ex: pre-cognition (in knowing), pre-sentiment (in feeling)
    - Ex: retro-cognition (in knowing), retro-sentiment (in feeling)

- **Superior Contacts**
  - —*With living minds*
    - Ex: telepathy
  - —*With the dead*
    - Ex: mediumship
  - —*With other-living entities*
    - Ex: telekinesis

Notes: The categories and examples are solely illustrative (not exhaustive), and the comparison is relative (not absolute), nor are they necessarily mutually exclusive. And some can be easily re-classified elsewhere. As generalities, they allow exceptions.
Source: A summary of Ch.5 of *FPHU*

Table 1.28. The Future Exploration of Unfolding Unconsciousness

- **In the Context of Nature**
  - —Ex: the higher-dimensional space-time in hyperspace theory
  - —Ex: the particle-wave interactions in quantum mechanics
  - —Ex: the study of brain waves in electromagnetic theory

- **In the Context of the Mind**
  - —Ex: the unconscious fantasies in psychoanalysis
  - —Ex: the mind-altering drugs in biochemistry
  - —Ex: the manipulation of neural activity in neurobiology

- **In the Context of Culture**
  - —Ex: the correlation between anomalous experience and moral/religious/aesthetic interests in culture studies
  - —Ex: the role of myths and language in epistemology

- **In the Context of Society**
  - —Ex: different organizational agendas in anomalous research
  - —Ex: the scholarly divide on anomalous study
  - —Ex: interests and propaganda in institutioanl research
  - —Ex: the transformative power of technology in research on social systems
  - —Ex: the natural and non-natural selection of other worlds in exo-biology
  - —Ex: the role of the post-human conscious mind in qualitative demography

Notes: The examples in each category are solely illustrative (not exhaustive), and the comparison is relative (not absolute), nor are they necessarily mutually exclusive. And some can be easily re-classified elsewhere. As generalities, they allow exceptions.

Source: A summary of Chs.2-5 of *FPHU*, in conjunction with the rest of the book

Table 1.29. Creative Techniques and Traits

- **Creative Techniques**
  - —*Comprehensiveness*
    - Ex: Broadness of Scope
    - Ex: In-Depth Analysis
    - Ex: Multifaceted Taxonomy
    - Ex: Numerous Theories
  - —*Arrangement*
    - Ex: Separation (or Subtraction)
    - Ex: Combination (or Addition)
    - Ex: Replacement
    - Ex: Reversal
    - Ex: Accommodation
    - Ex: Stretching
  - —*Serendipity*
    - Ex: Play
    - Ex: Chance

- **Creative Traits**
  - —*Openness / Risk*
    - Ex: Ability to welcome new ideas or to do new things, with risk
  - —*Discipline*
    - Ex: Ability to sacrifice whatever it takes to succeed
  - —*Resilience / Confidence*
    - Ex: Ability to take failures to mind, not to heart
  - —*Trust*
    - Ex: Ability to cooperate with others for team work, if necessary

Notes: The examples in the categories are solely illustrative (not exhaustive), and the comparison is relative (not absolute), nor are they necessarily mutually exclusive. And some can be easily re-classified elsewhere. As generalities, they allow exceptions.
Source: From *Sec.4.2* of *FPHCT*. For more details, also read the rest of the book.

Table 1.30. The Desirability of Creativity, and Its Dark Sides (Part I)

- **In Relation to Instrumental Rationality**
  —*Desirability*
    - Ex: For the sake of efficiency and effectiveness in this capitalist era of our time.

  —*Undesirability*
    - Ex: What Max Weber (1930) called the "iron cage" of capitalism, where live the "sensualists without heart, specialists without spirit"—or something which the Frankfurt School has forcefully asked us to be freed from.

- **In Relation to Substantive Rationality**
  —*Desirability*
    - Ex: For the sake of God, the King, Motherland, or other comparable ideals.

  —*Undesirability*
    - Ex: Domination and oppression of various forms—something which the moderns had struggled to free themselves from in the first place, since the dawn of modernity.

- **In Relation to Autonomous Rationality**
  —*Desirability*
    - Ex: For the sake of itself, the autonomy of creative endeavor.

  —*Undesirability*
    - Ex: The decadence of its own degeneration (e.g., the donwsides of postmodernism in our postmodern times, or what Nietzsche once called the unbearable "unreality" and "falseness" of the autonomous artist's "innermost existence"—and, in other cases, the painful suffering from different mental illnesses for those highly creative individuals).

(continued on next page)

Table 1.30. The Desirability of Creativity, and Its Dark Sides (Part II)

Notes: The examples in the categories are solely illustrative (not exhaustive), and the comparison is relative (not absolute), nor are they necessarily mutually exclusive. And some can be easily re-classified elsewhere. As generalities, they allow exceptions.
Also, I already went to great lenghts to explain the desirability and its dark sides of all these three rationalities (although there may be others too) in the two volumes of *FHC*—and, for that matter, *FCD*.
Source: From *Sec.4.9* of *FPHCT*. For more details, also read the rest of the book.

Table 1.31. Posthuman-Ism, Post-Humanism, and Trans-Humanism

- **Post-Humanism**
  —The neologism "post-human" used in my books should *not* be confused with another term which looks similar but has a totally different meaning in the literature of postmodernism, namely, "post-humanism"—which constitutes a critique of "humanism" as tradionally understood (especially, though not exclusively, in relation to the idea of progress in science and reason in the Enlightenment project). (WK 2008)
  —My works reject the project of "postmodernism" and propose the future world of what I orignally called "after-postmodernity" in *FHC* and *FCD*, for instance.

- **Trans-Humanism**
  —Also, the neologism "post-human" used in my books should *not* be confused with a similar term which is used to champion the ideology of technology for the fturue co-existence between humans and cyborgs in "trans-humanism." (WK 2008a)
  —Instead, my term "post-human" in relation to "posthuman-ism" also rejects "trans-humanism" (especially, though not exclusively, in relation to the promises of technology) and refers to something else altogether, that is, the future extinction of humans and its post-human successors in deep space and beyond unto multiverses.
  —Chapter Two of my book on ethics (*BEPE*) provides a more comprehensive critique of trans-humanism.

- **Posthuman-Ism**
  —With these two clarifications in mind, the "post-humans" (as envisioned in my books) can take different forms, and I proposed, in my different books, some of them, such as "unfolding unconsciousness," "floating consciousness," "hyper-spatial consciousness," "thinking machines," "thinking robots," "genetically altered superior beings," "cyborgs," and others (as already analyzed in my previous works).
  —They will evolve in conjunction with other visions of mine in relation to nature, society, and culture.

Sources: From *Sec.1.6* of *FPHE* (and also *BEPE*). For more details, also read the rest of the books (and other books of mine).

Table 1.32. Three Great Future Transformations of the Martial Body (Part I)

- **Virtual Battle**
  —Ex: virtual fight
  —Ex: virtual memory

- **The Hyper-Martial Body**
  —*In relation to the physical dimension*
  - Ex: striking (e.g., punching, kicking, trapping, acupressure-striking, and so on in an amazing way)
  - Ex: grapping (e.g., throwing, pinning, joint-locking, and so on in an amazing way)
  - Ex: running and walking (e.g., on different surfaces)
  - Ex: jumping (e.g., through walls, trees, etc.)
  - Ex: flying (e.g., through space)
  - Ex: enduring pain (e.g., absorbing punches, kicks, and so on in an amazing way)
  - Ex: using extremely advanced hi-tech weapons
  - Ex: healing (e.g., with special energy, etc.)
  - Ex: entering (e.g., into different dimensions of space)
  - Ex: sensing (e.g., in extraordinary ways through space and time, etc.)
  - Ex: wearing hi-tech suits for defensive and offensive purposes (e.g., like a hi-tech armor)

  —*In relation to the mental dimension*
  - Ex: the ability to relax the martial body in a way that current humans cannot.
  - Ex: the ability to concentrate the martial mind in a way that current humans are not accustomed to.
  - Ex: the ability to breathe and be timely in preparing the martial body for fighting in a way that current humans are not good at.

- **The Post-Martial Floating Mind**
  —Ex: the mind without the human body
  —Ex: the quest for spirituality beyond martial arts

(continued on next page)

Table 1.32. Three Great Future Transformations of the Martial Body (Part II)

Notes: The examples in the categories are solely illustrative (not exhaustive), and the comparison is relative (not absolute), nor are they necessarily mutually exclusive. And some can be easily re-classified elsewhere. As generalities, they allow exceptions.
Source: From *Sec. 2.5.1* of *FPHMA*. See text for citations.

Table 1.33. Three Great Future Transformations of the Sexual Body

- **Virtual Pleasure**
  —Ex: virtual Sex
  —Ex: virtual Recall

- **The Hyper-Sexual Body**
  —*In relation to the physical dimension*
  - Ex: the ability to perform differenet sexual positions without the various physical limitations that humans currently have.
  - Ex: the ability to produce unusual amount of sexual energy to endure in sexual acts in a way that humans currently cannot.
  - Ex: the ability to engage in multiple sexual experiences comparable to (but different from) non-human sexuality (e.g., hermaphrodite, monoecious, sex-switching, and many other types) that current humans cannot.

  —*In relation to the mental dimension*
  - Ex: the ability to relax the sexual body in a way that current humans are not accustomed to.
  - Ex: the ability to concentrate the sexual mind in a way that current humans are not good at.
  - Ex: the ability to breathe and be patient in preparing the sexual body for sexuality in a way that current humans are not able to.

- **The Post-Sexual Floating Mind**
  —Ex: the mind without the human body
  —Ex: the quest for spirituality beyond sexuality

Notes: The examples in the categories are solely illustrative (not exhaustive), and the comparison is relative (not absolute), nor are they necessarily mutually exclusive. And some can be easily re-classified elsewhere. As generalities, they allow exceptions.
Source: From *Sec. 3.4.2* of *FPHS*. See text for more info.

Table 1.34. The Trinity of Pre-Modernity

- **Pre-Free-Spirited Pre-Modernity (Pre-Modernism) and Its Internal Split**
  —Competing worldviews and values both within and between linear centric (e.g., Islamic, Christian, Judaic, Imperial Roman) and cyclical-centric (e.g., Confucian, Taoist, Hindu, and Buddhist) orientations
  —Compare modernism with pre-modernism here in relation to the seven dimensions of human existence like the true and the holy (e.g., different versions of epistemic dogmas and religious superstitions), the everyday and the technological (e.g.,different versions of non-technophilism and non-consumerism), the beautiful/sublime (e.g., different versions of aesthetic non-autonomy), and the good and the just (e.g., different versions of moral particularism).

- **Pre-Capitalist Pre-Modernity (Pre-Modernization) and Its Own Discontents**
  —Competing versions of societal arrangements (e.g., feudalism, monarchism, and the holy order)

- **Hegemonic Pre-Modernity and Its Countervailing Forces**
  —Different power centers and their enemies (e.g., the Roman Empire and the "barbarian hordes," the "Holy Crusades" and the Muslims, the Middle Kingdom and the invading tribes, different social castes in India, and warring Greek city-states)

Notes: The examples in each category are solely illustrative (not exhaustive) nor necessarily mutually exclusive, and the comparison is relative (not absolute). As generalities, they allow exceptions. Also, it does not matter what the "base" era is in the analysis of any trinity. And in the present context, the "base" era is modernity (for instance, with its "free-spirited modernity" and the other two parts). So, for pre-modernity, the trinity takes the form of, say, "pre-free-spirited pre-modernity," together with the other two parts.
Sources: From Ch.2 of *BCIV* and also the 2 volumes of *FHC*

Table 1.35. The Trinity of Modernity (Part I)

- **Free-Spirited Modernity (Modernism) and Its Internal Split**

  —*On the True and the Holy*
  - The freedom from the dogmas of the past to the better understanding of, and union with, the world and self (Ch.3 of *FHC*)
  - Alternative discourses: about the true (e.g., anti-science discourses) and the holy (non-mainstream theologies) (Ch.3 of *FHC*)

  —*On the Technological and the Everyday*
  - The freedom from life harshness to the higher technophilic, consumeristic lifeform (Ch.2 of *FHC*)
  - Alternative discourses: about the everyday (e.g., transcendental mindsets) and the technological (e.g., Arcadianism) (Ch.2 of *FHC*)

  —*On the Good and the Just*
  - The freedom from the theo-aristocratic tyranny to the moral universality for a just society (Ch.5 of *FHC*)
  - Alternative discourses: about the just (e.g., Communism, Anarchism) and the good (e.g., Nazism/Fascism, and Zarathustrianism) (Chs.5-6 of *FHC*)

  —*On the Beautiful and the Sublime*
  - The freedom from the external distortion of aesthetic pleasure to the boundless infinity of totality in artistic autonomy (Ch.4 of *FHC*)
  - Alternative discourses: about the beautiful/sublime (e.g., kitsch and historical avant-gardism) (Ch.4 of *FHC*)

- **Capitalist Modernity (Modernization) and Its Own Discontents**

  —*During the Industrial Revolution*
  - Ex: Marx on the institution of inequality (Ch.1 of *FHC*)

  —*During the Modern Rational-Instrumental Epoch*
  - Ex: Weber on the politics of soft liberal institutions (Ch.5 of *FHC*)

  —*During the Great Depression*
  - Ex: Keynes on the myth of the free market (Chs.1-3 of *FHC*)

  —*During the Cold War*
  - Ex: Lasch on the narcissistic culture industry (Chs.2-3 of *FHC*)

(continued on next page)

Table 1.35. The Trinity of Modernity (Part II)

- **Hegemonic Modernity and Its Countervailing Forces**

—*The Legacies of Colonialism and Imperialism*
  - Ex: European colonization of most of the modern world (Ch.1 of *FHC*)

—*The Struggle for Decolonialization*
  - Ex: The countervailing forces of resentment, rechantment, and regionalism (Chs.1 & 6 of *FHC*)

Notes: The examples in each category are solely illustrative (not exhaustive) nor necessarily mutually exclusive, and the comparison is relative (not absolute). As generalities, they allow exceptions.
Sources: From the 2 volumes of *FHC*—and also from *FCD*

Table 1.36. The Trinity of Post-Modernity

- **Free-Spirited Postmodernity (Postmodernism) and Its Internal Split**
  —*On the True and the Holy*
    - Postmodern performative turn for knowing and its enemies (Ch.3 of *FHC*)
    - Postmodern comparative theology and its opponents (Ch.3 of *FHC*)

  —*On the Technological and the Everyday*
    - Postmodern corporate technological mindset and its adversaries (Ch.2 of *FHC*)
    - Postmodern postmaterialism and its critics (Ch.2 of *FHC*)

  —*On the Good and the Just*
    - Postmodern politics of difference and its foes (Ch.5 of *FHC*)

  —*On the Beautiful and the Sublime*
    - Postmodern deconstruction and its dissenters (Ch.4 of *FHC*)

- **Capitalist Postmodernity (Postmodernization) and Its Own Discontents**
  —*During the Post-Cold War and Beyond*
    - Ex: post-Fordism and its shortcomings (Ch.6 of *FHC*; Chs.6-7 of *FCD*)

- **Hegemonic Postmodernity and Its Countervailing Forces**
  —*The Debate on the Global Village*
    - Ex: uni-civilizationalism vs. multi-civilizationalism (Ch.6 of *FHC*)

  —*The Resistance Movement*
    - Ex: rechantment and the politics of civilizational claims (e.g., Islamic, Confucian and other ethos in relation to the Same) (Ch.6 of *FHC*; Ch.10 of *FCD*)
    - Ex: resentment and the politics of resurgence (e.g., the rising Chinese superpower, the growing EU, and other players in relation to the U.S. and her allies) (Ch.6 of *FHC*; Ch.8 of *FCD*)
    - Ex: regionalism and the politics of inequality (e.g., trans- or international blocs, the North-South divide, NGO's) (Ch.6 of *FHC*; Ch.5 of *FCD*)

Notes: The examples in each category are solely illustrative (not exhaustive) nor necessarily mutually exclusive, and the comparison is relative (not absolute). As generalities, they allow exceptions.
Sources: From *FCD* and the 2 volumes of *FHC*

Table 1.37. The Trinity of After-Postmodernity

- **Free-Spirited After-Postmodernity (After-Postmodernism) and Its Internal Split**
  —The discourse of naked contingency (Ch.10 of *FCD*; Ch.4 of *FPHC*)

- **Post-Capitalist After-Postmodernity (After-Postmodernization) and Its Own Discontents**
  —Different versions of post-capitalism and post-democracy, and their enemies (Ch.10 of *FCD*; Chs.3-4 of *FPHC*)

- **Hegemonic After-Postmodernity and Its Countervailing Forces**
  —The Cyclical Progression of Hegemony in Multiverses (Chs.9-10 of *FCD*; Ch.4 of *FPHC*)

Notes: The examples in each category are solely illustrative (not exhaustive) nor necessarily mutually exclusive, and the comparison is relative (not absolute). As generalities, they allow exceptions.
Sources: From *FCD* and also *FHC*

• PART TWO •

Sacredness

CHAPTER 2
SACREDNESS AND ITS LIMITS

> Where there is evidence, no one speaks of 'faith.' We do not speak of faith that two and two are four or that the earth is round. We only speak of faith when we wish to substitute emotion for evidence.
> —Bertrand Russell (WK 2010o)

The Importance of Sacredness

The term "sacredness" is derived from the adjective "sacred," which in turn is from "Middle English, from past participle of *sacren* to consecrate, from Anglo-French *sacrer*, from Latin *sacrare*, from *sacr-*, *sacer* sacred; akin to Latin *sancire*...." (MWD 2010)

In one formal definition, "sacredness" refers to the state of being "dedicated or set apart for the service or worship of a deity," "worthy of religious veneration," or "entitled to reverence and respect...relating to religion." (MWD 2010)

In this way, the opposite of being "sacred" is "secular or profane"; so sacredness and secularness are two opposites. (MWD 2010)

Any study of religion, therefore, requires an examination of the nature of sacredness and secularness.

This book offers a dialectic treatment of sacredness and secularness, in that, if sacredness has its importance, it has its limitation too—just as, if secularnes has its promise, it likewise has its pitfall.

The inquiry concernng sacredness is the subject matter of this chapter (Chapter Two), whereas that of secularness will be addressed in the next chapter (Chapter Three).

A good way to examine the limits of sacredness is by way of the evaluation of the extent to which it (sacredness) is in fact both possible and desirabe.

This chapter thus takes the challenging task to provide a comprehensive analysis of sacredmess in the context of religion from the four perspectives of the mind, nature, society, and culture (in accordance to my sophisticated methodological holism, as explained in *Sec. 1.9*).

In other words, this chapter is organized in four main sections, in relation to (2.2) sacredness and the mind, (2.3) sacredness and nature, (2.4) sacredness and society, and (2.5) sacredness and culture—to be examined hereafter, in that order (and summarized in *Table 2.1*).

Sacredness and the Mind

Sacredness, when examined from the perspective of the mind, can cast some illuminating light on its possibility and desirability, and this can be shown by way of two case studies, namely, (2.2.1) faith, reason, and religion, and (2.2.2) magical thinkng, and religion—to be addressed in what follows, respectively.

Faith, Reason, and Religion

The term "faith" can be traced back to 1200–50 A.D., "from the Latin *fidem* or *fidēs*, meaning trust, derived from the verb *fīdere*, to trust." (WK 2010o)

In other words, faith refers to "the confident belief or trust in the truth or trustworthiness of a person, concept or thing." WK 2010o)

Generally speaking, "faith is…the persuasion of the mind that a certain statement is true, belief in and assent to the truth of what is declared by another, based on his or her supposed authority and truthfulness. Informal usage can be quite broad, and the word is often used as a mere substitute for trust or belief." (WK 2010o)

But specifically speaking, when used "in a religious or theological context," the word refers to "a confident belief in a transcendent reality, a religious teacher, a set of teachings or a Supreme Being." (WK 2010o)

This is true, even though, for the atheist and agnostic critics, the term "faith" is just "a euphemism for religious superstition"—and "since faith implies a trusting reliance upon future events or outcomes, it is often taken by its detractors as inevitably synonymous with a belief 'not resting on logical proof or material evidence.'" (WK 2010o)

Fideism and the Question about the Epistemological Validity of Faith

A critical question which is often asked in the study of religion concerns the epistemological validity of faith. There are, however, no lack of arguments to defend faith.

An excellent example concerns "fideism," which is "from *fides*, the Latin word for faith, and literally means 'faith-ism'"—and refers to "an epistemological theory which maintains that faith is independent of reason, or that reason and faith are hostile to each other and faith is superior at arriving at particular truths." (WK 2010p; R. Amesbury 2005)

However, "the term fideist, one who argues for fideism, is very rarely self applied. Support of fideism is most commonly ascribed to four philosophers: Pascal, Kierkegaard, William James, and Wittgenstein"—as summarized below. (WK 2010p)

(a) Blaise Pascal

Pascal offered a challenge known as "Pascal's Wager" to the atheists, in order "to see faith in God as a cost-free choice that carries a potential reward. He does not attempt to argue that God indeed exists, only that it might be valuable to assume that it is true." (WK 2010p)

The reason is that, for Pascal, "the various proposed proofs of the existence of God as irrelevant. Even if the proofs were valid, the beings they propose to demonstrate are not congruent with the deity worshiped by historical faiths, and can easily lead to deism instead of revealed religion: 'The God of Abraham, Isaac, and Jacob—not the god of the philosophers!'" (WK 2010p)

(b) Soren Kierkegaard

Kierkegaard offered his version of fideism in the context of Christian existentialism, especially in the book titled *Fear and Trembling* published in 1843 under the pseudonym Johannes de silentio (John the Silent). (WK 2010p)

Kierkegaard used the story of Abraham's willingness to sacrifice Isaac to make the case of fideism. The conventional wisdom at the time was that "the New Testament apostles repeatedly argued that Abraham's act was an admirable display of faith. To the eyes of a non-believer, however, it must necessarily have appeared to be an unjustifiable attempted murder, perhaps the fruit of an insane delusion." (WK 2010p)

But for Kierkegaard, "to believe in the incarnation of Christ, in God made flesh, was to believe in the 'absolute paradox,' since it implies that an eternal, perfect being would become a simple human. Reason cannot possibly comprehend such a phenomenon; therefore, one can only believe in it by taking a 'leap of faith.'" (WK 2010p)

(c) William James

James gave a lecture titled "The Will to Believe" in 1897 to "defend...the right to violate the principle of evidentialism in order to justify hypothesis venturing. Although this doctrine is often seen as a way for William James to justify religious beliefs, his philosophy of pragmatism allows him to use the results of his hypothetical venturing as evidence to support the hypothesis' truth. Therefore, this doctrine allows one to assume belief in God and prove its existence by what the belief brings to one's life." (WK 2010q)

There are three major claims in his philosophy of religion which are worth mentioning here, as shown below:

- "Religious genius (experience) should be the primary topic in the study of religion, rather than religious institutions—since institutions are merely the social descendant of genius." (WK 2010q)
- "The intense, even pathological varieties of experience (religious or otherwise) should be sought by psychologists, because they represent the closest thing to a microscope of the mind—that is, they show us in drastically enlarged form the normal processes of things." (WK 2010q)
- "In order usefully to interpret the realm of common, shared experience and history, we must each make certain 'over-beliefs' in things which, while they cannot be proven on the basis of experience, help us to live fuller and better lives." (WK 2010q)

Surely, there can be other claims, but these three are the most important for the purpose at hand.

(d) Ludwig Wittgenstein

Wittgenstein was much interested in religion as a "form of life" in language games. But because he did not explicitly write about the topic except lecturing on it, his view is often based on his students' notes which do not always agree with each other.

For instance, "[i]n his 1967 article, entitled 'Wittgensteinian Fideism,' Kai Nielsen evaluated one suggested interpretation of Wittgenstein's view, in that "religion is a self-contained—and primarily expressive—enterprise, governed by its own internal logic or 'grammar,'" which can be summarized in three major claims, as shown below: (WK 2010p; R. Amesbury 2005)

- "that religion is logically cut off from other aspects of life"
- "that religious concepts and discourse are essentially self-referential"

- "that religion cannot be criticized from an external (i.e., non-religious) point of view"

But Nielsen (2005) went on to argue that this interpretation, if true, could not be tenable, because "the position is socially and politically irresponsible since it ignores prudential, practical, and pragmatic considerations as a basis for criticizing different language games." (WK 2010p)

But for D. Z. Phillips, "the position is not Wittgensteinian at all, and that Wittgenstein's considered view not only allows for the possibility of external, cultural criticism, but also 'advances' philosophical discussion concerning it." (WK 2010p; K. Nielsen 2005)

In any event, the point here is not to side with either Nielsen or Phillips but to understand the opposing sides of the debate.

The Criticisms of Fideism

This dispute between Nielsen and Phillips aside—fideism has been subject to a lot of criticisms. Consider four most serious ones below, for illustration.

Firstly, one criticism of fideism is that "fideism is not a proper way to worship God. According to this position, if one does not attempt to understand what one believes, one is not really believing. 'Blind faith' is not true faith." (WK 2010p) Peter Abelard and Lord Herbert made precisely this point.

Secondly, another criticism of fideism is that fideism has no answer to the problem of relativism. For instance, "the existence of other religions puts a fundamental question to fideists—if faith is the only way to know the truth of God, how are we to know which God to have faith in? Fideism alone is not considered an adequate guide to distinguish true or morally valuable revelations from false ones. An apparent consequence of fideism is that all religious thinking becomes equal. The major monotheistic religions become on par with obscure fringe religions, as neither can be advocated or disputed." (WK 2010p)

Friedrich Nietzsche once apty said: "A casual stroll through the lunatic asylum shows that faith does not prove anything." (WK 2010p)

Thirdly, still another criticism of fideism is that reason is not as useless as the fideists would like us to believe. For instance, "people successfully use reason in their daily lives to solve problems and that reason has led to progressive increase of knowledge in the sphere of science. This gives credibility to reason and argumentative thinking as a proper method for seeking truth." (WK 2010p)

Even worse, "according to these critics, there is no evidence that a religious faith that rejects reason would also serve us while seeking truth. In situations in which our reason is not sufficient to find the truth (for example, when trying to answer a difficult mathematical question) fideism also fails." (WK 2010p)

And fourthly, the last criticism of fideism is that to have faith is the wrong way to make a decision when there is no compelling evidence.

For instance, "Carl Sagan states that faith is the belief in the absence of evidence. 'For me, believing when there is no compelling evidence is a mistake. The idea is to withhold belief until there is compelling evidence, and if the universe does not comply with our predispositions, okay then we have the wrenching obligation to accommodate to the way the universe really is.'" (WK 2010o; C. Rose 1996)

A Lesson to Learn

These criticisms of fideism do not mean to dismiss the usefulness of fideism to help us live fuller and better lives (as William James had argued); instead, they allow us to learn from the two opposing sides of the debate, such that the possibility and desirability of sacredness (from the perspective of the mind with fideism as a case study here) is not to the extent that its respective defenders would like us to believe.

More importantly, the analysis of fideism can teach us something insightful about the ontological principles in existential dialectics, and good examples include the formalness-informalness principle, the absoluteness-relativeness principle, the partiality-totality principle, the predictability-unpredictability principle, the explicability-inexplicability principle, the finiteness-transfiniteness principle, the preciseness-vagueness principle, the simpleness-complicatedness principle, the openness-hiddenness principle, the denseness-emptiness principle, the slowness-quickness principle, the expansion-contraction principle, the theory-praxis principle, the convention-novelty principle, the evolution-transformation principle, the symmetry-asymmetry principle, the softness-hardness principle, the regression-progression principle, and the same-difference principle.

For instance, in relation to the formalness-informalness principle, if there is formalness (e.g., the formal logical requirement of completeness for a system of ideas, as in science), there is informalness (e.g., the nonformal allowance of faith too in religion without complete proof, in addition to the use of reason—as in fideism) And the reverse direction also holds true.

In relation to the absoluteness-relativeness principle, if there is absoluteness (e.g., the absolute view of fideism that faith can be used in situations when there is no compelling evidence), there is relativeness (e.g., what is right for a fideist to appeal to faith is not so for a scientist like Sagan "to withhold belief until there is compelling evidence"). And the reverse direction also holds true.

In relation to the partiality-totality principle, if there is partiality (e.g., the partial view of each religious individual to use faith for knowing his own God), there is totality (e.g., the more holistic picture of all the views of religious individuals, each with faith for knowing his own God, such that the whole is not the sum of its parts, in that there are many incompatible positions about what the true God is). And the reverse direction also holds true.

In relation to the predictability-unpredictability principle, if there is predictability (e.g., the predictable tendency of a fideist to appeal to faith in situations where there is no compelling evidence about God), there is unpredictability (e.g., the more difficult task to predict which God a fideist is to have faith in, because "an apparent consequence of fideism is that all religious thinking becomes equal"). And the reverse direction also holds true.

In relation to the explicability-inexplicability principle, if there is explicability (e.g., the explanation by Kierkegaard that the "leap of faith" is necessary, because "reason cannot possibly comprehend such a phenomenon" like Abraham's act of sacrificing Isaac), there is inexplicability (e.g,. the lack of sufficient explanation by Kierkegaard of why Abraham could not withhold his belief in God if he could not comprehend the need to sacrifice Isaac, as someone like Sagan would say). And the reverse direction also holds true.

In relation to the finiteness-transfiniteness principle, if there is finiteness (e.g., the finite nature of a "simple" or ordinary human being, in the view of Kierkegaard), there is transfiniteness (e.g., the transfinite nature of an "eternal, perfect being" like God, in the view of Kierkegaard). And the reverse direction also holds true.

In relation to the preciseness-vagueness principle, if there is preciseness (e.g., the precise identification of God as "eternal" and "perfect" in Kierkegaard's Christian existentialism), there is vagueness (e.g,, the vagueness in the attributes of "eternity" and "perfection" of God, in Kierkegaard's Christian existentialism, since there can be different intepretations of why they actually refer to). And the reverse direction also holds true.

In relation to the simpleness-complicatedness principle, if there is simpleness (e.g., the relatively simple analysis of the need for faith in religious issues, in accordance to fideism), there is complicatedness (e.g., the relatively more complicated analysis of the nature of faith by including the different problems as pointed out by the critics). And the reverse direction also holds true.

In relation to the openness-hiddenness principle, if there is openness (e.g., the open exploration of the relationship between the use of faith and its contribution "to live fuller and better lives"), there is hiddenness (e.g., the hidden bias in downgrading the role of reason and exaggerating the power of faith in fideism, as revealed in the criticisms by the critics). And the reverse direction also holds true.

In relation to the denseness-emptiness principle, if there is denseness (e.g., the relatively denser concentration of individuals who have lesser education to believe in God, or more precisely, 62% for college graduates, as shown in a research study by Frank Sulloway at M.I.T. and Michael Shermer at California State University), there is emptiness (e.g., the relatively less dense, or more empty, concentration of adults with Ph.D.s to believe in God, or more precisely, 12% for Ph.D.'s, as shown by the research study by Sulloway and Shermer). (WK 2010j; M. Shermer 1999) And the reverse direction also holds true.

In relation to the slowness-quickness principle, if there is slowness (e.g., the relatively slower readiness of someone like Sagan to appeal to faith when there is no compelling evidence), there is quickness (e.g., the relatively quicker readiness of someone like Kierkegaard to take "the leap of faith" when there is no compelling evidence). And the reverse direction also holds true.

In relation to the expansion-contraction principle, if there is expansion (e.g., the relatively more developed ability of someone like Sagan to use reason to solve problems in life), there is contraction (e.g., the relatively less developed ability of someone like Sagan to use faith to solve problems in life). And the reverse direction also holds true.

In relation to the theory-praxis principle, if there is theory (e.g., the theoretical construction of fideism for the appeal to faith more than reason), there is praxis (e.g., the practical application of fideism for everyday life, as shown by those followers of Christian existentialism). And the reverse direction also holds true.

In relation to the convention-novelty principle, if there is conventional wisdom (e.g., the conventional wisdom about the importance of reason in life, as elegantly put by Galileo Galilei, who once said: "I not feel obliged to believe that the same God who has endowed us with sense, reason and intellect has intended us to forego their use"), there is novelty (e.g., the alternative novel challenge to the conventional wisdom about reason by William James to "defend...the right to violate the principle of evidentialism in order to justify hypothesis venturing," in his Will-to-Believe Doctrine). (WK 2010p & 2010q) And the reverse direction also holds true.

In relation to the evolution-transformation principle, if there is evolution (e.g., the natural evolution of humans to use reason, emotions, and other faculties for survival in the state of nature), there is transformation (e.g., the technical transformation of human life by way of the invention of the epistemological theory known as fideism). And the reverse direction also holds true.

In relation to the symmetry-asymmetry principle, if there is symmetry (e.g., the co-existence of different views concerning the epistemological validity of faith in intellectual history, be they fideist, scientific, or else), there is asymmetry (e.g., the acceptance of fideism among those in the tradition of Pascal, Kierkegaard, Wittgenstein, and James—but the popularity of the scientific spirit among those in the tradition of Sagan and his follow scientists). And the reverse direction also holds true.

In relation to the softness-hardness principle, if there is softness (e.g., the praise of those who appeal to faith for the defense of religious experience, especially by those in the tradition of fideism), there is hardness (e.g., the punishment of those who use reason for the defense of science, with negative implications for religion, as shown in the Galileo affair). And the reverse direction also holds true.

In relation to the regression-progression principle, if there is regression (e.g., the regression made by fideism, as shown in the problems pointed out by the critics), there is progression (e.g., the progress made by fideism in exploring the relationship between faith and its contribution "to live fuller and better lives"). And the reverse direction also holds true.

And in relation to the same-difference principle, if there is similarity in outcome (e.g., the contribution to the varieties of life experience, regardless of whether this is done with the use of reason or the appeal to faith), there is difference in outcome (e.g., the contribution to the enrichment of life experience in a more emotional way with the appeal to faith—but the contribution to the enrichment of life experience in a more sober way with the use of reason). And the reverse direction also holds true.

Magical Thinking, and Religion

Another way to evaluate the possibility and desirability of sacredness from the perspective of the mind is to explore the relationship among magical thinkng and religion.

The Conception of Magic

The term "magical thinking" refers to the appeal of "magic" (which is also known as "sorcery," from "Old French *sorcerie*, which is from Vulgar Latin *sortiarius*, from *sors* 'fate,' apparently meaning 'one who influences fate'"). (WK 2010r)

By definition, magic is "the practice of consciousness manipulation and/or autosuggestion to achieve a desired result, usually by techniques described in various conceptual systems…Magical thinking…often includes such ideas as associative thinking, the ability of the mind to affect the physical world…, and correlation mistaken for causation. Symbolic expression may be brought into play, as well as the use of metaphor, metonym, and synchronicity….[S]ome theorists maintain that the magician's goals are not necessarily physical, and that magical practices are, in some cases, genuinely efficacious." (WK 2010r)

In general, the practice of magic involves some basic components, as shown below:

- "Mystical power"—This refers to something like "mana, numen, chi, or kundalini, that exists in all things. Sometimes this power is concentrated in a magical object, such as a ring, a stone, a charm, or dehk, which the magician can manipulate." (WK 2010r)

- "Spirits"—This refers to the unuusal forces "with their own consciousness and intelligence. Believers in spirits will often describe a whole cosmos of beings of many different kinds, sometimes organized into a hierarchy." (WK 2010r)

- "Elements"—This refers to the things represented by "symbols or objects" used by the magician. "Western practitioners typically use the Classical elements of Earth, Air, Water, and Fire." (WK 2010r)

- "Symbols"—This refers to the signs which "can magically take on a physical quality of the phenomenon or object that they represent. Another view is that sigils [symbols] in particular can be 'charged' with magical powers. By manipulating symbols or sigils, one is said to be able to impact reality, or the reality that this symbol represents." (WK 2010r)

- "Energy"—This refers to the force "from the human body,...by the usage of the hands while the mouth uses a command of power." (WK 2010r)

- "Principles of Sympathetic Magic"—This refers to the two principles suggested by Sir James George Frazer to understand magic, namely, the "law of similarity" and the "law of contact" or "contagion." As Frazer put it: "If we analyze the principles of thought on which magic is based, they will probably be found to resolve themselves into two: first, that like produces like, or that an effect resembles its cause; and, second, that things which have once been in contact with each other continue to act on each other at a distance after the physical contact has been severed. The former principle may be called the Law of Similarity, the latter the Law of Contact or Contagion. From the first of these principles, namely the Law of Similarity, the magician infers that he can produce any effect he desires merely by imitating it: from the second he infers that whatever he does to a material object will affect equally the person with whom the object was once in contact, whether it formed part of his body or not." (WK 2010r)

- "Concentration or Meditation"—This refers to "amount of focusing or restricting the mind to some imagined object (or will)," which, "according to Aleister Crowley, produces mystical attainment or 'an occurrence in the brain characterized essentially by the uniting of subject and object.' Magic, as defined previously, seeks to aid concentration by constantly recalling the attention to the chosen object (or Will), thereby producing said attainment. For example, if one wishes to concentrate on a god, one might memorize a system of correspondences (perhaps chosen arbitrarily, as this would not affect its usefulness for mystical purposes) and then make every object that one sees 'correspond' to said God." (WK 2010r)

- "Subconscious Mind"—This refers to the need of the magicians "to convince the... subconscious mind to make the changes that they desire," since "all spirits and energies are projections and symbols that make sense to the subconscious. A variant of this belief is that the subconscious is capable of contacting spirits, who in turn can work magic." (WK 2010r)

Surely, there can be other components, but the ones listed above are the most important for illustration.

Religious Magic

The summary of these components of magic aside—the practice of magic is "often influenced by ideas of religion, mysticism, occultism, science, and psychology." (WK 2010r)

Thus, in this view, magic does not have to be religious (as it is also influenced by other ideas in "mysticism, occultism, science, and psychology," for instance). In cases like this, magic is non-religious.

However, when magic "involves requesting the intervention of a personal deity or deities—or often an impersonal divinity or spiritual force—to enact the desired effect," the outcome is called "religious magic." (WK 2010s)

Even then, religious magic does not guarantee successful outcome, since, so the excuse goes, "it is up to the deity in question whether or not to grant the request. In the case of an impersonal spiritual force, as in Taoism or other eastern or shamanic or pagan religions, it may require some specific religious or spiritual discipline, such as esoteric meditation methods or fasting or vision questing, to attune oneself to the divine power that is capable of effecting the desired magical change." (WK 2010s)

In other cases of religious magic, "especially neopagan witchcraft and magical traditions, deities may be called upon as tutors or guides in magic—to assist the individual in learning to develop his or her own magical abilities, and in learning the principles and practices of magic. Such tutelary deities are sometimes called 'hermetic deities' or 'spirit guides.' Such deities would include gods and goddesses such as Exu or Legba in African-based religion, Thoth in Kemetic (Egyptian) religion, and the Greek goddess Hecate in Wicca." (WK 2010s)

Magic and Religion

To understand religious magic better, it is important to know some similarities and differences between "magic" and "religion" (so as to be familiar with their subtle interrelationships).

Scholars like Marcel Mauss (1972), S. J. Tambiah (1990), Bronisław Malinowski (1954), and others, for instance, have much to say about their subtle interrelationships, that is, in relation to (a) the similarities between magic and religion and (b) the differences between magic and religion—as shown hereafter (and summarized in *Table 2.2*).

(a) The Similarities between Magic and Religon

Here are some major similarities between magic and religion. Surely, there can be others, but these four suffice for illustration here.

- For Mauss—"Both use similar types of rites, materials, social roles and relationships to accomplish aims and engender belief. They both operate on similar principles, in particular those of consecration and sacredness of objects and places, interaction with supernatural powers mediated by an expert, employment of symbolism, sacrifice, purification and representation in rites, and the importance of tradition and continuation of knowledge." (WK 2010r)
- For Mauss—"Magic and religion also share a collective character and totality of belief. The rules and powers of each are determined by the community's ideals and beliefs and so may slowly evolve. Additionally neither supports partial belief. Belief in one aspect of the phenomena necessitates belief in the whole, and each incorporates structural loopholes to accommodate contradictions." (WK 2010r)
- For Tambiah—"Magic, science, and religion all have their own 'quality of rationality,' and have been influenced by politics and ideology….[T]he perceptions of these three ideas have evolved over time as a result of Western thought. The lines of demarcation between these ideas depend upon the perspective of a variety of anthropologists…." (WK 2010r)
- In general—"Related to both magic and prayer [in religion] is…supplication. This involves a prayer, or even a sacrifice to a supernatural being or god. This god or being is then asked to intervene on behalf of the person offering the prayer." (WK 2010r)

If there are similarities between magic and religion, there are likewise differences between them, as shown below.

(b) The Differences between Magic and Religion

Here are some major differences between magic and religion. Surely, there can be others, but these six suffice for illustration here.

- For Mauss—"Magic is secretive and isolated, and rarely performed publicly in order to protect and to preserve occult knowledge. Religion is predictable and proscribed and is usually performed openly in order to impart knowledge to the community." (WK 2010r)
- For Mauss: "In practice, magic differs from religion in desired outcome. Religion seeks to satisfy moral and metaphysical ends, while magic is a functional art which often seeks to accomplish

tangible results. In this respect magic resembles technology and science....Yet,...science is based in experimentation and development, while magic is an "a priori belief." (WK 2010r)

- For Tambiah—"Magic is a strictly ritualistic action that implements forces and objects outside the realm of the gods and the supernatural. These objects and events are said to be intrinsically efficacious, so that the supernatural is unnecessary. To some, including the Greeks, magic was considered a "proto-science." (WK 2010r)
- For Tambiah—"Whereas science could be revised and developed through rational thought, magic was seen as less scientific and systematic than science and religion, making it the least respected of the three." (WK 2010r)
- For Malinowski—"The difference is that magic is more about the personal power of the individual and religion is about faith in the power of God. Magic is also something that is passed down over generations to a specific group while religion is more broadly available to the community." (WK 2010r)
- In general—"Prayer [in religion] requires the assent of a deity with an independent will, who can deny the request. Magic, by contrast is thought to be effective...by virtue of the operation itself," "by the strength of the magician's will," or "because the magician believes he can command the spiritual beings addressed by his spells." (WK 2010r)

The understanding of these differences between magic and religion (and for that matter, the similarities between magic and religion) can offer us a more sophisticated grasp of religious magic, when the two are combined.

Religious Magic in Action

Although there can be many different ways in which religious magic can have a role to play, hereafter are three often cited examples for illustrations, namely, (a) the naming of the Gods, (b) the practice of religious artifacts, and (c) sacrifice. (WK 2010s)

These examples of religious magic dffer from those of non-religious magic (like "divination...to reveal information about the past, present or future," "necromancy...to involve the summoning of, and conversation with, spirits of the dead," "the spell...to bring about a specific effect," etc.). (WK 2010r)

(a) The Naming of the Gods

The first example of religious magic in action concerns the naming of the gods, in that "there is a long-standing belief in the power of 'true names'; this often descends from the magical belief that knowing a being's true name grants you power over it. This is often seen as a requirement in spiritualism; knowing the identity of a spirit greatly aids in soliciting information from it." (WK 2010s)

When put in the context of religion, "knowing the name of a god that is regarded as supreme in your religion should grant the greatest power of all. This belief is reflected in traditional Wicca, where the names of the Goddess and the Horned God—the two supreme deities in Wicca—are usually held as a secret to be revealed only to initiates." (WK 2010s)

For instance, "ancient Judaism...used the Tetragrammaton (YHWH, usually translated as 'Lord' in small caps) to refer to God 'safely' in the Tanakh. Saying the name of God without good reason ('taking the Lord's name in vain,' one of the Ten Commandments) could result in stoning.(Rabbi Joseph Telushkin has claimed that the commandment is simply to not use God's name to deceive or to bully.) The same belief is seen in Hinduism, but with different conclusions; rather, attaining transcendence and the power of God is seen as a good thing. Thus, some Hindus chant the name of their favorite deities as often as possible, the most common being Krishna." (WK 2010s; L. Gonick 1990)

(b) The Practice of Religious artifacts

The second example of religious magic in action concerns the practice of religious artifacts, in that "some religions believe in transferring holiness to objects and places; this is often seen in even simple things like 'christening' ceremonies for a new boat. Churches and certain religiously-minded individuals often consecrate the ground where a building will be constructed." (WK 2010s)

In fact, "the practice was common during the Middle Ages, where a large market for spiritual trinkets existed. Fragments of the true cross and bones of saints were often brought back by Crusaders from the Holy Land, where they were sold to the peasantry as cure-alls. Most scholarly sources agree that the vast majority of these sales were frauds and simply a form of supplemental income for the Crusaders. This practice somewhat fell into disrepute during the Reformation; it became associated with idol worship. As a result, this is less seen in Protestantism than Roman Catholicism or Eastern Orthodoxy." (WK 2010s)

(c) Sacrifice

And the third example of religious magic in action concerns "a sacrifice to a supernatural being, such as a god, angel, or demon, who is asked to intervene on behalf of the person performing the sacrifice." (WK 2010s)

Although "sacrifice can take many forms," some "most common forms of supplication and sacrifice in pagan and neopagan religious practice involves the burning of oils or incense. Other common forms of supplication may include the offering of personal objects to a deity, offering chants, and the offering of drinks and food." (WK 2010s)

Some other forms may be bloody. For instance, "[i]n early history, blood sacrifice was common; a goat or calf would be sacrificed....Most strands of modern Judaism believe that with the destruction of the Temple in Jerusalem, there is no place to sacrifice to any more, and thus the need is negated (modern Samaritans disagree, and maintain the practice). In Christianity, it is believed that Jesus's final sacrifice renders any further sacrifices unnecessary. Some syncretic blends of Islam and native practices in places such as Indonesia feature sacrifice as an element of worship." (WK 2010s)

But the most bloody form of sacrifice is "human sacrifice. The moloch is one famous but disputed example of the practice; the Carthaginians seemingly sacrificed young children when circumstances looked grim, hoping to regain their gods' favor....The book Genesis contains the famous story of the 'Binding of Isaac'; Abraham is ordered to sacrifice his son Isaac by God, but it turns out that God was only performing a mysterious test, and a ram is sent instead." (WK 2010s)

Religious Magic under Attack

Yet, religious magic (and magic, in general) are not immune from criticisms. In fact, there are a lot of criticisms against them. Consider some of them below, for illustration.

Firstly, one criticism of magic (religious or not) is that it often does not work as initially hoped for, and when this happens, ad hoc excuses are given to explain away the failure.

For instance, a magician can excuse himself by pointing out any of several possibilities like the refusal of "the deity in question...to grant the request," "a failure to follow the exact formula," "unconducive" (or unfavorable) "general circumstances," "a lack of magical ability," "a lack of willpower," or else. (WK 2010r & 2010s)

Secondy, another criticism of magic (religious or not) is that, even when it works sometimes, it is not clear if it is merely a coincidence.

For instance, a well-known principle used by magicians is called "the law of similarity," in that the magician looks for some "associative" events based on "nonscientific causal reasoning that often includes...correlation mistaken for causation." (WK 2010r) This "associative" causal reasoning...accords unwarranted weight to correlation or coincidence." (WK 2010t)

As an illustration, in a case study by E. E. Evans-Pritchard (1976), "amongst the Azande one rubs crocodile teeth on banana plants to make them fruitful, because crocodile teeth are curved (like bananas) and grow back if they fall out. The Azande observe this similarity and want to impart this capacity of regeneration to their bananas. To them, the rubbing constitutes a means of transference" (a kind of mistaken causation). (WK 2010t)

Thirdly, still another criticism of magic (religious or not) is that, even when the effect is not a coincidence, it can be a question of "perception" (psychological), but not "an actual change (material)." (WK 2010s)

For instance, "whether prayer or some type of spell is used, it can either bring about an actual change (material) or a change in the way the subject feels (perception). The same prayer, for it to be 'cooler' could therefore either actually raise the temperature, or simply alter the praying subject and any other targets feeling of the temperature." (WK 2010s)

This is true, even though perceptual change can be psychosomatic, in that, in the above example about a a prayer for being "cooler," the perception "could be used in healing to numb the sensation of pain, allowing healing to take place more easily." (WK 2010s)

And finally, still one more criticism of magic (religious or not) is that its status is historically contingent on the politics and ideology of a given point of time. Tambiah once argued, for instance that "magic, science, and religion all have their own 'quality of rationality,' and have been influenced by politics and ideology....[T]he perceptions of these three ideas have evolved over time as a result of Western thought. The lines of demarcation between these ideas depend upon the perspective of a variety of anthropologists...." (WK 2010r)

A More Detached Perspective

Once more, these criticisms of magic (religious or not) are not meant to reject it but to let us learn from the two opposing sides of the debate, such that the possibility and desirability of sacredness (from the perspective of the mind with religious magic as a case study here) is not to the extent that its respective defenders would like us to believe.

More importantly, the analysis of religious magic can reveal something refreshiing about the ontological principles in existential dialectics, and good examples include the formalness-informalness principle, the absoluteness-relativeness principle, the predictability-unpredictability principle, the explicability-inexplicability principle, the finiteness-transfiniteness principle, the preciseness-vagueness principle, the simpleness-complicatedness principle, the openness-hiddenness principle, the denseness-emptiness principle, the slowness-quickness principle, the expansion-contraction principle, the theory-praxis principle, the convention-novelty principle, the evolution-transformation principle, the symmetry-asymmetry principle, the softness-hardness principle, the regression-progression principle, and the same-difference principle.

For instance, in relation to the formalness-informalness principle, if there is formalness (e.g., the formal logical requirement of soundness in a system of ideas, as in science), there is informalness (e.g., the non-formal allowance of coincidence too, without complete proof of causation for soundness, in magic, as Ramsey Dukes once said that "questions such as 'Are you sure it was your magic that cured her?' are irrelevant to the magician. 'If it was a coincidence, it doesn't matter just so long as he can bring about such coincidences'"). (WK 2010s) And the reverse direction also holds true.

In relation to absoluteness-relativeness principle, if there is absoluteness (e.g., the absolute view of the practitioners of magic that it should be "secretive and isolated, and rarely performed publicly in order to protect and to preserve occult knowledge"), there is relativeness (e.g., what is important for magic to be "secretive and isolated" is not so for religion to be "predictable and proscribed and…usually performed openly in order to impart knowledge to the community"). And the reverse direction also holds true.

In relation to the predictability-unpredictability principle, if there is predictability (e.g., the predictable tendency of a magician to emphasize such things as "mystical power," "elements," "symbols," "energy," "law of similarity," "law of contact," "concentration," "subconscious mind," and so on), there is unpredictability (e.g., the more difficult task to predict when a particular magical practice will produce the desired outcome, since magic does not always work as initially hoped for). And the reverse direction also holds true.

In relation to the explicability-inexplicability principle, if there is explicability (e.g., the explanation of the efficacy of magic, by its practitioners, on the basis of the law of similarity for associate thinking, for instance), there is inexplicability (e.g, the lack of sufficient explanation by the magician of why correlation is causation at all). And the reverse direction also holds true.

In relation to the finiteness-transfiniteness principle, if there is finiteness (e.g., the finite nature of the power of a magician in religious magic, since "it is up to the deity in question whether or not to grant the request"), there is transfiniteness (e.g., the transfinite nature of the power of the deity in religious magic, since it can grant any request if it so wishes, according to the believers in religious magic). And the reverse direction also holds true.

In relation to the preciseness-vagueness principle, if there is preciseness (e.g., the precise identification of some of the basic components of religious magic, like "spirits," "elements," "symbols," "energy," etc. by the practitioners of religious magic), there is vagueness (e.g.., the vagueness in understanding the nature of these components like "spirits," "deities," etc., since a magiican cannot exactly spell out the specific circumstances under which a deity in question will grant a specific request or not). And the reverse direction also holds true.

In relation to the simpleness-complicatedness principle, if there is simpleness (e.g., the relatively simple analysis of the working of magic by its practitioners), there is complicatedness (e.g., the relatively more complicated analysis of the nature of magic, as shown in the different problems pointed out by the critics). And the reverse direction also holds true.

In relation to the openness-hiddenness principle, if there is openness (e.g., the open exploration of the relationship between the practice of magic and the obtainment of certain tangible outcomes), there is hiddenness (e.g., the "secretive and isolated" nature of magic, such that its failures can be easily covered up with excuses). And the reverse direction also holds true.

In relation to the denseness-emptiness principle, if there is denseness (e.g., the relatively denser concentration of magicians in non-religious magic who emphasizes more on "the personal power" of the magician or "the strength of the magician's will"), there is emptiness (e.g., the relatively less dense, or more empty, concentration of magicians in non-religious magic who also focus on "faith in the power of God," because non-religious magic does not "involves requesting the intervention of a personal deity or deities"). And the reverse direction also holds true.

In relation to the slowness-quickness principle, if there is slowness (e.g., the relatively slower readiness of a scientist to practice the naming of the gods, religious artifacts, or sacrifice), there is quickness (e.g., the relatively quicker readiness of a religious magician to practice the naming of the gods, religious artifacts, or sacrifice). And the reverse direction also holds true.

In relation to the expansion-contraction principle, if there is expansion (e.g., the relative expansion of the power and influence of science in our time), there is contraction (e.g., the relative contraction of power and influence of magic in our time). And the reverse direction also holds true.

In relation to the theory-praxis principle, if there is theory (e.g., the theoretical construction of magic in accordance to some components like "spirits," "energy," "meditation," "law of similarity," etc.), there is praxis (e.g,. the practical application of magic in everyday life like "the burning of oil or incense," "christening," etc.). And the reverse direction also holds true.

In relation to the convention-novelty principle, if there is convention (e.g., the conventional wisdom about the differences betwee magic and religion), there is novelty (e.g., the alternative novel challenge to the conventional wisdom about the differences between magic and religion by way of combining the two into "religious magic"). And the reverse direction also holds true.

In relation to the evolution-transformation principle, if there is evolution (e.g, the natural evolution of humans to live and encounter many seemingly inexplicable natural phenomena in the state of nature), there is transformation (e.g., the technical transformation of human relationship with nature by way of the invention of religious magic, together with its different stories for different adherents). And the reverse direction also holds true.

In relation to the symmetry-asymmetry principle, if there is symmetry (e.g,. the co-existence of different forms of rationality in human history, regardless of whether they are about magic, religion, or science), there is asymmetry (e.g., the more influence of science in our time—but the popularity of magic in antiquity). And the reverse direction also holds true.

In relation to the softness-hardness principle, if there is softness (e.g., the use of magic to improve life, like its use "in healing to numb the sensation of pain, allowing healing to take place more easily," even if only perceptually), there is hardness (e.g., the punishment by "stoning" against those who do not practice religious magic correctly in "ancient Judaism," as in "Saying the name of God without good reason"). And the reverse direction also holds true.

In relation to the regression-progression principle, if there is regression (e.g., the regression made in religious magic as shown in the problems pointed out by the critics), there is progression (e.g., the progress made in religious magic for healing and other tangible results, under certain circumstances). And the reverse direction also holds true.

And in relation to the same-difference principle, if there is similarity in outcome (e.g, the contribution to life improvement and transformation, regardless of whether this is done by magic, religion, or science), there is difference in outcome (e.g., the contribution to life improvement and transformation by religious magic in terms of the practice of religious artifacts, sacrifice, etc.—but the contribution to life improvement and transformation by science in terms of medications, physical therapy, etc.). And the reverse direction also holds true.

Sacredness and Nature

Religion, when examined from the perspective of nature, can show us in a different way its possibility and desirability, and this can be done by way of two case studies, namely, (2.3.1) religious cosmolgy, and the teleological argument, and (2.3.2) evolutionary theory, and religion—to be addressed hereafter, in that order.

Religious Cosmology, and the Teleological Argument

The word "teleological" here is "from the Greek word *telos*, meaning 'end' or 'purpose,'" and its noun *teleology* refers to the view that "there is purpose or directive principle in the works and processes of nature. Immanuel Kant called this argument the Physico–theological proof." (WK 2010u)

So, the "teleological argument" (or "argument from design") is "an argument for the existence of God or a creator based on perceived evidence of order, purpose, design, or direction—or some combination of these—in nature." (WK 2010u; K. Himma 2006; D. Ratzsch 2009; P. Toner 1909)

The Teleological Argument

There are different ways to understand the teleological argument in detail, but one most often cited way can be stated in five major steps as shown below: (WK 2010u)

- "Nature exhibits complexity, order, adaptation, purpose and/or beauty."

- "The exhibited feature(s) cannot be explained by random or accidental processes, but only as a product of mind."
- "Therefore, there exists a mind that has produced or is producing nature."
- "A mind that produces nature is a definition of "God."
- "Therefore, God exists."

Another variant of the telological argument is shown below: (WK 2010u)

- "All things that are designed were preconceived, intended, purposed or contrived."
- "Preconception, intention, purpose, and contrivance necessitate an intellect, mind or will."
- "All things that are irreducibly complex display intention and preconception."
- "The universe contains non-man made things that are irreducibly complex."
- "Those things display intention and preconception."
- "Those things necessitate an intellect, mind or will."

Or in the funny parlance of G. K. Chesterton in 1908: "So one elephant having a trunk was odd; but all elephants having trunks looked like a plot." (WK 2010u)

Notable Contributors

There is no lack of scholars who have contributed to the telological argument in history. Consider a few of them below, for illustration.

For Socrates (c. 469–399 B.C.), " the adaptation of human parts to one another, such as the eyelids protecting the eyeballs, could not have been due to chance and was a sign of wise planning in the universe." (WK 2010u; J. Franklin 2001)

For Plato (c. 427–c. 347 B.C.), there must be "a 'demiurge' of supreme wisdom and intelligence as the creator of the cosmos in his work *Timaeus*." (WK 2010u)

For Aristotle (c. 384–322 B.C.), "all nature reflects inherent purposiveness and direction. In his *Metaphysics*, he demonstrated the existence of God, not a creator (for Aristotle the cosmos always existed) but as a 'Prime Mover' who kept nature in motion. He described the prime mover as 'self-thinking thought,' but believed that it did not lower itself to consider nature or relate to human beings." (WK 2010u)

For Cicero (c. 106–c. 43 B.C.), "the divine power is to be found in a principle of reason that pervades the whole of nature....When you see a sundial or a water-clock, you see that it tells the time by design and not by chance. How then can you imagine that the universe as a whole is devoid of purpose and intelligence, when it embraces everything, including these artifacts themselves and their artificers?" (WK 2010u)

For Thomas Aquinas (1225–1274), the argument from design is not hard to understand: "We see that things which lack knowledge, such as natural bodies, act for an end, and this is evident from their acting always, or nearly always, in the same way, so as to obtain the best result. Hence it is plain that they achieve their end, not fortuitously, but designedly. Now whatever lacks knowledge cannot move towards an end, unless it be directed by some being endowed with knowledge and intelligence; as the arrow is directed by the archer. Therefore, some intelligent being exists by whom all natural things are directed to their end; and this being we call God." (WK 2010u)

For Voltaire (1694–1778), in his usually sarcastic way, "l'univers m'embarrasse, et je ne puis songer Que cette horloge existe, et n'ait point d'horloger (The universe embarrasses me; I cannot think that the watch exists, but does not have a watchmaker)." (WK 2010u)

In more modern times, the teleological argument underwent some further refinements, with the advancement of physics.

For instance, "a modern variation of the teleological argument is built upon the anthropic principle. The anthropic principle is derived from the apparent delicate balance of conditions necessary for human life. In this line of reasoning, speculation about the vast, perhaps infinite, range of possible conditions in which life could not exist is compared to the speculated improbability of achieving conditions in which life does exist, and then interpreted as indicating a fine-tuned universe specifically designed so human life is possible. This view is shared by John D. Barrow and Frank J. Tipler in *The Anthropic Cosmological Principle* (1986)." (WK 2010u)

John Polkinghorne also argued, back in 1985, that "just one factor among many in the cosmos, the difference between expansive and contractive forces in the expanding cosmos according to then-currently accepted theory, depends upon an extremely fine balance of the total energy involved to within one in 10^{60}, a sixty-one digit number equivalent to taking aim from Earth and hitting an inch-wide target at the farthest reaches of the observable universe." (WK 2010u)

George Wald also shared the same view, in that "the conditions for something as fundamental as the atom depend on a balance of forces to within one in 10^{18}. Proponents of the fine-tuned universe form of teleological argument typically argue that taken together, the various fine-tuned balances appear quite improbable, and hint strongly at something designed rather than accidental." (WK 2010u)

Surely, there can be more thinkers who have contributed to the teleological argument than the list as shown above, but the examples here are deemed sufficient to illustrative the teleological argument in question.

The Counterarguments

However, there are quite a lot of counterarguments to the teleological argument. Consider some of the major criticisms as shown below, for illustration, and summarized in *Table 2.3*.

Firstly, one criticism of the teleological argument (especially in relation to "the anthropic principle" and its "fine-tuned universe" version) is that the statistics as shown by its ideologues are faulty or manipulative at best.

For instance, for the critics, "a key problem in terms of being able to verify whether the hypothesized probabilities are correct is that the improbable conditions were identified after the event, so they cannot be checked by experiment. And very importantly, there is no ability to sample a large enough set of alternatives (indeed we know of no other cosmos to sample) in order to be able to properly attach any odds or probabilities to these natural situations in the cosmos." (WK 2010u)

Secondly, another criticism of the teleological argument is that "complexity does not imply design." (WK 2010u)

For instance,"the teleological argument assumes that because life is complex, it must have been designed. It is argued that this is non-sequitur logic. Life or objects are described as 'orderly' or 'ordered,' which implies that an intelligent designer has ordered them. However, in reality, there are examples of systems that are non-random or ordered simply because it is following natural physical processes, for example diamonds or snowflakes." (WK 2010u)

In fact, the teleological argument "is often challenged as an argument from ignorance, since it is often unexplained or unsupported, or explained by unscientific conjecture. Supporters of design assume that natural objects and man-made objects have similar properties, therefore both must be designed. However, different objects can have similar properties for different reasons, such as stars and light bulbs. Proponents must therefore demonstrate that only design can cause orderly systems or the argument is invalid." (WK 2010u)

Thirdly, still another criticism of the teleological argument is that it confuses "a powerful intelligent designer" with "a God." (WK 2010u)

For insance, for the critics, "even if the argument from design proved the existence of a powerful intelligent designer, it would not prove that the designer is God. Voltaire [1901] observed in his Traité de métaphysique: '...from this sole argument I cannot conclude anything further than that it is probable that an intelligent and superior being has skillfully prepared and fashioned the matter. I cannot conclude from that alone that this being has made matter out of nothing and that he is infinite in every sense.'" (WK 2010u)

David Hume advanced the same point, when he asked, "Why may not several deities combine in contriving and framing the world?" (WK 2010u)

Fourthly, one more criticism of the teleological argument is that it can lead to "an infinite regress." (WK 2010u)

For instance, Richard Dawkins pointed out that "the teleological argument would in turn apply to the proposed designer, arguing any designer must be at least as complex and purposeful as the designed object....This...would create the absurdity of an infinite series of designers." (WK 2010u)

But if the proponent of the teleological argument responds by saying that "the designer exists outside of the natural laws of the universe" and "is therefore exempt from any laws requiring a design to have a designer"—then the critics will follow up and suggest that "this does not explain why the improbable event of the designer's existence does take place. While the designer might not require a cause, he still requires a reason as to why he exists, since he could just as well not exist at all." (WK 2010u)

And fifthly, still another criticism of the teleological argument is that it is "incoherent." (WK 2010u)

For instance, George H. Smith (1989) in *Atheism: The Case Against God* made this very point: "Consider the idea that nature itself is the product of design. How could this be demonstrated? Nature, as we have seen, provides the basis of comparison by which we distinguish between designed objects and natural objects. We are able to infer the presence of design only to the extent that the characteristics of an object differ from natural characteristics. Therefore, to claim that nature as a whole was designed is to destroy the basis by which we differentiate between artifacts and natural objects. Evidences of design are those characteristics not found in nature, so it is impossible to produce evidence of design within the context of nature itself. Only if we first step beyond nature, and establish the existence of a supernatural designer, can we conclude that nature is the result of conscious planning." (WK 2010u)

A Bigger Picture

Needless to say, these criticisms of the teleological argument do not imply that one should throw it out of the window but reveal to us the two opposing sides of the debate, such that the possibility and desirability of sacredness (from the perspective of the mind with the teleological argument as a case study here) is not to the extent that its respective defenders would like us to believe.

In addition, the analysis of the teleological can show us the usefulness of the ontological principles in existential dialectics, and good examples include the formalness-informalness principle, the absoluteness-relativeness principle, the predictability-unpredictability principle, the explicability-inexplicability principle, the preciseness-vagueness principle, the simpleness-complicatedness principle, the openness-hiddenness principle, the denseness-emptiness principle, the slowness-quickness principle, the expansion-contraction principle, the theory-praxis principle, the convention-novelty principle, the evolution-transformation principle, the symmetry-asymmetry principle, the regression-progression principle, and the same-difference principle.

For instance, in relation to the formalness-informalness principle, if there is formalness (e.g., the formal logical requirement of consistency and completeness in a system of ideas), there is informalness (e.g., the non-formal allowance of inconsistency and incompleteness in the teleological argument, which is "incoherent" and incapable of proving itself in some ways, since everything is known after the fact, as pointed out by the critics, but many people throughout history still believe in religious cosmology). And the reverse direction also holds true.

In relation to the absoluteness-relativeness principle, if there is absoluteness (e.g., the absolute viewpoint of the ideologues of religious cosmology like Plato, in that there must be "a 'demiurge' of supreme wisdom and intelligence as the creator of the cosmos"), there is relativeness (e.g., what is true for Plato in relation to the argumend from design is not so for the critics of religious cosmology like Richard Dawkins and George Smith). And the reverse direction also holds true.

In relation to the predictability-unpredictability principle, if there is predictability (e.g., the predictable tendency of a proponent of the teleological argument to claim that there is an intelligent designer in the cosmos), there is unpredictability (e.g., the more difficult task for a proponent of the teleological argument to predict other worlds because "there is no ability to sample a large enough set of alternatives" and "indeed we know of no other cosmos to sample). And the reverse direction also holds true.

In relation to the explicability-inexplicability principle, if there is explicability (e.g., the explanation of the orderly nature of the universe by the ideologues of the teleological argument on the basis of the existence of "a powerful intelligent designer"), there is inexplicability (e.g., the lack of sufficient explanation by the ideologues of the ideological argument to explain why this "powerful intelligent designer" must be "a God" in the first place, as questioned by Voltaire, or "why may not several deities combine in contriving and framing the world?" as asked by Hume). And the reverse direction also holds true.

In relation to the preciseness-vagueness principle, if there is preciseness (e.g., the precise identification of "a powerful intelligent designer" by the proponents of the teleological argument), there is vagueness (e.g., the vagueness in this idea of "a powerful intelligent designer," since it can mean different things for different thinkers, like "a God" for some, possibly multiple "deities" for others, perhaps a prior designer for the designer for still others, etc.). And the reverse direction also holds true.

In relation to the simpleness-complicatedness principle, if there is simpleness (e.g., the relatively simple construction of the teleological argument by its proponents), there is complicatedness (e.g., the relatively more complicated analysis of the teleogical argument as shown by the criticisms that the critics have made over time). And the reverse direction also holds true.

In relation to the openness-hiddenness principle, if there is openness (e.g., the open exploration of the relationship between the orderly universe and the existence of an intelligent designer, accordance to the teleological argument), there is hiddeness (e.g., the hidden bias of the teleological argument, since it does not consider alternatives like the confusion between a designer and a God in the argument, the inability of the argument to prove itself, etc.). And the reverse direction also holds true.

In relation to the denseness-emptiness principle, if there is denseness (e.g., the relatively denser concentration of the believers in the teleological argument in ancient Greece, like Plato, Aristotle, Socrates, Cicero, etc.), there is emptiness (e.g., the relatively less dense, or more empty, concentration of believers in the teleological argument among contemporary scientists). And the reverse direction also holds true.

In relation to the slowness-quickness principle, if there is slowness (e.g., the relatively slower readiness of an atheist like Dawkins to defend the teleological argument), there is quickness (e.g., the relatively quicker readiness of a theist like Thomas Aquinas to defend the teleological argument). And the reverse direction also holds true.

In relation to the expansion-contraction principle, if there is expansion (e.g., the relative expansion of the influence of the Big Bang theory in the scientific community since modern times), there is contraction (e.g., the relative contraction of the influence of the teleological argument in the scientific community since modern times). And the reverse direction also holds true.

In relation to the theory-praxis principle, if there is theory (e.g., the theoretical construction of the teleological argument), there is praxis (e.g., the practical application of the teleological argument for Christian conversion by the Catholic Church under Thomas Aquinas in the 13th century). (WK 2010u) And the reverse direction also holds true.

In relation to the convention-novelty principle, if there is convention (e.g., the conventional wisdom about "a powerful intelligent designer" in the teleological argument), there is novelty (e.g., the alternative novel challenge to the conventinal wisdom about "a powerful intelligent designer" by David Hume, in that there may be "several deities combine in contriving and framing the world" instead). And the reverse direction also holds true.

In relation to the evolution-transformation principle, if there is evolution (e.g., the natural evolution of humans to live in the state of nature, with no systematic cosmologies), there is transformation (e.g., the technical transformation of human thought by way of the invention of religious cosmology in a systematic way, as shown in the intellectual tradition of the teleological argument). And the reverse direction also holds true.

In relation to the symmetry-asymmetry principle, if there is symmetry (e.g., the co-existence of different ways to think about the cosmos, regardless of whether this is by way of the teleological argument, the Big Bang theory, or else), there is asymmetry (e.g., the popularity of the teleological argument in antiquity—but the influential rise of the Big Bang theory in our times). And the reverse direction also holds true.

In relation to the regression-progression principle, if there is regression (e.g., the regression made by the teleological argument, as shown in the unresolved problems pointed out by the critics), there is progression (e.g., the progress made by the teleological argument in helping us be more aware of the possible existence of an intelligent designer in the metaphysical realm beyond the reach of science). And the reverse direction also holds true.

And in relation to the same-difference principle, if there is similarity in outcome (e.g., the contribution to the understanding of the universe, regardless of whether this is achieved by way of the teleological argument, the Big Bang theory, or else), there is difference in outcome (e.g., the contribution to the understanding of the universe by way of the teleological argument for the possible existence of an intelligent designer in the metaphysical realm—but the contribution to the understanding of the universe by way of the Big Bang theory for a beginning without an intelligent designer). And the reverse direction also holds true.

Evolutionary Theory, and Religion

Another way to evaluate the possibility and desirability of sacredness from the perspective of nature has to do with the use of evolutionary theory for the understanding of religion in relation to nature.

The Evolutionary Origin of Religions

The term "evolutionary origin of religions" refers to "the emergence of religious behavior during the course of human evolution. When humans first became religious remains unknown, but there is credible evidence of religious behavior from the Middle Paleolithic era (300-50 thousand years ago) and possibly earlier." (WK 2010v)

If traced even earlier, it was also suggested, by Barbara King (2007), for example, that "chimpanzees and bonobos" (which are "humanity's closest living relatives") have "some traits that would have been necessary for the evolution of religion. These traits include high intelligence, a capacity for symbolic communication, a sense of social norms, realization of 'self' and a concept of continuity." (WK 2010v)

In the case of humans, a good question to ask here is, What exactly are the requirements for the evolutionary origin of religions? Four major requirements have been proposed in the literature to answer this question, namely, (a) "increased brain size," (b) "tool use," (c) "development of language," and (d) "morality and group living"—as described below. (WK 2010v)

(a) Increased Brain Size

The first requirement for the development of "the religious mind" concerns brain size, because it allows "a brain that is large enough to formulate religious and philosophical ideas." (WK 2010v; P. Ehrlich 2000)

In the process of "human evolution, the hominid brain tripled in size, peaking 500,000 years ago. Much of the brain's expansion took place in the neocortex. This part of the brain is involved in processing higher order cognitive functions that are necessary for human religiosity. The neocortex is responsible for self consciousness, language and emotion. According to [Robin] Dunbar's theory, the relative neocortex size of any species correlates with the level of social complexity of the particular species. The neocortex size correlates with a number of social variables that include social group size and complexity of mating behaviors. In chimpanzees the neocortex occupies 50% of the brain, whereas in modern humans it occupies 80% of the brain." (WK 2010v)

(b) Tool Use

The second requirement for the development of "the religious mind" concerns "tool use." (WK 2010v)

For instance, "Lewis Wolpert [2006] argues that causal beliefs that emerged from tool use played a major role in the evolution of belief. The manufacture of complex tools requires creating a mental image of an object that does not exist naturally before actually making the artefact. Furthermore, one must understand how the tool would be used, which requires an understanding of causality." (WK 2010v)

Therefore, "the level of sophistication of stone tools is a useful indicator of causal beliefs. Wolpert contends use of tools composed of more than one component, such as hand axes, represents an ability to understand cause and effect." (WK 2010v)

(c) Development of Language

The third requirement for the development of "the religious mind" concerns the "development of language." (WK 2010v)

The reason is that "religion requires a system of symbolic communication, such as language, to be transmitted from one individual to another. Philip Lieberman [1991] states 'human religious thought and moral sense clearly rest on a cognitive-linguistic base.'" (WK 2010v)

And Nicholas Wade (2006) made a comparable point, when he wrote: "Like most behaviors that are found in societies throughout the world, religion must have been present in the ancestral human population before the dispersal from Africa 50,000 years ago. Although religious rituals usually involve dance and music, they are also very verbal, since the sacred truths have to be stated. If so, religion, at least in its modern form, cannot pre-date the emergence of language. It has been argued earlier that language attained its modern state shortly before the exodus from Africa. If religion had to await the evolution of modern, articulate language, then it too would have emerged shortly before 50,000 years ago." (WK 2010v)

(d) Morality and Group Liviing

The fourth requirement for the development of "the religious mind" concerns "morality and group living." (WK 2010v)

For instance, "Frans de Waal and Barbara King both view human morality as having grown out of primate sociality. Though morality may be a unique human trait, many social animals, such as primates, dolphins and whales, have been known to exhibit pre-moral sentiments." (WK 2010v)

Michael Shermer (2004) was more specific when he idenified "the following characteristics...shared by humans and other social animals, particularly the great apes"—namely, "attachment and bonding, cooperation and mutual aid, sympathy and empathy, direct and indirect reciprocity, altruism and reciprocal altruism, conflict resolution and peacemaking, deception and deception detection, community concern and caring about what others think about you, and awareness of and response to the social rules of the group." (WK 2010v)

In group living, there is a need for cooperation; for De Waal, "all social animals have had to restrain or alter their behavior for group living to be worthwhile. Pre-moral sentiments evolved in primate societies as a method of restraining individual selfishness and building more cooperative groups. For any social species, the benefits of being part of an altruistic group should outweigh the benefits of individualism. For example, lack of group cohesion could make individuals more vulnerable to attack from outsiders. Being part of group may also improve the chances of finding food. This is evident among animals that hunt in packs to take down large or dangerous prey." (WK 2010v)

This does not mean, however, that all should be treated equally, because "all social animals have hierarchical societies in which each member knows its own place. Social order is maintained by certain rules of expected behavior and dominant group members enforce order through punishment." (WK 2010v)

For de Waal, "human morality has two extra levels of sophistication that are not found in primate societies. Humans enforce their society's moral codes much more rigorously with rewards, punishments and reputation building. People also apply a degree of judgment and reason, not seen in the animal kingdom." (WK 2010v)

For Matt J. Rossano (2007), "religion emerged after morality and built upon morality by expanding the social scrutiny of individual behavior to include supernatural agents. By including ever-watchful ancestors, spirits and gods in the social realm, humans discovered an effective strategy for restraining selfishness and building more cooperative groups. The adaptive value of religion would have enhanced group survival." (WK 2010v; N. Wade 2007; M. Rutherford 2008)

The Debate on the Evolutionary Psychology of Religion

However, it is one thing to say that there are some requirements for the development of "the religious mind," but it is something else to answer whether or not this development is subject to "natural selection" or, alternatively, simply a "by-product" of other evolutionary traits.

So, there are two opposing schools of thought here in the field of the evolutionary psychology of religion, namely, (a) "religion as an adaptation," and (b) "religion as a by-product" (or an "exaptation") as explained below (and summarized in *Table 2.4*). (WK 2010w)

(a) Religion as an Adaptation

On one side of the debate are those for the "adaptive value of religion."

For instance, "social solidarity theories" regard "religion as having evolved to enhance cooperation and cohesion within groups. Group membership in turn provides benefits which can enhance an individual's chances for survival and reproduction." (WK 2010w; R. Sosis 200)

In "social solidarity theories," one aim is "to explain the painful or dangerous nature of many religious rituals. Costly-signaling theory suggests that such rituals might serve as public and hard to fake signals that an individual's commitment to the group is sincere. Since there would be a considerable benefit in trying to cheat the system—taking advantage of group living benefits without taking on any possible costs—the ritual would not be something simple that can be taken lightly." (WK 2010w) R. Sosis 2003)

A good example is "warfare," as "Richard Sosis, Howard C. Kress (2007), and James S. Boster carried out a cross-cultural survey which demonstrated that men in societies which engage in war do submit to the costliest rituals." (WK 2010w)

Another example concerns "positive associations between religious practice and health and longevity; for instance, Harold G. Koenig (2001) and Harvey J. Cohen in their "100 evidence-based studies" found that "79% showed a positive influence." (WK 2010w)

However, for the critics like Richard P. Sloan, "there is no really good compelling evidence that there is a relationship between religious involvement and health," so "there is still debate over the validity of these findings, and they do not necessarily prove a direct cause-and-effect relationship between religion and health." (WK 2010w; M. Duenwald 2002)

(b) Religion as an "Exaptation"

On the other side of the debate are those for the "by-product" (or "exaptation" nature of religion.

For instance, Stephen Jay Gould (1991) and Elisabeth Vrba "proposed the term exaptation...to mean 'features that now enhance fitness, but were not built by natural selection for their current role.' Gould and R. C. Lewontin compared such features to spandrels, 'an architectural term for spaces left over between structural elements of a building.' A more complete explanation of this metaphor can be found in Gould and Lewontin's 1979 paper, 'The Spandrels of San Marco and the Panglossian Paradigm: A Critique of the Adaptationist Programme.'"

However, for the critics, "Gould...does not himself select a definite trait which he thinks was actually acted on by natural selection" which then subsequently led to the by-product of religion, although Gould (1991) appealed to "Freud's suggestion that our large brains, which evolved for other reasons, led to consciousness. The beginning of consciousness forced humans to deal with the concept of personal mortality. Religion may have been one solution to this problem." (WK 2010W)

In light of this problem, "Pierre Lienard [2006] and Pascal Boyer suggest that humans have evolved a 'hazard-precaution system' which allows us to detect potential threats in the environment and attempt to respond appropriately. Several features of ritual behaviors, often a major feature of religion, trigger this system. These include the occasion for the ritual, often the prevention or elimination of danger or evil, the harm believed to result from nonperformance of the ritual, and the detailed proscriptions for proper performance of the ritual. Lienard and Boyer discuss the possibility that a sensitive hazard-precaution system itself may have provided fitness benefits, and that religion then 'associates individual, unmanageable anxieties with coordinated action with others and thereby makes them more tolerable or meaningful.'" (WK 2010w)

Above the Fray

The fact that there is a debate on whether religion is "adaptive" or "exaptative," together with the criticisms against each, should caution us agianst any hasty acceptance of either side of the debate.

But this does not mean that the introduction of this debate is useless. On the contrary, it has the scholarly value to show us the two opposing sides of the debate, such that the possibility and desirability of sacredness (from the perspective of the mind with the evolutionary argument as a case study here) is not to the extent that its respective defenders would like us to believe.

Besides, the analysis of the evolutionary origin of religions can reveal the usefulness of the ontological principles in existential dialectics, and good examples include the absoluteness-relativeness principle, the partiality-totality principle, the predictability-unpredictability principle, the explicability-inexplicability principle, the preciseness-vagueness principle, the simpleness-complicatedness principle, the openness-hiddenness principle, the denseness-emptiness principle, the slowness-quickness principle, the expansion-contraction principle, the convention-novelty principle, the evolution-transformation principle, the symmetry-asymmetry principle, the softness-hardness principle, the regression-progression principle, and the same-difference principle.

For instance, in relation to the absoluteness-relativeness principle, if there is absolute viewpoint (e.g., the absolute view of creation theory in regard to the necessity of religion for the understanding of God), there is relative counterpart (e.g., what is true for creation theory is not so for the "exaptative" version of the evolutionary psychology of religion in regard to religion as a "by-product" of evolution instead). And the reverse direction also holds true.

In relation to the partiality-totality principle, if there is partial viewpoint (e.g., the partial view from each individual for his survival by using tools, language, living together, etc.), there is holistic view (e.g, the more holistic view that there is the emergent phenomenon of religion as a by-product of the evolution of tool use, language, group living, etc., such that the whole is not the sum of its parts). And the reverse direction also holds true.

In relation to the predictability-unpredictability principle, if there is predictabilty (e.g, the predictable claim by those for the evolutionary origin of religions that there are some major requirements such as "increased brain size," "tool use," etc.), there is unpredictability (e.g, the more difficult task to predict, if viewed solely within the evolutionary origin of religions, what other alternative religions and, for that matter, what other things can emerge out of these major requirements). And the reverse direction also holds true.

In relation to the explicability-inexplicability principle, if there is explicability (e.g, the explanation by those for the "adaptive value of religion" that religion evolves due to "natural selection"), there is inexplicability (e.g., the inexplicability, by those in the camp for the "adaptive value of religion," of why the benefits for health and solidarity, for instance, are necessarily "adaptive," as they may well be "exaptative" by the critics). And the reverse direction also holds true.

In relation to the preciseness-vagueness principle, if there is preciseness (e.g., the precise identification of religion, by Gould, as a "by-product" of the natural selection of something else), there is vagueness (e.g., the vagueness in Gould's argument, since he "does not himself select a definite trait which he thinks was actually acted on by natural selection"). And the reverse direction also holds true.

In relation to the simpleness-complicatedness principle, if there is simpleness (e.g., the relatively simple analysis of the four major requirements for the evolutionary origin of religions), there is complicatedness (e.g., the relatively more complicated analysis of the evolutionary origin of religions by pointing out the disagreements among scholars on whether religion is "adaptive" or "exaptative"). And the reverse direction also holds true.

In relation to the openness-hiddenness principle, if there is openenss (e.g,. the open exploration of the "positive associations between religious practice and health and longevity" by Koenig and Cohen), there is hiddenness (e.g., the hidden bias in the work by Koenig and Cohen, since, for the critics like Richard P. Sloan, "there is no really good compelling evidence that there is a relationship between religious involvement and health"). And the reverse direction also holds true.

In relation to the denseness-emptiness principle, if there is denseness (e.g, the relatively denser concentration of creation believers among Christians), there is emptiness (e.g., the relatively less dense, or more empty, concentration of creation believers among scientists in the evolution origin of religions). And the reverse direction also holds true.

In relation to the slowness-quickness principle, if there is slowness (e.g., the relatively slower readiness of people like Sosis and Kress to accept religion as an "adaptation"), there is quickness (e.g., the relatively quicker readiness of people like Gould and Lewontin to accept religion as an "exaptation"). And the reverse direction also holds true.

In relation to the expansion-contraction principle, if there is expansion (e.g., the relative expansion of the influence of evolutionary theory since the modern era), there is contraction (e.g., the relative contraction of the influence of creation theory since the modern era). And the reverse direction also holds true.

In relation to the convention-novelty principle, if there is convention (e.g., the conventional wisdom about religion as necessary in creation theory), there is novelty (e.g., the alternative novel challenge to the conventional wisdom about religion as necessary, by Gould and Lewontin for the "by-product" view of the evolutionary origin of religions). And the reverse direction also holds true.

In relation to the evolution-transformation principle, if there is evolution (e.g., the natural evolution of humans to use tools and live together in the state of nature), there is transformation (e.g, the technical transformation of human life by way of the invention of systematic religions in the evolution of civilization). And the reverse direction also holds true.

In relation to the symmetry-asymmetry principle, if there is symmetry (e.g., the co-existence of different schools of thought about religion through the ages, be they creation theory, the exaptative view of religion, etc.), there is asymmetry (e.g, the popularity of creation theory in medieval times—but the rise of the evolutionary view of religion in our times). And the reverse direction also holds true.

In relation to the softness-hardness principle, if there is softness (e.g., the use of cooperation in religious living), there is hardness (e.g., the use of competition for "the survival of the fittest"). And the reverse direction also holds true.

In relation to the regression-progression principle, if there is regression (e.g., the regression made in the history of religion, as shown in holy crusades where countless individuals were killed), there is progress (e.g., the progress made in the history of religion, as shown in cooperative living). And the reverse direction also holds true.

And the same-difference principle, if there is similarity in outcome (e.g., the contribution to the regulation and control of members in societies, regardless of whether this is true for primate societies or human societies), there is differrence in outcome (e.g., the contribution to the regulation and control of members in primate societies by way of social norms in group living—but the contribution to the regulation and control of members in human societies by way of "two extra levels of sophistication," namely, "much more rigorous" moral codes, and "a degree of judgment and reason, not seen in the animal kingdom," as shown by de Waal). And the reverse direction also holds true.

Sacredness and Society

Sacredness, when examined from the perspective of society, can illuminate some contrastive features on its possibility and desirability, and this can be shown by way of two case studies, namely, (2.4.1) religious conversion, and the politics of rights, and (2.4.2) new religious movements, and the sociology of religion—to be addressed hereafter, in that order.

Religious Converson, and the Politics of Rights

The term "religious conversion" refers to "the adoption of new religious beliefs that differ from the convert's previous beliefs. It involves a new religious identity, or a change from one religious identity to another." (WK 2010x)

Religious conversion so understood in terms of "changes from one religion to another" is "not to be confused with religious reaffiliation which refers to changes from one denomination to another within the same faith. Examples of religious reaffiliation include switching from being Southern Baptist to Methodist (within Christianity) or from Sunni to Shiite (within Islam)." (WK 2010x; R. Stark 2000)

This clarification aside—a controversy here concerns who is to decide what is legitimate or illegimatie conversion in the context of society. For instance, is "forced conversion" allowed?

The answer often depends on (a) the views on legal rights and their limits and (b) the disagreements about legal rights and their limits, to be summarized below.

The Views on Legal Rights and Their Limits

The views on legal rights and their limits can be divided into two parts, namely, (a) legal rights and (b) their limits—as explained below.

(a) In the area of international law, a good guidance about the legal rights of religious conversion is based on the United Nations Universal Declaration of Human Rights, which "defines religious conversion as a human right," in that "[e]veryone has the right to freedom of thought, conscience and religion; this right includes freedom to change his religion or belief" in Article 18. (WK 2010x)

This declaration of the United Nations became the foundation of another document known as "the International Covenant on Civil and Political Rights" drafted by "the United Nations Commission on Human Rights (UNCHR),"which states that "[e]veryone shall have the right to freedom of thought, conscience and religion. This right shall include freedom to have or to adopt a religion or belief of his choice...[Article 18.1] No one shall be subject to coercion which would impair his freedom to have or to adopt a religion or belief of his choice" (Article 18.2). (WK 2010x)

From the legal vantage point of these documents, some scholars suggest that the following rights about religious conversion are legitimate.

- "Freedom of Religion"—"All humans have the right to have religious beliefs, and to change these beliefs, even repeatedly, if that is their desire." (WK 2010x)
- "Freedom of Association"—"They have the right to form religious organizations for the purpose of worship, as well as for promoting their cause." (WK 2010x)
- "Freedom of Speech"—"They have the right to speak to others about their convictions, with the purpose of influencing the others." (WK 2010x)

By the same logic, if there are rights, there are also obligations (or limits).

(b) In the case of legal limits, "these very rights exercise a limiting influence on the freedoms of others. For instance, the right to have one's religious beliefs presumably includes the right not to be coerced into changing these beliefs by threats, discrimination, or similar inducements." (WK 2010x)

Therefore, the following acts are regarded by the scholars as not legitimate (or illegitimate):

- "It would not be proper to use coercion, threats, the weight of authority of the educational system, access to health care or similar facilities in order to induce people to change their religion." (WK 2010x)
- "It would be improper to try to impose one's beliefs on a 'captive audience', where the listeners have no choice but to be present. This would presumably require restraint in the exercise of their right to free speech, by teachers in the classroom, army officers to their inferiors, prison officers in prison, medical staff in hospitals, so as to avoid impinging on the rights of others." (WK 2010x)
- "It would not be proper to offer money, work, housing or other material inducements as a means of persuading people to adopt another religion." (WK 2010x)

In the broader case of conversion in general (not just religious conversion), as in "proselytism," which is defined as "the act of attempting to convert people to another opinion..., religious or not"—there are likewise limits, as shown below.

- "Making unjust or uncharitable references to other churches' beliefs and practices and even ridiculing them" (WK 2010y)
- Conversing in certain environments open to the public or…owned privately: government buildings, public education (grade schools and college campuses), the workplace and private properties like ones' home or front yard" (WK 2010y)
- "Comparing two Christian communities by emphasizing the achievements and ideals of one, and the weaknesses and practical problems of the other" (WK 2010y)
- "Employing any kind of physical violence, moral compulsion and psychological pressure e.g., the use of certain advertising techniques in mass media that might bring undue pressure on readers/viewers" (WK 2010y)
- "Using political, social and economic power as a means of winning new members for one's own church" (WK 2010y)
- "Extending explicit or implicit offers of education, health care or material inducements or using financial resources with the intent of making converts" (WK 2010y)
- Exercising "manipulative attitudes and practices that exploit people's needs, weaknesses or lack of education especially in situations of distress, and fail to respect their freedom and human dignity" (WK 2010y)

Of course, these limits are not exhaustive, so their citation here is for illustration only.

The Disagreements about Legal Rights and Their Limits

However, the views on the legal rights of religious conversion and their limits (as shown above) are one thing, but the enforcement of them is often subject to the politics of rights, which varies from one country to another and from an individual to another, for instance.

Consider some disagreements about legal rights and their limits, especially (a) among countries and (b) among individuals below, for illustration.

(a) In the case of the disagreements about the legal rights of religious conversion and their limits among countries, consider the following conflicts, for illustration. (WK 2010x)

- In Russa—"Since the collapse of the former Soviet Union and the rise of democracy in the Eastern Bloc, the Russian Orthodox Church has enjoyed a revival. However, it takes exception to what it considers illegitimate proselytizing by the Roman Catholic Church, the Salvation Army, Jehovah's Witnesses and other religious movements in what it refers to as its canonical territory." (WK 2010x)

- In Greece—The country "has a long history of conflict, mostly with Jehovah's Witnesses but also with some Pentecostals over its laws on proselytism. This situation stems from a law passed in the 1930s by the dictator Ioannis Metaxas. A Jehovah's Witness, Minos Kokkinakis, won the equivalent of US $14,400 in damages from the Greek state after being arrested for trying to preach his faith from door to door. In another case, Larissis vs. Greece, a member of the Pentecostal church, also won a case in the European Court of Human Rights." (WK 2010x)
- In Islamic Countries—"Some Islamic countries with Islamic law outlaw and carry strict sentences for proselytizing. Several Islamic countries under Islamic law, Saudi Arabia, Yemen, Afghanistan and Pakistan, Egypt, Iran, and Maldives outlaw apostasy and carry imprisonment or the death penalty for those leaving Islam and those enticing Muslims to leave Islam." (WK 2010x)
- In Canada and Some Parts of the U.S.—"Sociocultural norms suggest proselytism is improper." (WK 2010y)

Surely, there can be other examples too, but the ones above are deemed sufficient for the purpose of illustration.

(b) In the case of the disagreements about the legal rights of religious conversion and their limits among individuals, it is often observed by scholars in the field that "[w]hat one person considers legitimate evangelizing, or witness bearing" is something that "another may consider intrusive and improper." (WK 2010x)

A good illustration of findings like this about "subjective viewpoints" on the legitimacy of religious conversion is "this extract from an article by Dr. C. Davis [1996], published in Cleveland State University's 'Journal of Law and Health,'" in which he wrote: "According to the Union of American Hebrew Congregations, Jews for Jesus and Hebrew Christians constitute two of the most dangerous cults, and its members are appropriate candidates for deprogramming. Anti-cult evangelicals ...protest that 'aggressiveness and proselytizing...are basic to authentic Christianity,' and that Jews for Jesus and Campus Crusade for Christ are not to be labeled as cults. Furthermore, certain Hassidic groups who physically attacked a meeting of the Hebrew Christian 'cult' have themselves been labeled a 'cult' and equated with the followers of

Reverend Moon, by none other than the President of the Central Conference of American Rabbis." (WK 2010x)

In another finding, this time on "the propriety of proselytism, or even evangelism," the responses by individuals "differ radically. Some feel that freedom of speech should have no limits and that virtually anyone, anywhere should have the right to talk about anything they see fit. Others see all sorts of evangelism as a nuisance and an intrusion and would like to see them proscribed. Thus, Natan Lerner observes that the issue is one of a clash of rights—the right of a person to express his views versus the right of a person not to be exposed to views that he does not wish to hear." (WK 2010x)

A Redemptive Lesson

These disagreements about the legal rights of religious conversion and their limits among countries and individuals say a lot about the two opposing sides of the debate, such that the possibility and desirability of sacredness (from the perspective of society with religious conversion as a case study here) is not to the extent that its respective defenders would like us to believe.

In addition, the disagreements give us a redemptive lesson on the usefulness of the ontological principles in existential dialectics, and good examples include the absoluteness-relativeness principle, the predictability-unpredictability principle, the explicability-inexplicability principle, the preciseness-vagueness principle, the simpleness-complicatedness principle, the openness-hiddenness principle, the denseness-emptiness principle, the change-constancy principle, the slowness-quickness principle, the expansion-contraction principle, the theory-praxis principle, the convention-novelty principle, the evolution-transformation principle, the symmetry-asymmetry principle, the softness-hardness principle, the regression-progression principle, and the same-difference principle.

For instance, in relation to the absoluteness-relativeness principle, if there is absolute viewpoint (e.g., the absolute view of the United Nations Universal Declaration of Human Rights, since it is supposed to be "universal"), there is relative counterpart (e.g., what is right for the UN in regard to religious conversion as a human right is not so for the Russian Orthodox Church, which "takes exception to what it considers illegitimate proselytizing by the Roman Catholic Church, the Salvation Army, Jehovah's Witnesses and other religious movements in what it refers to as its canonical territory"). And the reverse direction also holds true.

In relation to the predictability-unpredictability principle, if there is predictability (e.g, the predictable tendency of officials from the UN to speak for religious conversion as a human right), there is unpredictability (e.g., the more difficult task to predict which specific country and specific indivdual will accept the legitimacy of proselitsing in a particular case at a given time, because of the disagreements about the legal rights of religious conversion and their limits among countries and individuals). And the reverse direction also holds true.

In relation to the explicability-inexplicability principle, if there is explicability (e.g, the explanation, if viewed within the United Nations Universal Declaration of Human Rights, of its defense of religious conversion on the basis of its being "a human right"), there is inexplicability (e.g, the lack of sufficient explanation, if viewed within the United Nations Universal Declaration of Human Rights, of why this universality of religious conversion as a human right is necessarily true in the first place, in light of the disagreements among countries and individuals). And the reverse direction also holds true.

In relation to the preciseness-vagueness principle, if there is preciseness (e.g., the precise identification of "religious conversion" as a human right by the United Nations Universal Declaration of Human Rights), there is vagueness (e.g., the vagueness in the nature of this "right," since it is subject to different interpretations by different countries and by different individuals, because "the boundary between them [what is legitimate and what is not] is not easily defined"). (WK 2010x) And the reverse direction also holds true.

In relation to the simpleness-complicatedness principle, if there is simpleness (e.g., the relatively simple formulation of religious conversion as a human right by the United Nations Universal Declaration of Human Rights), there is complicatedness (e.g., the more complicated analysis of religoius conversion in terms of the disagreements about its legal rights and limits among different countries and different individuals). And the reverse direction also holds true.

In relation to the openness-hiddenness principle, if there is openness (e.g., the open exploration of the relationship between religious conversion and human rights by the United Nations Universal Declaration of Human Rights), there is hiddenness (e.g., the hidden bias for universality in the United Nations Universal Declaration of Human Rights, without sufficient attention to the fundamental disagreements on legal rights and their limits among different countries and different individuals). And the reverse direction also holds true.

In relation to the denseness-emptiness principle, if there is denseness (e.g., the relatively denser concentration of individuals advocating religious converson as a human right among UN officials), there is emptiness (e.g., the relativley less dense, or more empty, concentration of individuals advocating the human right of religious conversion "for those leaving Islam and those enticing Muslims to leave Islam" in many Islamic countries). And the reverse direction also holds true.

In relation to the change-constancy principle, if there is change (e.g., individuals adopt new religious beliefs that differ from their previous beliefs), there is constancy (e.g., the ever constancy of the phenomenon of religious conversion). And the reverse direction also holds true.

In relation to the slowness-quickness principle, if there is slowness (e.g., the relatively slower readiness of a Muslim to leave Islam in Islamic countries), there is quickness (e.g., the relatively quicker readiness of individual in an Islamic family in Islamic countries to be converted into Islam). And the reverse direction also holds true.

In relation to the expansion-contraction principle, if there is expansion (e.g., the relative expansion of the influence of "new relgious movements" after WWII), there is contraction (e.g., the relative contraction of the influence of "mainstream" religious organizations after WWII). (WK 2010x) And the reverse direction also holds true.

In relation to the theory-praxis principle, if there is theory (e.g., the theoretical construction of "human rights," especially, though not exclusively, since modern times), there is praxis (e.g., the practical application of "human rights" for religious conversion as shown by the United Nations Universal Declaration of Human Rights). And the reverse direction also holds true.

In relation to the convention-novelty principle, if there is convention (e.g, the conventional wisdom in favor of "mainstream" religious traditions), there is novelty (e.g., the alternative novel challenge to the established views of "mainstream" religious traditions by the rise of "new religious movements" after WWII). And the reverse direction also holds true.

In relation to the evolution-transformation principle, if there is evolution (e.g, the natural evolution of humans to live in the state of nature without any knowledge of "human rights"), there is transformation (e.g., the technical transformation of human living together by way of the invention of the philosophy of "human rights"). And the reverse direction also holds true.

In relation to the symmetry-asymmetry principle, if there is symmetry (e.g., the co-existence of different views on religious conversion in the world), there is asymmetry (e.g.., the rise of th discourse on religious conversion as a "human right" after WWII—but the disagreements about religious conversion as a "human right" among countries, since some Islamic countries "carry imprisonment or the death penalty for those leaving Islam and those enticing Muslims to leave Islam"). And the reverse direction also holds true.

In relation to the softness-hardness principle, if there is softness (e.g., the existence of voluntary or "active" conversion), there is hardness (e.g., the existence of coerced or "forced" conversion). (WK 2010x) And the reverse direction also holds true.

In relation to the regression-progression principle, if there is regression (e.g., the regression made by the politics of religious conversion, as shown by the disagreements among different countries and individuals about the legal rights of religious conversion and its limits), there is progression (e.g., the progress made by the United Nations Universal Declaration of Human Rights to encourage religious conversion as a human right). And the reverse direction also holds true.

And in relation to the same-difference principle, if there is similarity in outcome (e.g., the contribution to the molding of human behaviors and beliefs, regardless of whether this be done by lax legal rights for religious conversion or strict limits on its exercise), there is difference in outcome (e.g., the contribution to the molding of human behaviors and beliefs by way of lax legal rights for religious conversion to encourage ideational individualism—but the contribution to the molding of human behaviors and beliefs by way of strict limits on religious conversion to encourage ideational collectivism). And the reverse direction also holds true.

New Religious Movements, and the Sociology of Religion

Another way to evaluate the possibility and desirability of sacredness from the perspective of society is to explore "the new religious movements" from the vantage point of the sociology of religion.

The Problem of Definition

The term "new religious movement" refers to "a intentional community, or ethical, spiritual, or philosophical group of recent origin. NRMs may be novel in origin or they may be part of a wider religion, such as Christianity, Hinduism, or Buddhism in which case they will be distinct from pre-existing denominations. Scholars studying the sociology of religion have almost unanimously adopted this term as a neutral alternative to the word 'cult.'" (WK 2010z; M. Introvigne 2001)

However, there is a heated debate in the field of "new religious studies" about how it can be clearly defined, because "there is no one criterion or set of criteria for describing a group as a 'new religious movement,'" so any "use of the term usually requires that the group be both of recent origin and different from existing religions." (WK 2010z)

Even then, the debate continues, especially about "the phrase 'of recent origin': some authors use World War II as the dividing line after which anything is 'new', whereas others define as 'new' everything after the advent of the Bahá'í Faith (mid-19th century)." (WK 2010z)

In addition, "some scholars also have a more restricted approach to what counts as 'different from existing religions.' For them, 'difference' applies to a faith that, though it may be seen as part of an existing religion, meets with rejection from that religion for not sharing the same basic creed or declares itself either separate from the existing religion or even 'the only right' faith. Other scholars expand their measurement of difference, considering religious movements new when, taken from their traditional cultural context, they appear in new places, perhaps in modified forms. Examples of these kinds of 'new movements' would be the Western importation and establishment of Hindu or Buddhist groups." (WK 2010z)

The Diversity of New Religious Movements

To make things worse, "NRMs vary in terms of leadership; authority; concepts of the individual, family, and gender; teachings; organizational structures; etc. These variations have presented a challenge to social scientists in their attempts to formulate a comprehensive and clear set of criteria for classifying NRMs." (WK 2010z)

For this reason, "Irving Hexham and Karla Poewe have consequently proposed that there are NRMs [not just NRM] particularly those who have gained adherents in a number of nations, which can be understood as forming global sub-cultures." (WK 2010z)

In any event, "the number of people who have affiliated with NRMs worldwide is small when compared to major world religions. However, the diversity of NRMs has seen the emergence of different groups in Africa, Japan, and Melanesia. In Africa, David Barrett has documented the emergence of 6,000 new indigenous churches since the late 1960s. In Japan a number of NRMs based on revitalised Shinto belief, as well as neo-Buddhist and New Age groups, have emerged, some of which originated in the late Nineteenth century in the Meiji Era and others in the aftermath of World War Two." (WK 2010z)

In fact, because "around twenty-five percent of the world's distinct cultures are found in Melanesia, spanning the island nations from Papua

New Guinea, the Solomon Islands, Vanuatu and Fiji," so it is therefore not surprising that "it was here that the phenomena of Cargo Cults were first discerned by anthropologists and religious studies scholars. The Cargo Cults are interpreted as indigenous NRMs that have arisen in response to colonial and post-colonial cultural changes, including the influx of modernisation and capitalist consumerism." (WK 2010z)

Reasons for Joining and Leaving

An interesting question for the sociologists of religion concerns the reasons of why individuals bother to join NRMs and later leave.

Consider first (a) reasons for joining and (b) reasons for leaving, in what follows.

(a) Reasons for Joining

For Marc Gallanter (1989), there are two main reasons for individuals to joion NRMs, namely, "a search for community and a spiritual quest." (WK 2010z)

And Jeffrey Hadden is more specific to summarize some reasons of why individuals to join "new religious movements, a term Hadden uses to include both cults and sects" (as shown below): (WK 2010z)

- "Belonging to groups is a natural human activity"
- "People belong to religious groups for essentially the same reasons they belong to other groups"
- "Conversion is generally understood as an emotionally charged experience that leads to a dramatic reorganization of the convert's life"
- "Conversion varies enormously in terms of the intensity of the experience and the degree to which it actually alters the life of the convert"
- "Conversion is one, but not the only reason people join religious groups"
- "Social scientists have offered a number of theories to explain why people join religious groups"
- "Most of these explanations could apply equally well to explain why people join lots of other kinds of groups"
- "No one theory can explain all joinings or conversions"
- "What all of these theories have in common is the view that joining or converting is a natural process"

Now, these reasons are by no means exhaustive, but the examples here suffice to illustrate the point of why individuals join NRMs.

(b) Reasons for Leaving

But, if individuals join, they can also leave later. So, the next question is, Why do individuals leave the NRMs that they once belonged to?

In general, there are three main reasons of why individuals leave the NRMs that they once belonged to, namely, (i) "by one's own decision," (ii) "through expulsion," and (iii) "through intervention" (like "exit counseling" and "deprogramming"). (WK 2010z; J. Duhaime 2003; C. Giambalvo 1993)

In one study by D. Bromley and J. Hadden (1993), "the overwhelming proportion of people who get involved in NRMs leave, most short of two years; the overwhelming proportion of people...leave of their own volition; and...two-thirds (67%) felt 'wiser for the experience.'" (WK 2010z)

One disturbing question concerns the phenomenon of "psychological trauma" for those who leave. (WK 2010z)

For instance, for Eileen Barker (1983), "the greatest worry of potential harm concerns the central and most dedicated followers of a new religious movement. Barker mentions that some former members may not take new initiatives for quite a long time after disaffiliation from the NRM. This generally does not concern the many superficial, short-lived, or peripheral supporters of an NRM." (WK 2010z; M. Galanter 1983)

For David Barret, "leaving can be difficult for some members and may include psychological trauma. Reasons for this trauma may include: conditioning by the religious movement; avoidance of uncertainties about life and its meaning; having had powerful religious experiences; love for the founder of the religion; emotional investment; fear of losing salvation; bonding with other members; anticipation of the realization that time, money, and efforts donated to the group were a waste; and the new freedom with its corresponding responsibilities, especially for people who lived in a community. Those reasons may prevent a member from leaving even if the member realizes that some things in the NRM are wrong." (WK 2010z)

For Reender Kranenborg, "in some religious groups, members have all their social contacts within the group, which makes disaffection and disaffiliation very traumatic." (WK 2010z)

However, F. Derks and J. van der Lans cautioned us that "there is no uniform 'post-cult trauma' of people leaving NRMs. While psychological and social problems upon resignation are not uncommon, their character and intensity are greatly dependent on the personal history and on the traits of the ex-member, and on the reasons for and way of resignation." (WK 2010z)

Four Models to Explain the Rise of NRMs

A more profound question which interests those in the sociology of religion concerns the explanation of the rise of NRMs in the first place.

Rodney Stark and William Sims Bainbridge (1987) offered their answer by way of four models for four possible explanations, as summarized below. (WK 2010z)

- "The Psycho-Pathological Model"—which explains that "the cult founder suffers from psychological problems; they develop the cult in order to resolve these problems for themselves, as a form of self-therapy."
- "The Entrepreneurial Model"—which explains that "the cult founder acts like an entrepreneur, trying to develop a religion which they think will be most attractive to potential recruits, often based on their experiences from previous cults or other religious groups they have belonged to."
- "The Social model"—which explains that "the cult is formed through a social implosion, in which cult members dramatically reduce the intensity of their emotional bonds with non-cult members, and dramatically increase the intensity of those bonds with fellow cult members....[T]his emotionally intense situation naturally encourages the formation of a shared belief system and rituals."
- "The Normal Revelations Model"—which explains that "the cult is formed when the founder chooses to interpret ordinary natural phenomena as supernatural, such as by ascribing his or her own creativity in inventing the cult to that of the deity."

Surely, all four models can be used simultaneously for the explanation of the rise of a given cult, depending on a particular case in question.

The Need for Caution

However, there is a need for caution in explainng the rise of NRMs on the basis of these different models, because not everyone agrees with them in the debate.

On one side of the fence are the critics of cults (or more broadly speaking, the new religious movements), who are more likely to use models like this to deconstruct NRMs (e.g., the claim that cult founders suffer from "psychological problems").

On the other side of the fence are the defenders of cults (or more broadly speaking, the new religious movements), who are more likely to question any models which do not flatter or speak more favorably about NRMs.

Thus, the critics of NRMs tend to call the defenders of NRMs "cult apologists"—whereas the defenders of NRMs like to call the critics of NRMs "hate groups" (or alternatively, "'anti-cult' activists"). (WK 2010z & 2010aa)

For instance, the critics of cults (or more broadly speaking, the new religious movements) like "Anton Hein...severely criticize scholars...who disagree with their views. Hein uses the term 'cult apologist' for them. Those offering such criticism accuse such scholars of naïveté and poor scholarship; and above all they reproach them for not warning people who need warning, as well as of receiving funding from the cults themselves." (WK 2010aa)

On the other hand, the defenders of cults (or more broadly speaking, the new religious movements) like "CESNUR's president Massimo Introvigne" (1999) argue that "fringe and extreme anti-cult activism resorts to tactics that may create a background favorable to extreme manifestations of discrimination and hate against individuals that belong to new religious movements." (WK 2010z)

The point here is not to favor either side of the debate but to show us the two opposing sides of the debate, such that the possibility and desirability of sacredness (from the perspective of society with the rise of NRMs as a case study here) is not to the extent that its respective defenders would like us to believe.

In fact, the contention between the critics and defenders of NRMs reveals something valuable about the ontological principles in existential dialectics, and good examples include the absoluteness-relativeness principle, the predictability-unpredictability principle, the explicability-inexplicability principle, the preciseness-vagueness principle, the simpleness-complicatedness principle, the openness-hiddenness principle, the denseness-emptiness principle, the change-constancy principle, the slowness-quickness principle, the expansion-contraction principle, the convention-novelty principle, the evolution-transformation principle, the symmetry-asymmetry principle, the softness-hardness principle, the regression-progression principle, and the same-difference principle.

For instance, in relation to the absoluteness-relativeness principle, if there is absolute viewpoint (e.g., the absolute view of the critics of cults like Anton Hein, who "severely criticize scholars…who disagree with their views" and call them "cult apologists"), there is relative counterpart (e.g., what is right for the critics of cults like Hein to call their enemies "cult apologists" is not so for the defenders of cults like Massimo Introvigne who call the critics of cults "hate groups" or alternatively, "'anti-cult' activists"). And the reverse direction also holds true.

In relation to the predictability-unpredictability principle, if there is predictability (e.g., the predictable tendency of an individual who is dissatisifed with "mainstream" or "established" religious organizations to join a NRM), therre is unpredictability (e.g., the more difficult task to predict exactly how long this individual will stay in that NRM or how he exactly he will leave later on). And the reverse direction also holds true.

In relation to the explicability-inexplicability principle, if there is explicability (e.g., the explanation of the rise of NRMs accordiing to different models by Stark and Bainbridge), there is inexplicability (e.g,. the lack of sufficient explanation of why these four models are sufficient to explain the rise of NRMs, since not everyone agress with them, and the defenders of cults often question any models which do not speak more favorably about NRMs). And the reverse direction also holds true.

In relation to the preciseness-vagueness principle, if there is preciseness (e.g., the precise identification of such features as "of recent origin" and "difference" in the definition of NRM), there is vagueness (e.g., the vagueness in the phrases "of recent origin" and "difference," since there is a debate among scholars about them). And the reverse direction also holds true.

In relation to the simpleness-complicatedness principle, if there is simpleness (e.g., the relatively simple analysis of the rise of NRMs on the basis of four models), there is complicatedness (e.g, the relatively more complicated analysis of the rise of NRMs, as shown in the debate between the critics of cults and the defenders of cults). And the reverse direction also holds true.

In relation to the openness-hiddenness principle, if there is openness (e.g., the open exploration of the rise of NRMs and their subsequent dark side, as revealed by some disaffected ex-members), there is hiddenness (e.g., the hidden bias in the account of NRMs by these disaffected ex-members, because their character, motivation, and credibility have been questioned). (WK 2010z) And the reverse direction also holds true.

In relation to the denseness-emptiness principle, if there is denseness (e.g., the relatively denser concentration of NRMs after WWII, with about 6,000 of them, according to Barrett), there is emptiness (e.g., the relatively less dense, or more empty, concentration of NRMs in medieval Europe). And the reverse direction also holds true.

In relation to the change-constancy principle, if there is change (e.g., the ever changing face of religion with the emergence of new religious movements throughout the ages), there is constancy (e.g, the ever constant search for "community" and "spiritual identity" by religion throughout the ages). And the reverse direction also holds true.

In relation to the slowness-quickness principle, if there is slowness (e.g., the relatively slower readiness of someone like Hein to be supportive of NRMs), there is quickness (e.g., the relatively quicker readness of someone like Introvigne to be supportive of NRMs). And the reverse direction also holds true.

In relation to the expansion-contraction principle, if there is expansion (e.g., the relative expansion of the influence of NRMs after WWII), there is contraction (e.g., the relative contraction of the influence of mainstream organizations after WWII). And the reverse direction also holds true.

In relation to the convention-novelty principle, if there is convention (e.g,. the conventional wisdom about spirituality by "mainstream" religions), there is novelty (e.g., the alternative novel challenge to conventional wisdom about spirituality by NRMs, which often offer something "different" from the "mainstream" views). And the reverse direction also holds true.

In relation to the evolution-transformation principle, if there is evolution (e.g,. the natural evolution of humans to live in the state of nature), there is transformation (e.g., the technical transformation of human living by way of the invention of NRMs for a different quest for community and spirituality). And the reverse direction also holds true.

In relation to the symmetry-asymmetry principle, if there is symmetry (e.g., the co-existence of "mainstream" and "new" religions after WWII), there is asymmetry (e.g., the larger number of NRMs, when compared with the number of "mainstream" world religions, after WWII—but the greater number of followers of "mainstream" world religions, when compared with the number of followers of NRMs, after WWII). And the reverse direction also holds true.

In relation to the softness-hardness principle, if there is softness (e.g., the joining of a NRM by an enthusiastic new member), there is hardness (e.g., the leaving of a NRM by a disaffected member). And the reverse direction also holds true.

In relation to the regression-progression principle, if there is regression (e.g., the regression made by NRMs as revealed by the criticisms from disaffected ex-members who "seek…redress for perceived wrongs or look…to expose perceived wrongdoings"), there is progression (e.g., the progress made by NRMs as shown by satisfied members who stay). (WK 2010z) And the reverse direction also holds true.

And in relation to the same-difference principle, if there is similarity in outcome (e.g., the contribution to the regulation and control of behaviors and beliefs, regardless of whether this be done in "mainstream" religious organizations or in NRMs), there is difference in outcome (e.g, the contribution to the regulation and control of behaviors and beliefs by way of the teaching of "mainstream" religious organizations, for instance, in regard to the existence of a monolithic deity in Christianity—but the contribution to the regulation and control of behaviors and beliefs by way of the teaching of NRMs, for instance, in regard to the view of "God" only as a "metaphor" by some "naturalistic" new religious groups). (WK 2010z) And the reverse direction also holds true.

Sacredness and Culture

Sacredness, when examined from the perspective of culture, teaches us something different on its possibility and desirability, and this can be shown by way of two case studies, namely, (2.5.1) shamanism, the outer-world, and the role of culture, and (2.5.2) animsm, the spirits, and cultural traditions—to be addressed hereafter, in that order.

Shamanism, the Outer-World, and the Role of Culture

A good starting point to understand sacredness from the perspective of culture concerns shamanism, the outer-world, and the role of culture.

The term "shamanism" refers to "an anthropological term referencing a range of beliefs and practices regarding communication with the spiritual world." (WK 2010bb)

Etymologically, the word "shaman" is "a loan from the Turkic word *šamán*, the term for such a practitioner [of shamanism], which also gained currency in the wider Turko-Mongol and Tungusic cultures in ancient Siberia. Shamanism played an important role in Altaic mythology. Tengriism which was the major belief of Xiongnu, Turkic, Hungarian and Bulgar peoples in ancient times incorporates elements of shamanism." (WK 2010bb)

Historical Origins and Development

Anthony Wallace once classified "four categories of religion, each subsequent category subsuming the previous"—with "shamanism" as the second of the four categories (i.e., "individualistic," "shamanistic," "communal," and "ecclesiastical"), although the critics have much questioned this classification with a Christian bias. (WK 2010cc)

In this way, shamanism is an old version of religion which precedes organized religions as we now known them. For many scholars, shamanism is often thought as a very old "Paleolithic" religion "predating all organized religions" and can certainly be dated back "as early as the Neolithic period." (WK 2010bb; J. Clottes, 2010; K. Narr 2008)

For instance, "shamanism is...widespread among hunter-gatherers and...Upper Paleolithic people were admittedly hunter-gatherers, looking to shamanism as a likely religion for them." (J. Clottes 2010)

In fact, "archaeological evidence exists for Mesolithic shamanism. In November 2008, researchers announced the discovery of a 12,000-year-old site in Israel that they regard as one of the earliest known shaman burials. The elderly woman had been arranged on her side, with her legs apart and folded inward at the knee. Ten large stones were placed on the head, pelvis and arms. Among her unusual grave goods were 50 complete tortoise shells, a human foot, and certain body parts from animals such as a cow tail and eagle wings. Other animal remains came from a boar, leopard, and two martens. 'It seems that the woman...was perceived as being in a close relationship with these animal spirits,' researchers noted." (WK 2010bb; M. Kahn 2008)

Later, as organized religions developed, the influence of shamanism could still be seen. For instance, "aspects of shamanism are encountered in later, organized religions, generally in their mystic and symbolic practices. Greek paganism was influenced by shamanism, as reflected in the stories of Tantalus, Prometheus, Medea, and Calypso among others, as well as in the Eleusinian Mysteries, and other mysteries. Some of the shamanic practices of the Greek religion later merged into the Roman religion." (WK 2010bb)

However, as organized religions gained more infuence, shamanism suffered. For instance, "during the early centuries AD, the shamanic practices of many subject cultures were marginalized with the spread of Abrahamic religion throughout the Roman Empire and its northern neighbors."

In early modern times, "Spanish repression of shamanism forced Roman Catholicism upon the peoples of the Western Hemisphere as an integral part of Spanish colonization. In Latin America, Catholic priests dedicated to the destruction of non-Abrahamic traditions followed the Conquistadors, denouncing practitioners as 'devil worshippers' and having them executed." (WK 2010bb)

And in the United States, "shamanism was brutally suppressed by the United States Government's military. In the massacre of Wounded Knee, a whole band of Lakota Sioux under Chief Big Foot were gunned down with automatic Hotchkiss guns and left to die in a snow storm." (WK 2010bb)

Shamanism vs. Magic

To avoid confusion, one should not confuse "shamanism" with "magic" (the latter of which was already analyzed in *Sec. 2.2.2*).

The first distinction between shamanism and magic is that the former is a form of religion (albeit a very old one dating back to the Paleolithic period), whereas the latter is not (with "religious magic" as an exceptional case).

In fact, it can be argued that, as shamanism later evolved into organized religions in the history of religion, its magical part was separated and became more independent from religion.

The reason is that "just as tribal elders were consolidated and transformed in kings and bureaucrats, so too were shamans and adepts changed into priests and a priestly caste. This shift is by no means in nomenclature alone. While the shaman's task was to negotiate between the tribe and the spirit world, on behalf of the tribe, as directed by the collective will of the tribe, the priest's role was to transfer instructions from the deities to the city-state, on behalf of the deities, as directed by the will of those deities. This shift represents the first major usurpation of power by distancing magic from those participating in that magic. It is at this stage of development that highly codified and elaborate rituals, setting the stage for formal religions, began to emerge, such as the funeral rites of the Egyptians and the sacrifice rituals of the Babylonians, Persians, Aztecs and Mayans." (WK 2010r)

And the second distinction between shamanism and magic is that they do not use the same materials and techniques to fulfill their respective functions (as will be further elaborated in a later section), although they may have something in common (like the use of rituals and others).

The Theoretical Construct of Shamanism

This qualification about shamanism vs. magic aside—shamanic religions can have many different characteristics, but there are two which stand out, for Jean Clottes (2010).

The first major characteristic of shamanism is "their concept of a complex cosmos in which at least two worlds—or more—coexist, be they side by side or one above the other. Those worlds interact with one another and in our own world most events are believed to be the consequence of an influence from the other-world(s)." (J. Clottes 2010)

And the second major characteristic of shamansm is "the belief of the group in the ability for certain persons to have at will a direct controlled relationship with the other-world. This is done for very practical purposes: to cure the sick, to maintain a good relationship with the powers in the other-world, to restore an upset harmony, to reclaim a lost soul, to make good hunting possible, to forecast the future, to cast spells, etc. Contact happens in two ways: spirit helpers, very often in animal form, come to the shaman and inhabit him/her when he/she calls on them; the shaman may also send his/her soul to the other-world in order to meet the spirits there and obtain their help and protection. Shamans will do so through trance. A shaman thus has a most important role as a mediator between the real world and the world of the spirits, as well as a social role." (J. Clottes 2010)

The Practical Application of Shamanism

With this theoretical construct of shamanism (and its distinction from magic) in mind—shamanism has been aplied in different cultures for various functions.

Some often cited functions performed by shamans are shown below. (WK 2010bb; T. Sem 2010)

- Ex: "healing"
- Ex: "leading a sacrifice"
- Ex: "acting as a psychopomp (literal meaning, 'guide of souls')"
- Ex: "preserving the tradition by storytelling and songs"
- Ex: "fortune-telling"

Of course, all of these functions are not always so separated, as "in some cultures, a shaman may fulfill several functions in one person." (WK 2010bb)

There are, however, two qualifications about these functions.

The first qualification about the functions of shamans is that each of these functions can be more complicated that it may seem.

For instance, in the first case (e.g., "healing"), "the ailments may be...purely physical afflictions." (WK 2010bb) If the ailments are "physical," then the shaman in question can have the disease "cured by gifting, flattering, threatening, or wrestling the disease-spirit (sometimes trying all these, sequentially)," and the curing process "may be completed by displaying some supposedly extracted token of the disease-spirit (displaying this, even if 'fraudulent,' is supposed to impress the disease-spirit that it has been, or is in the process of being, defeated, so that it will retreat and stay out of the patient's body)." (WK 2010bb) And if the ailments are "psychological," then the shaman in question can have it "likewise cured by similar methods." (WK 2010bb)

In the second case (e.g., "leading a sacrifice"), different cultures may require different shamans. For instance, in some instances, "a different term other than the one translated 'shaman' is applied to a religious official leading sacrificial rites ('priest'), or to a raconteur ('sage') of traditional lore; there may be more of an overlap in functions (with that of a shaman)." (WK 2010bb)

And in the third case (e.g., "acting as a psychopomp"), "there may be additional types of shaman, who perform more specialized functions. For example, among the Nanai people, a distinct kind of shaman acts as a psychopomp. Other specialized shaman may be distinguished according to the type of spirits, or realms of the spirit world, with which the shaman most commonly interacts. These roles vary among the Nenets, Enets, and Selkup shaman…." (WK 2010bb; M. Czaplicka 1914)

The second qualification about the functions of shamans is that they also need the help of some materials (e.g., "entheogens") and techniques (e.g., "autohypnosis") to perform their functions.

For instance, in general, "the shaman traverses the axis mundi and enters the spirit world by effecting a transition of consciousness, entering into an ecstatic trance, either autohypnotically or through the use of entheogens." (WK 2010bb)

The psychoactive substances (often from plants) used in entheogens include, for instance, "psilocybin mushrooms," "cannabis," "tobacco," "San Pedro cactus," "peyote," "ayahuasca," "cedar," "datura," "deadly nightshade," "fly agaric," "iboga," "sweetgrass," "salvia divinorum," and so on. (WK 2010bb; K. Salak 2010 & 2010a)

And the hypnotic techniques used in shaman practices include, for instance, "drumming," "dancing," "singing," "music," "vigils," "fasting," "sweat lodge," "swordfighting," "bladesmithing," and so on. (WK 2010bb; K. Salak 2010a)

The Criticisms of the Discourse on Shamanism

Yet, the discourse on shamanism has been subject to a lot of criticisms. Consider four of them below, for illustration.

Firstly, one criticism of the discourse on shamanism is that the literature is often full of works which "may not only misrepresent or 'dilute' genuine indigenous practices but do so in a way that...reinforces racist ideas such as the Noble Savage." (WK 2010bb)

For instance, Alice Kehoe (2000) in her book titled *Shamans and Religion: An Anthropological Exploration in Critical Thinking* was "highly critical of the term" (viz., shamanism) used in the literature, which is "an invention synthesized from various sources unsupported by more direct research. To Kehoe, what some scholars of shamanism treat as being definitive of shamanism, most notably drumming, trance, chanting, entheogens and hallucinogenics, spirit communication and healing, are practices" that are problematic, in that they are: (WK 2010bb)

- "exist outside of what is defined as shamanism and play similar roles even in non-shamanic cultures (such as the role of chanting in Judeo-Christian rituals)."
- "in their expression are unique to each culture that uses them and cannot be generalized easily, accurately or usefully into a global 'religion' such as shamanism."

Surely, Kehoe may have exaggerated quite a bit here, since she targeted her critique especially against the work of Mircea Eliade.

Secondly, another criticism of the discourse on shamanism is that more works are needed to "stress...the diversity and the specific features of the discussed cultures" of shamanism. (WK 2010bb)

For instance, "Mihály Hoppál...recommends using the term 'shamanhood' or 'shamanship' for stressing the diversity and the specific features of the discussed cultures. This is a term used in old Russian and German ethnographic reports at the beginning of the 20th century. He believes that this term is less general and places more stress on the local variations, and it emphasizes also that shamanism is not a religion of sacred dogmas, but linked to the everyday life in a practical way." (WK 2010bb)

In fact, others like Piers Vitebsky also had mentioned that "despite really astonishing similarities, there is no unity in shamanism. The various, fragmented shamanistic practices and beliefs coexist with other beliefs everywhere. There is no record of pure shamanistic societies (although, as for the past, their existence is not impossible)." (WK 2010bb)

Thirdly, still another criticism of the discourse on shamanism is that "the New Age movement has appropriated some ideas from shamanism" to the point that shamanism often becomes "misunderstood, sensationalized, or superficially understood and/or applied." (WK 2010bb; AICS 2010)

For instance, "there is an endeavor in some occult and esoteric circles to reinvent shamanism in a modern form, drawing from core shamanism—a set of beliefs and practices synthesized by the controversial Michael Harner—often revolving around the use of ritual drumming and dance, and Harner's interpretations of various indigenous religions. Harner has faced much criticism for implying that pieces of diverse religions can be taken out of context to form some sort of 'universal' shamanic tradition." (WK 2010bb)

And fourthly, still one more criticism of the discourse on shamanism is that the history of shamanic practices is full of "fraudulent shamans" in different cultures, such that it is not as effective as its practitioners would like us to believe. (WK 2010bb)

For instance, in a study by Richard L. Allen (2001), a Research & Policy Analyst for the Cherokee Nation, the natives "are overwhelmed with fraudulent Shamans," as Allen thus concluded: "One may assume that anyone claiming to be a Cherokee 'shaman, spiritual healer, or pipe-carrier,' is equivalent to a modern day medicine show and snake-oil vendor." (WK 2010bb)

Siding with Neither

Lest any misunderstanding occurs, the introduction to this debate on the nature of shamanism is not to favor either side of the debate but to give us the opportunity to learn from the two opposing sides, such that the possibility and desirability of sacredness (from the perspective of culture with shamanism as a case study here) is not to the extent that its respective defenders would like us to believe.

In addition, the debate on shamanism shows us the usefulness of the ontological principles in existential dialectics, and good examples include the absoluteness-relativeness principle, the predictability-unpredictability principle, the explicability-inexplicability principle, the preciseness-vagueness principle, the simpleness-complicatedness principle, the openness-hiddenness principle, the denseness-emptiness principle, the slowness-quickness principle, the expansion-contraction principle, the theory-praxis principle, the convention-novelty principle, the evolution-transformation principle, the symmetry-asymmetry principle, the softness-hardness principle, the regression-progression principle, and the same-difference principle.

For instance, in relation to the absoluteness-relativeness principle, if there is absolute viewpoint (e.g., "the belief" of a shaman "in the ability…

to have at will a direct controlled relationship with the other-world"), there is relative counterpart (e.g., what is true for a shaman in regard to his ability "to have at will a direct controlled relationship with the other-world" is not so for a contemporary scientist who is skeptical to the existence of this other-world and to the shaman's claim of his ability). And the reverse direction also holds true.

In relation to the predictability-unpredictability principle, if there is predictability (e.g., the predictable tendency of a shaman to use any of the substances and techniques to perform his functions), there is unpredictability (e.g,. the more difficult task to predict which particular combination of substances and techniques a shaman will use on a particular occasion and when exactly his attempt is successful or not). And the reverse direction also holds true.

In relation to the explicability-inexplicability principle, if there is explicability (e.g, the explanation of those like Hamer "in some occult and esoteric circles to reinvent shamanism in a modern form, drawing from core shamanism…often revolving around the use of ritual drumming and dance"), there is inexplicability (e.g, the lack of sufficient explanation by those like Hamer in these "occult and esoteric circles" of why "pieces of diverse religions can be taken out of context to form some sort of 'universal' shamanic tradition" in the first place). And the reverse direction also holds true.

In relation to the preciseness-vagueness principle, if there is preciseness (e.g, the precise identification of "drumming, trance, chanting, entheogens and hallucinogenics, spirit communication and healing" as shamanistic practices), there is vagueness (e.g., the vagueness in the identification of these shamanistic practices, since, for the critics like Kehoe, they "in their expression are unique to each culture that uses them and cannot be generalized easily, accurately or usefully into a global 'religion' such as shamanism"). And the reverse direction also holds true.

In relation to the simpleness-complicatedness principle, if there is simpleness (e.g., the relatively simple analysis of shamanism in terms of its concepts, techniques, histories, etc.), there is complicatedness (e.g, the relatively more complicated analysis of shamanism, as shown in the problems pointed out by the critics). And the reverse direction also holds true.

In relation to the openness-hiddenness principle, if there is openness (e.g., the open exploration of the relationship between an individual like a shaman and the ability to connect with the other-world for healing, etc.), there is hiddenness (e.g., the hidden bias in shamanistic practices, as they can be "fraudulent shamans," as shown in the research by Richard Allen on the Cherokee Nation). (WK 2010bb) And the reverse direction also holds true.

In relation to the denseness-emptiness principle, if there is denseness (e.g,. the relatively denser concentration of shamans in "Paleolithic" period), there is emptiness (e.g, the relatively less dense, or more empty, concentration of shamans in our times). And the reverse direction also holds true.

In relation to the slowness-quickness principle, if there is slowness (e.g., the relatively slower readiness of a contemporary mainstream doctor to use trance, chanting, etc. to cure his patients for ailments), there is quickness (e.g, the relatively quicker readiness of a Paleolithic shaman to use trance, chanting, etc. to cure the ailments of a patient). And the reverse direction also holds true.

In relation to the expansion-contraction principle, if there is expansion (e.g., the relative rise of shamanism in Paleothic period), there is contraction (e.g., the relative decline of shamanism in our times). And the reverse direction also holds true.

In relation to the theory-praxis principle, if there is theory (e.g, the theoretical construction of shamanism in regard to the existence of two different but interconnected worlds in the cosmos and the ability of some individuals to "have at will a direct controlled relationship with the other-world"), there is praxis (e.g., the practical application of the theoretical construct of shamanism "for very practical purposes: to cure the sick, to restore an upset harmony, etc.). And the reverse direction also holds true.

In relation to the convention-novelty principle, if there is convention (e.g., the conventional wisdom about ancient forms of shamanism as in "core shamanism"), there is novelty (e.g., the alternative novel challenge to the conventional wisdom about "core shamanism" by Hamer by way of his original attempt to "reinvent shamanism in a modern form, drawing from core shamanism"). And the reverse direction also holds true.

In relation to the evolution-transformation principle, if there is evolution (e.g., the natural evolution of humans to live in the state of nature, with such hazards as illness, injury, death, etc.), there is transformation (e.g, the technical transformation of human life by way of the invention of religions, such as shamanism and later more organized religions, for a systematic systems of ideas for the explanation and even treatment of these hazards). And the reverse direction also holds true.

In relation to the symmetry-asymmetry principle, if there is symmetry (e.g., the co-existence of different religions throughout the ages), there is asymmetry (e.g., the popularity of shamanism in Paleolithic times—but the popularity of medical science in our times). And the reverse direction also holds true.

In relation to the softness-hardness principle, if there is softness (e.g,. the spirits in the world of shamanism can help the cure of ailments), there is hardness (e.g., the spirits in the world shamanism can inflict harm too). And the reverse direction also holds true.

In relation to the regression-progression principle, if there is regression (e.g, the regression made by shamanism, as shown by the phenomenon of "fraudulent shamans" in different cultures and the "shamanic mass movement, the Ghost Dance, [which] swept through many tribes of Native Americans" to unsuccessfully get rid of the white invaders in the late 19th century), there is progression (e.g., the progress made by shamanism, as shown by the history of healing, etc. by shamans). (WK 2010bb) And the reverse direction also holds true.

Amd in relation to the same-difference principle, if there is similarity in outcome (e.g., the contribution to the curing of ailments in human life, regardless of whether this be done by shamanism or by modern science), there is difference in outcome (e.g., the contribution to the curing of ailments in human life by way of shamanism, especially with more success in psychosomatic cases—but the contribution to the curing of ailments in human life by way of modern science, with more success in physical cases). And the reverse direction also holds true.

Animism, the Spirits, and Cultural Traditions

Another way to evaluate the possibility and desirability of sacredness from the perspective of culture concerns animism, the spirits, and cultural traditions.

The Definition of Animism

The term "animism" is from Latin *anima* to mean "soul, life" and refers to the idea that "souls or spirits exist not only in humans but also in animals, plants, rocks, natural phenomena such as thunder, geographic features such as mountains or rivers, or other entities of the natural environment." (WK 2010dd; R. Segal 2004; AHDEL 2006)

In fact, "animism" can also be extended to "attribute souls to abstract concepts such as words, true names or metaphors in mythology. Animism is particularly widely found in the religions of indigenous peoples, although it is also found in Shinto, and some forms of Hinduism, Sikhism, Pantheism and Neopaganism." (WK 2010dd; N. Bird-David 1999)

Later, "the term was taken and redefined by the anthropologist Sir Edward Tylor in his 1871 book *Primitive Culture*, in which he defined it as being 'the theory of the universal animation of nature.'" (WK 2010dd)

Animism as Distinct from Related Terms

There are, however, some terms which are related to "animism" but are not the same as the latter. Consider three of them below, for illustration.

Firstly, the term "animism" should not be confused with "totemism."

The reason is that, "whilst having similarities to totemism, animism differs in that it, according to the anthropologist Tim Ingold [2000], focuses on individual spirit beings which help to perpetuate life, whilst totemism more typically holds that there is a primary source, such as the land itself, or the ancestors, who provide the basis to life. Certain indigenous religious groups, such as that of the Australian Aborigines are more typically totemic, whilst others, like the Inuit are more typically animistic in their worldview." (WK 2010dd)

Secondly, the term "animism" should not be confused with "pantheism."

The reason is that, "while animists believe everything to be spiritual in nature, they do not necessarily see the spiritual nature of everything in existence as being united, the way pantheists do." (WK 2010dd)

And thirdly, the term "animism" should not be confused with "mythology."

The reason is that, although "a large part of mythology is based upon a belief in souls and spirits—that is, upon animism in its more general sense," it is not true that it is the same as animism, because "many mythologies focus largely on corporeal beings rather than 'spiritual' ones; the latter may even be entirely absent. Stories of transformation, deluge and doom myths, and myths of the origin of death do not necessarily have any animistic basis. As mythology began to include more numerous and complex ideas about a future life and purely spiritual beings, the overlap between mythology and animism widened. However, a rich mythology does not necessarily depend on a belief in many spiritual beings." (WK 2010dd)

Notable Thinkers on Animism

With these distinctions in mind—in European history, there is no lack of contributors to the understanding of animism.

For instance, "philosophers such as Plato, Aristotle and Thomas Aquinas, among others, contemplated the possibility that souls exist in animals, plants and people." (WK 2010dd)

Jean Piaget related the term to his study of child psychology, "in reference to an implicit understanding of the world in a child's mind which assumes all events are the product of intention or consciousness. Piaget explains this with a cognitive inability to distinguish the external world from one's own psyche. Developmental psychology has since established that the distinction of animate vs. inanimate things is an abstraction acquired by learning." (WK 2010dd)

David Hume (1956) made the same point in his *Natural History of Religion* (Section III): "There is a universal tendency among mankind to conceive all beings like themselves, and to transfer to every object those qualities with which they are familiarly acquainted, and of which they are intimately conscious." (WK 2010dd)

And Sigmund Freud (1950) suggested that "'primitive men' came up with the animistic system by observing the phenomena of sleep (including dreams) and of death which so much resembles it, and by attempting to explain those states. Freud regarded it as perfectly natural for man to react to the phenomena which aroused his speculations by forming the idea of the soul and then extending it to objects in the external world." (WK 2010dd)

Animism and Religion

The theoretical relationship between animism and religion can be summarized in four major aspects, as shown below (and in *Table2.5*).

Firstly, animism is related to religion in that "the belief in animism among early humans was the basis for the later evolution of religions." (WK 2010dd)

For instance, for E. B. Tylor, "early humans initially worshipped local deities of nature, in a form of animism. These eventually grew into larger, polytheistic deities, such as gods of the sun and moon." (WK 2001dd)

Secondly, animism is related to religion in that it offers an egalitarian view of dealing with nature in a spiritual way.

For instance, "in many animistic world views found in hunter-gatherer cultures, the human being is often regarded as on a roughly equal footing with other animals, plants, and natural forces. Therefore, it is morally imperative to treat these agents with respect. In this world view, humans are considered a part of nature, rather than superior to, or separate from it. In such societies, ritual is considered essential for survival, as it wins the favor of the spirits of one's source of food, shelter, and fertility and wards off malevolent spirits." (WK 2010dd; F. Fernandez-Armesto 2003)

Thirdly, animism is related to religion in that it offers a view about life after death.

For instance, "most animistic belief systems hold that the spirit survives physical death. In some systems, the spirit is believed to pass to an easier world of abundant game or ever-ripe crops, while in other systems, the spirit remains on earth as a ghost, often malignant. Still other systems combine these two beliefs, holding that the soul must journey to the spirit world without becoming lost and thus wandering as a ghost (e.g., the Navajo religion). Funeral, mourning rituals, and ancestor worship performed by those surviving the deceased are often considered necessary for the successful completion of this journey." (WK 2010dd)

Later, this belief about life after death was further developed into "the practice of offering food, lighting fires, etc., at the grave, at first, maybe, as an act of friendship or filial piety, later as an act of ancestor worship. The simple offering of food or shedding of blood at the grave develops into an elaborate system of sacrifice. Even where ancestor worship is not found, the desire to provide the dead with comforts in the future life may lead to the sacrifice of wives, slaves, animals, and so on, to the breaking or burning of objects at the grave or to the provision of the ferryman's toll: a coin put in the mouth of the corpse to pay the traveling expenses of the soul." (WK 2010dd)

Even then, "all is not finished with the passage of the soul to the land of the dead. The soul may return to avenge its death by helping to discover the murderer, or to wreak vengeance for itself. There is a widespread belief that those who die a violent death become malignant spirits and endanger the lives of those who come near the haunted spot. In Malay folklore, the woman who dies in childbirth becomes a pontianak, a vampire-like spirit who threatens the life of human beings. People resort to magical or religious means of repelling spiritual dangers from such malignant spirits." (WK 2010dd)

In fact, "the practice of head shrinking among Jivaroan and Urarina peoples derives from an animistic belief that if the spirit of one's mortal enemies, i.e., the nemesis of ones being, are not trapped within the head, they can escape slain bodies. After the spirit transmigrates to another body, they can take the form of a predatory animal and even exact revenge." (WK 2010dd)

And fourthly, animism is related to religion in that it offers a view about the diversity of spirits in the cosmos.

For instance, "modern Neopagans, especially Eco-Pagans, sometimes like to describe themselves as animists, meaning that they respect the diverse community of living beings and spirits with whom humans share the world/cosmos." (WK 2010dd; M. Adler 2006; J. Higginbotham 2002)

In fact, "polytheist Pagans may extend the idea of many gods and goddesses to encompass the many spirits of nature, such as those embodied in holy wells, mountains and sacred springs. While some of these many spirits may be seen as fitting into rough categories and sharing similarities with one another, they are also respected as separate individuals." (WK 2010dd)

Animism in Different Cultural Traditions

The theoretical relationship between animism and religion is abstract enough, since in practice, animism has different expressions in different cultural traditions. Consider a few below, for illustration.

For instance, in many African traditional religions, "'animism' is a term that is used as shorthand to describe a richer and more complex interplay between elders, ancestors and nature spirits." (WK 2010dd)

In Eastern religions, "Shinto, the traditional religion of Japan, is highly animistic. In Shinto, spirits of nature, or kami, exist everywhere, from the major (such as the goddess of the sun), who can be considered polytheistic, to the minor, who are more likely to be seen as a form of animism. There are some Hindu groups which may be considered animist. The coastal Karnataka has a different tradition of praying the spirits for their God." (WK 2010dd)

In Native American religions, many of them are "fundamentally animistic. See, for example, the Lakota Sioux prayer Mitakuye Oyasin. The Haudenausaunee Thanksgiving Address, which can take an hour to recite, directs thanks towards every being—plant, animal and other." (WK 2010dd)

And in new religious movements, "many, though not all, Neopagan religions, practice a form of animism. Most followers of Germanic Neopaganism believe in spirits that are, or live in Nature and technology, which stems from their effort to reconstruct historical Norse Paganism. The New Age movement commonly purports animism in the form of the existence of nature spirits and fairies." (WK 2010dd)

The Criticisms of Animism

Impressive as the different versions of animism are, there are a lot of criticisms against the discourse and practice of animism in general. Consider three major ones below, for illustration.

Firstly, one criticism of animism is that, as Edward Tylor was blunt in saying it, "such a view was 'childish' and typical of 'cognitive underdevelopment,' and…it was therefore common in 'primitive' peoples such as those living in hunter gatherer societies." (WK 2010dd; N. Bird-David 1999)

However, "some anthropologists, such as Nurit Bird-Davis [1999] have criticised the Tylorian concept of animism, believing it to be outdated." (WK 2010dd)

Secondly, another criticism of animism is that its religious views about the cosmos cannot be proved, be they about the egalitarian view of humans with nature, the existene of life after death, the diversity of spirits in the cosmos, etc.

And finally (or thirdly), still another criticism of animism is that there are so many different versions of animism in the world that it is not clear if it is inherently coherent as a whole.

For instance, although some "lists of phenomena [e.g., "trance states," "dreams and hallucinations," etc.] from the contemplation of which 'the savage' was led to believe in animism have been given by Sir E. B. Tylor, Herbert Spencer, Andrew Lang and others"—"an animated controversy arose between the former [and others] as to the priority of their respective lists." (WK 2010dd)

Or in another case about life after death, "in some systems, the spirit is believed to pass to an easier world of abundant game or ever-ripe crops, while in other systems, the spirit remains on earth as a ghost, often malignant," whereas others try to combine the two. (WK 2010dd)

From a Broader Horizon

Yet, from a broader horizon, these criticisms of animism do not mean to dismiss it but to show us the two opposing sides of the debate, such that the possibility and desirability of sacredness (from the perspective of culture with animism as a case study here) is not to the extent that its respective defenders would like us to believe.

Furthermore, the debate on animism reveals something valuable about the ontological principles in existential dialectics, and good examples include the absoluteness-relativeness principle, the predictability-unpredictability principle, the explicability-inexplicability principle, the finiteness-transfiniteness principle, the preciseness-vagueness principle, the simpleness-complicatedness principle, the openness-hiddenness principle, the denseness-emptiness principle, the slowness-quickness principle, the expansion-contraction principle, the theory-praxis principle, the convention-novelty principle, the evolution-transformation principle, the symmetry-asymmetry principle, the softness-hardness principle, the regression-progression principle, and the same-difference principle.

For instance, in relation to the absoluteness-relativeness principle, if there is absolute viewpoint (e.g., the absolute view in the Abrahamic tradition that there exists only one God), there is relativeness (e.g., what is true for the Abrahamic tradition in regard to the existence of only one God is not so for animism in regard to the existence of many spirits in the cosmos). And the reverse direction also holds true.

In relation to the predictability-unpredictability principle, if there is predictability (e.g., the predictable tendency of animists to believe in life after death), there is unpredictability (e.g, the more difficult task to predict where exactly the spirit of a deceased will actually go, since "in some systems, the spirit is believed to pass to an easier world of abundant game or ever-ripe crops, while in other systems, the spirit remains on earth as a ghost, often malignant," whereas others try to combine the two). And the reverse direction also holds true.

In relation to the explicability-inexplicability principle, if there is explicability (e.g, the explanation by animists that humans are just part of nature on the egalitarian basis of many spirits in the cosmos, both human and non-human), there is inexplicability (e.g., the lack of sufficient explanation by animists of why some spirits cannot be superior than others, or why this egalitarian view is necessarily true). And the reverse direction also holds true.

In relation to the finiteness-transfiniteness principle, if there is finiteness (e.g., the finite number of years that the body of an animal like a human being can remain alive), there is transfiniteness (e.g., the transfinite number of years that the soul of a human body can live, even after the decomposition of the body after death, in accordance to animism). And the reverse direction also holds true.

In relation to the preciseness-vagueness principle, if there is preciseness (e.g., the precise identification of "trance states," "dreams and hallucinations," etc. as the things that animists engage in), there is vagueness (e.g., the vagueness about the priority of the things on the list, since scholars like "E. B. Tylor, Herbert Spencer, Andrew Lang and others" disagreed "as to the priority of their respective lists"). And the reverse direction also holds true.

In relation to the simpleness-complicatedness principle, if there is simpleness (e.g,. the relatively simple analysis of animism in terms of its major features as shown in the relationship between animism and religion), there is complicatedness (e.g., the relatively complicated analysis of animism as revealed in the problems pointed out by the critics). And the reverse direction also holds true.

In relation to the openness-hiddenness principle, if there is openness (e.g., the open exploration of the relationship between animism and the "primitive" nature of the beliefs, as pointed out by Tylor), there is hiddenness (e.g., the hidden bias in Tylor's view, with its European ethnocentrism, for the critics). And the reverse direction also holds true.

In relation to the denseness-emptiness principle, if there is denseness (e.g., the relatively denser concentration of animists in hunting-gathering societies), there is emptiness (e.g., the relatively less dense, or more empty, concentration of animists in industrial societies). And the reverse direction also holds true.

In relation to the slowness-quickness principle, if there is slowness (e.g., the relatively slower readiness of an atheist to practice ancestor worship), there is quickness (e.g., the relatively quicker readness of an animist to practice ancetor worship). And the reverse direction also holds true.

In relation to the expansion-contraction principle, if there is expansion (e.g., the relative rise of the organized versions of religion like the Abrahamic tradition in agricultural and industrial societies), there is contraction (e.g., the relative decline of the animistic versions of religion in agricultural and industrial societies). And the reverse direction also holds true.

In relation to the theory-praxis principle, if there is theory (e.g., the theoretical construction of animism in relation to its views on the cosmos, life after death, and the diversity of spirits), there is praxis (e.g., the practical application of animism for the practices of ancestor worship, rituals to honor animals, etc.). And the reverse direction also holds true.

In relation to the convention-novelty principle, if there is convention (e.g., the conventional wisdom by ancient animists that "souls or spirits exist not only in humans but also in animals, plants, rocks,…and other entities of the natural environment"), there is novelty (e.g., the alternative novel challenge to this ancient animistic conventional wisdom by the followers of the New Age Movement in our time who reconstruct ancient animism by believing "in spirits that are, or live in…technology" too, not just in nature). (WK 2010dd) And the reverse direction also holds true.

In relation to the evolution-transformation principle, if there is evolution (e.g., the natural evolution of humans to live with nature in the state of nature), there is transformation (e.g., the technical transformation of human living with nature by the invention of a religion along the animistic way for ancestor worship, rituals to honor animals, etc.). And the reverse direction also holds true.

In relation to the symmetry-asymmetry principle, if there is symmetry (e.g., the co-existence of different versions of religion in history), there is asymmetry (e.g., the greater influence of animism in hunting-gathering societies—but the rise of organized religions in agricultural and industrial societies). And the reverse direction also holds true.

In relation to the softness-hardness principle, if there is softness (e.g., the egalitarian view of humans "on a roughly equal footing with other animals, plants, and natural forces," as taught in animism), there is hardness (e.g., the hunting and killing of animals by humans for their consumption, as permitted in animism). And the reverse direction also holds true.

In relation to the regression-progression principle, if there is regression (e.g., the regression made by animism, as shown by the problems pointed out by the critics), there is progression (e.g., the progress made by animism to help us understand the close relationship between humans and others in nature). And the reverse direction also holds true.

And in relation to the same-difference principle, if there is similarity in outcome (e.g., the contribution to the regulation and control of human beliefs and behaviors, regardless of whether this be done by way of animism or of organized religions like Christianity), there is difference in outcome (e.g., the contribution to the regulation and control of human beliefs and behaviors by way of animism for a more egalitarian treatment of nature—but the contribution to the regulation and control of human beliefs and behaviors by way of organized religions like Christianity for humans to play the role of stewardship of nature in an inegalitarian way). And the reverse direction also holds true.

The Limitation of Sacredness

This comprehensive analysis of the possibility and desirability of sacredness, from the perspectives of the mind, nature, society, and culture, enhances our understanding of the different ways in which sacredness is both possible and desirable, but not to the extent that the spokespersons from each side would like us to believe.

Sacredness thus has its limitation, just as it has its importance too, as another side of the same mirror.

But this is only one part of a larger story, since the other side of the same mirror is secularness, the opposite of sacredness. Since this chapter already deals with sacredness, the next chapter will therefore address the issue of secularness.

These dual analyses are vital, because those on the side of sacredness often understimate secularness merely as the opposite of sacredness without really appreciating it from the vantage point of secularness too.

With this in mind, let's now turn to Chapter Three for the study of secularness and its faults—for which we now turn to chapter three.

Table 2.1. Sacredness and Its Limits

- **Sacredness and the Mind**
  —Ex: faith, reason, and religion
  —Ex: magical thinking, and religion

- **Sacredness and Nature**
  —Ex: religious cosmology, and the teleological argument
  —Ex: evolutionary theory, and religion

- **Sacredness and Society**
  —Ex: religious conversion, and the politics of rights
  —Ex: new religious movements, and the sociology of religion

- **Sacredness and Culture**
  —Ex: shamanism, the outer-world, and the role of culture
  —Ex: animism, the spirits, and cultural traditions

Notes: The examples in the categories are solely illustrative (not exhaustive), and the comparison is relative (not absolute), nor are they necessarily mutually exclusive. And some can be easily re-classified elsewhere. As generalities, they allow exceptions.
Source: A summary of Ch.2 of *FPHR*

Table 2.2. The Comparison and Contrast Between Magic and Religion (Part I)

• **The Similarities between Magic and Religion**

—For Mauss: "Both use similar types of rites, materials, social roles and relationships to accomplish aims and engender belief. They both operate on similar principles, in particular those of consecration and sacredness of objects and places, interaction with supernatural powers mediated by an expert, employment of symbolism, sacrifice, purification and representation in rites, and the importance of tradition and continuation of knowledge." (WK 2010r)

—For Mauss: "Magic and religion also share a collective character and totality of belief. The rules and powers of each are determined by the community's ideals and beliefs and so may slowly evolve. Additionally neither supports partial belief. Belief in one aspect of the phenomena necessitates belief in the whole, and each incorporates structural loopholes to accommodate contradictions." (WK 2010r)

—For Tambiah: "Magic, science, and religion all have their own 'quality of rationality,' and have been influenced by politics and ideology….[T]he perceptions of these three ideas have evolved over time as a result of Western thought. The lines of demarcation between these ideas depend upon the perspective of a variety of anthropologists…." (WK 2010r)

—In general: "Related to both magic and prayer [in religion] is…supplication. This involves a prayer, or even a sacrifice to a supernatural being or god. This god or being is then asked to intervene on behalf of the person offering the prayer." (WK 2010r)

industry (Chs.2-3 of *FHC*)

(continued on next page)

Table 2.2. The Comparison and Contrast Between Magic and Religion (Part II)

- **The Differences between Magic and Religion**

—For Mauss: "Magic is secretive and isolated, and rarely performed publicly in order to protect and to preserve occult knowledge. Religion is predictable and proscribed and is usually performed openly in order to impart knowledge to the community." (WK 2010r)

—For Mauss: "In practice, magic differs from religion in desired outcome. Religion seeks to satisfy moral and metaphysical ends, while magic is a functional art which often seeks to accomplish tangible results. In this respect magic resembles technology and science....Yet,...science is based in experimentation and development, while magic is an "a priori belief." (WK 2010r)

—For Tambiah: "Magic is a strictly ritualistic action that implements forces and objects outside the realm of the gods and the supernatural. These objects and events are said to be intrinsically efficacious, so that the supernatural is unnecessary. To some, including the Greeks, magic was considered a "proto-science." (WK 2010r)

—For Tambiah: "Whereas science could be revised and developed through rational thought, magic was seen as less scientific and systematic than science and religion, making it the least respected of the three." (WK 2010r)

—For Malinowski: "The difference is that magic is more about the personal power of the individual and religion is about faith in the power of God. Magic is also something that is passed down over generations to a specific group while religion is more broadly available to the community." (WK 2010r)

—In general: "Prayer [in religion] requires the assent of a deity with an independent will, who can deny the request. Magic, by contrast is thought to be effective...by virtue of the operation itself," "by the strength of the magician's will," or "because the magician believes he can command the spiritual beings addressed by his spells." (WK 2010r)

Notes: The examples in the categories are solely illustrative (not exhaustive), and the comparison is relative (not absolute), nor are they necessarily mutually exclusive. And some can be easily re-classified elsewhere. As generalities, they allow exceptions.

Source: From *Sec. 2.2.2* of *FPHR*. See book for citations.

Table 2.3. The Problems with the Argument from Design

• Firstly, one criticism of the teleological argument (especially in relation to "the anthropic principle" and its "fine-tuned universe" version) is that the statistics as shown by its ideologues are faulty or manipulative at best.

• Secondly, another criticism of the teleological argument is that "complexity does not imply design." (WK 2010u)

• Thirdly, still another criticism of the teleological argument is that it confuses "a powerful intelligent designer" with "a God." (WK 2010u)

• Fourthly, one more criticism of the teleological argument is that it can lead to "an infinite regress." (WK 2010u)

• And fifthly, still another criticism of the teleological argument is that it is "incoherent." (WK 2010u)

Notes: The examples are solely illustrative (not exhaustive), and the comparison is relative (not absolute), nor are they necessarily mutually exclusive. And some can be easily re-classified elsewhere. As generalities, they allow exceptions.
Source: From *Sec. 2.3.1* of *FPHR*. See book for more details and citations.

Table 2.4. The Debate on the Evolutionary Psychology of Religion (Part I)

• **Religion as an Adaptation**

—For instance, "social solidarity theories" regard "religion as having evolved to enhance cooperation and cohesion within groups. Group membership in turn provides benefits which can enhance an individual's chances for survival and reproduction." (WK 2010w; R. Sosis 200)

—In "social solidarity theories," one aim is "to explain the painful or dangerous nature of many religious rituals. Costly-signaling theory suggests that such rituals might serve as public and hard to fake signals that an individual's commitment to the group is sincere. Since there would be a considerable benefit in trying to cheat the system—taking advantage of group living benefits without taking on any possible costs—the ritual would not be something simple that can be taken lightly." (WK 2010w) R. Sosis 2003)

—A good example is "warfare," as "Richard Sosis, Howard C. Kress (2007), and James S. Boster carried out a cross-cultural survey which demonstrated that men in societies which engage in war do submit to the costliest rituals." (WK 2010w)

—Another example concerns "positive associations between religious practice and health and longevity; for instance, Harold G. Koenig (2001) and Harvey J. Cohen in their "100 evidence-based studies" found that "79% showed a positive influence." (WK 2010w)

—However, for the critics like Richard P. Sloan, "there is no really good compelling evidence that there is a relationship between religious involvement and health," so "there is still debate over the validity of these findings, and they do not necessarily prove a direct cause-and-effect relationship between religion and health." (WK 2010w; M. Duenwald 2002)

(continued on next page)

Table 2.4. The Debate on the Evolutionary Psychology of Religion (Part II)

- **Religion as an Exaptation**
  —For instance, Stephen Jay Gould (1991) and Elisabeth Vrba "proposed the term exaptation…to mean 'features that now enhance fitness, but were not built by natural selection for their current role.' Gould and R. C. Lewontin compared such features to spandrels, 'an architectural term for spaces left over between structural elements of a building.' A more complete explanation of this metaphor can be found in Gould and Lewontin's 1979 paper, 'The Spandrels of San Marco and the Panglossian Paradigm: A Critique of the Adaptationist Programme.'"
  —However, for the critics, "Gould…does not himself select a definite trait which he thinks was actually acted on by natural selection" which then subsequently led to the by-product of religion, although Gould (1991) appealed to "Freud's suggestion that our large brains, which evolved for other reasons, led to consciousness. The beginning of consciousness forced humans to deal with the concept of personal mortality. Religion may have been one solution to this problem." (WK 2010W)
  —In light of this problem, "Pierre Lienard [2006] and Pascal Boyer suggest that humans have evolved a 'hazard-precaution system' which allows us to detect potential threats in the environment and attempt to respond appropriately. Several features of ritual behaviors, often a major feature of religion, trigger this system. These include the occasion for the ritual, often the prevention or elimination of danger or evil, the harm believed to result from nonperformance of the ritual, and the detailed proscriptions for proper performance of the ritual. Lienard and Boyer discuss the possibility that a sensitive hazard-precaution system itself may have provided fitness benefits, and that religion then 'associates individual, unmanageable anxieties with coordinated action with others and thereby makes them more tolerable or meaningful.'" (WK 2010w)

Notes: The examples in the categories are solely illustrative (not exhaustive), and the comparison is relative (not absolute), nor are they necessarily mutually exclusive. And some can be easily re-classified elsewhere. As generalities, they allow exceptions.
Source: From *Sec. 2.3.2* of *FPHR*. See book for citations.

Table 2.5. The Relationshisp between Animism and Religion

• Firstly, animism is related to religion in that "the belief in animism among early humans was the basis for the later evolution of religions." (WK 2010dd)

• Secondly, animism is related to religion in that it offers an egalitarian view of dealing with nature in a spiritual way.

• Thirdly, animism is related to religion in that it offers a view about life after death.

• And fourthly, animism is related to religion in that it offers a view about the diversity of spirits in the cosmos.

Notes: The examples in the categories are solely illustrative (not exhaustive), and the comparison is relative (not absolute), nor are they necessarily mutually exclusive. And some can be easily re-classified elsewhere. As generalities, they allow exceptions.
Source: From *Sec. 2.5.2* of *FPHR*. See book for more details and citations.

• Part Three •

Secularness

CHAPTER 3
SECULARNESS AND ITS FAULTS

> Specialists without spirit, sensualists without heart; this nullity imagines that it has attained a level of civilization never before achieved.
> —Max Weber (1930)

The Promise of Secularness

Sacredness and secularness are two opposites. If sacredness is important, it is also limited. And if secularness has its promise, it likewise has its pitfall.

This chapter here is to explore these dual faces of secularness (whereas the double sides of sacredness were already addressed in Chapter Two).

A good way to explore the dual faces of secularness is by way of the evaluation of the extent to which secularness is in fact both possible and desirabe.

Thus, this chapter is to provide a comprehensive analysis of secularness in the context of religion from the four perspectives of the mind, nature, society, and culture (in accordance to my sophisticated methodological holism, as explained in *Sec. 1.9*).

With this aim in mind, this chapter is organized in four main sections, in relation to (3.2) secularness and the mind, (3.3) secularness and nature, (3.4) secularness and society, and (3.5) secularness and culture—to be examined in what follows, respectively (and summarized in *Table 3.1*).

Secularness and the Mind

Secularness, when examined from the perspective of the mind, can cast some light on its possibility and desirability, and this can be shown by way of two case studies, namely, (3.2.1) mental delusion, and the secular origin of religions, and (3.2.2) power drive, developmental stages, and the search for faith—to be addressed hereafter, in what follows.

Mental Delusion, and the Secular Origin of Religions

A good way to examine secularness from the perspective of the mind is to address the disturbing relationship between mental delusion and the secular origin of religious experiences.

There are quite a number of scholars who have researched on this topic.

Mental Disorders and the Temporal Lobe

For instance, back in 1954, "Canadian neurologist, Wilder Penfield, reported that our temporal lobe is the only part of the brain from which one could elicit, by physical stimulation alone, a feelingful memory reaction accompanied by the possibility of an interpretative response" related to various "psychic" and "spiritual" phenomena. (J. Speyrer 2010)

Penfield then realized that "the brain's temporal lobe was the location of the key hole or entry point to the release of 'referenced material' from other sections of the brain. The temporary removal of temporal lobe inhibition is what allows a large variety of 'psychic' or 'spiritual' phenomena to become conscious, including out-of-body and near-death experiences, alien abductions, past lives experiences, one's earlier repressed traumatic memories and the mystical or God experience." (J. Speyrer 2010)

Those who experienced "psychic" or "spiritual" phenomena like this were found to possess "a higher than average ability…to have one or more of the following characteristics" of mental disorders (and other kinds of suffering). (J. Speyrer 2010)

- Ex: "experience deja vu frequently"
- Ex: "sense the presence of spirits"
- Ex: "often feel that they are not alone"
- Ex: "have a history of hallucinogenic/psychedelic drug use"
- Ex: "have lots of sex or none at all"
- Ex: "frequently engage in repetitive prayers"
- Ex: "have limbic epileptic seizures"
- Ex: "do vipassana meditation"
- Ex: "have kuldalini-type experiences"
- Ex: "think often of suicide"
- Ex: "find that being in love is all consuming"

- Ex: "have been sexually or physically abused as children"
- Ex: "be homosexual"
- Ex: "be under deep hypnosis"
- Ex: "have anxiety attacks"
- Ex: "have a seemingly disproportionate fear of death"
- Ex: "fast frequently"
- Ex: "have endured recent sleep loss"
- Ex: suffer from "starvation"
- Ex: "are on their death bed"
- Ex: "being at high altitudes, as there is less oxygen there....Remember how cartoons often show gurus residing on tops of mountains?...Having less oxygen than normal available to breathe helps to induce spiritual and regressive experiences"
- Ex: suffer from "physical aging of the brain"
- Ex: "having had a traumatic birth"

In fact, the "Spiritual Aptitude Test" as designed by Todd Murphy includes some of these mental disorders. (J. Speyrer 2010)

One should not underestimate these abnormal states of mind, because, as Stanislav Grof pointed out, "these non-ordinary states of mind can be the beginning phases of emergences of spirituality. These spiritual emergences can become emergencies when they take on the characteristics of functional psychoses. Many such patients are often given large doses of anti-psychotic medication to stop their symptoms instead of being given an opportunity to regress and feel the real origins of their sufferings." (J. Speyrer 2010)

Medication and Therapy for Healing

This understanding of the relationship between mental disorders and the abnormal states of mind is the first step towards healing, with the help of medication, therapy, and other means.

For instance, John Speyrer (2010) thus confessed in his article: "Ten years ago, I experienced olfactory hallucinations which were accompanied by depression and a severe fear of dying. The fear was triggered when I read that the physical symptoms I was having were typical of those with a brain tumor."

Fortunately, as Speyrer (2010) continued, "the MRI and catscan revealed I did not have a brain tumor, but the repressed trauma of almost dying during my birth had become unrepressed due to my fear of having a brain tumor. I began suffering from severe anxiety/depression, with a quirky symptom of experiencing hallucinogenic odors. The olfactory hallucinations occurred about twice each week during a six weeks' period."

Worse, as Speyrer (2010) thus wrote, "I had begun smelling ether, freshly baked bread, cake, acetone and other non-existent odors. I surmise that the 'kitchen' odors were disinhibited temporal lobe memories from my childhood and the ether/acetone odors were associated with childhood traumas of two early surgeries as well as perhaps from olfactory memories of my mother's use of nail polish remover respectively."

However, Speyrer later recovered when he was "able to bring down…[the] psychiatric symptoms with primal-oriented regression therapy" and other medical means. (J. Speyrer 2010)

Of course, how much time a successful therapy needs for a given patient varies from case to case; quite often, however, if the patients "have an opening to their traumas…much additional work over long periods of time is required to resolve their ever unfolding issues and psychosomatic diseases." (J. Speyrer 2010)

Disinhibited Temporal Lobes and Religious Experiences

Stories like this about the traumas suffered by Speyrer and others thus point to the close relationship between disinhibited temporal lobes and religious experiences.

For instance, it was subsequently found that "the disinhibited temporal lobes and its structures allow for the access of early traumas" and therefrom increase "the opportunity to intensify the extraordinary potential for the God or Jesus, Allah or Vishnu experience" as "a built-in characteristic of brain function." (J. Speyrer 2010)

In fact, for some scholars like Michael Persinger (1983), "the use of the temporal lobe potentials may make it possible, in the future, for developing selective activations as specific treatments for psychiatric disorders. Spontaneous healings of long existent emotional and physical ills are commonly reported in the autobiographies of medieval mystics and well as in the lives of more modern ones." (J. Speyrer 2010)

As Persinger wrote, "in general, the more severe the disturbance, the more intense the God Experience." (J. Speyrer 2010) In fact, "the same effects can have their source in other transcendental experiences such as out-of-body feelings, near-death experiences and even by the electrical stimulation of the brain's temporal lobes." (J. Speyrer 2010; W. Penfield 1955)

Other "anomalous events, such as…apparitions of deceased loved ones, appearances of ghosts or demons, alien abductions, etc. are all associated with temporal lobe disinihibitions but as mentioned are not all wondrous, joyful, and exciting. Some such events can be quite disconcerting. Some who experience negative near death experiences truly believe that they are having a foretaste of the literal hell which awaits them." (J. Speyrer 2010; C. Bache 1996)

It is thus no wonder that, "the temporal lobe, which is the portion of the brain which mediates the sense of self, the sense of the visitor experience, the religious experience, and one's own previously repressed biographical memory with its accompanying emotion, has been named by some as the very seat of the God impulse." (J. Speyrer 2010)

The Case Study of the Visitor Experience

A good illustration of this relationship between disinhibited temporal lobes and religious experiences concerns "the visitor experience" (when "the visitor" can be a god, a demon, a spirit, etc.) as a case study.

For instance, "the bible recounts harassments of Jesus by Satan on three separate occasions. Mother Teresa of Calcutta, during a decades long 'dark night of the soul' trial, towards the end of her life, requested and received an exorcism from the Catholic church. Demonic 'presences' are not surprising....It is a normal and natural happening to a disinhibited temporal lobe and is usually proportional to the severity of repressed traumatic material (which temporarily becomes less well defended). Some institutionalized temporal lobe psychotics have daily communications with negative and positive spiritual entities." (J. Speyrer 2010)

In the case of "negative" spiritual entities, "seeming attempts by malevolent 'demonic spirits' to sabotage the prayer life of mystics can and do occur. These minor and major trials consist of negative 'sensed presences' and are self interpreted as demonic influences, e.g., Martin Luther throwing an inkwell at a demon. Sometimes they arise during the healing journey of the mystic as they continue their quest for an intimate experience with the deity or with holy persons." (J. Speyrer 2010)

Individuals who experienced "spiritual trials" like this often "had to temporarily endure profoundly disconcerting states of mind and body....Some had completely lost their ability to pray, others suffered continuous severe psychosomatic physical pains and illnesses and endured periods of painful alienation from God." (J. Speyrer 2010) Two well-known cases like this concern Teresa of Avila and John of the Cross. (J. Speyrer 2010; C. Bache 1985 & 1991)

In any event, "over the ages these touches by the divine have been called by many names: Ecstatic moment, mystical experience, God experience, transcendental unconsciousness, getting it, felt shift, objective consciousness, absolute tao, satori, peak experience, deep knowing, shamanic ecstasy, intensity experience, overmind, unclouded vision, divine intuition, luminosity, samadhi, peak state, mystic vision, divine hallucination, divine revelation, flash point, gestalt formation, spiritual epiphany, cosmic consciousness, and born-again experience." (J. Speyrer 2010)

Surely, "the list of their names is endless but these experiences all have the same origin. Their building blocks comprise our earliest selves. A dose of a psychedelic drug, such as LSD, could also permanently shift our balance into the sublime, but with proper stimulation our own brain chemicals can suffice to loosen our unconscious mind's shackles and thereby transport and transform us." (J. Speyrer 2010)

Michael A. Persinger, for instance, had precisely done some lab experiments with his subjects on this trick by "stimulat[ing]…the temporal lobes of the brain artificially with a magnetic field using a device nicknamed the 'God helmet,'" and "was able to artificially induce religious experiences along with near-death experiences and ghost sightings." (WK 2010ee; M. Shermer 1999a)

Persinger thus concluded: "Against data, social opinion, and sometimes direct confrontation that the experience was a lie, people will still persist (in the) validity of their own perceptions….I cannot overemphasize the importance of the sense of conviction produced by these experiences. Following these small alterations in the temporal lobe, the person becomes convinced that what he or she has experienced is absolutely right. No amount of rational conversation or data can sway the opinion." (J. Speyrer 2010)

These consciousness shifts can be quite powerful, to the extent that "sociopaths may acquire moral consciences. Some individuals even lose their normal interest in sexuality as the prurient no longer holds their attention. The brain has become washed and the old way of life no longer beckons them to follow its previously alluring, but compulsive, act outs. Magnanimity replaces self-centeredness. Brain circuits are rerouted or physically changed and enjoy a new way of looking at life….For some, the changes are much less dramatic than having a God experience, but the changes they perceive in themselves are nonetheless rewarding, undoubtedly, both to themselves and to their families." (J. Speyrer 2010)

In the end, for Arnold Mandell (1980), these changes constitute the "manifestations of the drive-arrest-release sequence in biogenic amine inhibitory systems, releasing temporal lobe limbic, hippocampal-septal hypersynchrony that lasts for long periods of afterdischarge. They all may reflect the neurobiological mechanisms underlying transcendence, God in the brain." (J. Speyrer 2010)

A Response from a Known Critic

Of course, this secular interpretation of the origin of religious experiences is not well accepted by the defenders of religion in general.

An excellent illustration of this is none other than the response by Keith Ward (2006), in regard to this new intellectual fashion about "God is in the brain."

Here is Ward's interesting counter-argument. He first "quotes the definition [of the word 'delusion'] in the *Oxford Companion to Mind* as 'a fixed, idiosyncratic belief, unusual in the culture to which the person belongs,' and notes that '[n]ot all false opinions are delusions.'" (WK 2010ee)

Then, Ward "characterizes a delusion as a 'clearly false opinion, especially as a symptom of a mental illness,' an 'irrational belief' that is 'so obviously false that all reasonable people would see it as mistaken.' He then says that belief in God is different, since '[m]ost great philosophers have believed in God, and they are rational people.' He argues that '[a]ll that is needed to refute the claim that religious belief is a delusion is one clear example of someone who exhibits a high degree of rational ability, who functions well in the ordinary affairs of life…and who can produce a reasonable and coherent defense of their beliefs' and claims that there are many such people, 'including some of the most able philosophers and scientists in the world today.'" (WK 2010ee)

Maneuvering between Two Sides

This counter-argument by Ward is not used here to dismiss the "God is in the brain" argument altogther but is intended to show us the two opposing sides of the debate, such that the possibility and desirability of secularness (from the perspective of the mind with mental delusion and the temporal lobe as a case study here) is not to the extent that its respective defenders would like us to believe.

In addition, the analysis of mental delusion and the temporal lobe can teach us an invaluable lesson about the ontological principles in existential dialectics, and good examples include the absoluteness-relativeness principle, the predictability-unpredictability principle, the explicability-inexplicability principle, the preciseness-vagueness principle, the simpleness-complicatedness principle, the openness-hiddenness principle, the denseness-emptiness principle, the slowness-quickness principle, the expansion-contraction principle, the theory-praxis principle, the convention-novelty principle, the evolution-transformation principle, the symmetry-asymmetry principle, the regression-progression principle, and the same-difference principle.

For instance, in relation to the absoluteness-relativeness principle, if there is absolute viewpoint (e.g., the absolute view of scholars like Mandell that "God is in the brain"), there is relative counterpart (e.g., what is true for scholars like Mandell that "God is in the brain" is not so for the critics like Ward). And the reverse direction also holds true.

In relation to the predictability-unpredictability principle, if there is predictability (e.g., the predictable tendency of those who experience "psychic" or "spiritual" phenomena to have "a higher than average ability…to have one or more…characteristics" of mental disorders, in accordance to researchers like Penfield and others), there is unpredictability (e.g., the more difficult task to predict, if viewed from the vantage point of Penfield and others, the particular combination of mental disorders that an individual who experiences "psychic" or "spiritual" phenomena really has at a given point of time). And the reverse direction also holds true.

In relation to the explicability-inexplicability principle, if there is explicability (e.g., the explanation of the experience of the "psychic" or "spiritual" phenomena on the basis of "disinhibited temporal lobes"), there is inexplicability (e.g., the lack of sufficient explanation, if viewed within the psychobiology of religion, of why some individuals who believe in God or something like that are "some of the most able philosophers and scientists in the world today" without mental delusion at all, as pointed out by Ward). And the reverse direction also holds true.

In relation to the preciseness-vagueness principle, if there is preciseness (e.g., the precise identification of the experience of "psychic" or "spiritual" phenomena in "disinhibited temporal lobes"), there is vagueness (e.g., the vagueness in the term like "psychic" or "spiritual," since it can mean different things to different people, like "ecstatic moment, mystical experience, God experience, transcendental unconsciousness, getting it, felt shift, objective consciousness, absolute tao, satori, peak experience, deep knowing, shamanic ecstasy, intensity experience, overmind, unclouded vision, divine intuition, luminosity, samadhi, peak state, mystic vision, divine hallucination, divine revelation, flash point, gestalt formation, spiritual epiphany, cosmic consciousness, and born-again experience"). And the reverse direction also holds true.

In relation to the simpleness-complicatedness principle, if there is simpleness (e.g., the relatively simple analysis of the linkage between the experience of "psychic" or "spiritual" phenomena and "disinhibited temporal lobes"), there is complicatedness (e.g., the relatively more complicated analysis of the linkage by way of questioning the usage of "mental delusion," since '[n]ot all false opinions are delusions,'" as pointed out by the critics like Ward). And the reverse direction also holds true.

In relation to the openness-hiddenness principle, if there is openness (e.g., the open exploration by Speyrer to understand his "olfactory hallucinations...accompanied by depression and a severe fear of dying" with the "physical symptoms...typical of those with a brain tumor"), there is hiddenness (e.g., the hidden nature of Speyrer's physical symptoms which can be traced back to his "childhood traumas of two early surgeries"). And the reverse direction also holds true.

In relation to the denseness-emptiness principle, if there is denseness (e.g., the relatively denser concentration of the experiences of "psychic" or "spiritual" phenemena in individuals with mental delusion, according to those like Penfield, Speyrer, and others), there is emptiness (e.g., the relatively less dense, or more empty, concentration of the experiences of "psychic" or "spiritual" phenemena in "some of the most able philosophers and scientists in the world today," according to Ward). And the reverse direction also holds true.

In relation to the slowness-quickness principle, if there is slowness (e.g., the relatively slower readiness of individuals who had their temporal lobes stimulated by Persinger in the experiment to question the conviction of what they experienced as true), there is quickness (e.g., the relatively quicker readiness of someone like Persinger to question the conviction of what his subjects experienced in his experiment). And the reverse direction also holds true.

In relation to the expansion-contraction principle, if there is expansion (e.g, the relative expansion of the influence of the psychobiology of religion in our times), there is contraction (e.g, the relative decline of the influence of fundamentalist organized religions in our times). And the reverse direction also holds true.

In relation to the theory-praxis principle, if there is theory (e.g., the theoretical construction of the psychobiology of religion), there is praxis (e.g,., the practical application of the psychobiology of religion for anti-faith politics, as Bunting once argued that "the books [by scholars like Richard Dawkins, Daniel Dennett, Sam Harris and Christopher Hitchens] are 'deeply political,' sharing a 'loathing' of the role of religion in U.S. politics"). (WK 2010k) And the reverse direction also holds true.

In relation to the convention-novelty principle, if there is convention (e.g., the conventional wisdom in organized religions about the validity of the belief in God), there is novelty (e.g, the alternative novel challenge to the conventional wisdom about the validity of the belief in God by those in the psychobiology of religion, in that "God is in the brain"). And the reverse direction also holds true.

In relation to the evolution-transformation principle, if there is evolution (e.g., the natural evolution of humans to live in the state of nature with their fear of, or awe toward, the powerful forces of nature, at times with some mental delusion about them), there is transformation (e.g., the technical tranfromation of human relation with nature by the invention of the psychobiology of religion, for a deeper understanding of the relationship between "disinhibited temporal lobes" and the experiences of "psychic" or "spiritual" phenemena, or of mental delusion like that). And the reverse direction also holds true.

In relation to the symmetry-asymmetry principle, if there is symmetry (e.g., the co-existence of different views about the validity of the beliefs in God, regardless of whether they are religious or scientific), there is asymmetry (e.g., the popularity of the theistic argument for the validity of the beliefs in God among those who are deeply religious—but the skepticism towards the validity of the belief in God among those like the new atheists in the 21st century, namely, Richard Dawkins, Daniel Dennett, Sam Harris and Christopher Hitchens, for instance). (WK 2010ff) And the reverse direction also holds true.

In relation to the regression-progression principle, if there is progression (e.g., the regression made in the experiences of "psychic" or "spiritual" phenemena by those individuals who, afterwards, "had completely lost their ability to pray, others suffered continuous severe psychosomatic physical pains and illnesses and endured periods of painful alienation from God"), there is progression (e.g., the progress made in the experiences of "psychic" or "spiritual" phenemena by those individuals who, afterwards, "may acquire moral consciences" as "magnanimity replaces self-centeredness," and "the changes they perceive in themselves are…rewarding, undoubtedly, both to themselves and to their families"). And the reverse direction also holds true.

And in relation to the same-difference principle, if there is similarity in outcome (e.g., the contribution to the molding of beliefs and behaviors, regardless of whether this be done by way of "psychic" or "spiritual" experiences or by way of rational conversion), there is difference in outcome (e.g., the contribution to the molding of beliefs and behaviors by way of "psychic" or "spiritual" experiences with their consequent traumatic "consciousness shifts"—but the contribution to the molding of beliefs and behaviors by way of rational conversion with their consequent ability to "produce a reasonable and coherent defense of their beliefs" in

God," especially among those of "the most able philosophers and scientists in the world today"). And the reverse direction also holds true.

Power Drive, Developmental Stages, and the Search for Faith

Another way to evaluate the possibility and desirability of sacredness from the perspective of the mind is to understand power drive, developmental stages, and the search for faith.

Power Drive, and the Religious Compensation for Inferiority

The idea of power drive in the context of religion refers to an interesting thesis by "Austrian psychiatrist Alfred Adler (1870–1937), who parted ways with Freud, emphasised the role of goals and motivation in his *Individual Psychology* [1956]." (WK 2010gg)

For Adler, "we try to compensate for inferiorities that we perceive in ourselves. A lack of power often lies at the root of feelings of inferiority. One way that religion enters into this picture is through our beliefs in God, which are characteristic of our tendency to strive for perfection and superiority. For example, in many religions God is considered to be perfect and omnipotent, and commands people likewise to be perfect. If we, too, achieve perfection, we become one with God. By identifying with God in this way, we compensate for our imperfections and feelings of inferiority." (WK 2010gg)

This idea about God in relation to power drive "to compensate for inferiorities," for Adler, is not static, in that it can be subject to different interpretations in different times.

In other words, "these ideas have changed over time, as our vision of the world—and our place in it—has changed"; for instance, "the traditional belief that people were placed deliberately on earth as God's ultimate creation is being replaced with the idea that people have evolved by natural selection. This coincides with a view of God not as a real being, but as an abstract representation of nature's forces. In this way our view of God has changed from one that was concrete and specific to one that is more general. From Adler's vantage point, this is a relatively ineffective perception of God because it is so general that it fails to convey a strong sense of direction and purpose," especially in relation to the power drive. (WK 2010gg)

In the end, for Adler, "God (or the idea of God) motivates people to act, and that those actions do have real consequences for ourselves and for others. Our view of God is important because it embodies our goals and directs our social interactions. Compared to science, another social movement, religion is more efficient because it motivates people more effectively. According to Adler, only when science begins to capture the same religious fervour, and promotes the welfare of all segments of society, will the two be more equal in peoples' eyes." (WK 2010gg)

The Developmental Stages of the Religious Quest

While Adler focused on the power drive in the search for faith "to compensate for inferiorities" and how it is subject to different interpretations in different times—James W. Fowler (1981) was devoted to how the search for faith itself has changed over time, especially in the context of his stage model of faith developpment across the lifespan of an individual. (WK 2010gg)

For Fowler, there are "six stages through which pilgrim of faith invariably travels," as summarized below (and in *Table 3.2*). (R. Croucher 2003)

(a) Stage 1: "'Intuitive-Projective' Faith (Ages of Three to Seven)"

The first stage, for Fowler, "usually occurs between the ages of three and seven, and is characterized by the psyche's unprotected exposure to the Unconscious. Imagination runs wild in this stage, uninhibited by logic. It is the first step in self-awareness and when one absorbs one's culture's strong taboos. The advantages of this stage are the birth of imagination and the growing ability to grasp and unify one's perception of reality. Stage one is also dangerous, though, in that the child's imagination can be 'possessed' by unrestrained images of terror and destruction from the unconscious, and the exploitation of the fertile imagination by enforced taboos and indoctrination." (R. Croucher 2003)

(b) Stage 2: "'Mythic-Literal' Faith (Mostly in School Children)"

The second stage, for Fowler, usually occurs in school children, when "symbol and ritual begin to be integrated by the child. These symbols, however, are one-dimensional. Only literal interpretations of myth and symbol are possible. The runaway imagination of stage one is here harnessed, and linear thinking becomes normative. Found mostly in school children (although one can maintain this state for life), stage two persons have a strong belief in the justice and reciprocity of the universe, and their cosmic powers are almost always anthropomorphic. Objective distance and critical evaluation of myth or symbology is impossible. Fowler describes a person in this stage as being both 'carried and…trapped…in' their own narrative. Stage two can be dangerous because the relentless belief in reciprocity forces the individual into a strict, overcontrolling perfectionism; their religious system will without doubt be either legalistic or else, in the case of abuse, the child may be convinced of his or her own irredeemability." (R. Croucher 2003)

(c) Stage 3: "'Synthetic-Conventional' Faith (Arising in Adolescence)"

The third stage, for Fowler, is where "the majority of the population finds its permanent home....Usually arising in adolescence, this stage demands a complex pattern of socialization and integration, and faith is an inseparable factor in the ordering of one's world. It is a stage characterized by conformity, where one finds one's identity by aligning oneself with a certain perspective, and lives directly through this perception with little opportunity to reflect on it critically. One has an ideology at this point, but may not be aware that one has it. Those who differ in opinion are seen as 'the Other,' as different 'kinds' of people. Authority derives from the top down, and is invested with power by majority opinion. Dangers in this stage include the internalization of symbolic systems (power, 'goodness' 'badness') to such a degree that objective evaluation is impossible. Furthermore, while one can at this stage enter into an intimate relationship with the divine, one's life situations may drive one into despair (the threshold to the next stage). Such situations may include contradictions between authorities, the revelation of authoritarian hypocrisy, and lived experiences which contradict one's convictions." (R. Croucher 2003)

(d) Stage 4: "'Individuative-Reflective' Faith" ("Mid-20s to Late 30s)"

The fourth stage, for Fowler, is "primarily a stage of angst and struggle, in which one must face difficult questions regarding identity and belief. Those that pass into stage four usually do so in their mid-thirties to early forties. At this time, the personality gradually detaches from the defining group from which it formerly drew its identity. The person is aware of him or herself as an individual and must—perhaps for the first time—take personal responsibility for his/her beliefs and feelings. This is a stage of de-mythologizing, where what was once unquestioned is now subjected to critical scrutiny. Stage four is heavily existential, where nothing is certain but one's own existence, and disillusionment reigns. This stage is not a comfortable place to be and, although it can last for a long time, those who stay in it do so in danger of becoming bitter, suspicious characters who trust nothing and no one. But most, after entering this stage, sense that not only is the world far more complex than his or her stage three mentality would allow for, it is still more complex and numinous than the agnostic rationality of stage four allows." (R. Croucher 2003)

(e) Stage 5: “'Conjunctive' Faith (Mid-Life Crisis)”

The fifth stage, for Fowler, “moves one from stage four’s rationalism to the acknowledgement of paradox and transcendence. It is in this stage that, in Washburnian terminology, one chooses regression in the service of transcendence. In this stage a person grasps the reality behind the symbols of his or her inherited systems, and is also drawn to and acknowledging of the symbols of other’s systems. This stage makes room for mystery and the unconscious, and is fascinated by it while at the same time apprehensive of its power. It sees the power behind the metaphors while simultaneously acknowledging their relativity. In stage five, the world, demythologized in stage four, is re-sacrilized, literally brimming with vision. It is also imbued with a new sense of justice that goes beyond justice defined by one’s own culture and people. Because one has begun to see 'the bigger picture' the walls culture and tradition have built between ourselves and others begins to erode. It is not easy to live on the cusp of paradox, and due to its radical drive towards inclusivity, the mind struggles to assimilate and integrate faster than it can work through its cultural and psychological baggage. It is an overwhelming, ecstatic stage in which one is radically opened to possibility and wonder.” (R. Croucher 2003)

(f) Stage 6: “'Universalizing' Faith” (or “Enlightenment”)

Finally, the sixth stage, for Fowler, is when “any such apprehensions dissolve and one becomes an activist for the unitive vision.” (R. Croucher 2003)

Fowler thus wrote: ”Persons described by stage six typically exhibit qualities that shake our usual criteria of normalcy. Their heedlessness to self-preservation and the vividness of their taste and feel for transcendent moral and religious actuality give their actions and words an extraordinary and often unpredictable quality. In their devotion to universalizing compassion they may offend our parochial perceptions of justice. In their penetration through the obsession with survival, security, and significance they threaten our measured standards of righteousness and goodness and prudence. Their enlarged visions of universal community disclose the partialness of our tribes and pseudo-species. And their leadership initiatives, often involving strategies of nonviolent suffering and ultimate respect for being, constitute affronts to our usual notions of relevance.” (R. Croucher 2003)

The Problems with the Psychology of Religion

Yet, there is no lack of criticisms against the idea of power drive in faith development and its different stages. Consider five of them below, for illustration.

Firstly, one criticism of Adler's idea of power drive in faith development "to compensate for inferiorities" is that not everyone is so obsessed with the striving for "perfection and superiority." Surely, some do, but it is not clear to what extent human population in general are so at all.

Secondly, another criticism of Adler's idea of power drive in faith development "to compensate for inferiorities" is that it is also not clear why "to strive for perfection and superiority" must be the goal in faith development, even if one feels insecure and imperfect. Is it possible that other goals in faith development (like humility, modesty, the acceptance of imperfection, etc.) can be important too for many in their spiritual quest?

Thirdly, one criticism of Fowler's stage model of faith development is that it lacks empirical support. For instance, the critics had pointed out that "only the first two [stages] found empirical support, and these were heavily based upon Piaget's stages of cognitive development. The tables and graphs in the book were presented in such a way that the last four stages appeared to be validated, but the requirements of statistical verification of the stages did not come close to having been met." (WK 2010gg)

Fourthly, another criticism of Fowler's stage model of faith development is that it is biased in favor of his own Christian faith. For instance, "other critics of Fowler have questioned whether his ordering of the stages really reflects his own commitment to a rather liberal Christian Protestant outlook, as if to say that people who adopt a similar viewpoint to Fowler are at higher stages of faith development." (WK 2010gg)

And fifthly, still another criticism of Fowler's stage model of faith development is that not everyone goes through his six stages or experiences them equally. For instance, some other critics pointed out that, "although there is evidence that children up to the age of twelve years do tend to be in the first two of these stages, there is evidence that adults over the age of sixty-one do show considerable variation in displays of qualities of Stages 3 and beyond." (WK 2010gg)

Looking Beyond

These criticisms of Adler's and Fowler's ideas in regard to faith development from the vantage point of the psychology of religion do not mean to reject it outright to favor the other side of the debate but are introduced here in order to teach us the two opposing sides of the debate, such that the possibility and desirability of secularness (from the perspective of the mind with faith development as a case study here) is not to the extent that its respective defenders would like us to believe.

More importantly, the analysis of power drive, developmental stages, and the spiritual quest can also teach us something insightful about the ontological principles in existential dialectics, and good examples include the absoluteness-relativeness principle, the predictability-unpredictability principle, the explicability-inexplicability principle, the preciseness-vagueness principle, the simpleness-complicatedness principle, the openness-hiddenness principle, the denseness-emptiness principle, the slowness-quickness principle, the expansion-contraction principle, the convention-novelty principle, the evolution-transformation principle, the symmetry-asymmetry principle, the softness-hardness principle, the regression-progression principle, and the same-difference principle.

For instance, in relation to the absoluteness-relativeness principle, if there is absolute viewpoint (e.g., the absolute view by Fowler about the six stages of faith development), there is relative counterpart (e.g., what is true for Fowler in regard to the six stages of faith development is not so for the critics in regard to the lack of sufficient empirical support of his stage model of faith development). And the reverse direction also holds true.

In relation to the predictability-unpredictability principle, if there is predictability (e.g, the predictable tendency of those supporters of Fowler's stage model to point out the six stages for individuals to go through in faith development), there is unpredictability (e.g, the more difficult task to predict, if looked within Fowler's stage model, whether a particular individual will go through the six stages in his lifespan, or, alternatively, to what extent he will go through his stages, or experiences them, when compared with others individuals). And the reverse direction also holds true.

In relation to the explicability-inexplicability principle, if there is explicability (e.g,. the explanation, by Adler, of the spiritual quest of people on the basis of the power drive "to compensate for inferiorities"), there is inexplicability (e.g., the lack of sufficient explanation, by Adler, of why "to strive for perfection and superiority" must be the goal in faith development, or why other goals in faith development like humility, modesty, the acceptance of imperfection, etc. are not important too for many in their spiritual quest). And the reverse direction also holds true.

In relation to the preciseness-vagueness principle, if there is preciseness (e.g., the precise identification of the six stages in faith development by Fowler), there is vagueness (e.g., the vagueness concerning the validity of the six stages in Fowler's model, because they "were presented in such a way that the last four stages appeared to be validated, but the requirements of statistical verification of the stages did not come close to having been met," so their validity remains unclear). And the reverse direction also holds true.

In relation to the simpleness-complicatedness principle, if there is simpleness (e.g., the relatively simple analysis of the six stages in faith development by Fowler), there is complicatedness (e.g., the relatively more complicated analysis of the stages in faith development, as shown in the criticisms by the critics). And the reverse direction also holds true.

In relation to the openness-hiddenness principle, if there is openness (e.g., the open exploration of the six stages in faith development by Fowler), there is hiddenness (e.g., the hidden bias in Fowler's exploration of the stages in faith development, as "other critics of Fowler have questioned whether his ordering of the stages really reflects his own commitment to a rather liberal Christian Protestant outlook, as if to say that people who adopt a similar viewpoint to Fowler are at higher stages of faith development"). And the reverse direction also holds true.

In relation to the denseness-emptiness principle, if there is denseness (e.g., the relatively denser concentration of concerns by people like Adler with power drive in faith development), there is emptiness (e.g., the relatively less dense, or more empty, concentration of concerns by people like Fowler with power drive in faith development). And the reverse direction also holds true.

In relation to the slowness-quickness principle, if there is slowness (e.g., the relatively slower readiness of "adults over the age of sixty-one" to be "in the first two of these stages"), there is quickness (e.g., the relatively quicker readiness of "children up to the age of twelve years" to be "in the first two of these stages"). And the reverse direction also holds true.

In relation to the expansion-contraction principle, if there is expansion (e.g., the relatively more developed ability of those who follow Adler's idea of power drive in faith development to strive for "perfection and superiority"), there is contraction (e.g., the relatively less developed ability of those who follow Adler's idea of power drive in faith development to strive for humility, modesty, or the acceptance of imperfection as a fact of life). And the reverse direction also holds true.

In relation to the convention-novelty principle, if there is convention (e.g., the conventional wisdom about "the traditional belief that people were placed deliberately on earth as God's ultimate creation"), there is novelty (e.g., the alternative novel challenge to this conventional wisdom about God by a "new idea that people have evolved by natural selection" in modern times, as pointed out by Adler). And the reverse direction also holds true.

In relation to the evolution-transformation principle, if there is evolution (e.g., the natural evolution of humans to live in the state of nature, with a sense of awe towards natural forces), there is transformation (e.g, the technical transformation of human awe towards nature by the invention of the idea of power drive in faith development, such that "we compensate for our imperfections and feelings of inferiority" to "become one with God"). And the reverse direction also holds true.

In relation to the symmetry-asymmetry principle, if there is symmetry (e.g., the co-existence of different schools of thought about God throughout the ages), there is asymmetry (e.g., the popularity in the older days of "the traditional belief that people were placed deliberately on earth as God's ultimate creation"—but the rise in our times of the evolutionary "idea that people have evolved by natural selection"). And the reverse direction also holds true.

In relation to the softness-hardness principle, if there is softness (e.g., to treat those who conform in relation to one's ideology as "good," in stage 3 of Fowler's stage model), there is hardness (e.g., to treat those who do not conform in relation to one's ideology as "bad," since they are seen as "the Other," in stage 3 of Fowler's stage model). And the reverse direction also holds true.

In relation to the regression-progression principle, if there is regression (e.g., the regression made in stage 1 of Fowler's stage model, in that "the child's imagination can be 'possessed' by unrestrained images of terror and destruction from the unconscious, and the exploitation of the fertile imagination by enforced taboos and indoctrination"), there is progression (e.g., the progress made in stage 1 of Fowler's stage model, in that "the advantages of this stage are the birth of imagination and the growing ability to grasp and unify one's perception of reality"). And the reverse direction also holds true.

And in relation to the same-difference principle, if there is similarity in outcome (e.g., the contribution to the motivation of people to act, regardless of whether this be done by science or by religion), there is difference in outcome (.e.g, the contribution to the motivation of people to act by way of religion with its "religious fervour" for "perfection" and "superiority"—but the contribution to the motivation of people to act by way of science with its "scientific" spirit for the discovery of "truth" in the physical world). And the reverse direction also holds true.

Secularness and Nature

Secularness, when examined from the perspective of nature, can show us something exotic on its possibility and desirability, and this can be shown by way of two case studies, namely, (3.3.1) evolutionary biology, and the debate on creation in religion, and (3.3.2) heliocentrism, and its conflict with organized religion—to be addressed hereafter, in that order.

Evolutionary Biology, and the Debate on Creation in Religion

An interesting way to examine secularness from the perspective of nature is to introduce the debate between evolutionary theory and creation theory (or creationism) in the context of religion.

In *BNN* (2006), I already provided an extensive analysis of evolutionary theory (in terms of the five processes of variation, mutation, inheritance, adaptation, and natural selection) and therefore do not want to repeat the extensive analysis here.

It suffices, however, for me to introduce evolutionary theory in relation to its debate with creationism in the context of religion hereafter.

Biological Evolution vs. Other Evolutions

The term "evolution" refers to "the change in the inherited traits of a population of organisms through successive generations. After a population splits into smaller groups, these groups evolve independently and may eventually diversify into new species. A nested hierarchy of anatomical and genetic similarities, geographical distribution of similar species and the fossil record indicate that all organisms are descended from a common ancestor through a long series of these divergent events, stretching back in a tree of life that has grown over the 3,500 million years of life on Earth." (WK 2010ii; D. Futuyma 2005; T. Cavalier-Smith 2006)

But the term "evolution" has been used in non-biological fields too. Thus, "to distinguish biological evolution from other senses of the term 'evolution' used outside of the field of biology, such as cultural evolution, technological evolution and the evolution of language, it is sometimes referred to as genetic evolution or organic evolution." (WK 2010ii; T. Walsh 2006; C. Kottak 2005)

The Evolution of Life vs. the Origin of Life

The study of "the evolution of life" in evolutionary biology should not be confused with a related but different research topic, namely, "the origin of life."

Although "the origin of life is a necessary precursor for biological evolution,...understanding that evolution occurred once organisms appeared and investigating how this happens does not depend on understanding exactly how life began." (WK 2010ii; M. Isaak 2005)

In fact, "the current scientific consensus is that the complex biochemistry that makes up life came from simpler chemical reactions, but it is unclear how this occurred. Not much is certain about the earliest developments in life, the structure of the first living things, or the identity and nature of any last universal common ancestor or ancestral gene pool." (WK 2010ii; P. Luisi 2006; J. Peretó 2005; J. Trevors 2004; P. Forterre 1992)

Therefore, currently, "there is no scientific consensus on how life began, but proposals include self-replicating molecules such as RNA, and the assembly of simple cells." (WK 2010ii; G. Joyce 2002; R. Psenner 2001)

The Rise of Evolutionary Biology in Modern Times

This distinctin aside—evolutionary biologists are interested not just in "the fact that evolution occurs" but also in the development and testing of the "theories that explain its causes. The study of evolutionary biology began in the mid-nineteenth century, when research into the fossil record and the diversity of living organisms convinced most scientists that species changed over time." (WK 2010ii; I. Johnston 1999; P. Bowler 2003)

This is true, especially when "the theories of natural selection were independently proposed by Charles Darwin [1859] and Alfred Wallace. In 1859, Darwin's seminal work *On the Origin of Species* brought the new theories of evolution by natural selection to a wide audience, leading to the overwhelming acceptance of evolution among scientists." (WK 2010ii; AAAS 1922 & 2006; IAP 2006)

By the 1930s, "Darwinian natural selection became understood in combination with Mendelian inheritance, forming the modern evolutionary synthesis, which connected the units of evolution (genes) and the mechanism of evolution (natural selection). This powerful explanatory and predictive theory has become the central organizing principle of modern biology, directing research and providing a unifying explanation for the history and diversity of life on Earth." (WK 2010ii; IAP 2006; AAAS 2006; U. Kutschera 2004; NS 2008)

Since then, evolutionary theory has been "applied and studied in fields as diverse as ecology, anthropology, conservation biology, paleontology, agriculture, medicine, psychology, philosophy and others." (WK 2010ii)

The Claim of Common Descent

One of the most remarkable findings of evolutionary theory is that "all organisms on Earth are descended from a common ancestor or ancestral gene pool"— not by a supernatural being in a stroke of creation. (WK 2010ii)

In accordance to evolutionary thoery, "current species are a stage in the process of evolution, with their diversity the product of a long series of speciation and extinction events. The common descent of organisms was first deduced from four simple facts about organisms," as shown below: (WK 2010ii; C. Darwin 1859)

- that "they have geographic distributions that cannot be explained by local adaptation"
- that "the diversity of life is not a set of completely unique organisms, but organisms that share morphological similarities"
- that "vestigial traits with no clear purpose resemble functional ancestral traits"
- that "organisms can be classified using these similarities into a hierarchy of nested groups—similar to a family tree"

However, things can be a bit more complicated than simply drawing a "tree of life" as claimed by those in evolutionary theory.

For instance, "modern research has suggested that, due to horizontal gene transfer, this 'tree of life' may be more complicated than a simple branching tree since some genes have spread independently between distantly related species." (WK 2010ii; W. Doolittle 2007; V. Kunin 2005)

The Evoluton of Life in Detail

These empirical limits aside—much work has been done to provide a more detailed picture of this common descent in the evolution of life.

For illustration, "it is generally accepted that prokaryotes inhabited the Earth from approximately 3–4 billion years ago. No obvious changes in morphology or cellular organization occurred in these organisms over the next few billion years." (WK 2010ii; T. Cavalier-Smith 2006; J. Schopf 1994 & 2006; W. Altermann 2003)

Then, "the eukaryotes were the next major change in cell structure. These came from ancient bacteria being engulfed by the ancestors of eukaryotic cells, in a cooperative association called endosymbiosis. The engulfed bacteria and the host cell then underwent co-evolution, with the bacteria evolving into either mitochondria or hydrogenosomes. An independent second engulfment of cyanobacterial-like organisms led to the formation of chloroplasts in algae and plants. It is unknown when the first eukaryotic cells appeared though they first emerged between 1.6–2.7 billion years ago." (WK 2010ii; A. Poole 2007; S. Dyall 2004; W. Martin 2005; B. Lang 1999; G. McFadden 1999)

Then, "about 610 million years ago…multicellular organisms began to appear in the oceans in the Ediacaran period. The evolution of multicellularity occurred in multiple independent events, in organisms as diverse as sponges, brown algae, cyanobacteria, slime moulds and myxobacteria." (WK 2010ii; T. Cavalier-Smith 2006; E. DeLong 2001; D. Kaiser 2001)

Soon afterwards, "a remarkable amount of biological diversity appeared over approximately 10 million years, in an event called the Cambrian explosion. Here, the majority of types of modern animals appeared in the fossil record, as well as unique lineages that subsequently became extinct. Various triggers for the Cambrian explosion have been proposed, including the accumulation of oxygen in the atmosphere from photosynthesis." (WK 2010ii; J. Valentine 1999 & 2003; S. Ohno 1997)

In any event, the biological diversity began "about 500 million years ago," when "plants and fungi colonized the land, and were soon followed by arthropods and other animals. Insects were particularly successful and even today make up the majority of animal species. Amphibians first appeared around 300 million years ago, followed by early amniotes, then mammals around 200 million years ago and birds around 100 million years ago (both from "reptile"-like lineages)." (WK 2010ii; E. Waters 2003; P. Mayhew 2007)

Even then, however, "despite the evolution of these large animals, smaller organisms similar to the types that evolved early in this process continue to be highly successful and dominate the Earth, with the majority of both biomass and species being prokaryotes." (WK 2010ii; P. Schloss 2004)

The Criticisms of Evolutionary Biology

In spite of "the fact that organisms evolve is uncontested in the scientific literature and the modern evolutionary synthesis is widely accepted by scientists," evolutionary biology has been subject to different criticisms, especially "for some theists." (WK 2010ii; U. Kutschera 2004; D. Dennett 2007)

There can be many criticisms of evolutionary biology, of course, especially from the religious community, and hereafter are some serious ones, for illustration, as summarized in *Table 3.3*.

Firstly, one criticism of evolutionary biology is that evolution's evidence is not complete.

For instance, for some critics, although "[p]ast species have also left records of their evolutionary history,...this approach is most successful for organisms that had hard body parts, such as shells, bones or teeth. Further, as prokaryotes such as bacteria and archaea share a limited set of common morphologies, their fossils do not provide information on their ancestry." (WK 2010ii)

Secondly, another criticism of evolutionary biology is that evolution's evidence is inconsistent.

For instance, for some critics, "there are too many 'gaps' in the fossil record, that fossil-dating is circular, or that certain fossils, such as polystrate fossils, are seemingly 'out of place'....It is argued that certain features of evolution support creationism's catastrophism (cf. Great Flood), rather than evolution's gradualistic punctuated equilibrium, which some assert is an 'ad-hoc' theory to explain the fossil gaps." (WK 2010jj; M. Isaak 2004)

Thirdly, still another criticism of evolutionary biology is that evolution's explanation is incomplete.

For instance, Michael Behe (1996) argued "that current evolutionary theory cannot account for certain complex structures, particularly in microbiology....In addition to complex structures and systems, among the phenomena that critics variously claim evolution cannot explain are consciousness, free will, hominid intelligence, instincts, emotions, metamorphosis, photosynthesis, homosexuality, music, language, religion, morality, and altruism." (WK 2010jj; P. Johnson 1990)

A counter-argument against this criticism is that "most of these such as homosexuality, hominid intelligence, instinct, emotion, photosynthesis, language, and altruism have, in fact, been well-explained by evolution," but, for the critics, "others remain largely mysterious, or only have preliminary explanations." (WK 2010jj)

And finally, one more criticism of evolutionary biology is that humans, unlike animals, are increasingly mastering nature, to the point that there will be what I already originally proposed in my previous works (like *FHC*, *FCD*, and so on) the emergence of "post-humans" in future times.

Transcending the Debate

These criticisms of evolutionary biology, by the way, do not mean to dismiss it but are used here to show the two opposing sides of the debate, such that the possibility and desirability of secularness (from the perspective of nature with evolutionary biology as a case study here) is not to the extent that its respective defenders would like us to believe.

In addition, the analysis of evolutionary biology reveals something powerful about the ontological principles in existential dialectics, and good examples include the formalness-informalness principle, the absoluteness-relativeness principle, the partiality-totality principle, the predictability-unpredictability principle, the explicability-inexplicability principle, the preciseness-vagueness principle, the simpleness-complicatedness principle, the openness-hiddenness principle, the denseness-emptiness principle, the change-constancy principle, the order-chaos principle, the slowness-quickness principle, the expansion-contraction principle, the theory-praxis principle, the convention-novelty principle, the evolution-transformation principle, the symmetry-asymmetry principle, the softness-hardness principle, the regression-progression principle, and the same-difference principle.

For instance, in relation to the formalness-informalness principle, if there is formalness (e.g. the formal logical requirements of a system of idea to be consistent and sound), there is informalness (e.g., the nonformal nature of evolutionary theory, such that its claims are consistent and sound in some ways, but inconsistent and unsound in some other ways). And the reverse direction also holds true.

In relation to the absoluteness-relativeness principle, if there is absoluteness (e.g., the absolute view of creationism that life and the world are the creation of God), there is relativeness (e.g., what is true for creationism in regard to the creation of God is not so for evolutionary biology in regard to natural selection and chance). And the reverse direction also holds true.

In relation to the partiality-totality principle, if there is partiality (e.g, the partial viewpoint of each animal to compete for the survival of the fittest in the state of nature), there is holistic counterpart (e.g, the holistic view of the outcome of all animals competing with each other in the state of nature, such that there is subsequently the emergence of new species and the extinction of old ones, so the whole is not the sum of its parts). And the reverse direction also holds true.

In relation to the predictability-unpredictability principle, if there is predictability (e.g., the predictable occurrence of "common descent" like "the tree of life" in evolutionary biology), there is unpredictability (e.g,. the more difficult task to predict the common ancestry of those "species" which have not "left records of their evolutionary history" because of soft "body parts," and those "prokaryotes such as bacteria and archaea" which "share a limited set of common morphologies," so "their fossils do not provide information on their ancestry"). And the reverse direction also holds true.

In relation to the explicability-inexplicability principle, if there is explicability (e.g., the explanation of variation in the evolution of life on the basis of natural selection and chance, for instance, in accordance to evolutionary biology), there is inexplicability (e.g, the lack of explanation of other phenomena like "consciousness," "free will," "music," "religion," etc., if examined solely on the basis of evolutionary biology, for the critics). And the reverse direction also holds true.

In relation to the preciseness-vagueness principle, if there is preciseness (e.g., the precise identification of "chance" as a process for the variation of traits in a population, in accordance to evolutionary biology), there is vagueness (e.g., the vagueness in the term "chance," since it means different things for different people, so that, for the critics like the creationists, life is too complex for chance to decide). (WK 2010jj) And the reverse direction also holds true.

In relation to the simpleness-complicatedness principle, if there is simpleness (e.g., the relatively simple analysis of the evolution of life on the basis of some processes like variation, mutation, inheritance, selection, and adaptation in evolutionary biology), there is complicatedness (e.g, the relatively more complicated analysis of the evolution of life as showed in the criticisms by the critics). And the reverse direction also holds true.

In relation to the openness-hiddenness principle, if there is openness (e.g., the open exploration of the evolution of life on the basis of such processes as natural selection, chance, etc., in evolutionary biology), there is hiddenness (e.g,. the hidden bias in evolutionary biology for its search for "the tree of life" without sufficiently accounting for other phenomena in life such as like "consciousness," "free will," "music," "religion," etc. and for other "species" which have not "left records of their evolutionary history" and which "share a limited set of common morphologies," so "their fossils do not provide information on their ancestry"). And the reverse direction also holds true.

In relation to the denseness-emptiness principle, if there is denseness (e.g., the relatively denser concentration of American scientists who believe in "evolution without God guiding the process," or 55% according to a poll conducted in 1997), there is emptiness (e.g., the relatively less dense, or more empty, concentration of American scientists who believe in "young earth creationism," or only 5% according to the poll). (WK 2010jj; E. Larson 1997 & 1997a) And the reverse direction also holds true.

In relation to the change-constancy principle, if there is change (e.g., "the change in the inherited traits of a population of organisms through successive generations," according to evolutionary biology), there is constancy (e.g,. the ever constant role of "natural selection" as a powerful process to affect the variation of traits over time, according to evolutionary biology). And the reverse direction also holds true.

In relation to the order-chaos principle, if there is order (e.g., the orderly pattern of the evolution of life as detected in "the tree of life," according to evolutionary biology), there is chaos (e.g., the role of "chance" to play, as in "genetic drift, an independent process that produces entirely random changes in how common traits are in a population"). And the reverse direction also holds true.

In relation to the slowness-quickness principle, if there is slowness (e.g., the relatively slower rate of the emergence of new lifeforms prior to the Cambrian era in the timeline of evolution on Earth, according to evolutionary biology), there is quickenss (e.g., the relatively quicker rate of the emergence of new lifeforms during the evolutionary period known as "the Cambrian explosion," according to evolutionary biology). And the reverse direction also holds true.

In relation to the expansion-contraction principle, if there is expansion (e.g., the relative expansion of the influence of humans in modern times, such that they dominate other animals), there is contraction (e.g., the relative contraction of the influence of other animals in modern times, such that quite a number of them now become "endangered species," because of the intrusion of humans). And the reverse direction also holds true.

In relation to the theory-praxis principle, if there is theory (e.g., the theoretical constraction of evolutionary theory in modern times, especially with the works of Darwin and Mendel), there is praxis (e.g., the practical application of evolutionary theory for "genetic engineering, with selectable markers such as antibiotic resistance genes being used to manipulate DNA in molecular biology"). (WK 2010ii) And the reverse direction also holds true.

In relation to the convention-novelty principle, if there is convention (e.g., the conventional wisdom about creationism prior to the works of Darwin and Mendel), there is novelty (e.g., the alternative novel challenge to the conventional wisdom about creationism by Darwin and Mendel for the modern evolutionary theory). And the reverse direction also holds true.

In relation to the evolution-transformation principle, if there is evolution (e.g., the natural evolution of lifeforms like plants and animals on Earth as depicted in "the tree of life," according to evolutionary biology), there is transformation (e.g., the technical transformation of lifeforms like those of humans by way of the invention of new technologies for humans to master nature). And the reverse direction also holds true.

In relation to the symmetry-asymmetry principle, if there is symmetry (e.g., the co-existence of different schools of thought about the emergence of lifeforms), there is asymmetry (e.g., the popularity of creationism in medieval Europe—but the rise of evolutionary theory in modern Europe). And the reverse direction also holds true.

In relation to the softness-hardness principle, if there is softness (e.g., the practice of cooperation among social insects "such as bees, termites and ants"), there is hardness (e.g., the practice of competition, like a predator killing its prey). And the reverse direction also holds true.

In relation to the regression-progression principle, if there is regression (e.g., the regression made by evolutionary theory, as revealed in the criticisms by the critics), there is progress (e.g., the progress made by evolutionary theory, for a better understanding of the evolution of life on Earth). And the reverse direction also holds true.

And in relation to the same-difference principle, if there is similarity in outcome (e.g., the contribution to the understanding of how lifeforms come into existence over time on Earth, regardless of whether it is shown by creationism or by evolutionary theory), there is difference in outcome (e.g., the contribution to the understanding of how lifeforms come into existence over time on Earth by way of creationism on the basis of a supernatural being—but the contribution to the understanding of how lifeforms come into existence over time on Earth by way of evolutionary theory on the basis of such processes like variation, mutation, inheritance, adapation, and selection, together with chance). And the reverse direction also holds true.

Heliocentrism, and Its Conflict with Organized Religion

A related controversy which can help us evaluate the possibility and desirability of secularness from the perspective of nature concerns heliocentrism and its conflict with organized religion.

The word "heliocentrism" (or "heliocentricism") is "from the Greek (ἥλιος *helios* 'sun' and κέντρον *kentron* 'center')" and thus refers to "the astronomical theory that the Earth and planets revolve around the Sun and that the Sun is stationary and at the center of the universe." (WK 2010kk; D. O' Leary 2006)

The opposite of heliocentrism is "geocentrism, which placed the Earth at the center." (WK 2010kk) To understand why heliocentrism is a theoretical reaction to (or critique of) geocentrism, it is important to first summarize what geocentrism is.

The Geocentric Model

In the history of astronomy, "the geocentric model (also known as 'geocentrism,' 'geocentricism,' or 'the Ptolemaic view of the universe'), is the theory, now superseded, that the Earth is the center of the universe and other objects go around it. Belief in this system was common in ancient Greece. It was embraced by both Aristotle…and Ptolemy, and most, but not all, Ancient Greek philosophers assumed that the Sun, Moon, stars, and naked eye planets circle the Earth." (WK 2010ll)

Later, the Catholic Church found this model comforting, because it was compatible with the Christian teaching that God created the world (with intelligent life on earth), which does not move, but the sun is to move around it. For instance, "in the King James Bible Chronicles 16:30 state that 'the world also shall be stable, that it be not moved.' Psalm 104:5 says, '[the Lord] Who laid the foundations of the earth, that it should not be removed for ever.' Ecclesiastes 1:5 states that 'The sun also ariseth, and the sun goeth down, and hasteth to his place where he arose.'" (WK 2010kk)

But even before the rise of Christianity—for the ancients, there were two major reasons at the time which contributed to this geocentric belief, based on two empirical observations, as shown below:

- The First Observation—revealed that "the stars, sun, and planets appear to revolve around the Earth each day, with the stars circling around the pole and those stars nearer the equator rising and setting each day and circling back to their rising point." (WK 2010ll; T. Kuhn 1957)

- "The Second Observation—revealed that "as the Earth is solid and stable it is not moving—but is at rest." (WK 2010ll)

In addition, "the geocentric model was usually combined with a spherical Earth by ancient Greek and medieval philosophers....The ancient Greeks believed that the motions of the planets were circular and not elliptical, a view that was not challenged in Western culture before the 17th century." (WK 2010ll) To avoid confusion, the geocentric model is "not the same as as the older flat Earth model implied in some mythology." (WK 2010ll)

However, although "the basic tenets of Greek geocentrism were established by the time of Aristotle, the details of his system did not become standard" until the work of "the Hellenistic astronomer Claudius Ptolemaeus in the 2nd century AD." (WK 2010ll)

For Ptolemaeus, "each planet is moved by two or more spheres: one sphere is its deferent," which is "a circle centered on a point halfway" between the earth and the "equant" (viz., a point "directly opposite the Earth from the center of the deferent"). (WK 2010ll & 2010mm) So, a planet does not rotate exactly around the earth but around the center of the deferent, and the center is where the earth is opposite the equant on two opposite sides (of the center).

The second sphere is "the epicycle which is embedded in the deferent. The planet is embedded in the epicycle sphere. The deferent rotates around the Earth while the epicycle rotates within the deferent, causing the planet to move closer to and farther from Earth at different points in its orbit, and even to slow down, stop, and move backward (in retrograde motion)." (WK 2010ll)

In the Ptolemaic model, "the order of spheres from Earth outward" in relation to other planets and objects is shown below: (WK 2010ll)

- "Moon"
- "Mercury"
- "Venus"
- "Sun"
- "Mars"
- "Jupiter"
- "Saturn"
- "Fixed Stars"
- "Sphere of Prime Mover"

But the Ptolemaic model, as we now know, is problematic.

For instance, "the system that was available in Ptolemy's time did not quite match observations, even though it was considerably improved over Aristotle's system. Sometimes the size of a planet's retrograde loop (most notably that of Mars) would be smaller, and sometimes larger. This prompted him to come up with the idea of an equant. The equant was a point near the center of a planet's orbit which, if you were to stand there and watch, the center of the planet's epicycle would always appear to move at the same speed. Therefore, the planet actually moved at different speeds when the epicycle was at different points on its deferent. By using an equant, Ptolemy claimed to keep motion which was uniform and circular, but many people did not like it because they did not think it was true to Plato's dictum of 'uniform circular motion.'" (WK 2010ll)

Thus, this claim by Ptolemy does not hold, because, within the system, "each planet required an epicycle revolving on a deferent, offset by an equant which was different for each planet." (WK 2010ll)

This problem remained, even though "it predicted various celestial motions, including the beginnings and ends of retrograde motion, fairly well at the time it was developed"—although not by modern standards. (WK 2010ll)

The Heliocentric Model

This problem in the Ptolemaic model had led to the rise of the heliocentric model later on.

Although the heliocentric model "can be found in a range of Greek, Arabic and Latin texts,…[t]hese early sources…do not provide techniques to compute any observational consequences of their proposed heliocentric ideas." (WK 2010kk)

Good examples of early scholars in the Western world who contributed to the heliocentric model in pre-modern times include Philolaus (d. 390 BC), Heraclides of Pontus (4th century BC), Aristarchus of Samos (c. 270 BC), Archimedes, Seleucus of Seleucia (b. 190 BC), Martianus Capella (5th century A.D.), and Bishop Nicole Oresme. (WK 2010kk)

(a) Copernicus

Later on, Nicolaus Copernicus (1473–1543) developed "the first computational system explicitly tied to a heliocentric model." (WK 2010kk)

What Copernicus did was that he "discussed the philosophical implications of his proposed system, elaborated it in full geometrical detail, used selected astronomical observations to derive the parameters of his model, and wrote astronomical tables which enabled one to compute the past and future positions of the stars and planets. In doing so, Copernicus moved heliocentrism from philosophical speculation to predictive geometrical astronomy." (WK 2010kk)

Copernicus was lucky enough, however, in that, although "his ideas contradicted the then-prevailing understanding of the Bible" (that the earth did not move, but the sun was to move around it, as shown in the quotes from the King James Bible aforeindicated), he was not persecuted. (WK 2010kk)

The reason is that Copernicus died in the year of his book publication, since he "published the definitive statement of his system in *De Revolutionibus* in 1543" (and then he died in that year). (WK 2010kk)

In addition, "he was in good standing with the Church and had dedicated the book to Pope Paul III," and "the published form contained an unsigned preface by Osiander defending the system and arguing that it was useful for computation even if its hypotheses were not necessarily true. Possibly because of that preface, the work of Copernicus inspired very little debate on whether it might be heretical during the next 60 years. There was an early suggestion among Dominicans that the teaching of heliocentrism should be banned, but nothing came of it at the time." (WK 2010kk)

(b) Galileo

Unfortunately, Galileo Galilei (1564–1642) was not so lucky, by comparison, as he was persecuted for his belief in heliocentrism.

Galileo had the empirical advantage to be "able to look at the night sky with the newly invented telescope. He published [in 1610] his discoveries in *Sidereus Nuncius* including (among other things) the moons of Jupiter and that Venus exhibited a full range of phases. These discoveries were not consistent with the Ptolemeic model of the solar system." (WK 2010kk)

Galileo also did some work on the tides on earth, in that they "were caused by the sloshing back and forth of water in the seas as a point on the Earth's surface speeded up and slowed down because of the Earth's rotation on its axis and revolution around the Sun." (WK 2010oo)

In 1615, Galileo wrote "a Letter to the Grand Duchess Christina" to "defend…heliocentrism, and claimed it was not contrary to Scriptures….He took Augustine's position on Scripture: not to take every passage literally when the scripture in question is a book of poetry and songs, not a book of instructions or history. The writers of the Scripture wrote from the perspective of the terrestrial world, and from that vantage point the sun does rise and set. In fact, it is the Earth's rotation which gives the impression of the sun in motion across the sky." (WK 2010kk)

The Letter also put pressure on "the papal authorities to decide whether heliocentrism was acceptable. Galileo was summoned to Rome to defend his position. The Church accepted the use of heliocentrism as a calculating device, but opposed it as a literal description of the solar system. Cardinal Robert Bellarmine himself considered that Galileo's model made 'excellent good sense' on the ground of mathematical simplicity; that is, as a hypothesis," but, as long as Galileo could not give "the conclusive proof," it was not right to oppose the Scripture to fvor heliocnetrism." (WK 2010kk & 2010nn)

Bellarmine thus explained: "If there were a real proof that the Sun is in the center of the universe, that the Earth is in the third sphere, and that the Sun does not go round the Earth but the Earth round the Sun, then we should have to proceed with great circumspection in explaining passages of Scripture which appear to teach the contrary, and we should rather have to say that we did not understand them than declare an opinion false which has been proved to be true. But I do not think there is any such proof since none has been shown to me." (WK 2010kk; A. Koestler 1959)

This conclusion by Bellarmine "put Galileo in a difficult position, because he believed that the available evidence strongly favoured heliocentrism,...but he did not have the conclusive proof necessary to satisfy Bellarmine's requirements." (WK 2010nn; M. Sharratt 1994)

So, in 1616, "Bellarmine...delivered to Galileo the papal command not to 'hold or defend' the heliocentric idea. The Vatican files suggest that Galileo was forbidden to teach heliocentrism in any way whatsoever, but whether this ban was known to Galileo is a matter of dispute." (WK 2010kk; A. Koestler 1959)

However, in 1632, Galileo had his *Dialogue Concerning the Two Chief World Systems* published, which "clearly advocated heliocentrism and appeared to make fun of the Pope. Urban VIII became hostile to Galileo and he was again summoned to Rome. Galileo's trial in 1633 involved making fine distinctions between 'teaching' and 'holding and defending as true.' For advancing heliocentric theory Galileo was put under house arrest for the last few years of his life." (WK 2010kk; A. Koestler 1959)

In Historical Retrospect

In historical retrospect, however, things are still not so crystally final in the early 21st century, as two sides continue to provide new arguments to defend their respective views.

For instance, on one side of the debate, "Pope John Paul II [in 2000] issued a formal apology for all the mistakes committed by some Catholics in the last 2,000 years of the Catholic Church's history, including the trial of Galileo among others." (WK 2010nn; R. Carroll 2000; NH 2000)

This, for the supporters of Galileo, showed that he was finally "vindicated." (WK 2010nn)

On the other side of the debate, however, there are still critics of Galileo's stand. For instance, Pope Benedict XVI (who officially became the Pople in 2005) delivered a speech on February 15, 1990 at La Sapienza University in Rome, when he was "Cardinal Ratzinger." (WK 2010nn)

In the speech, Ratzinger (now Pope Benedict XVI) questioned Galileo's stand by citing "the views of a few prominent philosophers including Ernst Bloch and Carl Friedrich von Weizsäcker, as well as Paul Feyerabend, whom he quoted as saying: 'The Church at the time of Galileo kept much more closely to reason than did Galileo himself, and she took into consideration the ethical and social consequences of Galileo's teaching too. Her verdict against Galileo was rational and just, and the revision of this verdict can be justified only on the grounds of what is politically opportune.'" (WK 2010nn)

In fact, we now know that the proof by Galileo for heliocentrism is defective (or not quite correct), so Feyerabend's comment (as aforecited by Ratzinger) is not so outrageous as it may appear.

For instance, "as general account of the cause of tides [to defend heliocentrism], however, his theory [Galileo's] was a failure. If this theory were correct, there would be only one high tide per day. Galileo and his contemporaries were aware of this inadequacy because there are two daily high tides at Venice instead of one, about twelve hours apart. Galileo dismissed this anomaly as the result of several secondary causes, including the shape of the sea, its depth, and other factors....Galileo dismissed as a 'useless fiction' the idea, held by his contemporary Johannes Kepler, that the moon caused the tides. Galileo also refused to accept Kepler's elliptical orbits of the planets, considering the circle the 'perfect shape for planetary orbits." (WK 2010oo; M. Finocchiaro 1989; S. Kusukawa 1999)

In any event, the controversy of the Galileo's affair continued in January, 2008, when "Pope Benedict XVI [formerly Cardinal Ratzinger] canceled a visit to La Sapienza University,...following a protest letter signed by 67 of its 4,500 academics, as well as a few dozen of its 135,000 students." (WK 2010nn)

But "La Sapienza's rector, Renato Guarini, has been quoted as stating that the cancellation was a 'defeat for the freedom of expression'; Italian Prime Minister Romano Prodi echoed such concerns. Also notable were public counter-statements by La Sapienza professors Giorgio Israel and Bruno Dalla Piccola." (WK 2010nn; BG 2008; CAN 2008)

Yet, this continued heated disagreement between the two sides of the debate should teach us the two opposing sides of the fence, such that the possibility and desirability of secularness (from the perspective of nature with heliocentrism as a case study here) is not to the extent that its respective defenders would like us to believe.

In addition, the analysis of the debate on heliocentrism reveals something refreshing about the ontological principles in existential dialectics, and good examples include the formalness-informalness principle, the absoluteness-relativeness principle, the predictability-unpredictability principle, the explicability-inexplicability principle, the preciseness-vagueness principle, the simpleness-complicatedness principle, the openness-hiddenness principle, the denseness-emptiness principle, the slowness-quickness principle, the expansion-contraction principle, the theory-praxis principle, the convention-novelty principle, the evolution-transformation principle, the symmetry-asymmetry principle, the softness-hardness principle, the regression-progression principle, and the same-difference principle.

For instance, in relation to the formalness-informalness principle, if there is formalness (e.g., the formal logical requirements of a system of ideas to be complete and sound), there is informalness (e.g., the nonformal nature of the heliocentric model as proposed by Galileo, such that it is complete and sound in some ways but not in other ways, as "he believed that the available evidence strongly favoured heliocentrism,...but he did not have the conclusive proof necessary to satisfy Bellarmine's requirements"). And the reverse direction also holds true.

In relation to the absoluteness-relativeness principle, if there is absoluteness (e.g., the absolute view of the Catholic Church in the time of Galileo that the earth did not move but the sun was to move around it), there is relativeness (e.g., what is true for the Catholic Church in regard to the geocentric model is not so for Galileo in regard to the heliocentric model). And the reverse direction also holds true.

In relation to the the predictability-unpredictability principle, if there is predictability (e.g., the prediction by the Ptolemaic model of "various celestial motions, including the beginnings and ends of retrograde motion" of the planets in the solar system, generally speaking), there is unpredictability (e.g., the failure of the Ptolemaic model to predict precisely or accurately "various celestial motions, including the beginnings and ends of retrograde motion" of the planets, because the prediction was only "fairly well at the time it was developed" in antiquity, but not by modern standards). And the reverse direction also holds true.

In relation to the explicability-inexplicability principle, if there is explicability (e.g., the explanation of the cause of tides on earth by Galileo, on the basis that they "were caused by the sloshing back and forth of water in the seas as a point on the Earth's surface speeded up and slowed down because of the Earth's rotation on its axis and revolution around the Sun"), there is inexplicability (e.g., the failure of Galileo's theory of tides to explain why "there are two daily high tides at Venice instead of one, about twelve hours apart," and to take into account of the moon which can cause the tides, as suggested by Kepler but ignored by Galileo). And the reverse direction also holds true.

In relation to the preciseness-vagueness principle, if there is preciseness (e.g., the precise identification of "the Sun…at the center of the universe" in heliocentrism as "found in a range of Greek, Arabic and Latin texts"), there is vagueness (e.g., the vagueness in these "Greek, Arabic and Latin texts," because they "do not provide techniques to compute any observational consequences of their proposed heliocentric ideas" in an accurate and precise way). And the reverse direction also holds true.

In relation to the simpleness-complicatedness principle, if there is simpleness (e.g., the relatively simple view of Galileo affair, in that he was persecuted for his view of heliocentrism, as opposed to the geocentric model held by the Catholic Church at the time), there is complicatedness (e.g., the relatively more complicated analysis of Galileo affair, in that Galileo was not as innocent as portrayed by his defenders, as shown in the criticisms by the critics). And the reverse direction also holds true.

In relation to the openness-hiddenness principle, if there is openness (e.g., the open exploration, by Galileo, of the nature of the tides on earth, in that they "were caused by the sloshing back and forth of water in the seas as a point on the Earth's surface speeded up and slowed down because of the Earth's rotation on its axis and revolution around the Sun"), there is hiddeness (e.g., the hidden bais in Galileo's theory of tides, because he "dismissed th[e] anomaly [of two daily high tides at Venice] as the result of several secondary causes, including the shape of the sea, its depth, and other factors" and also "the idea, held by his contemporary Johannes Kepler, that the moon caused the tides"). And the reverse direction also holds true.

In relation to the denseness-emptiness principle, if there is denseness (e.g., the relatively denser concentration of the ideologues of the Ptolemaic model in pre-modern times), there is emptiness (e.g., the relatively less dense, or more empty, concentration of the ideologues of the Ptolemaic model in our times). And the reverse direction also holds true.

In relation to the slowness-quickness principle, if there is slowness (e.g., the relatively slower pace of reaction towards the work of Copernicus, since it "inspired very little debate on whether it might be heretical during the next 60 years" after his death), there is quickness (e.g., the relatively faster pace of reaction towards the work of Galileo, because he was put on trial in 1633, only one year after the publication of his controversial *Dialogue Concerning the Two Chief World Systems* in 1632). And the reverse direction also holds true.

In relation to the expansion-contraction principle, if there is expansion (e.g., the relative expansion of the influence of heliocentrism in modern times), there is contraction (e.g., the relative contraction of the influence of geocentrism in modern times). And the reverse direction also holds true.

In relation to the theory-praxis principle, if there is theory (e.g., the theoretical construction of geocentrism, like the Ptolemaic model, in ancient times), there is praxis (e.g., the practical application of the Ptolemaic model by the Catholic Church for the defense of Christian teaching). And the reverse direction also holds true.

In relation to the convention-novelty principle, if there is convention (e.g., the conventional wisdom held by the ancient Greeks that "the motions of the planets were circular and not elliptical"), there is novelty (e.g., the alternative novel challenge to the conventional wisdom about the ancient Greek claim of the circular motions of the planets by a more modern view in Western culture in the 17th century and beyond, that the motions of the planets are elliptical). And the reverse direction also holds true.

In relation to the evolution-transformation principle, if there is evolution (e.g., the natural evolution of humans to live in the state of nature with a primitive understanding of the working of the universe), there is transformation (e.g., the technical transformation of human understanding of the universe by the invention of heliocentrism by Copernicus, Galileo, and other thinkers). And the reverse direction also holds true.

In relation to the symmetry-asymmetry principle, if there is symmetry (e.g., the co-existence of different sides in the debate about the Galileo affair), there is asymmetry (e.g., the formal apology by Pope John Paul II in 2000 in regard to the Galileo affair—but the criticism of Galileo by Cardinal Ratzinger in 1990, who later became Pope Benedict XVI in 2005). And the reverse direction also holds true.

In relation to the softness-hardness principle, if there is softness (e.g., the acceptance of those in defense of geocentrism by the Catholic Church in the time of Galileo), there is hardness (e.g., the house arrest of those like Galileio by the Catholic Church for his belief in heliocenrism). And the reverse direction also holds true.

In relation to the regression-progression principle, if there is regression (e.g., the regression made by the heliocentric model, as shown in the failure of Galileo's theory of tides in his attempt to defend heliocentrism), there is progression (e.g., the progress made by the heliocentric model in helping us understand why the sun is the center of the solar system). And the reverse direction also holds true.

And in relation to the same-difference principle, if there is similarity in outcome (e.g., the contribution to the prediction of "various celestial motions" of the planets, regardless of whether this be achieved by way of the Ptolemaic model or the heliocentric model), there is difference in outcome (e.g., the contribution to the prediction of "various celestial motions" of the planets by way of the Ptolemaic model, if needed on a "fairly well" basis, by pre-modern standards—but the contribution to the prediction of "various celestial motions" of the planets by way of the heliocentric model, if needed on a more accurate basis, by modern standards). And the reverse direction also holds true.

Secularness and Society

Secularness, when scrutinized from the perspective of society, can show us in a different way its possibility and desirability, and this can be shown by way of two case studies, namely, (3.4.1) religion, and the challenge of secularization, and (3.4.2) religion, and the politics of antireligion—to be addressed hereafter, respectively.

Religion, and the Challenge of Secularization

A good point of departure to understand secularness from the perspective of society is to address religion and the challenge of secularization in modern times.

Secularization and Secularism

The term "secularization" refers to "the transformation of a society from close identification with religious values and institutions toward non-religious (or 'irreligious') values and secular institutions. Secularisation thesis refers to the belief that as societies 'progress,' particularly through modernization and rationalization, religion loses its authority in all aspects of social life and governance." (WK 2010pp; P. Norris 2004)

However, "secularization" can mean different things to different scholars, depending on their respective focus. For instance, "social theorists such as Karl Marx, Sigmund Freud, Max Weber, and Émile Durkheim, postulated that the modernization of society would include a decline in levels of religiosity. Study of this process seeks to determine the manner in which, or extent to which religious creeds, practices and institutions are losing social significance." (WK 2010pp)

Other therorists argue "that the secularization of modern civilization partly results from our inability to adapt broad ethical and spiritual needs of mankind to the increasingly fast advance of the physical sciences." (WK 2010pp; R. Niebuhr 2010)

Still others think that, for instance, "in Catholic theology, the term can also denote the permission or authorization given for an individual (typically clergy, who become secular clergy) to live outside his or her religious colony (monastery), either for a fixed or permanent period." (WK 2010pp; CE 2007)

In any event, the secularization thesis is related to a larger theoretical debate on "secularism," which was first used by the agnostic George Holyoake (1896) in 1851. (WK 2010qq) The term "secularism" refers to the argument that "government or other entities should exist separately from religion and/or religious beliefs." (WK 2010qq)

Like "secularization"—the term "secularism" has different meanings to different people. For instance, "in one sense, secularism may assert the right to be free from religious rule and teachings, and the right to freedom from governmental imposition of religion upon the people within a state that is neutral on matters of belief." (WK 2010qq)

But "in another sense, it [secularism] refers to the view that human activities and decisions, especially political ones, should be based on evidence and fact unbiased by religious influence." (WK 2010qq; B. Kosmin 2007)

Major contributors to "secularism" include "Greek and Roman philosophers such as Marcus Aurelius and Epicurus, medieval Muslim polymaths such as Ibn Rushd, Enlightenment thinkers like Denis Diderot, Voltaire, John Locke, James Madison, Thomas Jefferson, and Thomas Paine, and modern freethinkers, agnostics and atheists such as Bertrand Russell and Robert Ingersoll." (WK 2010qq)

In practice, the ideology of secularism has its influence on both political society (as in "secular state") and civil society (as in secular society") and thus contributes to secularization in society, as described below, in that order.

Secular State

In political society, "secularism is a movement towards the separation of religion and government (often termed the separation of church and state). This can refer to reducing ties between a government and a state religion, replacing laws based on scripture (such as the Torah and Sharia law) with civil laws, and eliminating discrimination on the basis of religion." (WK 2010qq; N. Feldman 2005)

In the West, "secularism is often associated with the Age of Enlightenment…and plays a major role in Western society. The principles, but not necessarily practices, of separation of church and state in the United States and Laïcité in France draw heavily on secularism. Secular states also existed in the Islamic world during the Middle Ages." (WK 2010qq; I. Lapidus 1975)

In more specific practical terms, "secularists tend to prefer that politicians make decisions for secular rather than religious reasons. In this respect, policy decisions pertaining to topics like abortion, contraception, embryonic stem cell research, same-sex marriage, and sex education are prominently focused upon by American secularist organizations such as the Center for Inquiry." (WK 2010qq; N. Feldman 2005; M. Kaufman 2006; CI 2010)

Even then, different religious organizations react differently to this separation of church and state.

For instance, on one side of the debate, some "major religions accept the primacy of the rules of secular, democratic society but may still seek to influence political decisions or achieve specific privileges or influence through church-state agreements such as a concordat. Many Christians support a secular state, and may acknowledge that the conception has support in Biblical teachings, particularly Jesus' statement, 'Then give to Caesar what is Caesar's, and to God what is God's.'" (WK 2010qq)

On the other side of the debate, however, "some Christian fundamentalists (notably in the United States) oppose secularism, often claiming that there is a 'radical secularism' ideology being adopted in current days and see secularism as a threat to 'Christian rights' and national security. The most significant forces of religious fundamentalism in the contemporary world are Fundamentalist Christianity and Fundamentalist Islam." (WK 2010qq; B. Lewis 2007; J. Falwell 2001)

With this contention in mind—good examples of secular states in modern times include "France, India, Mexico, South Korea, and Turkey although none of these nations have identical forms of governance." (WK 2010qq; R. Blancarte 2006; K. Schmitt 1962)

This is so, even though one should not confuse "secular states" with "liberal democracy" (which means something else), because secular states do not necessarily imply being liberal-democratic (in a small sense) or democratic (in a general sense).

Secular Society

In the case of secular society, "modern Western societies are generally recognized as secular. This is due to the near-complete freedom of religion (beliefs on religion generally are not subject to legal or social sanctions), and the lack of authority of religious leaders over political decisions." (WK 2010qq)

D. L. Munby (1963) once proposed the following "characterizes" of "a secular society," in that a secular society: (WK 2010qq)

- Ex: "refuses to commit itself as a whole to any one view of the nature of the universe and the role of man in it."
- Ex: "is not homogenous, but is pluralistic."
- Ex: "is tolerant. It widens the sphere of private decision-making."
- Ex: imposes limits "on methods of problem-solving, and a common framework of law; in a secular society."
- Ex: Requires "problem solving…rationally, through examination of the facts."
- Ex: "is a society without any official images. Nor is there a common ideal type of behavior with universal application."

Surely, there can be other characteristics, but for Munby, these are the most representative.

Good examples of secular organizations in civil society include "National Secular Society (United Kingdom)," "Secular Coalition for America," "Freethought Association of West Michigan," "Toronto Secular Alliance," "Atatürk Thought Association," "Leicester Secular Society," and so on. (WK 2010qq)

The Problems with the Secular Order

Yet, the secular order, be it achieved in the process of secularization or understood in the ideology of secularism, has its own inherent problems. Consider the following criticisms by the critics, for illustration, as summarized in *Table 3.4*.

Firstly, one major criticism of the secular order is that "secularization as understood in the West…is being debated in the sociology of religion"; "scholars [like Rodney Stark and Peter Berger] have argued that levels of religiosity are not declining." (WK 2010pp)

In fact, "many contemporary theorists have critiqued secularisation thesis, arguing that religion has continued to play a vital role in the lives of individuals worldwide. In the United States, in particular, church attendance has remained relatively stable in the past 40 years. In Africa, the emergence of Christianity has occurred at a startling rate. While Africa could claim roughly 10 million Christians in 1900, recent estimates put that number closer to 200 million. The rise of Islam as a major world religion, especially its new-found influence in the West, is another significant development." (WK 2010rr)

In addition, the rise of the "new religious movements" (as discussed in *Sec. 2.4.2*) is another good counter-argument to the secularization thesis in modern times. However, as I already showed in Ch.3 of *FHC* (and also in *Sec. 2.4.2* here), the new religious movements have their own problems too.

Secondly, another major criticism of the secular order is that it is not as desirable (e.g., liberating) as its ideologues would like us to believe.

For instance, I already went to great lengths in Ch.3 of *The Future of Human* Civilization (*FHC*) to argue that, as I wrote, "the idea of a post-secular society is a postmodern myth, just as the vision of a liberating secular society was a modern myth." I elaborated further this issue in *The Future of Capitalism and Democracy* (or *FCD*)

My argument in *FHC* thus targets both sides of the debate, in that both the secular order in modern discourse and its alternative post-secular order in postmodern discourse are equally questionable, in regard to the extent of its respective possibility and desirability.

And thirdly, still another major criticism of the secular order is that a secular state does not "add to democracy by protecting the rights of religious minorities" and other achievements as popularly claimed by its ideologues. (WK 2010qq)

In *FHC*, I precisely made this argument by showing that the secular state, even when it is embedded in a liberal democracy (for the separation of church and state), has a long history of failure, in four major ways, namely, (a) that it is "morally disorientating," (b) that "it marginalizes circumstantially disadvantaged others," (c) that "it is hegemonic to its enemies," and (d) that "it is in-efficacious in achieving justice under modern (and now especially postmodern) conditions."

Beyond Both the Secular Order and Its Post-Secular Alternative

These criticisms of the secular order should not be misunderstood as an endorsement of its post-secular alternative (as popular in postmodern discourse).

As already mentioned above, my view in *FHC* went beyond both the secular order in modern discourse and its post-secular alternative in postmodern one.

In the present context, my intention is to show the two opposing sides of the debate, such that the possibility and desirability of secularness (from the perspective of society with the secular order as a case study here) is not to the extent that its respective defenders would like us to believe.

Moreover, the analysis of the challenge of secularization in this section casts an illuminating light on the ontological principles in existential dialectics, and good examples include the absoluteness-relativeness principle, the predictability-unpredictability principle, the explicability-inexplicability principle, the preciseness-vagueness principle, the simpleness-complicatedness principle, the openness-hiddenness principle, the denseness-emptiness principle, the change-constancy principle, the slowness-quickness principle, the expansion-contraction principle, the theory-praxis principle, the convention-novelty principle, the evolution-transformation principle, the symmetry-asymmetry principle, the softness-hardness principle, the regression-progression principle, and the same-difference principle.

For instance, in relation to the absoluteness-relativeness principle, if there is absoluteness (e.g., the absolute view of the secularists that secularization is "progressive"), there is relativeness (e.g., what is good for the secularists in regard to the separation of church and state is not so for the Christian fundamentalists who oppose it). And the reverse direction also holds true.

In relation to the predictability-unpredictability principle, if there is predictability (e.g., the predictable tendency of a secular state to argue for the separation of church and state), there is unpredictability (e.g., the more difficult task to predict whether, or to what extent, a particular secular state is necessarily able to achieve its ideals like "equality of all people"). (WK 2010qq; D. Munby 1963) And the reverse direction also holds true.

In relation to the explicability-inexplicability principle, if there is explicability (e.g., the explanation of the desirability of a secular state on the basis of its contribution to "democracy by protecting the rights of religious minorities"), there is inexplicability (e.g., the lack of sufficient explanation by the ideologues of the secular state about its four failures in the modern era, contrary to its essential claim, as shown by my analysis in *FHC*). And the reverse direction also holds true.

In relation to the preciseness-vagueness principle, if there is preciseness (e.g., the precise identification of the separation of church and state in the definition of "secularism"), there is vagueness (e.g., the vagueness in what is exactly meant by the separation of church and state, which means different things to different scholars). And the reverse direction also holds true.

In relation to the simpleness-complicatedness principle, if there is simpleness (e.g., the relatively simple view of the secular state as "progressive" by its defenders), there is complicatedness (e.g., the relatively more complicated analysis of the secular state by including its failures, as analyzed in *FHC*). And the reverse direction also holds true.

In relation to the openness-hiddenness principle, if there is openness (e.g., the open exploration of the relationship between the secular state and the promotion of democracy, like the protection of the rights of minorities), there is hiddenness (e.g., the hidden bias in the discourse on secularism by downplaying its long history of marginalizing "circumstantially disadvantaged others" and glorifying the role of reason, as shown in *FHC*). And the reverse direction also holds true.

In relation to the denseness-emptiness principle, if there is denseness (e.g., the relatively denser concentration of secularists, especially those who accept the dictum that "Then give to Caesar what is Caesar's, and to God what is God's"), there is emptiness (e.g., the relatively less dense, or more empty, concentration of secularists among the Christian fundamentalists). And the reverse direction also holds true.

In relation to the change-constancy principle, if there is change (e.g., the change in some nation-states in modern times "from close identification with religious values and institutions toward non-religious...values and secular institutions," as in Turkey), there is constancy (e.g., the ever constancy of the search for law and order in society, be it secular or religious). And the reverse direction also holds true.

In relation to the slowness-quickness principle, if there is slowness (e.g., the relatively slower readiness of a Christian fundamentalist to accept the separation of church and state), there is quickness (e.g., the relatively quicker readiness of the followers of Ataturk in Turkey to accept the separation of church and state). And the reverse direction also holds true.

In relation to the expansion-contraction principle, if there is expansion (e.g., the relatively more developed ability of secular leaders to solve problems by the rationality based on reason), there is contraction (e.g., the relatively less developed ability of secular leaders to solve problems by the rationality based on faith in the Scripture). And the reverse direction also holds true.

In relation to the theory-praxis principle, if there is theory (e.g., the theoretical construction of secularism, especially though not exclusively, during the Enlightenment), there is praxis (e.g., the practical application of secularism for the process of secularization, as in modern Turkey under Ataturk for the strict separation of church and state). And the reverse direction also holds true.

In relation to the convention-novelty principle, if there is convention (e.g., the conventional wisdom in pre-modern times for the fusion of church and state), there is novelty (e.g., the alternative novel challenge to the pre-modern conventional wisdom about the fusion of church and state by the secularists in modern times for the separation of church and state).

In relation to the evolution-transformation principle, if there is evolution (e.g., the natural evolution of humans to live in the state of nature in a group like a clan, a tribe, etc.), there is transformation (e.g. the technical transformation of human grouping by way of the invention of a political system based on the separation of church and state in a large community). And the reverse direction also holds true.

In relation to the symmetry-asymmetry principle, if there is symmetry (e.g., the co-existence of different political systems in human history), there is asymmetry (e.g., the pervasiveness of the fusion of church and state in pre-modern states—but the rise of the secular states in modern times). And the reverse direction also holds true.

In relation to the softness-hardness principle, if there is softness (e.g., the welcome to the secularists in power in modern Turkey), there is hardness (e.g., the discrimination against the Islamic fundamentalists who do not accept secularism in modern Turkish politics). And the reverse direction also holds true.

In relation to the regression-progression principle, if there is regression (e.g., the regression made in the secular order, as shown in the four failures as analyzed in *FHC*), there is progression (e.g., the progress made in secularism for the separation of church and state). And the reverse direction also holds true.

And in relation to the same-difference principle, if there is similarity in outcome (e.g., the contribution to law and order in political society, be this done by the secular state or the religious state), there is difference in outcome (e.g., the contribution to law and order in political society by the secular state for the separation of church and state—but the contribution to law and order in political society by the religious state for the fusion of religion and state). And the reverse direction also holds true.

Religion, and the Politics of Antireligion

Another way to evaluate the possibility and desirability of secularness from the perspective of society concerns a phenomenon, which, though related to secularization (in the previous section), yet is distinctive enough for a separate analysis, namely, "antireligion."

Antireligion vs. Related Terms

The term "antireligion" refers to the "opposition to organized religion, or to describe a broader opposition to any form of belief in the supernatural or the divine." (WK 2010ss)

In this sense, the term "antireligion" should not be confused with two related terms.

Firstly, "antireligion" is not the same as "atheism" and "antitheism," in that it is "distinct from atheism and antitheism (opposition to belief in deities) by banning all forms of religion, although antireligionists may be atheists or antitheists." (WK 2010ss)

Secondly, "antireligion" is not the same as "religious persecution," although antireligionists may end up persecuting religious groups.

On the one hand, "religious persecution" refers to the persecution based on "religious bigotry (i.e., the denigration of practitioners religions other than those of the oppressors) or by the State when it views a particular religious group as a threat to its interests or security." (WK 2010tt)

On the other hand, "antireligion" is not based on "the denigration of practitioners religions other than those of the oppressors" (as in religious persecution), since antireligionists do not have their own religion at all to favor. In addition, an antireligious state does not discriminate against certain religious groups on the sole basis of their being "a threat to its interests or security" (as in religious persecution) but simply do not want them at all, because of its opposition to all religions, even if they pose no threat. Then, of course, when they pose a threat to its interests or security, this will be an additional good reason for the antireligious state to oppose them.

Antireligion and Its Followers

These two distinctions aside—there is no lack of (a) antireligious individuals and (b) antireligious organizations throughout history—as shown below.

(a) Antireligious Individuals

Hereafter are some notable individuals in history who are antireligious. Some of them are agnostic, some others are atheist, and still others are something else.

- Ex: Georges Bataille—"Nietzsche-influenced surrealist, journalist and philosopher who held that modern Western civilization was characterized by the myth of 'the absence of myth.'" (WK 2010ss)
- Ex: William Blake—"poet and painter. Although he remained very spiritual, he viewed organised religion as oppressive." (WK 2010ss)
- Ex: George Carlin—"who expressed religion as the biggest human accomplishment in terms of 'bullshit.'" (WK 2010ss)
- Ex: Richard Dawkins—"a prominent atheist and evolutionary biologist. He wrote *The God Delusion* criticizing belief in god(s) in 2006." (WK 2010ss; GR 2001)
- Ex: John Dewey—"an atheistic American pragmatic philosopher, psychologist, and educational reformer, believed neither religion nor metaphysics could provide legitimate moral or social values, though scientific empiricism could." (WK 2010ss; W. Adrian 2005)
- Ex: Harlan Ellison—"science fiction writer, called religion 'the last vestige of barbarism.'" (WK 2010ss)
- Ex: Johann Hari—"British atheist journalist and a self-described antitheist." (WK 2010ss)
- Ex: Sam Harris (2006)—"author and scientist, who argues that religious moderation provides cover for dangerous fundamentalism." (WK 2010ss)
- Ex: Christopher Hitchens (2007)—"outspoken and uncompromising antitheist, journalist and literary critic, author of the book *God Is Not Great: How Religion Poisons Everything*." (WK 2010ss)
- Ex: Alistair Horne—"British historian, believes peace follows when prosperity reduces religious influence." (WK 2010ss; G. Kamiya 2007)
- Ex: Enver Hoxha—"former head-of-state of Albania, the only state to ever officially ban religion." (WK 2010ss)
- Ex: David Hume (1779)—"the Scottish agnostic philosopher, known for his skepticism, who wrote that human reason is wholly inadequate

to make any assumptions about the divine, whether through a priori reasoning or observation of nature." (WK 2010ss)

- Ex: Robert Maynard Hutchins—"past president of the University of Chicago. Although religious, thought religion was not adequate for organizing modern universities and educational institutions, preferring metaphysics." (WK 2010ss; M. Dzuback 1990)
- Ex: Vladimir Lenin—"like most Marxists, he believed all religions to be 'the organs of bourgeois reaction, used for the protection of the exploitation and the stupefaction of the working class.'" (WK 2010ss)
- Ex: John Lennon—"singer. Famously sang 'and no religion too' in his song, 'Imagine.' Lennon commented that the song was 'an anti-religious, anti-nationalistic, anti-conventional, anti-capitalistic song, but because it's sugar-coated, it's accepted.'" (WK 2010ss)
- Ex: Friedrich Nietzsche—"*Der Antichrist*, general anti-Christian statements in many other works. Nietzsche believed Christianity, and specifically Christian morality, to be the product of a transvaluation of values amongst the Jewish lower classes who bucked at Roman rule, and ascribed its other-worldly nature as the product of ressentiment, or the desire to devalue the things of this world out of spite. Famous for popularizing the phrase, 'God is dead.'" (WK 2010ss)
- Ex: Madalyn Murray O'Hair—"founder of American Atheists, plaintiff of *Murray v. Curlett*, and self-proclaimed sexual libertarian. Allegedly once said that she wanted to be buried in an anonymous grave because she 'didn't want any christers comin' around and prayin' over [her] dead body.'" (WK 2010ss)
- Ex: Ayn Rand—"novelist and philosopher, founder of the objectivist school of metaphysics, famous for writing *Atlas Shrugged* and *The Virtue of Selfishness*." (WK 2010ss)
- Ex: Bertrand Russell—"British logician, and analytic philosopher." (WK 2010ss)
- Ex: Marquis de Sade—"French aristocrat and writer of philosophy-laden and often violent pornography." (WK 2010ss)
- Ex: Max Stirner—"anarcho-egoist and proto-existentialist nihilist who penned *The Ego And Its Own*." (WK 2010ss)

Surely, there are other notable contributors too to the discourse on antireligon, so the list above is illustrative, not exhaustive.

(b) Antireligous Organizations

Just as there are individuals who have contributed to the discourse on antireligion, there are organizations which have contributed to the movement of antireligion.

For instance, the anti-religious activist group called *The Rational Response Squad* is "a group of American antitheists who lobby for atheism. They are most famous for their controversial 'Blasphemy Challenge' on YouTube." (WK 2010ss)

Another one like *The Society of the Godless* is "a mass volunteer antireligious organization of Soviet workers and others in 1925-1947." (WK 2010ss)

Still another one like <Antireligion.com> is "an open forum for discussion on the harmful nature of organized religion and its negative historical impact on society." (WK 2010ss)

But the most influential organizations for the antireligious movement are related to what is known as "state atheism" (as described below).

Antireligion and State Atheism

The term "state atheism" was once "defined by David Kowalewski [1980] as the official 'promotion of atheism' by a government, typically by active suppression of religious freedom and practice." (WK 2010uu)

The best examples of state atheism are (a) Revolutionary France in the 18th century and (b) the Communist Bloc in the 20th century, as discussed below, in that order.

(a) Revolutionary France

The French Revolution in 1789 produced something important for the history of antireligion, since "for the first time in history, a society delved into the prospect of an atheist state." (WK 2010uu; A. McGrath 2006)

Shortly "after the Revolution, Jacques Hébert, a radical revolutionary journalist, and Anacharsis Cloots, a politician, both anticlerical, had successfully campaigned for the proclamation of the atheistic Cult of Reason, which was adopted by the French Republic on November 10, 1793, though abandoned May 7, 1794 in favor of its deistic replacement as the state religion, the Cult of the Supreme Being." (WK 2010uu; G. Fremont-Barnes 2007; A. McGrath 2006)

The reason is that, as Cloots claimed, "'Reason' and Truth' were 'supremely intolerant' and that the daylight of atheism would make the lesser lights of religious night disappear. The state then further pushed its campaign of dechristianization, which included removal and destruction of religious objects from places of worship and the transformation of churches into 'Temples of the Goddess of Reason,' culminating in a celebration of Reason in Notre Dame Cathedral." (WK 2010uu; A. McGrath 2006; A. Latreille 2002; J. Spielvogel 2005; F. Tallet 1991)

(b) The Communist Bloc

But it was the 20th century that the antireligious movement was most impactful, because of the rise of the Communist Bloc.

For instance, "by 1970 all 22 nations of central and eastern Europe which were behind the Iron Curtain were de jure atheistic, promoting it, ideologically linked to it and opposed on principle to all religion. Communist regimes elsewhere took similar approaches." (WK 2010uu; J. Haynes 2009)

After all, it was Karl Marx (1844) who regarded "religion as the 'opium of the people' in the sense that it gives illusory happiness—real happiness for Marx coming only when a worker controls the fruits of his own labor, which he says is achieved only in a communist society. Critics argue that this has motivated certain communist regimes to curtail religious freedom or seek to suppress religion because they considered it a suppressive, subversive set of guidelines, and thereby attached the charge of sedition to certain religions." (WK 2010uu)

For instance, in the Soviet Union, "state atheism...was known as 'gosateizm,' and was based on the ideology of Marxism-Leninism.... Marxism-Leninism has consistently advocated the control, suppression, and, ultimately, the elimination of religious beliefs. Within about a year of the revolution the state expropriated all church property, including the churches themselves, and in the period from 1922 to 1926, 28 Russian Orthodox bishops and more than 1,200 priests were killed (a much greater number was subjected to persecution)....Most seminaries were closed, publication of religious writing was banned. The Russian Orthodox Church, which had 54,000 parishes before World War I, was reduced to 500 by 1940." (WK 2010uu; D. Kowalewski 1980; TIME 1931)

The case of Albania is more extreme, because "Enver Hoxha's regime in Albania set out to abolish all religion with the intention of making the country officially atheistic: Article 37 of the Albanian constitution of 1976 stated that 'The State recognizes no religion, and supports atheistic propaganda in order to implant a scientific materialistic world outlook in people.'" (WK 2010uu)

Antireligion and Its Mixed Legacy

An interesting question to ask of course is, To what extent did the campaign for "state atheism" succeed in achieving its goal in the historical examples as presented above?

Just consider two most serious criticisms as shown below, for illustration.

Firstly, one major criticism of state atheism is that it is not effective. For instance, "the French Revolutionary experiment was short (7 months), incomplete and inconsistent." (WK 2010uu; A. McGrath 2006)

In the case of the Soviet Union, the regime later collapsed, and in post-Soviet Russia, by the early 2000s, "approximately 100 million citizens consider themselves Russian Orthodox Christians, amounting to 70% of population, although the Church claims a membership of 80 million." (WK 2010uu; J. Page 2005; USDS 2007)

In other post-Soviet republics, state atheism also did not succeed in eradicating religion. For instance, "in Ukraine [after its independence in the post-Soviet era], 96.1% of the Ukrainian population is Christian. In Lithuania, a 2005 report stated that 79% of Lithuanians belonged to the Roman Catholic Church. Most Poles—approximately 88.4% in 2007, are members of the Roman Catholic Church." (WK 2010uu)

In other post-Soviet areas, "Armenia, Kazakhstan, Uzbekistan, Turkmenistan, Kyrgyzstan, Tajikistan, Belarus, Moldova and Georgia have high religious populations." (WK 2010uu; USDS 2009; NM 2010, 2010a & 2010b)

And secondly, another major criticism of state atheism is that it is not desirable, in that the experiment in the Communist Bloc degenerated into religious persecution. For instance, "Richard Dawkins [2006] argues that Stalin's atrocities were influenced not by atheism but by their dogmatic Marxism, saying that while Stalin and Mao were atheists and antitheists, they did not do their deeds in the name of atheism." (WK 2010uu; BBC 2007)

Beyond Religion and Antireligion

These criticisms of state athesim, however, should not be taken as a defense of religion; rather, it serves the important scholarly exercise to show us the two opposing sides of the debate, such that the possibility and desirability of secularness (from the perspective of society with antireligion as a case study here) is not to the extent that its respective defenders would like us to believe.

Furthermore, the analysis of antireligion in this section can also teach us something valuable about the ontological principles in existential dialectics, and good examples include the absoluteness-relativeness principle, the predictability-unpredictability principle, the explicability-inexplicability principle, the preciseness-vagueness principle, the simpleness-complicatedness principle, the openness-hiddenness principle, the denseness-emptiness principle, the change-constancy principle, the slowness-quickness principle, the expansion-contraction principle, the theory-praxis principle, the convention-novelty principle, the evolution-transformation principle, the symmetry-asymmetry principle, the softness-hardness principle, the regression-progression principle, and the same-difference principle.

For instance, in relation to the absoluteness-relativeness principle, if there is absoluteness (e.g., the absolute view of of Marxism-Leninism that religion is what Marx once called "the opium of the people" and is to be eliminated, as during the existence of the Soviet Union), there is relativeness (e.g., what is good for the Soviet Union to suppress the religions is not so for the Russian Orthodox Church which was suppressed). And the reverse direction also holds true.

In relation to the predictability-unpredictability principle, if there is predictability (e.g., the predictable tendency of a state which advocates state atheism to try to suppress and eliminate all religious beliefs), there is unpredictability (e.g., the more difficult task to predict to what extent the effort of state atheism in a particular country at a given point in history will succeed in achieving its central goal). And the reverse direction also holds true.

In relation to the explicability-inexplicability principle, if there is explicability (e.g., the explanation of religion by Marx on the basis of class struggle), there is inexplicability (e.g,. the lack of sufficient explanation of religion, if looked only from the narrow Marxist viewpoint, in regard to other phenomena of religion as explained by alternative theories in, say, evolutionary biology, neuroscience, etc.). And the reverse direction also holds true.

In relation to the preciseness-vagueness principle, if there is preciseness (e.g, the precise identification of state atheism as a political version of antireligion), there is vagueness (e.g., the vagueness in the term "state atheism," since it meant and was praticed differently in different countries, be they in Revolutionary France, the Soviet Union, Communist Albania, etc.). And the reverse direction also holds true.

In relation to the simpleness-complicatedness principle, if there is simpleness (e.g., the relativley simple analysis of state atheism for the eradication of "the opium of the people," as the Marxist-Leninists put it), there is complicatedness (e.g., the relatively more complicated analysis of state atheism in terms of its failures by the critics). And the reverse direction also holds true.

In relation to the openness-hiddenness principle, if there is openness (e.g., the open exploration of religion on the basis of "the opium of the people," as in Marxist-Leninism), there is hiddenness (e.g., the hidden class bias for the lower class against the upper one in Marxist-Leninism in its campaign for state atheism). And the reverse direction also holds true.

In relation to the denseness-emptiness principle, if there is denseness (e.g., the relatively denser concentration of state atheists in the Communist Bloc), there is emptiness (e.g., the relatively less dense, or more empty, concentration of state atheists in pre-Soviet Russia). And the reverse direction also holds true.

In relation to the change-constancy principle, if there is change (e.g., the change from the support of the Russian Orthodox Church in pre-Soviet era to its condemnation in the Soviet era), there is constancy (e.g, the recurrent debate on the nature of religion, regardless of whether it was promoted in pre-Soviet Russia or condemned in the Soviet era). And the reverse direction also holds true.

In relation to the slowness-quickness principle, if there is slowness (e.g., the relatively slower readiness of someone like Lenin to endorse religion), there is quickness (e.g., the relatively quicker readiness of someone like the Pope to endorse religion). And the reverse direction also holds true.

In relation to the expansion-contraction principle, if there is expansion (e..g., the relative expansion of the influence of Marxist-Leninism in the Soviet Union), there is contraction (e.g., the relative contraction of the influence of Russian Orthodox religion in the Soviet Union). And the reverse direction also holds true.

In relation to the theory-praxis principle, if there is theory (e.g., the theoretical construction of state atheism, in that religion is "the opium of the people"), there is praixs (e.g.., the practical application of state atheism in the Soviet Union for the suppression of all religions). And the reverse direction also holds true.

In relation to the convention-novelty principle, if there is convention (e.g., the conventional wisdom about the importance of religious faith in human life, as championed by those followers of the Abrahamic tradition), there is novelty (e.g., the alternative novel challenge to the conventional wisdom about the importance of religious faith by Marx and other state atheists, in that religion is instead "the opium of the people"). And the reverse direction also holds true.

In relation to the evolution-transformation principle, if there is evolution (e.g,. the natural evolution of humans to live in awe towards nature in the state of nature, with their superstitious beliefs), there is transformation (e.g., the technical transformation of human view about the world by the invention of state atheism to eradicate all such superstitious beliefs, especially in regard to religion). And the reverse direction also holds true.

In relation to the symmetry-asymmetry principle, if there is symmetry (e.g., the co-existence of different views about religion throughout human history), there is asymmetry (e.g., the dominance of religion in the medieval era—but the dominance of state atheism in the modern Communist Bloc). And the reverse direction also holds true.

In relation to the softness-hardness principle, if there is softness (e.g., the praise of those who accepted state atheism in the Soviet Union), there is hardness (e.g., the punishment of those who accepted Russian Orthodox Christianity in the Soviet Union). And the reverse direction also holds true.

In relation to the regression-progression principle, if there is regression (e.g., the regression made in antireligion, as revealed in the failures of state atheism as pointed out by the critics), there is progression (e.g., the progress made in antireligion to help us understand the dark sides of religion, as pointed out by various notable individuals on antireligion). And the reverse direction also holds true.

And in relation to the same-difference principle, if there is similarity in outcome (e.g., the contribution to the molding and control of human beliefs and behaviors, regardless of whether this be achieved by way of state atheism or by way of organized religion), there is difference in outcome (e.g., the contribution to the molding and control of human beliefs and behaviors by way of state atheism for the suppression of all religious beliefs and practices—but the contribution to the molding and control of human beliefs and behaviors by way of organized religion for the glorification of religious beliefs and practices). And the reverse direction also holds true.

Secularness and Culture

Secularness, when examined from a different perspective, this time the perspective of culture, can also cast an illuminating light on its possibility and desirability, and this can be shown by way of two case studies, namely, (3.5.1) the anti-Christian, and the quest for life affirmation, and (3.5.2) the philosophy of religion, and the critique of religion—to be addressed hereafter, in that order.

The Anti-Christian, and the Quest for Life Affirmation

A good case study here concerns the anti-Christian and the quest for life affirmation.

The word "anti-Christian" here refers to the 1895 book titled *Der Antichrist* by the philosopher Friedrich Nietzsche (1990). (WK 2010ww)

Although the title was translated into English as "the anti-Christ," it is more correct to call it "the anti-Christian," because it "is not intended to refer to the biblical Antichrist but is rather an attack on the 'slave morality' and apathy of Western Christianity....After all, even to acknowledge the existence of an Antichrist, let alone to prop oneself up as one, presupposes the existence of a Christ, of a Messiah. Nietzsche recognized no such entity. His argument is entirely with those who would attempt to make a Christ, a Messiah, out of Jesus of Nazareth, which is to say, with 'Christians.'" (WK 2010ww)

The Origin of Christianity

To understand Nietzsche's critique of Christianity, it is important to first address his analysis of the origin of Christianity, in three major aspects, namely, (a) "Jewish priesthood," (b) "the revolt against Jewish priesthood," and (c) "the redeemer type"—as summarized hereafter, in that order.

(a) Jewish Priesthood

For Nietzsche, "Jewish, and subsequently, to a greater degree, Christian, priests survived and attained power by siding with decadents.... They turned against the natural world. Their resentment against those who were well–constituted led them to... 'invent another world from which that life–affirmation would appear evil'....In order to survive, the Jewish priests made use of the decadents and their large population." (WK 2010ww)

But this does not mean that "the Jews were...decadents, themselves. According to Nietzsche, they have...'the toughest national will to life which has ever existed on earth.' However, they pretended to be decadents so they could...'place themselves at the head of all decadence movements (—as the Christianity of Paul—) so as to make of them something stronger than any party that affirms life." (WK 2010ww)

The Jews achieved this goal of denaturizing life-affirmation in five major steps, as shown below.

- "Israel's Yahweh"—"'was the expression of their consciousness of power, of their delight in themselves, their hopes of themselves.' Because he was their God, they considered him to be the God of justice. The Jews affirmed themselves, realized their own power, and had a good conscience." (WK 2010ww)
- "Concept of God is falsified"—Yahweh became a demanding god of justice who is...'no longer at one with Israel or an expression of national self-confidence....'" (WK 2010ww)
- "Concept of morality is falsified"—"Morality is no longer an expression of life and growth. Instead, morality opposes life by presenting well–being as a dangerous temptation. Priestly agitators...'interpret all good fortune as a reward, all misfortune as punishment, for disobedience of God,'" which is "sin." (WK 2010ww)
- "History of Israel is falsified"—"The past is translated into religious terms. It was a record of guilt, punishment, piety, and reward in relation to Yahweh. A moral world order is established which assigns value to actions that obey the will of God (and which claims that this general will, i.e. the right way of life for everyone, is eternal and unchanging)." (WK 2010ww)
- "God's will is revealed in the holy scripture"—"The sacred book formulates the will of God and specifies what is to be given to the priests": "[A]ll things of life are so ordered that the priest is everywhere indispensable; at all the natural events of life, at birth, marriage, sickness, death. Not to speak of 'sacrifice' (meal–times)...." (WK 2010ww) "Natural values become utterly valueless. The priest sanctifies and bestows all value. Disobedience of God (the priest) is 'sin.' Subjection to God (the priest) is redemption. Priests use 'sin' to gain and hold power." (WK 2010ww)

But the Jewish prisethood created its own rebellious child, Christianity.

(b) The Revolt against Jewish Priesthood

For Nietzsche, "the Jewish church opposed and negated nature, reality, and the world as being sinful and unholy. Christianity then negated the Jewish church and its holy, chosen people": "[T]he little rebellious movement which is baptized with the name Jesus of Nazareth represents the Jewish instinct once more—in other words, the priestly instinct which can no longer stand the priest as a reality, the invention of an even more abstract form of existence, an even more unreal vision of the world...." (WK 2010ww) "The Jewish church and the Jewish nation received this rebellion as a threat to its existence. 'That holy anarchist who roused up the people at the bottom, the outcasts...[as sinners], the Chandalas within

Judaism, to opposition against the dominant order…was a political criminal….That is what brought him to the cross…where he died for his own guilt.'" (WK 2010ww)

(c) The Redeemer Type

For Nietzsche, the rebellious child, Christianity, belongs to "the redeemer type" for "a new way of life," a life of more decadence. "Nietzsche thought that the word idiot best described Jesus….With an antipathy toward the material world, Jesus was…'at home in a world undisturbed by reality of any kind….The kingdom of God is *within* you'….According to Nietzsche, the redeemer type is determined by a morbid intolerance of pain. Extreme sensitivity results in avoidance of the world. Also, any feeling of resistance to the world is experienced as pain. Even evil is therefore not resisted….Jesus was a distorted version of the redeemer type….According to Jesus,…'the kingdom of heaven belongs to 'children'….Jesus does not resist or contend with the world because he doesn't recognize the importance of the world. His life is its own kingdom of God at every moment." (WK 2010ww)

The Psychology of Christian Belief

For Nietzsche, the psychology of Christian belief is distinctive enough, and two most important ones are worth mentioning here, namely, (a) life negation, and (b) the holy falsehood, as summarized hereafter (and in *Table 3.5*).

(a) Life Negation

The psychology of Christian belief is decadent, for Nietzsche, because it is life-negating, not life-affirming, as he once wrote that "one is not 'converted' to Christianity—one must be sufficiently sick for it." (WK 2010ww)

For Nietzsche, "[t]he decadent and sick types of people came to power through Christianity. From everywhere, the aggregate of the sick accumulated in Christianity and outnumbered the healthy. 'The majority became master; the democratism of the Christian instincts conquered….' The meaning of the God on the Cross is that…'[e]verything that suffers, everything that hangs on the Cross, is divine….'" (WK 2010ww)

In fact, "[b]ecause sickness belongs to the essence of Christianity, the typical Christian condition, 'belief,' has to be a form of sickness. Every straightforward, honest, scientific road to knowledge has to be repudiated by the Church as a forbidden road. Even doubt is a sin.'" (WK 2010ww)

But this is contrary to the nature of true lnowledge, which "requires caution, intellectual moderation, discipline, and self–overcoming. But

Christianity uses sick reasoning, such as martyrdom, to try to prove its truth....In response, Nietzsche quoted a passage from his earlier work: '[T]he need for belief, for some unconditional Yes and No,...is a need born of weakness.'" (WK 2010ww)

(b) The Holy Falsehood

Also, the psychology of Christian belief, for Nietzsche, is obsessed with lying, as he once wrote: "Lying, or not wanting to see as one sees, is a trait of those who are devoted to a party or faction. Lying is utilized by all priests, whether pagan, Jewish, or Christian." (WK 2010ww)

In this sense, "the right to lie and the shrewdness of a 'revelation' (Offenbarung) pertains to the priestly type....The 'Law,' the 'will of God,' the 'sacred book,' 'inspiration'—all merely words for the conditions under which the priest comes to power, by which he maintains his power." (WK 2010ww)

And "Christianity's lies...serve...bad ends: the poisoning, slandering, denying of life, contempt for the body, the denigration and self–violation of man through the concept of sin...." (WK 2010ww)

The Quest for Life Affirmation

In response, Nietzsche advoated a new way of life, which is to "affirm life," not to deminish it, in three major ways, namely, (a) the will to power, (b) the overman, and (c) the eternal recurrence—as summarized below, respectively.

(a) The Will to Power

A good place to start for the quest for life affirmation is Nietzsche's idea of the "will to power" (der Wille zur Macht), which "provides a basis for understanding motivation in human behavior. This concept...suggests that the will to power is a more important element than pressure for adaptation or survival." (WK 2010xx)

The only exception to the will to power, for Nietzsche, is when "in limited situations the drive for conservation is precedent over the will to power: namely, when life is reduced to a condition of poverty and limitation. The natural condition of life...is one of profusion. In its later forms Nietzsche's concept of the will to power applies to all living things, suggesting that adaptation and the struggle to survive is a secondary drive in the evolution of animals, less important than the desire to expand one's power. Nietzsche eventually took this concept further still, and speculated that it may apply to inorganic nature as well. He transformed the idea of matter as centers of force into matter as centers of will to power. Nietzsche wanted to dispense with the atomistic theory of matter, a theory which he viewed as a relic of the metaphysics of substance." (WK 2010xx; G. Whitlock 1996)

(b) The Overman

But how this new era for the will to power to take hold in human society for life affirmation (not life negation) remains problematic.

However, Nietzsce provided some hope in his idea of the leadership under "the overman" (Übermensch). (WK 2010xx)

Although "interpretations of Nietzsche's overman vary wildly, here are a few of his quotes from *Thus Spoke Zarathustra* (Prologue, §§3–4): "I teach you the overman. Man is something that shall be overcome. What have you done to overcome him?....All beings so far have created something beyond themselves; and do you want to be the ebb of this great flood, and even go back to the beasts rather than overcome man? What is ape to man? A laughing stock or painful embarrassment. And man shall be that to overman: a laughingstock or painful embarrassment. You have made your way from worm to man, and much in you is still worm....The overman is the meaning of the earth. Let your will say: the overman shall be the meaning of the earth....Man is a rope, tied between beast and overman—a rope over an abyss....what is great in man is that he is a bridge and not an end." (WK 2010xx)

(c) Eternal Recurrence

In the end, to overcome man is an attempt to search for a new way of life (for life affirmation, not life negation), such that one can affirm the same life time and again.

This then leds to Nietzsche's idea of "the Eternal Recurrence" originally found "in the works of Heinrich Heine, who speculated that one day a person would be born with the same thought-processes as himself, and that the same applied to every other individual. Nietzsche expanded on this thought to form his theory, which he put forth in *The Gay Science* and developed in *Thus Spoke Zarathustra*. Schopenhauer directly influenced this theory. Schopenhauer postulated that a person who unconditionally affirms life would do so even if everything that has happened were to happen again repeatedly." (WK 2010vv; S. Luper 1999)

Besides Schopenhauer, Nietzsche also found inspiration from David Hume, who proposed "the idea that an eternal recurrence of blind, meaningless variation—chaotic, pointless shuffling of matter and law—would inevitably spew up worlds whose evolution through time would yield the apparently meaningful stories of our lives. This idea of eternal recurrence became a cornerstone of his nihilism, and thus part of the foundation of what became existentialism." (WK 2010vv; D. Dennett 1995)

In fact, "Nietzsche was so impressed by this idea, that he at first thought he had discovered a new scientific proof of the greatest importance....He gradually backed off of this view, and in later works referred to it as a thought-experiment...." (WK 2010vv; D. Dennett 1995)

Some Criticisms from the Critics

Yet, the Nietzschean suggestion for a new way of life which is to affirm life, not to negate it, is not be so promising as its rhetoric would sound.

Consider three major criticisms below, for illustration—as this is something that I already pointed out back in *BEPE*.

Firstly, one criticism of Nietsche's proposal is that the Nietzschean will to power can be inherently "destructive" and "harmful" to life in practice.

For instance, Abir Taha claimed that the Nietzschean proposal is "elitist" and "aristocratic" for "domination" and "destruction," as Taha thus wrote: "Nietzsche, in fact, explicitly and specifically defined the egalitarian state-idea as the embodiment of the will to power in decline," when he (Nietzsche) argued in *On the Genealogy of Morality* (Second Essay, §11): "To speak of just or unjust in itself is quite senseless; in itself, of course, no injury, assault, exploitation, destruction can be 'unjust,' since life operates essentially, that is in its basic functions, through injury, assault, exploitation, destruction and simply cannot be thought of at all without this character." (WK 2010yy)

Secondly, another criticism of Nietsche's proposal is that it is compatible with the disturbing ideologies advocated by political groups like the Nazis, the Fascists, and other militarists.

For instance, "by World War I,...he [Nietzsche] had acquired a reputation as an inspiration for right-wing German militarism. German soldiers even received copies of *Thus Spoke Zarathustra* as gifts during World War I." (WK 2010xx; S. Aschheim 2000)

After WWI, "the concept [by Nietzsche] was appropriated by some Nazis like Alfred Bäumler, etc., who may have drawn influence from it or used it to justify their expansive quest for power and world domination." (WK 2010yy)

Even "Hitler...was a frequent visitor to the Nietzsche museum in Weimar and did use expressions of Nietzsche's, such as 'lords of the earth' in *Mein Kampf*. The Nazis made very selective use of Nietzsche's philosophy....Mussolini certainly read Nietzsche." (WK 2010xx; W. Shirer 1960; P. Morgan 2003; S. Falasca-Zamponi 2000)

Not surprisingly, Jacques Derrida (1984:24) thus criticized Nietzsche: "One may wonder why the only teaching institution or the only beginning of a teaching institution that ever succeeded in taking as its model the teaching of Nietzsche on teaching will have been a Nazi one."

And thirdly, another criticism of Nietsche's proposal raises the issue concerning his mental health.

For instance, "Bertrand Russell [2004] in his *History of Western Philosophy* was scathing in his chapter on Nietzsche, calling his work the 'mere power-phantasies of an invalid' and referring to Nietzsche as a 'megalomaniac.'" (WK 2010xx) After all, one should remember that "on January 3, 1889, Nietzsche...suffered a mental collapse" (which lasted almost a decade, before he died in 1900). (WK 2010xx) Sadly speaking, Nietzsche thus became insane (or mad) in those last years of his life.

A Sober Reflection

These criticisms of Nietzsche's quest for life affirmation, however, does not mean to dismiss it but have the scholarly virtue to show us the two opposing sides of the debate, such that the possibility and desirability of secularness (from the perspective of culture with the anti-Christian as a case study here) is not to the extent that its respective defenders would like us to believe.

In addition, the analysis of the anti-Christian in this section reveals something important about the ontological principles in existential dialectics, and good examples include the absoluteness-relativeness principle, the predictability-unpredictability principle, the explicability-inexplicability principle, the preciseness-vagueness principle, the simpleness-complicatedness principle, the openness-hiddenness principle, the denseness-emptiness principle, the change-constancy principle, the slowness-quickness principle, the expansion-contraction principle, the theory-praxis principle, the convention-novelty principle, the evolution-transformation principle, the symmetry-asymmetry principle, the softness-hardness principle, the regression-progression principle, and the same-difference principle.

For instance, in relation to the absoluteness-relativeness principle, if there is absoluteness (e.g., the absolute view of the Jews that they are the "holy, chosen people"), there is relativeness (e.g., what is true for the Jews in regard to the "holy, chosen people" is not necessarily so for a gentile). And the reverse direction also holds true.

In relation to the predictability-unpredictability principle, if there is predictability (e.g., the predictable requirement of the Jews in antiquity to to obey the commandment that "[d]isobedience of God [the priest] is 'sin'" and "[s]ubjection to God [the priest] is redemption"), there is unpredictability (e.g., the Jews in antiquity failed to predict the rebellious child "wihtin Judaism," with "the name Jesus of Nazareth," for the "opposition against the dominant order," such that "[t]he Jewish church and the Jewish nation received this rebellion as a threat to its existence"). And the reverse direction also holds true.

In relation to the explicability-inexplicability principle, if there is explicability (e.g., the explanation of truth by the Christians, for Nietzsche, on the basis of faith in regard to blessedness, in that "[b]elief makes blessed: thus it is true"), there is inexplicability (e.g., the lack of convincinng explanation by the Christians, for Nietzsche, of why faith or blessedness can be a proof of truth at all, since "blessedness is something that the priest promises for the future. It, itself, is an object of belief. Also, blessedness, or pleasure, cannot be a proof of truth. '[W]hen on earth was it established that true judgments give more enjoyment than false ones...?' It could be said, 'Belief makes blessed: thus it is lies'"). (WK 2010ww) And the reverse direction also holds true.

In relation to the preciseness-vagueness principle, if there is preciseness (e.g., the precise identification of "the overman" for the leadership of the quest for life affirmation in the future, for Nietzsche), there is vagueness (e.g., the vagueness in the idea of this "overman," since "interpretations of Nietzsche's overman vary wildly," from one scholar to another). And the reverse direction also holds true.

In relation to the simpleness-complicatedness principle, if there is simpleness (e.g., the relatively simple analysis of the origin of Christianity by Nietzsche and his solution for life affirmation), there is complicatedness (e.g., the relatively more complicated analysis of Nietzsche's work on the origin of Christianity and his solution, as shown by the damaging criticisms from his critics). And the reverse direction also holds true.

In relation to the openness-hiddenness principle, if there is openness (e.g., the open exploration of a new way of life by the Christians to address human suffering, according to Nietzsche), there is hiddenness (e.g., the hidden bias of this Christian new way of life, which is "decadent" and "life-negating," for Nietzsche). And the reverse direction also holds true.

In relation to the denseness-emptiness principle, if there is denseness (e.g., the relatively denser concentration of concerns, among the

Christians, with pain in the sufferers, or with what Nietzsche called the "morbid intolerance of pain. Extreme sensitivity results in avoidance of the world"), there is emptiness (e.g., the relatively less dense, or more empty, concentration of concerns, among the Nazis, with pain in the sufferers). And the reverse direction also holds true.

In relation to the change-constancy principle, if there is change (e.g., the ever changing nature of the ways of life in human society, ranging from the Jewish through the Christian to the Nietzschean versions), there is constancy (e.g., the ever constancy of seeking a new way of life in human history). And the reverse direction also holds true.

In relation to the slowness-quickness principle, if there is slowness (e.g, the relatively slower readiness of a Jew or Christian to question the claims that "[d]isobedience of God…is 'sin'" and "[s]ubjection to God…is redemption"), there is quickness (e.g., the relativey quicker readiness of someone like Nietzsche to question the claims that "[d]isobedience of God…is 'sin'" and "[s]ubjection to God…is redemption"). And the reverse direction also holds true.

In relation to the expansion-contraction principle, if there is expansion (e.g., the relative expansion of the influence of Nietzsche's work in Nazi Germany), there is contraction (e.g., the relative decline of the influence of Judaism in Nazi Germany). And the reverse direction also holds true.

In relation to the theory-praxis principle, if there is theory (e.g., the theoretical construction of the Nietzsche quest for life affirmation), there is praxis (e.g., the practical application of Nietzsche's work by the Nazi during the inter-war period, as "the Nazis made very selective use of Nietzsche's philosophy"). And the reverse direction also holds true.

In relation to the convention-novelty principle, there is convention (e.g., the conventional wisdom about Christianity as a new way of life for "peace," "tolerance," "love," etc.), there is novelty (e.g, the alternative novel challenge to this conventional wisdom about Christianity by Nietzsche with his critique of the "decadent" values and holy falsehood in Christianity). (WK 2010ww) And the reverse direction also holds true.

In relation to the evolution-transformation principle, if there is evolution (e.g., the natural evolution of humans to live in the state of nature, with their "natural" values, which also allow violence, war, etc., for Nietzsche), there is transformation (e.g., the technical transformation of human values in the state of nature by the invention of the theologies of Judaism and Christianity, such that, for Nietzsche, "[n]atural values become utterly valueless. The priest sanctifies and bestows all value. Disobedience of God…is 'sin.' Subjection to God…is redemption"). And the reverse direction also holds true.

In relation to the symmetry-asymmetry principle, if there is symmetry (e.g., the co-existence of different ways of life in human history), there is asymmetry (e.g., the acceptance of the Jewish way of life among the Jews in antiquity—but the rise of the Christian way of life among the Christians later, as the rebellious child "within Judaism"). And the reverse direction also holds true.

In relation to the softness-hardness principle, if there is softness (e.g., the promise of "redemption" to those who accept the "subjection to God [the priest]"), there is hardness (e.g., the punishment of those who dare the "disobedience of God [the priest]," which is cursed as a "sin"). And the reverse direction also holds true.

In relation to the regression-progression principle, if there is regression (e.g., the regression made in religions like Judaism and Christianity as shown in the criticisms by Nietzsche in regard to their "decadence" and "lies"), there is progression (e.g., the progress made in religious like Judaism and Christianity for the better understanding of the need to search for spirituality in human life). And the reverse direction also holds true.

And in relation to the same-difference principle, if there is similarity (e.g., the contribution to the molding of human beliefs and values, regardless of whether this be done by way of Judaism, Christanity, and Nazism, for instance), there is difference in outcome (e.g., the contribution to the molding of human beliefs and values by way of Judaism and Christanity for "peace," "love," etc.—but the contribution to the molding of human beliefs and values by way of Nazism for "war," "power," etc.). And the reverse direction also holds true.

Philosophy of Religion, and Its Critical Questions for Religion

Another way to evaluate the possibility and desirability of secularmess from the perspective of culture concerns the philosophy of religion, and its critical questions for religion

Philosophy of Religion vs. Two Related Terms

The term "philosophy of religion" refers to "a branch of philosophy that asks questions about religion. As with all philosophies, the topics at hand are generated by those who participate. In the philosophy of religion, these may include but are not limited to the nature and existence of God, religious language, miracles, prayer, the problem of evil, and how religion and other belief systems such as ethics interrelate." (WK 2010zz)

However, the term "philosophy of religion" should not be confused with two related terms, namely, "sociology of religion" and "religious philosophy."

In the first case, "the philosophy of religion broadly differs to the sociology of religion in assessing the validity of religious truth-claims, rather than examining social or cultural functions." (WK 2010zz)

And in the second case, "the philosophy of religion is the philosophical thinking about religion. It is designed such that it can be carried out dispassionately by what are thought of as those in two 'camps': adherents or believers, and non-believers"; but "[r]eligious philosophy, on the other hand, is the philosophical thinking that is inspired and directed by religion, such as Christian philosophy and Islamic philosophy." (WK 2010zz; S. Evans 1985)

For instance, a good expression of religious philosophy in action is when theologians discuss some philosophical issues from the vantage point of certain religions that they want to defend: "Theologians sometimes consider the existence of God as axiomatic, or self-evident. Most theological treatises seek to explain, justify or support religious claims by two primary epistemic means: rationalization or intuitive metaphors." (WK 2010zz)

By contrast, "a philosopher of religion examines and critiques the epistemological, logical, aesthetic and ethical foundations inherent in the claims of a religion. Whereas a theologian could elaborate metaphysically on the nature of God either rationally or experientially, a philosopher of religion is more interested in asking what may be knowable and opinable with regards to religions' claims." (WK 2010zz)

Philosophy of Religion vs. Metaphysics

Traditionally, "philosophy of religion" is "regarded as a part of metaphysics. In Aristotle's *Metaphysics*, he described first causes as one of the subjects of his investigation. For Aristotle, the first cause was the unmoved mover, which has been read as God, particularly when Aristotle's work became prevalent again in the Medieval West." (WK 2010zz)

However, "today,…the term philosophy of religion…is regarded as a separate field of specialization,…In fact the subject has long involved important questions in areas such as epistemology, philosophy of language, philosophical logic, and moral philosophy." (WK 2010zz)

Even with this distinction between the two in mind—philosophy of religion has much in common with metaphysics. For instance, "the traditional objects of religious discussion have been very special sorts of entities (such as gods, angels, supernatural forces, and the like) and events, abilities, or processes (the creation of the universe, the ability to do or know anything, interaction between humans and gods, and so forth). Metaphysicians (and ontologists in particular) are characteristically interested in understanding what it is for something to exist—what it is for something to be an entity, event, ability, process, and so forth. Because many members of religious traditions believe in things that exist in profoundly different ways from more everyday things, objects of religious belief both raise special philosophical problems and, as extreme or limiting cases, invite us to clarify central metaphysical concepts." (WK 2010zz)

In any event, philosophy of religion asks some critical questions about religion, and good examples include the following questions: (WK 2010zz)

- Ex: "What, if anything, would give us good reason to believe that a miracle has occurred?"
- Ex: "What is the relationship between faith and reason?"
- Ex: "What is the relationship between morality and religion?"
- Ex: "What is the status of religious language?"
- Ex: "Does petitionary prayer (sometimes still called impetratory prayer) make sense?"

Surely, there are other questions too, and perhaps the two most critical questions which have often been asked in the literature on religion are, namely, (a) "What is God?" And (b) "Does God exist?"

Let's consider these two most critical questions in what follows, in that order.

The First Critical Question: What is God?

This question "What is God?" can be asked in a different way, "What is the meaning of the word 'God'?" (WK 2010zz)

However, there is no best answer to this question, because "there are a number of widely different senses of the word 'God,'" depending on the philosophical bias of the scholar in question. (WK 2010zz)

For instance, in Western culture, "monotheistic conception of God… has been the primary source of investigation in philosophy of religion….One likely reason as to why the Western conception of God is dominant in the canon of philosophy of religion is that philosophy of religion is primarily an area of analytic philosophy, which is primarily Western." (WK 2010zz)

By contrast, in the non-Western world, "people...such as Hindus...believe in many different deities..., while maintaining that all are manifestations of one God. Hindus also have a widely followed monistic philosophy that can be said to be neither monotheistic nor polytheistic [like Advaita Vedanta]....Since Buddhism tends to deal less with metaphysics and more with ontological...questions, Buddhists generally do not believe in the existence of a creator God similar to that of the Abrahamic religions, but direct attention to a state called Nirvana [like Mu]." (WK 2010zz)

With this philosophical bias in the literature in mind—let's consider three major definitions of "God," for illustration, as a way to answer the question "What is God?" from the standpoint of the philosophy of religion. These three are, (a), "monotheistic definitions," (b), "polytheistic definitions," and (c) "pantheistic definitions," to be summarized hereafter, in that order.

(a) Monotheistic Definitions

The term "monotheism" refers to "the view that only one God exists (as opposed to multiple gods). In Western thought, God is traditionally described as a being that possesses at least three necessary properties: omniscience (all-knowing), omnipotence (all-powerful), and omnipresence (present every where). In other words, God knows everything, has the power to do anything, and is present where He wishes." (WK 2010zz)

Surely, they can be "[m]any other properties (e.g., omnibenevolence)" which "have been alleged to be necessary properties of a god," but "these are the three most uncontroversial and dominant in Christian tradition. By contrast, Monism is the view that all is of one essential essence, substance or energy. Monistic theism, a variant of both monism and monotheism, views God as both immanent and transcendent. Both are dominant themes in Hinduism." (WK 2010zz)

But the critical problems in monotheistic definitions are: "For example, what does it mean for something to be created? How can something be 'all-powerful'?" (WK 2010zz)

(b) Polytheistic Definitions

The term "polytheism" refers to the "belief in more than one god(dess). There can be as few as two (such as a classical Western understanding of Zoroastrian dualism) or an innumerably large amount, as in Hinduism (as the Western world perceives it)." (WK 2010zz)

In addition, "[t]here are many varieties of polytheism; they all accept that many gods exist, but differ in their responses to that belief. Henotheists, for example, worship only one of the many gods, either because it is held to be more powerful or worthy of worship than the others (some pseudo-Christian sects take this view of the Trinity, holding that only God the Father should be worshipped, Jesus and the Holy Spirit being distinct and lesser gods), or because it is associated with their own group, culture, state, etc." (WK 2010zz)

But the critical problems in polytheistic definitions are: "The distinction isn't a clear one, of course, as most people consider their own culture superior to others, and this will also apply to their culture's God. Kathenotheists have similar beliefs, but worship a different god at different times or places." (WK 2010zz)

(c) Pantheistic Definitions

The term "pantheism" refers to the belief that "God is itself the natural universe. The most famous Western pantheist is Baruch Spinoza." (WK 2010zz)

But the often cited critical problem in pantheistic definitions is that there are different interpretations. For instance, a different view is "panentheism," which "holds that the physical universe is part of God, but that God is more than this. While pantheism can be summed up by 'God is the world and the world is God,' panentheism can be summed up as 'The world is in God and God is in the world, but God is more than the world and is not synonymous with the world.'" (WK 2010zz)

Another critical question concerns whether or not it is an appropriate usage of the word "God" to be equated with the "natural universe" at all, because, for the critics, "Pantheism is little more than a redefinition of the word 'God' to mean 'Nature,' 'Universe,' or 'reality.'" (WK 2010e)

The Second Critical Question: Does God Exist?

And the second critical question to religion is not less important, as it asks: "Does God exist?" This question can also be asked in a different way: "Do we have any good reason to think that God does or does not exist?" (WK 2010zz)

Like the first critical question—there is also no best answer to the second critical questions, because it also depends on the philosophical orienation of a scholar in question.

For instance, throughout the ages, different answers have been given to this critical question, as shown below: (WK 2010zz)

- "Theism"—This is "the belief in the existence of one or more divinities or deities." There are at least the following three versions.

–"Pantheism" is "the belief that God exists as all things of the cosmos, that God is one and all is God; God is immanent."
–"Panentheism" is "the belief that God encompasses all things of the cosmos but that God is greater than the cosmos; God is both immanent and transcendent."
–"Deism" is "the belief that God does exist but does not interfere with human life and the laws of the universe; God is transcendent."

- "Agnosticism"—This is "the belief that the existence or non-existence of deities is currently unknown or unknowable, or that the existence of a God or of gods cannot be proven."
- "Atheism"—This is "the rejection of belief, or absence of belief, in deities."
- "Retreism"—This is "the belief in the ending or previous existence of god or gods."

Of course, things can be a bit more complicated than this classification here. After all, "some of these positions are not mutually exclusive. For example, agnostic theists choose to believe God exists while asserting that knowledge of God's existence is inherently unknowable. Similarly, agnostic atheists reject belief in the existence of all deities, while asserting that whether any such entities exist or not is inherently unknowable." (WK 2010zz)

A more detailed summary of the theoretical debate on the existence of God was already provided in *Sec. 1.5*.

The Dilemma of Critical Reason

These diverse (sometimes even incompatible) answers to the two often cited critical questions to religion should suffice to show us why the philosophy of religion does not provide answers (to the critical questions) that can satisfy everyone (or at least most people).

In fact, in *FHC*, I already went to great lengths to show the limits of critical reason, such that it has its dark side too (leading to destructive consequences, be they nihilistic, despotic, or else).

There is no lack of critics who have questioned the virtue of critical reason in history. For instance, the "excesses of the French Revolution" as criticized by "writers such as Joseph-Marie de Maistre and Edmund Burke" had raised serious "doubts that reason and rationalism…could solve all problems." (WK 2010g; E. Mossner 1967)

Isaiah Berlin (1969:144,152-4) once wrote this damaging critique of reason: "This is the positive doctrine of liberation by reason….I must assume that if the law I impose is rational (and I can only consult my own reason) it will automatically be approved by all the members of my society so far as they are rational beings. For if they disapprove, they must, *pro tanto*, be irrational; then they will need to be repressed by reason: whether their own or mine cannot matter, for the pronouncements of reason must be the same in all minds….If this leads to despotism, albeit by the best or the wisest…, can it be that there is something amiss in the premises of the argument?...Can it be that Socrates and the creators of the central Western tradition…who followed him have been mistaken, for more than two millennia, that virtue is not knowledge, nor freedom identical with either? That despite the fact that it rules the lives of more men than ever before in its long history, not one of the basic assumptions of this famous view is demonstrable, or, perhaps, even true."

This constitutes what I call, in the absence of better words, "the dilemma of critical reason"—in that, if it can be liberating, it can likewise be destructive.

When put in the current context of the philosophy of religion for the use of critical reason—the introduction to the contentious debate on the critical questions to religion reveals to us the opposing sides of the fence, such that the possibility and desirability of secularness (from the perspective of culture with the two critical questions to religion as two case studies here) is not to the extent that its respective defenders would like us to believe.

In addition, the analysis of the dilemma of critical reason (with the two critical questions to religion as a case study here) can reveal something about the ontological principles in existential dialectics, and good examples include the absoluteness-relativeness principle, the predictability-unpredictability principle, the explicability-inexplicability principle, the preciseness-vagueness principle, the simpleness-complicatedness principle, the openness-hiddenness principle, the denseness-emptiness principle, the slowness-quickness principle, the expansion-contraction principle, the convention-novelty principle, the evolution-transformation principle, the symmetry-asymmetry principle, the softness-hardness principle, the regression-progression principle, and the same-difference principle.

For instance, in relation to the absoluteness-relativeness principle, if there is absoluteness (e.g., the absolute view about the monotheistic definition of God in Christianity), there is relativeness (e.g., what is right for Christianity in regard to its monotheistic definition of God is not so for Hinduism in regard to its polytheistic definition of God). And the reverse direction also holds true.

In relation to the predictability-unpredictability principle, if there is predictability (e.g., the predictable tendency of a theist to believe in God), there is unpredictability (e.g., the more difficult task to even predict the particular outcome of a conversation among different theists in the traditions of pantheism, panentheism, and deism). And the reverse direction also holds true.

In relation to the explicability-inexplicability principle, if there is explicability (e.g., the explanation of the Western concern with the monotheistic definitions of God on the basis that "philosophy of religion is primarily an area of analytic philosophy, which is primarily Western"), there is inexplicability (e.g., the lack of convincing explanation, by those pointing out the Western basis in this way, of why, in this age of globalization, the West cannot be seriously interested in other definitions too). And the reverse direction also holds true.

In relation to the preciseness-vagueness principle, if there is precisensss (e.g., the precise identification of some critical questions like "What is God" in the philosophy of religion), there is vagueness (e.g., the vagueness in the word "God" in the question, since "there are a number of widely different senses of the word 'God'"). And the reverse direction also holds true.

In relation to the simpleness-complicatedness principle, if there is simpleness (e.g., the relatively simple way of understanding God in the West, mostly along the monotheistic tradition), there is complicatedness (e.g., the relatively more complicated analysis of the meaning of God by includiing other definitions in the non-West too). And the reverse direction also holds true.

In relation to the openness-hiddenness principle, if there is openness (e.g., the open exploration of the meaning of God by way of the monotheistic definitions in the West), there is hiddenness (e.g., the hidden bias in this obsession with the monotheistic definitions of God in the West, because of its neglect of other definitions in the non-West). And the reverse direction also holds true.

In relation to the denseness-emptiness principle, if there is denseness (e.g., the relatively denser concentration of the philosophers of religion in the West who devote their works on the monotheistic definitions of God), there is emptiness (e., the relatively less dense, or more empty, concentration of the philosophers of religion in the West who devote their works on the non-monotheistic definitions of God). And the reverse direction also holds true.

In relation to the slowness-quickness principle, if there is slowness (e.g. the relatively slower readiness of an atheist to accept the existence of

God), there is quickness (e.g., the relatively quicker readiness of a theist to accept the existence of God). And the reverse direction also holds true.

In relation to the expansion-contraction principle, if there is expansion (e.g., the relatively more developed ability of a philosopher of religion in the West to deal with religious questions in the analytic way), there is contraction (e.g, the relatively less developed ability of a philosopher of religion in the West to deal with religious questions in the intuitive or mystical way). And the reverse direction also holds true.

In relation to the convention-novelty principle, if there is convention (e.g., the conventional wisdom in religious philosophy about "the philosophical thinking that is inspired and directed by religion," such as Christianity), there is novelty (e.g., the alternative novel challenge to the conventional wisdom about defending religion in religious philosohy by the philosophers of religion who examine religious issues "dispassionately by what are thought of as those in two 'camps': adherents or believers, and non-believers"). And the reverse direction also holds true.

In relation to the evolution-transformation principle, if there is evolution (e.g., the natural evolution of humans to live in the state of awe towards nature, in the pre-historical days), there is transformation (e.g., the technical transformation of human view towards nature by the invention of systematic religious philosophies like Christianity, Islam, Hinduism, etc.). And the reverse direction also holds true.

In relation to the symmetry-asymmetry principle, if there is symmetry (e.g.., the co-existence of different philosophical views about religion throughout the ages), there is asymmetry (e.g., the prevalence of religious philosophy in the older days—but the rise of the philosophy of religion as a separate field of study in the modern days). And the reverse direction also holds true.

In relation to the softness-hardness principle, if there is softness (e.g., the polytheistic tolerance towards the existence of different gods in Hinduism), there is hardness (e.g., the monotheistic exclusiveness in accepting only one god among the Christians). And the reverse direction also holds true.

In relation to the regression-progression principle, if there is regression (e.g., the regression made in the philosophy of religion, in that it is unable to provide answers to the critical questions for religion that can satisfy everyone or at least most people), there is progression (e.g., the progress made in the philosophy of religion to clarify the usage of such words like "God," etc.). And the reverse direction also holds true.

And in relation to the same-difference principle, if there is similarity in outcome (e.g., the contribution to the molding of different beliefs about the larger universe, regardless of whether this be accomplished by way of theism, agnostism, atheism, etc.), there is difference in outcome (e.g., the contribution to the molding of different beliefs about the larger universe by way of theism for the existence of a supernatural reality—but the contribution to the molding of different beliefs about the larger universe by way of atheism for the non-existence of a supernatural reality). And the reverse direction also holds true.

The Pitfall of Secularness

This comprehensive analysis of the possibility and desirability of secularness, from the perspectives of the mind, nature, society, and culture, is no idle academic exercise but to show the different ways in which secularness is both possible and desirable, but not to the extent that the spokespersons from each side would like us to believe.

If secularness has its promise, it likewise has its pitfall—just as, in the previous chapter, if sacredness has its importance, it has its limitation too.

This comparison and contrast are important, because those on the side of sacredness often dismiss secularness merely as the opposite of sacredness without really trying to appreciate it from the vantage point of secularness itself. And the reverse also holds true.

Now that this intellectual journey comes to an end, what then can be concluded about the future of sacredness and secularness—or, more broadly speaking, about the future of religion itself.

This is the question which the next chapter, that is, Chapter Four on the future of religion, will answer, and for which we now turn to the concluding chapter hereafter.

Table 3.1. Secularness and Its Faults

- **Secularness and the Mind**
  —Ex: mental delusion, and the secular origin of religions
  —Ex: power drive, developmental stages, and the search for faith

- **Secularness and Nature**
  —Ex: evolutionary biology, and the debate on creation in religion
  —Ex: heliocentrism, and its conflict with organized religion

- **Secularness and Society**
  —Ex: religion, and the challenge of secularization
  —Ex: religion, and the politics of anitreligion

- **Secularness and Culture**
  —Ex: the anti-Christian, and the quest for life affirmation
  —Ex: philosophy of religion, and its critical questions for religion

Notes: The examples in the categories are solely illustrative (not exhaustive), and the comparison is relative (not absolute), nor are they necessarily mutually exclusive. And some can be easily re-classified elsewhere. As generalities, they allow exceptions.
Source: A summary of Ch.3 of *FPHR*

Table 3.2. Six Developmental Stages in the Search for Faith

- **Stage 1: "'Intuitive-Projective' Faith (Ages of Three to Seven)"**
  The first stage, for James Fowler, "usually occurs between the ages of three and seven, and is characterized by the psyche's unprotected exposure to the Unconscious. Imagination runs wild in this stage, uninhibited by logic." (R. Croucher 2003)
- **Stage 2: "'Mythic-Literal' Faith (Mostly in School Children)"**
  The second stage, for Fowler, usually occurs in school children, when "symbol and ritual begin to be integrated by the child. These symbols, however, are one-dimensional….[as] stage two persons have a strong belief in the justice and reciprocity of the universe, and their cosmic powers are almost always anthropomorphic." (R. Croucher 2003)
- **Stage 3: "'Synthetic-Conventional' Faith (Arising in Adolescence)"**
  The third stage, for Fowler, is where "the majority of the population finds its permanent home….Usually arising in adolescence, this stage demands a complex pattern of socialization and integration, and faith is an inseparable factor in the ordering of one's world. It is a stage characterized by conformity…." (R. Croucher 2003)
- **Stage 4: "'Individuative-Reflective' Faith" ("Mid-20s to Late 30s)"**
  The fourth stage, for Fowler, is "primarily a stage of angst and struggle, in which one must face difficult questions regarding identity and belief….At this time, the personality gradually detaches from the defining group from which it formerly drew its identity." (R. Croucher 2003)
- **Stage 5: "'Conjunctive' Faith (Mid-Life Crisis)"**
  The fifth stage, for Fowler, "moves one from stage four's rationalism to the acknowledgement of paradox and transcendence….In this stage a person grasps the reality behind the symbols of his or her inherited systems, and is also drawn to and acknowledging of the symbols of other's systems." (R. Croucher 2003)
- **Stage 6: "'Universalizing' Faith" (or "Enlightenment")**
  Finally, the sixth stage, for Fowler, is when "any such apprehensions dissolve and one becomes an activist for the unitive vision." (R. Croucher 2003)

Source: From *Sec. 3.2.2.* of *FPHR*. See book for more details and citations.

. **Table 3.3. Four Major Criticisms of Evolutionary Biology**

• Firstly, one criticism of evolutionary biology is that evolution's evidence is not complete. For instance, for some critics, although "[p]ast species have also left records of their evolutionary history,...this approach is most successful for organisms that had hard body parts, such as shells, bones or teeth. Further, as prokaryotes such as bacteria and archaea share a limited set of common morphologies, their fossils do not provide information on their ancestry." (WK 2010ii)

• Secondly, another criticism of evolutionary biology is that evolution's evidence is inconsistent. For instance, for some critics, "there are too many 'gaps' in the fossil record, that fossil-dating is circular, or that certain fossils, such as polystrate fossils, are seemingly 'out of place'....It is argued that certain features of evolution support creationism's catastrophism (cf. Great Flood), rather than evolution's gradualistic punctuated equilibrium, which some assert is an 'ad-hoc' theory to explain the fossil gaps." (WK 2010jj; M. Isaak 2004)

• Thirdly, still another criticism of evolutionary biology is that evolution's explanation is incomplete. For instance, Michael Behe (1996) argued "that current evolutionary theory cannot account for certain complex structures, particularly in microbiology....In addition to complex structures and systems, among the phenomena that critics variously claim evolution cannot explain are consciousness, free will, hominid intelligence, instincts, emotions, metamorphosis, photosynthesis, homosexuality, music, language, religion, morality, and altruism." (WK 2010jj; P. Johnson 1990) Alhtough some of these "have, in fact, been well-explained by evolution," for the critics, "others remain largely mysterious, or only have preliminary explanations." (WK 2010jj)

• And finally, one more criticism of evolutionary biology is that humans, unlike animals, are increasingly mastering nature, to the point that there will be what I already originally proposed in my previous works (like *FHC*, *FCD*, and so on) the emergence of "post-humans" in future times.

Source: From *Sec. 3.3.1* of *FPHR*. See book for more details and citations.

. **Table 3.4. Three Main Problems with the Secular Order**

• Firstly, one major criticism of the secular order is that "secularization as understood in the West…is being debated in the sociology of religion"; "scholars [like Rodney Stark and Peter Berger] have argued that levels of religiosity are not declining." (WK 2010pp) In addition, the rise of the "new religious movements" (as discussed in *Sec. 2.4.2*) is another good counter-argument to the secularization thesis in modern times. However, as I already showed in Ch.3 of *FHC* (and also in *Sec. 2.4.2* here), the new religious movements have their own problems too.

• Secondly, another major criticism of the secular order is that it is not as desirable (e.g., liberating) as its ideologues would like us to believe. For instance, I already went to great lengths in Ch.3 of *The Future of Human* Civilization (*FHC*) to argue that, as I wrote, "the idea of a post-secular society is a postmodern myth, just as the vision of a liberating secular society was a modern myth." I elaborated further this issue in *The Future of Capitalism and Democracy* (or *FCD*) My argument in *FHC* thus targets both sides of the debate, in that both the secular order in modern discourse and its alternative post-secular order in postmodern discourse are equally questionable, in regard to the extent of its respective possibility and desirability.

• And thirdly, still another major criticism of the secular order is that a secular state does not "add to democracy by protecting the rights of religious minorities" and other achievements as popularly claimed by its ideologues. (WK 2010qq) In *FHC*, I precisely made this argument by showing that the secular state, even when it is embedded in a liberal democracy (for the separation of church and state), has a long history of failure, in four major ways, namely, (a) that it is "morally disorientating," (b) that "it marginalizes circumstantially disadvantaged others," (c) that "it is hegemonic to its enemies," and (d) that "it is in-efficacious in achieving justice under modern (and now especially postmodern) conditions."

Source: From *Sec. 3.4.1* of *FPHR*. See book for more details and citations.

Table 3.5. A Critqiue of the Christian Psychology of Belief

- **Life Negation**
  The psychology of Christian belief is decadent, for Nietzsche, because it is life-negating, not life-affirming, as he once wrote that "one is not 'converted' to Christianity—one must be sufficiently sick for it." (WK 2010ww)
  For Nietzsche, "[t]he decadent and sick types of people came to power through Christianity. From everywhere, the aggregate of the sick accumulated in Christianity and outnumbered the healthy. 'The majority became master; the democratism of the Christian instincts conquered....' The meaning of the God on the Cross is that...'[e]verything that suffers, everything that hangs on the Cross, is divine....'" (WK 2010ww)
  In fact, "[b]ecause sickness belongs to the essence of Christianity, the typical Christian condition, 'belief,' has to be a form of sickness. Every straightforward, honest, scientific road to knowledge has to be repudiated by the Church as a forbidden road. Even doubt is a sin.'" (WK 2010ww)
  But this is contrary to the nature of true lnowledge, which "requires caution, intellectual moderation, discipline, and self–overcoming. But Christianity uses sick reasoning, such as martyrdom, to try to prove its truth....In response, Nietzsche quoted a passage from his earlier work: '[T]he need for belief, for some unconditional Yes and No,...is a need born of weakness.'" (WK 2010ww)

- **The Holy Falsehood**
  Also, the psychology of Christian belief, for Nietzsche, is obsessed with lying, as he once wrote: "Lying, or not wanting to see as one sees, is a trait of those who are devoted to a party or faction. Lying is utilized by all priests, whether pagan, Jewish, or Christian." (WK 2010ww)
  In this sense, "the right to lie and the shrewdness of a 'revelation' (Offenbarung) pertains to the priestly type....The 'Law,' the 'will of God,' the 'sacred book,' 'inspiration'—all merely words for the conditions under which the priest comes to power, by which he maintains his power." (WK 2010ww)
  And "Christianity's lies...serve...bad ends: the poisoning, slandering, denying of life, contempt for the body, the denigration and self–violation of man through the concept of sin...." (WK 2010ww)

Source: From *Sec. 3.5.1* of *FPHR*. See book for more details and citations.

• PART FOUR •

Conclusion

CHAPTER 4
CONCLUSION—THE FUTURE OF RELIGION

> [E]ach of our leading conceptions —each branch of our knowledge— passes successively through three different theoretical conditions: the theological, or fictitious; the metaphysical, or abstract; and the scientific, or positive.
> —Auguste Comte (WK 2010ee)

Beyond Sacredness and Secularness

The analyses of sacredness (in Chapter Two) and secularness (in Chapter Three) are important for the scholarly virtue of understanding the extent of the possibility and desirability of religion in human history, in the context of both sacredness and secularness.

This is all the more relevant in our time, when there is this secular underestimation of religion by a known scholar in 2007, who wrote that "in about twenty-five years almost all religions will have evolved into very different phenomena, so much so that in most quarters religion will no longer command the awe it does today"? In fact, Auguste Comte committed a similar underestimation of religion in his classic passage that the evolution of history moves from the theological mode of thinking through the metaphysical to the scientific. (WK 2010ee)

What then should we make with this ignorant nonsense in underestimating the future of religion? This secular underestimation can be well contrasted with an opposing idea back in the old days, when Francois-Marie Arouet Voltaire once sarcastically said that "[i]f God did not exist, it would be necessary to invent Him." (A. Rocco 2007)

One need not side with either of these two opposing sides of the debate on the future of religion, since the promise of secularness (on one side of the fence, as already discussed in Chapter Three) and the importance of sacredness (on the other side of the fence, as already analyzed in Chapter Two) are neither possible nor desirable to the extent that their respective ideologues would like us to believe.

But one should not misinterpret this dual critique of the two contrastive versions (and other views as already discussed in the last two chapters) of the conventional wisdom on the future of religion as a suggestion that religion is an useless field of study, or that other fields of study (related to religion) like philosophy, psychology, biology, or even cosmology are to be dismissed. Of course, neither of these two extreme views is plausible either.

As already indicated in *Sec. 1.1*, this book provides an alternative (better) way to understand the future of religion, especially in the dialectic context of sacredness and secularness—while learning from different approaches in the literature but without favoring any one of them (nor integrating them, since they are not necessarily compatible with each other).

Thus, this book offers a new theory (that is, *the comparative-substitutive theory of religion*) to go beyond the existing approaches in the literature on religion in a new way not thought of before.

This theory was first proposed in a preliminary way in Ch.9 of *The Future of Capitalism and Democracy* (or *FCD*) and in Ch.3 of the 2 volumes titled *The Future of Human* Civilization (*FHC*), especially with the conclusion in Ch.3 of *FHC*, where I wrote: "The idea of a post-secular society is a postmodern myth, just as the vision of a liberating secular society was a modern myth."

This view was then known as "the comparative theory of religion" in Ch.1 of *The Future of Post-Human Knowledge* (or *FPHK*). And this book (*FPHR*) provides a solid foundation for the *comparative-substitutive* argument here.

As a reminder, there are two words here, *comparative* and *substitutive*, in the title of the argument.

My argument is "comparative" because it provides a comparative analysis of different theoretical approaches in the literature by learning from them but without favoring any of them nor trying to integrate them (as they are not necessarily compatible with each other).

And my argument is also "substitutive," because it offers a visionary prediction of different forms of religion that the post-humans will use as substitutes for the human ones (hitherto existing in human history) which will no longer be much useful in the post-human future.

With this clarification in mind—the comparative-substitutive theory of religion has four distinctive features to remember.

Firstly, my theory makes good use of all theoretical approaches in the literature on religion, be they about the theist argument, the skeptical argument, or the critical argument—especially from the most comprehensive combined perspectives of the mind, nature, society, and culture (as already analyzed in Chapter Two and Chapter Three).

Secondly, just like many other theories of mine in my previous books, my theory here does not heavily favor any specific theory over others in the literature, nor trying to integrate them (as they are not necessarily compatible with each other).

Thirdly, my theory treats the issue of religion in the distinctive dialectic context of sacredness and secularness—especially in the larger dialectic context of no sacredness without secularness, and vice versa, together with the subsequent transcendence of both.

And fourthly, it contains sixteen major theses, namely, (a) the first thesis: the absoluteness-relativeness principle, (b) the second thesis: the predictability-unpredictability principle, (c) the third thesis: the explicability-inexplicability principle, (d) the fourth thesis: the preciseness-vagueness principle, (e) the fifth thesis: the simpleness-complicatedness principle, (f) the sixth thesis: the openness-hiddenness principle, (g) the seventh thesis: the denseness-emptiness principle, (h) the eighth thesis: the slowness-quickness principle, (i) the nineth thesis: the expansion-contraction principle, (j) the tenth thesis: the convention-novelty principle, (k) the eleventh thesis: the evolution-transformation principle, (l) the twelveth thesis: the symmetry-asymmetry principle, (m) the thirteenth thesis: the softness-hardness principle, (n) the fourteenth thesis: the regression-progression principle, (o) the fifteenth thesis: the sameness-difference principle, and (p) the sixteenth thesis: the post-human substitution—to be elaborated in the rest of this concluding chapter.

If successful, this seminal project is to fundamentally change the way that we think about religion, from the combined perspectives of the mind, nature, society, and culture, with enormous implications for the human future and what I originally called its "post-human" fate.

Other Relevant Principles

Lest misunderstanding hastily occurs (as this is something that I regularly did in my previous books, *almost verbatim*), it should be clarified at the outset that, if other ontological principles in existential dialectics (other than the 15 as listed in the 16 theses) are not explicitly included in the listing of the theses in the Table of Contents, it is not because they are not important, but merely because they are not as equally relevant as the others in the current case study (in terms of the number of citations of each principle in the book), although different case studies will, of course, reveal different degrees of relevance of the principles.

Even then, in some cases (like this one), the difference between any two given principles, for instance, in terms of the number of citations in a book, is rather small, so the reason in those cases is more aesthetic (than otherwise), because it looks nicer to list only 15 theses for 15 principles (than 21 theses for all of the 21 principles) in the Table of Contents.

This is true, even if different studies of the same kind can yield different views about the degree of relevance for each ontological principle, depending on the specific nature of a research in question, needless to say. So, if a different author analyzes the subject matter in a different way, the relevance of the ontological principles will be different.

After all, the symmetry-asymmetry principle already implies that not all principles are equally relevant in any topic under examination, as they are not created equal for all cases under all circumstances (which would be an extreme view, of course).

In any event, the relevancy of other principles (besides the ones as already listed in the theory above) for the present study can be summarized below, in relation to the five categories of ontological principles in existential dialectics.

In the Category of Method

Firstly, in regard to the formalness-informalness principle (on the formal requirements of logical systems), if there is formalness (e.g., the formal logical requirement of completeness for a system of ideas, as in science, in *Sec. 2.2.1*; the formal logical requirement of soundness in a system of ideas, as in science, in *Sec. 2.2.2*; the formal logical requirement of consistency and completeness in a system of ideas, in *Sec. 2.3.1*; the formal logical requirements of a system of idea to be consistent and sound, in *Sec. 3.3.1*; and the formal logical requirements of a system of ideas to be complete and sound, in *Sec. 3.3.2*), there is informalenss too (e.g., the nonformal allowance of faith too in religion without complete proof, in addition to the use of reason—as in fideism, in *Sec. 2.2.1*; the non-formal allowance of coincidence too, without complete proof of causation for soundness, in magic, as Ramsey Dukes once said that "questions such as 'Are you sure it was your magic that cured her?' are irrelevant to the magician. 'If it was a coincidence, it doesn't matter just so long as he can bring about such coincidences,'" in *Sec. 2.2.2*; the non-formal allowance of inconsistency and incompleteness in the teleological argument, which is "incoherent" and incapable of proving itself in some ways, since everything is known after the fact, as pointed out by the critics, but many people throughout history still believe in religious cosmology, in *Sec. 2.3.1*; the nonformal nature of evolutionary theory, such that its claims are consistent and sound in some ways, but inconsistent and unsound in some other ways, in *Sec. 3.3.1*; and the nonformal nature of the heliocentric model as proposed by Galileo, such that it is complete and sound in some ways but not in other ways, as "he believed that the available evidence strongly favoured heliocentrism,...but he did not have the conclusive proof necessary to satisfy Bellarmine's requirements," in *Sec. 3.3.2*). And the reverse direction also holds true.

And secondly, in regard to the partiality-totality principle (on the relationships between whole and parts), if there is partial analysis (e.g., the partial view of each religious individual to use faith for knowing his own God, in *Sec. 2.2.1*; the partial view from each individual for his survival by using tools, language, living together, etc., in *Sec. 2.3.2*; and the partial viewpoint of each animal to compete for the survival of the fittest in the state of nature, in *Sec. 3.3.1*), there is also holistic analysis (e.g., the more holistic picture of all the views of religious individuals, each with faith for knowing his own God, such that the whole is not the sum of its parts, in that there are many incompatible positions about what the true God is, in *Sec. 2.2.1*; the more holistic view that there is the emergent phenomenon of religion as a by-product of the evolution of tool use, language, group living, etc., such that the whole is not the sum of its parts, in *Sec. 2.3.2*; and the holistic view of the outcome of all animals competing with each other in the state of nature, such that there is subsequently the emergence of new species and the extinction of old ones, so the whole is not the sum of its parts, in *Sec. 3.3.1*). And the reverse direction also holds true.

In the Category of Structure

Firstly, in regard to the finiteness-transfiniteness principle (on the nature of numbers), if there is finiteness (e.g., the finite nature of a "simple" or ordinary human being, in the view of Kierkegaard, in *Sec. 2.2.1*; the finite nature of the power of a magician in religious magic, since "it is up to the deity in question whether or not to grant the request," in *Sec. 2.2.2*; and the finite number of years that the body of an animal like a human being can remain alive, in *Sec. 2.5.2*), there is also transfiniteness (e.g., the transfinite nature of an "eternal, perfect being" like God, in the view of Kierkegaard, in *Sec. 2.2.1*; the transfinite nature of the power of the deity in religious magic, since it can grant any request if it so wishes, according to the believers in religious magic, in *Sec. 2.2.2*; and the transfinite number of years that the soul of a human body can live, even after the decomposition of the body after death, in accordance to animism, in *Sec. 2.5.2*). And the reverse direction also holds true.

In the Category of Process

Firstly, in regard to the change-constancy principle (on the alteration of things), if there is change (e.g., individuals adopt new religious beliefs that differ from their previous beliefs, in *Sec. 2.4.1*; the ever changing face of religion with the emergence of new religious movements throughout the ages, in *Sec. 2.4.2*; "the change in the inherited traits of a population of organisms through successive generations," according to evolutionary biology, in *Sec. 3.3.1*; the change in some nation-states in modern times "from close identification with religious values and institutions toward non-religious…values and secular institutions," as in Turkey, in *Sec. 3.4.1*; the change from the support of the Russian Orthodox Church in pre-Soviet era to its condemnation in the Soviet era, in *Sec. 3.4.2*; and the ever changing nature of the ways of life in human society, ranging from the Jewish through the Christian to the Nietzschean versions, in *Sec. 3.5.1*), there is constancy too (e.g., the ever constancy of the phenomenon of religious conversion, in *Sec. 2.4.1*; the ever constant search for "community" and "spiritual identity" by religion throughout the ages, in *Sec. 2.4.2*; the ever constant role of "natural selection" as a powerful process to affect the variation of traits over time, according to evolutionary biology, in *Sec. 3.3.1*; the ever constancy of the search for law and order in society, be it secular or religious, in *Sec. 3.4.1*; the recurrent debate on the nature of religion, regardless of whether it was promoted in pre-Soviet Russia or condemned in the Soviet era, in *Sec. 3.4.2*; and the ever constancy of seeking a new way of life in human history, in *Sec. 3.5.1*). And the reverse direction also holds true.

And secondly, in relation to the order-chaos principle (on the pattern of things), if there is order (e.g., the orderly pattern of the evolution of life as detected in "the tree of life," according to evolutionary biology, in *Sec. 3.3.1*), there is chaos too (e.g., the role of "chance" to play, as in "genetic drift, an independent process that produces entirely random changes in how common traits are in a population," in *Sec. 3.3.1*). And the reverse direction also holds true.

In the Category of Agency

Firstly, in regard to the theory-praxis principle (on the duality of knowledge), on the one hand, there is theoretical construction (e.g., the theoretical construction of fideism for the appeal to faith more than reason, in *Sec. 2.2.1*; the theoretical construction of magic in accordance to some components like "spirits," "energy," "meditation," "law of similarity," etc., in *Sec. 2.2.2*; the theoretical construction of the teleological argument, in *Sec. 2.3.1*; the theoretical construction of "human rights," especially, though not exclusively, since modern times, in *Sec. 2.4.1*; the theoretical construction of shamanism in regard to the existence of two different but interconnected worlds in the cosmos and the ability of some individuals to "have at will a direct controlled relationship with the other-world," in *Sec. 2.5.1*; the theoretical construction of animism in relation to its views on the cosmos, life after death, and the diversity of spirits, in *Sec. 2.5.2*; the theoretical construction of the psychobiology of religion, in *Sec. 3.2.1*; the theoretical constraction of evolutionary theory in modern times, especially with the works of Darwin and Mendel, in *Sec. 3.3.1*; the theoretical construction of geocentrism, like the Ptolemaic model, in ancient times, in *Sec. 3.3.2*; the theoretical construction of secularism, especially though not exclusively, during the Enlightenment, in *Sec. 3.4.1*; the theoretical construction of state atheism, in that religion is "the opium of the people," in *Sec. 3.4.2*; and the theoretical construction of the Nietzsche quest for life affirmation, in *Sec.3.5.1*).

On the other hand, there is also its practical application (e.g., the practical application of fideism for everyday life, as shown by those followers of Christian existentialism, in *Sec. 2.2.1*; the practical application of magic in everyday life like "the burning of oil or incense," "christening," etc., in *Sec. 2.2.2*; the practical application of the teleological argument for Christian conversion by the Catholic Church under Thomas Aquinas in the 13th century, in *Sec. 2.3.1*; the practical application of "human rights" for religious conversion as shown by the United Nations Universal Declaration of Human Rights, in *Sec. 2.4.1*; the practical application of the theoretical construct of shamanism "for very practical purposes: to cure the sick, to restore an upset harmony, etc., in *Sec. 2.5.1*; the practical application of animism for the practices of ancestor worship, rituals to honor animals, etc., in *Sec. 2.5.2*; the practical application of the psychobiology of religion for anti-faith politics, as Bunting once argued that "the books [by scholars like Richard Dawkins, Daniel Dennett, Sam Harris and Christopher Hitchens] are 'deeply political,' sharing a 'loathing' of the role of religion in U.S. politics," in *Sec. 3.2.1*; the practical application of evolutionary theory for "genetic engineering, with selectable markers such as antibiotic resistance genes being used to manipulate DNA in molecular biology," in *Sec. 3.3.1*; the practical application of the Ptolemaic model by the Catholic Church for the defense of Christian teaching, in *Sec. 3.3.2*; the practical application of secularism for the process of secularization, as in modern Turkey under Ataturk for the strict separation of church and state, in *Sec. 3.4.1*; the practical application of state atheism in the Soviet Union for the suppression of all religions, in *Sec. 3.4.2*; and the practical application of Nietzsche's work by the Nazi during the inter-war period, as "the Nazis made very selective use of Nietzsche's philosophy," in *Sec. 3.5.1*).

And the reverse direction also holds true.

1st Thesis: The Absoluteness-Relativeness Principle

The first thesis refers to the absoluteness-relativeness principle (on the multiplicity of things) in the category of "method" in existential dialectics, which was first proposed in *FPHK*, in that there is the multiplicity of things in reality, be they about entities, qualities (or properties), and relationships. If there is something absolute, there is likewise something relative. And there is no absoluteness without relativeness—and vice versa.

Both absoluteness and relativeness here are also relevant to different modalities often cited in the literature on ontology, such as possibility (e.g., something "can" happen) and its opposite (e.g., impossibility), probability (e.g., something "will" happen) and its opposite (e.g., improbability), and necessity (e.g., something "should" happen) and its opposite (e.g., contingency).

For instance, on the one hand, there are absolute viewpoints (e.g., the absolute view of fideism that faith can be used in situations when there is no compelling evidence, in *Sec. 2.2.1*; the absolute view of the practitioners of magic that it should be "secretive and isolated, and rarely performed publicly in order to protect and to preserve occult knowledge," in *Sec. 2.2.2*; the absolute viewpoint of the ideologues of religious cosmology like Plato, in that there must be "a 'demiurge' of supreme wisdom and intelligence as the creator of the cosmos," in *Sec. 2.3.1*; the absolute view of creation theory in regard to the necessity of religion for the understanding of God, in *Sec. 2.3.2*; the absolute view of the United Nations Universal Declaration of Human Rights, since it is supposed to be "universal," in *Sec. 2.4.1*; the absolute view of the critics of cults like

Anton Hein, who "severely criticize scholars...who disagree with their views" and call them "cult apologists," in *Sec. 2.4.2*; "the belief" of a shaman "in the ability... to have at will a direct controlled relationship with the other-world," in *Sec. 2.5.1*; the absolute view in the Abrahamic tradition that there exists only one God, in *Sec. 2.5.2*; the absolute view of scholars like Mandell that "God is in the brain," in *Sec. 3.2.1*; the absolute view by Fowler about the six stages of faith development, in *Sec. 3.2.2*; the absolute view of creationism that life and the world are the creation of God, in *Sec. 3.3.1*; the absolute view of the Catholic Church in the time of Galileo that the earth did not move but the sun was to move around it, in *Sec. 3.3.2*; the absolute view of the secularists that secularization is "progressive," in *Sec. 3.4.1*; the absolute view of of Marxism-Leninism that religion is what Marx once called "the opium of the people" and is to be eliminated, as during the existence of the Soviet Union, in *Sec. 3.4.2*; the absolute view of the Jews that they are the "holy, chosen people," in *Sec. 3.5.1*; and the absolute view about the monotheistic definition of God in Christianity, in *Sec. 3.5.2*).

On the other hand, there are likewise relative counterparts (e.g., what is right for a fideist to appeal to faith is not so for a scientist like Sagan "to withhold belief until there is compelling evidence," in *Sec. 2.2.1*; what is important for magic to be "secretive and isolated" is not so for religion to be "predictable and proscribed and...usually performed openly in order to impart knowledge to the community," in *Sec. 2.2.2*; what is true for Plato in relation to the argumend from design is not so for the critics of religious cosmology like Richard Dawkins and George Smith, in *Sec. 2.3.1*; what is true for creation theory is not so for the "exaptative" version of the evolutionary psychology of religion in regard to religion as a "by-product" of evolution instead, in *Sec. 2.3.2*; what is right for the UN in regard to religious conversion as a human right is not so for the Russian Orthodox Church, which "takes exception to what it considers illegitimate proselytizing by the Roman Catholic Church, the Salvation Army, Jehovah's Witnesses and other religious movements in what it refers to as its canonical territory," in *Sec. 2.4.1*; what is right for the critics of cults like Hein to call their enemies "cult apologists" is not so for the defenders of cults like Massimo Introvigne who call the critics of cults "hate groups" or alternatively, "'anti-cult' activists," in *Sec. 2.4.2*; what is true for a shaman in regard to his ability "to have at will a direct controlled relationship with the other-world" is not so for a contemporary scientist who is skeptical to the existence of this other-world and to the shaman's claim of his ability, in *Sec. 2.5.1*; what is true for the Abrahamic tradition in regard to the existence of only one God is not so for animism in regard to the existence of many spirits in the cosmos, in *Sec. 2.5.2*; what is true for scholars like Mandell that "God is in the brain" is not so for the critics like Ward, in *Sec. 3.2.1*; what is true for Fowler in regard to the six stages of faith development is not so for the critics in regard to the lack of sufficient empirical support of his stage model of faith development, in *Sec. 3.2.2*; what is true for creationism in regard to the creation of God is not so for evolutionary biology in regard to natural selection and chance, in *Sec. 3.3.1*; what is true for the Catholic Church in regard to the geocentric model is not so for Galileo in regard to the heliocentric model, in *Sec. 3.3.2*; what is good for the secularists in regard to the separation of church and state is not so for the Christian fundamentalists who oppose it, in *Sec. 3.4.1*; what is good for the Soviet Union to suppress the religions is not so for the Russian Orthodox Church which was suppressed, in *Sec. 3.4.2*; what is true for the Jews in regard to the "holy, chosen people" is not necessarily so for a gentile, in *Sec. 3.5.1*; and what is right for Christianity in regard to its monotheistic definition of God is not so for Hinduism in regard to its polytheistic definition of God, in *Sec. 3.5.2*).

And the reverse direction also holds true.

However, it should be stressed (as this is something that I regularly did in my previous books, *almost verbatim*) that there are different shades of gray (or different degrees of truth) in the two opposites, and the classification is not necessarily mutually exclusive either. In fact, even when some combinations of the two occur, they only end up sharing the same dialectic relationship, but in a different degree.

Also, there are some other relationships (as a kind of family resemblance) which have something in common with the principle, but they are not exactly the same but only more or less comparable, which varies from case to case.

Good examples of family resemblance in relation to the principle are uniformity-diversity, internalness-externalness, immanence-transcendence, and so forth.

2nd Thesis: The Predictability-Unpredictability Principle

The second thesis is called the predictability-unpredictability principle (on the occurrence of events) in the category of "method" in existential dialectics (which was first proposed in *FC* and, later, other books of mine), in that both predictability and unpredictability have a major role to play in the occurrence of things, so that neither determinism nor indeterminism wins the centuries-old fight. There is no predictability without unpredictability—and vice versa.

There are events which are predictable, just as there are those which are not. Or what is regarded as unpredictable at one point in time may turn out to be predictable later, and, conversely, what is deemed as predictable may turn out to not be so predictable. Even in predictability, outcomes are subject to uncertainty, the degree of which varies from case to case.

For instance, on the one hand, there is predictability (e.g., the predictable tendency of a fideist to appeal to faith in situations where there is no compelling evidence about God, in *Sec. 2.2.1*; the predictable tendency of a magician to emphasize such things as "mystical power," "elements," "symbols," "energy," "law of similarity," "law of contact," "concentration," "subconscious mind," and so on, in *Sec. 2.2.2*; the predictable tendency of a proponent of the teleological argument to claim that there is an intelligent designer in the cosmos, in *Sec. 2.3.1*; the predictable claim by those for the evolutionary origin of religions that there are some major requirements such as "increased brain size," "tool use," etc., in *Sec. 2.3.2*; the predictable tendency of officials from the UN to speak for religious conversion as a human right, in *Sec. 2.4.1*; the predictable tendency of an individual who is dissatisifed with "mainstream" or "established" religious organizations to join a NRM, in *Sec. 2.4.2*; the predictable tendency of a shaman to use any of the substances and techniques to perform his functions, in *Sec. 2.5.1*; the predictable tendency of animists to believe in life after death, in *Sec. 2.5.2*; the predictable tendency of those who experience "psychic" or "spiritual" phenomena to have "a higher than average ability…to have one or more…characteristics" of mental disorders, in accordance to researchers like Penfield and others, in *Sec. 3.2.1*; the predictable tendency of those supporters of Fowler's stage model to point out the six stages for individuals to go through in faith development, in *Sec. 3.2.2*; the predictable occurrence of "common descent" like "the tree of life" in evolutionary biology, in *Sec. 3.3.1*; the prediction by the Ptolemaic model of "various celestial motions, including the beginnings and ends of retrograde motion" of the planets in the solar system, generally speaking, in *Sec. 3.3.2*; the predictable tendency of a secular state to argue for the separation of church and state, in *Sec. 3.4.1*; the predictable tendency of a state which advocates state atheism to try to suppress and eliminate all religious beliefs, in *Sec. 3.4.2*; the predictable requirement of the Jews in antiquity to to obey the commandment that "[d]isobedience of God [the priest] is 'sin'" and "[s]ubjection to God [the priest] is redemption," in *Sec.*

3.5.1; and the predictable tendency of a theist to believe in God, in *Sec. 3.5.2*).

On the other hand, there is unpredictability (e.g., the more difficult task to predict which God a fideist is to have faith in, because "an apparent consequence of fideism is that all religious thinking becomes equal," in *Sec. 2.2.1*; the more difficult task to predict when a particular magical practice will produce the desired outcome, since magic does not always work as initially hoped for, in *Sec. 2.2.2*; the more difficult task for a proponent of the teleological argument to predict other worlds because "there is no ability to sample a large enough set of alternatives" and "indeed we know of no other cosmos to sample, in *Sec. 2.3.1*; the more difficult task to predict, if viewed solely within the evolutionary origin of religions, what other alternative religions and, for that matter, what other things can emerge out of these major requirements, in *Sec. 2.3.2*; the more difficult task to predict which specific country and specific indivdual will accept the legitimacy of proselitsing in a particular case at a given time, because of the disagreements about the legal rights of religious conversion and their limits among countries and individuals, in *Sec. 2.4.1*; the more difficult task to predict exactly how long this individual will stay in that NRM or how he exactly he will leave later on, in *Sec. 2.4.2*; the more difficult task to predict which particular combination of substances and techniques a shaman will use on a particular occasion and when exactly his attempt is successful or not, in *Sec. 2.5.1*; the more difficult task to predict where exactly the spirit of a deceased will actually go, since "in some systems, the spirit is believed to pass to an easier world of abundant game or ever-ripe crops, while in other systems, the spirit remains on earth as a ghost, often malignant," whereas others try to combine the two, in *Sec. 2.5.2*; the more difficult task to predict, if viewed from the vantage point of Penfield and others, the particular combination of mental disorders that an individual who experiences "psychic" or "spiritual" phenomena really has at a given point of time, in *Sec. 3.2.1*; the more difficult task to predict, if looked within Fowler's stage model, whether a particular individual will go through the six stages in his lifespan, or, alternatively, to what extent he will go through his stages, or experiences them, when compared with others individuals, in *Sec. 3.2.2*; the more difficult task to predict the common ancestry of those "species" which have not "left records of their evolutionary history" because of soft "body parts," and those "prokaryotes such as bacteria and archaea" which "share a limited set of common morphologies," so "their fossils do not provide information on their ancestry," in *Sec. 3.3.1*; the failure of the Ptolemaic model to predict precisely or accurately "various celestial motions, including the beginnings and ends of retrograde motion" of the planets, because the prediction was only "fairly well at the time it was developed" in antiquity, but not by modern standards, in *Sec. 3.3.2*; the more difficult task to predict whether, or to what extent, a particular secular state is necessarily able to achieve its ideals like "equality of all people," in *Sec. 3.4.1*; the more difficult task to predict to what extent the effort of state atheism in a particular country at a given point in history will succeed in achieving its central goal, in *Sec. 3.4.2*; the Jews in antiquity failed to predict the rebellious child "wihtin Judaism," with "the name Jesus of Nazareth," for the "opposition against the dominant order," such that "[t]he Jewish church and the Jewish nation received this rebellion as a threat to its existence," in *Sec. 3.5.1*; and the more difficult task to even predict the particular outcome of a conversation among different theists in the traditions of pantheism, panentheism, and deism, in *Sec. 3.5.2*).

And the reverse direction also holds true.

Again, it should be stressed, however, that there are different shades of gray (or different degrees of truth) in the two opposites, and the classification is not necessarily mutually exclusive either. In fact, even when some combinations of the two occur, they only end up sharing the same dialectic relationship, but in a different degree.

Also, there are some other relationships (as a kind of family resemblance) which have something in common with the principle, but they are not exactly the same but only more or less comparable, which varies from case to case.

Good examples of family resemblance in relation to the principle are sureness-arbitrariness, and so forth.

3rd Thesis: The Explicability-Inexplicability Principle

The third thesis is called the explicability-inexplicability principle (on the underlying mechanisms of things) in the category of "method" in existential dialectics (which was proposed in *FPHU* and other books of mine), in that both explicability and inexplicability are part of the understanding of things. There is no explicability without inexplicability—and vice versa.

This principle tells us the dual nature of the research dilemma, in that, if reality can be explained in some ways, it also has its other ways which are not quite explainable, at a given point in time.

For instance, on the one hand, there is explicability (e.g., the explanation by Kierkegaard that the "leap of faith" is necessary, because "reason cannot possibly comprehend such a phenomenon" like Abraham's act of sacrificing Isaac, in *Sec. 2.2.1*; the explanation of the efficacy of magic, by its practitioners, on the basis of the law of similarity for associate thinking, for instance, in *Sec. 2.2.2*; the explanation of the orderly nature of the universe by the ideologues of the teleological argument on the basis of the existence of "a powerful intelligent designer," in *Sec. 2.3.1*; the explanation by those for the "adaptive value of religion" that religion evolves due to "natural selection," in *Sec. 2.3.2*; the explanation, if viewed within the United Nations Universal Declaration of Human Rights, of its defense of religious conversion on the basis of its being "a human right," in *Sec. 2.4.1*; the explanation of the rise of NRMs accordiing to different models by Stark and Bainbridge, in *Sec. 2.4.2*; the explanation of those like Hamer "in some occult and esoteric circles to reinvent shamanism in a modern form, drawing from core shamanism…often revolving around the use of ritual drumming and dance," in *Sec. 2.5.1*; the explanation by animists that humans are just part of nature on the egalitarian basis of many spirits in the cosmos, both human and non-human, in *Sec. 2.5.2*; the explanation of the experience of the "psychic" or "spiritual" phenomena on the basis of "disinhibited temporal lobes," in *Sec. 3.2.1*; the explanation, by Adler, of the spiritual quest of people on the basis of the power drive "to compensate for inferiorities," in *Sec. 3.2.2*; the explanation of variation in the evolution of life on the basis of natural selection and chance, for instance, in accordance to evolutionary biology, in *Sec. 3.3.1*; the explanation of the cause of tides on earth by Galileo, on the basis that they "were caused by the sloshing back and forth of water in the seas as a point on the Earth's surface speeded up and slowed down because of the Earth's rotation on its axis and revolution around the Sun," in *Sec. 3.3.2*; the explanation of the desirability of a secular state on the basis of its contribution to "democracy by protecting the rights of religious minorities," in *Sec. 3.4.1*; the explanation of religion by Marx on the basis of class struggle, in *Sec. 3.4.2*; the explanation of truth by the Christians, for Nietzsche, on the basis of faith in regard to blessedness, in that "[b]elief makes blessed: thus it is true," in *Sec. 3.5.1*; and the explanation of the Western concern with the monotheistic definitions of God on the basis that "philosophy of religion is primarily an area of analytic philosophy, which is primarily Western," in *Sec. 3.5.2*).

On the other hand, there is inexplicability (e.g., the lack of sufficient explanation by Kierkegaard of why Abraham could not withhold his belief in God if he could not comprehend the need to sacrifice Isaac, as someone like Sagan would say, in *Sec. 2.2.1*; the lack of sufficient explanation by the magician of why correlation is causation at all, in *Sec. 2.2.2*; the lack of sufficient explanation by the ideologues of the ideological argument to explain why this "powerful intelligent designer" must be "a God" in the first place, as questioned by Voltaire, or "why may not several deities combine in contriving and framing the world?" as asked by Hume, in *Sec. 2.3.1*; the inexplicability, by those in the camp for the "adaptive value of religion," of why the benefits for health and solidarity, for instance, are necessarily "adaptive," as they may well be "exaptative" by the critics, in *Sec. 2.3.2*; the lack of sufficient explanation, if viewed within the United Nations Universal Declaration of Human Rights, of why this universality of religious conversion as a human right is necessarily true in the first place, in light of the disagreements among countries and individuals, in *Sec. 2.4.1*; the lack of sufficient explanation of why these four models are sufficient to explain the rise of NRMs, since not everyone agress with them, and the defenders of cults often question any models which do not speak more favorably about NRMs, in *Sec. 2.4.2*; the lack of sufficient explanation by those like Hamer in these "occult and esoteric circles" of why "pieces of diverse religions can be taken out of context to form some sort of 'universal' shamanic tradition" in the first place, in *Sec. 2.5.1*; the lack of sufficient explanation by animists of why some spirits cannot be superior than others, or why this egalitarian view is necessarily true, in *Sec. 2.5.2*; the lack of sufficient explanation, if viewed within the psychobiology of religion, of why some individuals who believe in God or something like that are "some of the most able philosophers and scientists in the world today" without mental delusion at all, as pointed out by Ward, in *Sec. 3.2.1*; the lack of sufficient explanation, by Adler, of why "to strive for perfection and superiority" must be the goal in faith development, or why other goals in faith development like humility, modesty, the acceptance of imperfection, etc. are not important too for many in their spiritual quest, in *Sec. 3.2.2*; the lack of explanation of other phenomena like "consciousness," "free will," "music," "religion," etc., if examined solely on the basis of evolutionary biology, for the critics, in *Sec. 3.3.1*; the failure of Galileo's theory of tides to explain why "there are two daily high tides at Venice instead of one, about twelve hours apart," and to take into account of the moon which can cause the tides, as suggested by Kepler but ignored by Galileo, in *Sec. 3.3.2*; the lack of sufficient explanation by the ideologues of the secular state about its four failures in the modern era, contrary to its essential claim, as shown by my analysis in *FHC*, in *Sec. 3.4.1*; the lack of sufficient explanation of religion, if looked only from the narrow Marxist viewpoint, in regard to other phenomena of religion as explained by alternative theories in, say, evolutionary biology, neuroscience, etc., in *Sec. 3.4.2*; the lack of convincinng explanation by the Christians, for Nietzsche, of why faith or blessedness can be a proof of truth at all, since "blessedness is something that the priest promises for the future. It, itself, is an object of belief. Also, blessedness, or pleasure, cannot be a proof of truth. '[W]hen on earth was it established that true judgments give more enjoyment than false ones…?' It could be said, 'Belief makes blessed: thus it is lies,'" in *Sec. 3.5.1*; and the lack of convincing explanation, by those pointing out the Western basis in this way, of why, in this age of globalization, the West cannot be seriously interested in other definitions too, in *Sec. 3.5.2*).

And the reverse direction also holds true.

Once more, it should be stressed, however, that there are different shades of gray (or different degrees of truth) in the two opposites, and the classification is not necessarily mutually exclusive either. In fact, even when some combinations of the two occur, they only end up sharing the same dialectic relationship, but in a different degree.

Also, there are some other relationships (as a kind of family resemblance) which have something in common with the principle, but they are not exactly the same but only more or less comparable, which varies from case to case.

Good examples of family resemblance in relation to the principle are underlyingness-regularness, causation-regularity, causation-correlation and so forth.

4th Thesis: The Preciseness-Vagueness Principle

The fourth thesis is called the preciseness-vagueness principle (on the refinement of things) in the category of "structure" in existential dialectics (which was first out worked out in *FIA*), in that both preciseness and vagueness are important, not that one is better than the other, but that both are used, in different degrees of preference, in accordance to the contextual application from the perspectives of nature, the mind, culture, and society. There is no preciseness without vagueness—and vice versa.

For instance, on the one hand, there is preciseness (e.g., the precise identification of God as "eternal" and "perfect" in Kierkegaard's Christian existentialism, in *Sec. 2.2.1*; the precise identification of some of the basic components of religious magic, like "spirits," "elements," "symbols," "energy," etc. by the practitioners of religious magic, in *Sec. 2.2.2*; the precise identification of "a powerful intelligent designer" by the proponents of the teleological argument, in *Sec. 2.3.1*; the precise identification of religion, by Gould, as a "by-product" of the natural selection of something else, in *Sec. 2.3.2*; the precise identification of "religious conversion" as a human right by the United Nations Universal Declaration of Human Rights, in *Sec. 2.4.1*; the precise identification of such features as "of recent origin" and "difference" in the definition of NRM, in *Sec. 2.4.2*; the precise identification of "drumming, trance, chanting, entheogens and hallucinogenics, spirit communication and healing" as shamanistic practices, in *Sec. 2.5.1*; the precise identification of "trance states," "dreams and hallucinations," etc. as the things that animists engage in, in *Sec. 2.5.2*; the precise identification of the experience of "psychic" or "spiritual" phenomena in "disinhibited temporal lobes," in *Sec. 3.2.1*; the precise identification of the six stages in faith development by Fowler, in *Sec. 3.2.2*; the precise identification of "chance" as a process for the variation of traits in a population, in accordance to evolutionary biology, in *Sec. 3.3.1*; the precise identification of "the Sun…at the center of the universe" in heliocentrism as "found in a range of Greek, Arabic and Latin texts," in *Sec. 3.3.2*; the precise identification of the separation of church and state in the definition of "secularism," in *Sec. 3.4.1*; the precise identification of state atheism as a political version of antireligion, in *Sec. 3.4.2*; the precise identification of "the overman" for the leadership of the quest for life affirmation in the future, for Nietzsche, in *Sec. 3.5.1*; and the precise identification of some critical questions like "What is God" in the philosophy of religion, in *Sec. 3.5.2*).

On the other hand, there is vagueness (e.g., the vagueness in the attributes of "eternity" and "perfection" of God, in Kierkegaard's Christian existentialism, since there can be different intepretations of why they actually refer to, in *Sec. 2.2.1*; the vagueness in understanding the nature of these components like "spirits," "deities," etc., since a magiican cannot exactly spell out the specific circumstances under which a deity in question will grant a specific request or not, in *Sec. 2.2.2*; the vagueness in this idea of "a powerful intelligent designer," since it can mean different things for different thinkers, like "a God" for some, possibly multiple "deities" for others, perhaps a prior designer for the designer for still others, etc., in *Sec. 2.3.1*; the vagueness in Gould's argument, since he "does not himself select a definite trait which he thinks was actually acted on by natural selection," in *Sec. 2.3.2*; the vagueness in the nature of this "right," since it is subject to different interpretations by different countries and by different individuals, because "the boundary between them [what is legitimate and what is not] is not easily defined," in *Sec. 2.4.1*; the vagueness in the phrases "of recent origin" and "difference," since there is a debate among scholars about them, in *Sec. 2.4.2*; the vagueness in the identification of these shamanistic practices, since, for the critics like Kehoe, they "in their expression are unique to each culture that uses them and cannot be generalized easily, accurately or usefully into a global 'religion' such as shamanism," in *Sec. 2.5.1*; the vagueness about the priority of the things on the list, since scholars like "E. B. Tylor, Herbert Spencer, Andrew Lang and others" disagreed "as to the priority of their respective lists," in *Sec. 2.5.2*; the vagueness in the term like "psychic" or "spiritual," since it can mean different things to different people, like "ecstatic moment, mystical experience, God experience, transcendental unconsciousness, getting it, felt shift, objective consciousness, absolute tao, satori, peak experience, deep knowing, shamanic ecstasy, intensity experience, overmind, unclouded vision, divine intuition, luminosity, samadhi, peak state, mystic vision, divine hallucination, divine revelation, flash point, gestalt formation, spiritual epiphany, cosmic consciousness, and born-again experience," in *Sec. 3.2.1*; the vagueness concerning the validity of the six stages in Fowler's model, because they "were presented in such a way that the last four stages appeared to be validated, but the requirements of statistical verification of the stages did not come close to having been met," so their validity remains unclear, in *Sec. 3.2.2*; the vagueness in the term "chance," since it means different things for different people, so that, for the critics like the creationists, life is too complex for chance to decide, in *Sec. 3.3.1*; the vagueness in these "Greek, Arabic and Latin texts," because they "do not provide techniques to compute any observational consequences of their proposed heliocentric ideas" in an accurate and precise way, in *Sec. 3.3.2*; the vagueness in what is exactly meant by the separation of church and state, which means different things to different scholars, in *Sec. 3.4.1*; the vagueness in the term "state atheism," since it meant and was praticed differently in different countries, be they in Revolutionary France, the Soviet Union, Communist Albania, etc., in *Sec. 3.4.2*; the vagueness in the idea of this "overman," since "interpretations of Nietzsche's overman vary wildly," from one scholar to another, in *Sec. 3.5.1*; and the vagueness in the word "God" in the question, since "there are a number of widely different senses of the word 'God,'" in *Sec. 3.5.2*).

And the reverse direction also holds true.

Once more, it should be stressed, however, that there are different shades of gray (or different degrees of truth) in the two opposites, and the classification is not necessarily mutually exclusive either. In fact, even when some combinations of the two occur, they only end up sharing the same dialectic relationship, but in a different degree.

Also, there are some other relationships (as a kind of family resemblance) which have something in common with the principle, but they are not exactly the same but only more or less comparable, which varies from case to case.

Good examples of family resemblance in relation to the principle are clarity-ambiguity, directness-indirectness, quantitativeness-qualitativeness, specificity-obscurity, describability-nondescribability, specificity-generality, thickness-thinness, concretness-abstractness, and the like.

5th Thesis: The Simpleness-Complicatedness Principle

The fifth thesis refers to the simpleness-complicatedness principle (on the interconnection among things) in the category of "structure" in existential dialectics (which was first out worked out in *FIA*), in that both simpleness and complicatedness are vital, without favoring one over the other, and each is utilized, depending on the basis of the perspectives of nature, the mind, culture, and society. There is no simpleness without complicatedness—and vice versa.

For instance, on the one hand, there is simple analysis (e.g., the relatively simple analysis of the need for faith in religious issues, in accordance to fideism, in *Sec. 2.2.1*; the relatively simple analysis of the working of magic by its practitioners, in *Sec. 2.2.2*; the relatively simple construction of the teleological argument by its proponents, in *Sec. 2.3.1*; the relatively simple analysis of the four major requirements for the evolutionary origin of religions, in *Sec. 2.3.2*; the relatively simple formulation of religious conversion as a human right by the United Nations Universal Declaration of Human Rights, in *Sec. 2.4.1*; the relatively simple analysis of the rise of NRMs on the basis of four models, in *Sec. 2.4.2*; the relatively simple analysis of shamanism in terms of its concepts, techniques, histories, etc., in *Sec. 2.5.1*; the relatively simple analysis of animism in terms of its major features as shown in the relationship between animism and religion, in *Sec. 2.5.2*; the relatively simple analysis of the linkage between the experience of "psychic" or "spiritual" phenomena and "disinhibited temporal lobes," in *Sec. 3.2.1*; the relatively simple analysis of the six stages in faith development by Fowler, in *Sec. 3.2.2*; the relatively simple analysis of the evolution of life on the basis of some processes like variation, mutation, inheritance, selection, and adaptation in evolutionary biology, in *Sec. 3.2.2*; the relatively simple view of Galileo affair, in that he was persecuted for his view of heliocentrism, as opposed to the geocentric model held by the Catholic Church at the time, in *Sec. 3.3.2*; the relatively simple view of the secular state as "progressive" by its defenders, in *Sec. 3.4.1*; the relativley simple analysis of state atheism for the eradication of "the opium of the people," as the Marxist-Leninists put it, in *Sec. 3.4.2*; the relatively simple analysis of the origin of Christianity by Nietzsche and his solution for life affirmation, in *Sec. 3.5.1*; and the relatively simple way of understanding God in the West, mostly along the monotheistic tradition, in *Sec. 3.5.2*).

On the other hand, there is also complicated counterpart (e.g., the relatively more complicated analysis of the nature of faith by including the different problems as pointed out by the critics,in *Sec. 2.2.1*; the relatively more complicated analysis of the nature of magic, as shown in the different problems pointed out by the critics, in *Sec. 2.2.2*; the relatively more complicated analysis of the teleogical argument as shown by the criticisms that the critics have made over time, in *Sec. 2.3.1*; the relatively more complicated analysis of the evolutionary origin of religions by pointing out the disagreements among scholars on whether religion is "adaptive" or "exaptative," in *Sec. 2.3.2*; the more complicated analysis of religoius conversion in terms of the disagreements about its legal rights and limits among different countries and different individuals, in *Sec. 2.4.1*; the relatively more complicated analysis of the rise of NRMs, as shown in the debate between the critics of cults and the defenders of cults, in *Sec. 2.4.2*; the relatively more complicated analysis of shamanism, as shown in the problems pointed out by the critics, in *Sec. 2.5.1*; the relatively complicated analysis of animism as revealed in the problems pointed out by the critics, in *Sec. 2.5.2*; the relatively more complicated analysis of the linkage by way of questioning the usage of "mental delusion," since '[n]ot all false opinions are delusions,"' as pointed out by the critics like Ward, in *Sec. 3.2.1*; the relatively more complicated analysis of the stages in faith development, as shown in the criticisms by the critics, in *Sec. 3.2.2*; the relatively more complicated analysis of the evolution of life as showed in the criticisms by the critics, in *Sec. 3.2.2*; the relatively more complicated analysis of Galileo affair, in that Galileo was not as innocent as portrayed by his defenders, as shown in the criticisms by the critics, in *Sec. 3.3.2*; the relatively more complicated analysis of the secular state by including its failures, as analyzed in *FHC*, in *Sec. 3.4.1*; the relatively more complicated analysis of state atheism in terms of its failures by the critics, in *Sec. 3.4.2*; the relatively more complicated analysis of Nietzsche's work on the origin of Christianity and his solution, as shown by the damaging criticisms from his critics, in *Sec. 3.5.1*; and the relatively more complicated analysis of the meaning of God by includiing other definitions in the non-West too, in *Sec. 3.5.2*).

And the reverse direction also holds true.

Again, it should be stressed, however, that there are different shades of gray (or different degrees of truth) in the two opposites, and the classification is not necessarily mutually exclusive either. In fact, even when some combinations of the two occur, they only end up sharing the same dialectic relationship, but in a different degree.

Also, there are some other relationships (as a kind of family resemblance) which have something in common with the principle, but they are not exactly the same but only more or less comparable, which varies from case to case.

Good examples of family resemblance in relation to the principle are inflexibility-flexibility, standardization-specialization, imperfectness-perfectness, superficiality-depth, shallowness-deepness, economicalness-elaboratedness, plainness-circumspection, onesidedness-multisidedness, and the like.

6th Thesis: The Openness-Hiddenness Principle

The sixth thesis refers to the openness-hiddenenss principle (on the detection of things) in the category of "structure" in existential dialectics (which was already worked out in my previous books, especially in *FPHU*), in that reality has its hidden face, just as it is open to outside view in some other ways. There is no openness without hiddenness—and vice versa.

For instance, on the one hand, there is openness (e.g., the open exploration of the relationship between the use of faith and its contribution "to live fuller and better lives," in *Sec. 2.2.1*; the open exploration of the relationship between the practice of magic and the obtainment of certain tangible outcomes, in *Sec. 2.2.2*; the open exploration of the relationship between the orderly universe and the existence of an intelligent designer, accordance to the teleological argument, in *Sec. 2.3.1*; the open exploration of the "positive associations between religious practice and health and longevity" by Koenig and Cohen, in *Sec. 2.3.2*; the open exploration of the relationship between religious conversion and human rights by the United Nations Universal Declaration of Human Rights, in *Sec. 2.4.1*; the open exploration of the rise of NRMs and their subsequent dark side, as revealed by some disaffected ex-members, in *Sec. 2.4.2*; the open exploration of the relationship between an individual like a shaman and the ability to connect with the other-world for healing, etc., in *Sec. 2.5.1*; the open exploration of the relationship between animism and the "primitive" nature of the beliefs, as pointed out by Tylor, in *Sec. 2.5.2*; the open exploration by Speyrer to understand his "olfactory hallucinations…accompanied by depression and a severe fear of dying" with the "physical symptoms…typical of those with a brain tumor," in *Sec. 3.2.1*; the open exploration of the six stages in faith development by Fowler, in *Sec. 3.2.2*; the open exploration of the evolution of life on the basis of such processes as natural selection, chance, etc., in evolutionary biology, in *Sec. 3.3.1*; the open exploration, by Galileo, of the nature of the tides on earth, in that they "were caused by the sloshing back and forth of water in the seas as a point on the Earth's surface speeded up and slowed down because of the Earth's rotation on its axis and revolution around the Sun," in *Sec. 3.3.2*; the open exploration of the relationship between the secular state and the promotion of democracy, like the protection of the rights of minorities, in *Sec. 3.4.1*; the open exploration of religion on the basis of "the opium of the people," as in Marxist-Leninism, in *Sec. 3.4.2*; the open exploration of a new way of life by the Christians to address human suffering, according to Nietzsche, in *Sec. 3.5.1*; and the open exploration of the meaning of God by way of the monotheistic definitions in the West, in *Sec. 3.5.2*).

On the other hand, there is also hiddenness (e.g., the hidden bias in downgrading the role of reason and exaggerating the power of faith in fideism, as revealed in the criticisms by the critics, in *Sec. 2.2.1*; the "secretive and isolated" nature of magic, such that its failures can be easily covered up with excuses, in *Sec. 2.2.2*; the hidden bias of the teleological argument, since it does not consider alternatives like the confusion between a designer and a God in the argument, the inability of the argument to prove itself, etc., in *Sec. 2.3.1*; the hidden bias in the work by Koenig and Cohen, since, for the critics like Richard P. Sloan, "there is no really good compelling evidence that there is a relationship between religious involvement and health," in *Sec. 2.3.2*; the hidden bias for universality in the United Nations Universal Declaration of Human Rights, without sufficient attention to the fundamental disagreements on legal rights and their limits among different countries and different individuals, in *Sec. 2.4.1*; the hidden bias in the account of NRMs by these disaffected ex-members, because their character, motivation, and credibility have been questioned, in *Sec. 2.4.2*; the hidden bias in shamanistic practices, as they can be "fraudulent shamans," as shown in the research by Richard Allen on the Cherokee Nation, in *Sec. 2.5.1*; the hidden bias in Tylor's view, with its European ethnocentrism, for the critics, in *Sec. 2.5.2*; the hidden nature of Speyrer's physical symptoms which can be traced back to his "childhood traumas of two early surgeries," in *Sec. 3.2.1*; the hidden bias in Fowler's exploration of the stages in faith development, as "other critics of Fowler have questioned whether his ordering of the stages really reflects his own commitment to a rather liberal Christian Protestant outlook, as if to say that people who adopt a similar viewpoint to Fowler are at higher stages of faith development," in *Sec. 3.2.2*; the hidden bias in evolutionary biology for its search for "the tree of life" without sufficiently accounting for other phenomena in life such as like "consciousness," "free will," "music," "religion," etc. and for other "species" which have not "left records of their evolutionary history" and which "share a limited set of common morphologies," so "their fossils do not provide information on their ancestry," in *Sec. 3.3.1*; the hidden bais in Galileo's theory of tides, because he "dismissed th[e] anomaly [of two daily high tides at Venice] as the result of several secondary causes, including the shape of the sea, its depth, and other factors" and also "the idea, held by his contemporary Johannes Kepler, that the moon caused the tides," in *Sec. 3.3.2*; the hidden bias in the discourse on secularism by downplaying its long history of marginalizing "circumstantially disadvantaged others" and glorifying the role of reason, as shown in *FHC*, in *Sec. 3.4.1*; the hidden class bias for the lower class against the upper one in Marxist-Leninism in its campaign for state atheism, in *Sec. 3.4.2*; the hidden bias of this Christian new way of life, which is "decadent" and "life-negating," for Nietzsche, in *Sec. 3.5.1*; and the hidden bias in this obsession with the monotheistic definitions of God in the West, because of its neglect of other definitions in the non-West, in *Sec. 3.5.2*).

And the reverse direction also holds true.

Again, it should be stressed, however, that there are different shades of gray (or different degrees of truth) in the two opposites, and the classification is not necessarily mutually exclusive either. In fact, even when some combinations of the two occur, they only end up sharing the same dialectic relationship, but in a different degree.

Also, there are some other relationships (as a kind of family resemblance) which have something in common with the principle, but they are not exactly the same but only more or less comparable, which varies from case to case.

Good examples of family resemblance in relation to the principle are overtness-covertness, publicness-privateness, openness-closedness, transparency-secrecy, openness-biasedness, and so on.

7th Thesis: The Denseness-Emptiness Principle

The seventh thesis concerns the denseness-emptiness principle (on the distribution of entities in space) in the category of "structure" in existential dialectics, which is first proposed in *FPHUP*, in that both density and void are needed, in relation to the mind, nature, culture, and society, albeit in different ways. There is no denseness without emptiness—and vice versa.

Lest any misunderstanding occurs, the term "void" is used here only as an approximation of emptiness (depending on the degree of the lack of density), since, in physics, it is well known that "empty" space is not really empty all the way, because it can be full of energy (e.g., random quantum fluctuations at the sub-atomic level, and, for that matter, dark energy in the universe) and matter (e.g., different versions of sub-atomic particles, and, for that matter, dark matter in the universe). (F. Wilczek 2008)

For instance, on the one hand, there is denseness (e.g., the relatively denser concentration of individuals who have lesser education to believe in God, or more precisely, 62% for college graduates, as shown in a research study by Frank Sulloway at M.I.T. and Michael Shermer at California State University, in *Sec. 2.2.1*; the relatively denser concentration of magicians in non-religious magic who emphasizes more on "the personal power" of the magician or "the strength of the magician's will," in *Sec. 2.2.2*; the relatively denser concentration of the believers in the teleological argument in ancient Greece, like Plato, Aristotle, Socrates, Cicero, etc., in *Sec. 2.3.1*; the relatively denser concentration of creation believers among Christians, in *Sec. 2.3.2*; the relatively denser concentration of individuals advocating religious converson as a human right among UN officials, in *Sec. 2.4.1*; the relatively denser concentration of NRMs after WWII, with about 6,000 of them, according to Barrett, in *Sec. 2.4.2*; the relatively denser concentration of shamans in "Paleolithic" period, in *Sec. 2.5.1*; the relatively denser concentration of animists in hunting-gathering societies, in *Sec. 2.5.2*; the relatively denser concentration of the experiences of "psychic" or "spiritual" phenemena in individuals with mental delusion, according to those like Penfield, Speyrer, and others, in *Sec. 3.2.1*; the relatively denser concentration of concerns by people like Adler with power drive in faith development, in *Sec. 3.2.2*; the relatively denser concentration of American scientists who believe in "evolution without God guiding the process," or 55% according to a poll conducted in 1997, in *Sec. 3.3.1*; the relatively denser concentration of the ideologues of the Ptolemaic model in pre-modern times, in *Sec. 3.3.2*; the relatively denser concentration of secularists, especially those who accept the dictum that "Then give to Caesar what is Caesar's, and to God what is God's," in *Sec. 3.4.1*; the relatively denser concentration of state atheists in the Communist Bloc, in *Sec. 3.4.2*; the relatively denser concentration of concerns, among the Christians, with pain in the sufferers, or with what Nietzsche called the "morbid intolerance of pain. Extreme sensitivity results in avoidance of the world," in *Sec. 3.5.1*; and the relatively denser concentration of the philosophers of religion in the West who devote their works on the monotheistic definitions of God, in *Sec. 3.5.2*).

On the other hand, there is emptiness (e.g., the relatively less dense, or more empty, concentration of adults with Ph.D.s to believe in God, or more precisely, 12% for Ph.D.'s, as shown by the research study by Sulloway and Shermer, in *Sec. 2.2.1*; the relatively less dense, or more empty, concentration of magicians in non-religious magic who also focus on "faith in the power of God," because non-religious magic does not "involves requesting the intervention of a personal deity or deities," in *Sec. 2.2.2*; the relatively less dense, or more empty, concentration of believers in the teleological argument among contemporary scientists, in *Sec. 2.3.1*; the relatively less dense, or more empty, concentration of creation believers among scientists in the evolution origin of religions, in *Sec. 2.3.2*; the relativley less dense, or more empty, concentration of individuals advocating the human right of religious conversion "for those leaving Islam and those enticing Muslims to leave Islam" in many Islamic countries, in *Sec. 2.4.1*; the relatively less dense, or more empty, concentration of NRMs in medieval Europe, in *Sec. 2.4.2*; the relatively less dense, or more empty, concentration of shamans in our times, in *Sec. 2.5.1*; the relatively less dense, or more empty, concentration of animists in industrial societies, in *Sec. 2.5.2*; the relatively less dense, or more empty, concentration of the experiences of "psychic" or "spiritual" phenemena in "some of the most able philosophers and scientists in the world today," according to Ward, in *Sec. 3.2.1*; the relatively less dense, or more empty, concentration of concerns by people like Fowler with power drive in faith development, in *Sec. 3.2.2*; the relatively less dense, or more empty, concentration of American scientists who believe in "young earth creationism," or only 5% according to the poll, in *Sec. 3.3.1*; the relatively less dense, or more empty, concentration of the ideologues of the Ptolemaic model in our times, in *Sec. 3.3.2*; the relatively less dense, or more empty, concentration of secularists among the Christian fundamentalists, in *Sec. 3.4.1*; the relatively less dense, or more empty, concentration of state atheists in pre-Soviet Russia, in *Sec. 3.4.2*; the relatively less dense, or more empty, concentration of concerns, among the

Nazis, with pain in the sufferers, in *Sec. 3.5.1*; and the relatively less dense, or more empty, concentration of the philosophers of religion in the West who devote their works on the non-monotheistic definitions of God, in *Sec. 3.5.2*).

And the reverse direction also holds true.

Again, it should be stressed, however, that there are different shades of gray (or different degrees of truth) in the two opposites, and the classification is not necessarily mutually exclusive either. In fact, even when some combinations of the two occur, they only end up sharing the same dialectic relationship, but in a different degree.

Also, there are some other relationships (as a kind of family resemblance) which have something in common with the principle, but they are not exactly the same but only more or less comparable, which varies from case to case.

Good examples of family resemblance in relation to the principle are fullness-voidness, nearness-farness, concentration-dispersion, and the like.

8th Thesis: The Slowness-Quickness Principle

The eighth thesis concerns the slowness-quickness principle (on the speed of change) in the category of "process") in existential dialectics (which was first worked out in *FIA*), in that both slowness and quickness co-exist, with their own internal tension, to the extent that each fights for its own relevance with the other, in accordance to the perspectives of nature, the mind, culture, and society, without one being the victor and the other being the vanquished in the long haul. There is no slowness without quickness—and vice versa.

For instance, on the one hand, there is slowness (e.g., the relatively slower readiness of someone like Sagan to appeal to faith when there is no compelling evidence, in *Sec. 2.2.1*; the relatively slower readiness of a scientist to practice the naming of the gods, religious artifacts, or sacrifice, in *Sec. 2.2.2*; the relatively slower readiness of an atheist like Dawkins to defend the teleological argument, in *Sec. 2.3.1*; the relatively slower readiness of people like Sosis and Kress to accept religion as an "adaptation," in *Sec. 2.3.2*; the relatively slower readiness of a Muslim to leave Islam in Islamic countries, in *Sec. 2.4.1*; the relatively slower readiness of someone like Hein to be supportive of NRMs, in *Sec. 2.4.2*; the relatively slower readiness of a contemporary mainstream doctor to use trance, chanting, etc. to cure his patients for ailments, in *Sec. 2.5.1*; the relatively slower readiness of an atheist to practice ancestor worship, in *Sec. 2.5.2*; the relatively slower readiness of individuals who had their temporal lobes stimulated by Persinger in the experiment to question the conviction of what they experienced as true, in *Sec. 3.2.1*; the relatively slower readiness of "adults over the age of sixty-one" to be "in the first two of these stages," in *Sec. 3.2.2*; the relatively slower rate of the emergence of new lifeforms prior to the Cambrian era in the timeline of evolution on Earth, according to evolutionary biology, in *Sec. 3.3.1*; the relatively slower pace of reaction towards the work of Copernicus, since it "inspired very little debate on whether it might be heretical during the next 60 years" after his death, in *Sec. 3.3.2*; the relatively slower readiness of a Christian fundamentalist to accept the separation of church and state, in *Sec. 3.4.1*; the relatively slower readiness of someone like Lenin to endorse religion, in Sec. 3.4.2; the relatively slower readiness of a Jew or Christian to question the claims that "[d]isobedience of God…is 'sin'" and "[s]ubjection to God…is redemption," in *Sec. 3.5.1*; and the relatively slower readiness of an atheist to accept the existence of God, in *Sec. 3.5.2*).

On the other hand, there is quickness (e.g., the relatively quicker readiness of someone like Kierkegaard to take "the leap of faith" when there is no compelling evidence, in *Sec. 2.2.1*; the relatively quicker readiness of a religious magician to practice the naming of the gods, religious artifacts, or sacrifice, in *Sec. 2.2.2*; the relatively quicker readiness of a theist like Thomas Aquinas to defend the teleological argument, in *Sec. 2.3.1*; the relatively quicker readiness of people like Gould and Lewontin to accept religion as an "exaptation," in *Sec. 2.3.2*; the relatively quicker readiness of individual in an Islamic family in Islamic countries to be converted into Islam, in *Sec. 2.4.1*; the relatively quicker readness of someone like Introvigne to be supportive of NRMs, in *Sec. 2.4.2*; the relatively quicker readiness of a Paleolithic shaman to use trance, chanting, etc. to cure the ailments of a patient, in *Sec. 2.5.1*; the relatively quicker readness of an animist to practice ancetor worship, in *Sec. 2.5.2*; the relatively quicker readiness of someone like Persinger to question the conviction of what his subjects experienced in his experiment, in *Sec. 3.2.1*; the relatively quicker readiness of "children up to the age of twelve years" to be "in the first two of these stages," in *Sec. 3.2.2*; the relatively quicker rate of the emergence of new lifeforms during the evolutionary period known as "the Cambrian explosion," according to evolutionary biology, in *Sec. 3.3.1*; the relatively faster pace of reaction towards the work of Galileo, because he was put on trial in 1633, only one year after the publication of his controversial *Dialogue Concerning the Two Chief World Systems* in 1632, in *Sec. 3.3.2*; the relatively quicker readiness of the followers of Ataturk in Turkey to accept the separation of church and state, in *Sec. 3.4.1*; the relatively quicker readiness of someone like the Pope to endorse religion, in *Sec. 3.4.2*; the relativey quicker readiness of someone like Nietzsche to question the claims that "[d]isobedience of God...is 'sin'" and "[s]ubjection to God...is redemption," in *Sec. 3.5.1*; and the relatively quicker readiness of a theist to accept the existence of God, in *Sec. 3.5.2*).

And the reverse direction also holds true.

Again, it should be stressed, however, that there are different shades of gray (or different degrees of truth) in the two opposites, and the classification is not necessarily mutually exclusive either. In fact, even when some combinations of the two occur, they only end up sharing the same dialectic relationship, but in a different degree.

Also, there are some other relationships (as a kind of family resemblance) which have something in common with the principle, but they are not exactly the same but only more or less comparable, which varies from case to case.

Good examples of family resemblance in relation to the principle are inconvenience-convenience, passiveness-activenessness, gradualness-abruptness, deceleration-acceleration, and the like.

9th Thesis: The Expansion-Contraction Principle

The nineth thesis is called the expansion-contraction principle in the category of "process" in existential dialectics, in that entities in the world can both expand in some ways and contract in other ones, as part of their nature. There is no expansion without contraction—and vice versa.

This principle, although not so explicitly called, was already used in my previous works on different topics (e.g., the theory of floating consciousness in *FCD* and *FPHC*, the union of the unions in *BWT*, and the cyclical progression of system fragmentation and integration in *FCD*).

For instance, on the one hand, there is expansion (e.g., the relatively more developed ability of someone like Sagan to use reason to solve problems in life, in *Sec. 2.2.1*; the relative expansion of the power and influence of science in our time, in *Sec. 2.2.2*; the relative expansion of the influence of the Big Bang theory in the scientific community since modern times, in *Sec. 2.3.1*; the relative expansion of the influence of evolutionary theory since the modern era, in *Sec. 2.3.2*; the relative expansion of the influence of "new relgious movements" after WWII, in *Sec. 2.4.1*; the relative expansion of the influence of NRMs after WWII, in *Sec. 2.4.2*; the relative rise of shamanism in Paleothic period, in *Sec. 2.5.1*; the relative rise of the organized versions of religion like the Abrahamic tradition in agricultural and industrial societies, in *Sec. 2.5.2*; the relative expansion of the influence of the psychobiology of religion in our times, in *Sec. 3.2.1*; the relatively more developed ability of those who follow Adler's idea of power drive in faith development to strive for "perfection and superiority," in *Sec. 3.2.2*; the relative expansion of the influence of humans in modern times, such that they dominate other animals, in *Sec. 3.3.1*; the relative expansion of the influence of heliocentrism in modern times, in *Sec. 3.3.2*; the relatively more developed ability of secular leaders to solve problems by the rationality based on reason, in *Sec. 3.4.1*; the relative expansion of the influence of Marxist-Leninism in the Soviet Union, in *Sec. 3.4.2*; the relative expansion of the influence of Nietzsche's work in Nazi Germany, in *Sec. 3.5.1*; and the relatively more developed ability of a philosopher of religion in the West to deal with religious questions in the analytic way, in *Sec. 3.5.2*).

On the other hand, there is contraction (e.g., the relatively less developed ability of someone like Sagan to use faith to solve problems in life, in *Sec. 2.2.1*; the relative contraction of power and influence of magic in our time, in *Sec. 2.2.2*; the relative contraction of the influence of the teleological argument in the scientific community since modern times, in *Sec. 2.3.1*; the relative contraction of the influence of creation theory since the modern era, in *Sec. 2.3.2*; the relative contraction of the influence of "mainstream" religious organizations after WWII, in *Sec. 2.4.1*; the relative contraction of the influence of mainstream organizations after WWII, in *Sec. 2.4.2*; the relative decline of shamanism in our times, in *Sec. 2.5.1*; the relative decline of the animistic versions of religion in agricultural and industrial societies, in *Sec. 2.5.2*; the relative decline of the influence of fundamentalist organized religions in our times, in *Sec. 3.2.1*; the relatively less developed ability of those who follow Adler's idea of power drive in faith development to strive for humility, modesty, or the acceptance of imperfection as a fact of life, in *Sec. 3.2.2*; the relative contraction of the influence of other animals in modern times, such that quite a number of them now become "endangered species," because of the intrusion of humans, in *Sec. 3.3.1*; the relative contraction of the influence of geocentrism in modern times, in *Sec. 3.3.2*; the relatively less developed ability of secular leaders to solve problems by the rationality based on faith in the Scripture, in *Sec. 3.4.1*; the relative contraction of the influence of Russian Orthodox religion in the Soviet Union, in *Sec. 3.4.2*; the relative decline of the influence of Judaism in Nazi Germany, in *Sec. 3.5.1*; and the relatively eal with religious questions in the intuitive or mystical way, in *Sec. 3.5.2*).

And the reverse direction also holds true.

Again, it should be stressed, however, that there are different shades of gray (or different degrees of truth) in the two opposites, and the classification is not necessarily mutually exclusive either. In fact, even when some combinations of the two occur, they only end up sharing the same dialectic relationship, but in a different degree.

Also, there are some other relationships (as a kind of family resemblance) which have something in common with the principle, but they are not exactly the same but only more or less comparable, which varies from case to case.

Good examples of family resemblance in relation to the principle are conquest-autarky, rise-fall (or up-down), spread-shrink, extendingness-shorteningness, and so forth.

10th Thesis: The Convention-Novelty Principle

The tenth thesis is the convention-novelty principle (on the nature of creative thinking) in the category of "agency" in existential dialectics (which was first worked out in *FPHCT*), in that, if there is conventional wisdom, there is likewise novel challenge, to the extent that both convergent and divergent thinking are part of life. There is no convention without novelty—and vice versa.

As summarized from *FPHCT* (almost verbatim here), there are (a) "creative techniques" and (b) "creative traits," which, when satisfied—in relation to the larger context of the mind, nature, society, and culture—can be used to enhance creative works.

In addition, creative thinking has its own possibilities and limits (in relation to invention), just as it has its own promises and pitfalls (in relation to innovation)—as already analyzed in *FPHCT*.

In the end, creative thinking has its own desirability and dark sides (as also already analyzed in *FPHCT*).

With these clarifications in mind—there are good empirical examples for the convention-novelty princple.

For instance, on the one hand, there is convention (e.g., the conventional wisdom about the importance of reason in life, as elegantly put by Galileo Galilei, who once said: "I not feel obliged to believe that the same God who has endowed us with sense, reason and intellect has intended us to forego their use," in *Sec. 2.2.1*; the conventional wisdom about the differences betwee magic and religion, in *Sec. 2.2.2*; the conventional wisdom about "a powerful intelligent designer" in the teleological argument, in *Sec. 2.3.1*; the conventional wisdom about religion as necessary in creation theory, in *Sec. 2.3.2*; the conventional wisdom in favor of "mainstream" religious traditions, in *Sec. 2.4.1*; the conventional wisdom about spirituality by "mainstream" religions, in *Sec. 2.4.2*; the conventional wisdom about ancient forms of shamanism as in "core shamanism," in *Sec. 2.5.1*; the conventional wisdom by ancient animists that "souls or spirits exist not only in humans but also in animals, plants, rocks,...and other entities of the natural environment," in *Sec. 2.5.2*; the conventional wisdom in organized religions about the validity of the belief in God, in *Sec. 3.2.1*; the conventional wisdom about "the traditional belief that people were placed deliberately on earth as God's ultimate creation," in *Sec. 3.2.2*; the conventional wisdom about creationism prior to the works of Darwin and Mendel, in *Sec. 3.3.1*; the conventional wisdom held by the ancient Greeks that "the motions of the planets were circular and not elliptical," in *Sec. 3.3.2*; the conventional wisdom in pre-modern times for the fusion of church and state, in *Sec. 3.4.1*; the conventional wisdom about the importance of religious faith in human life, as championed by those followers of the Abrahamic tradition, in *Sec. 3.4.2*; the conventional wisdom about Christianity as a new way of life for "peace," "tolerance," "love," etc., in *Sec. 3.5.1*; and the conventional wisdom in religious philosophy about "the philosophical thinking that is inspired and directed by religion," such as Christianity, in *Sec. 3.5.2*).

On the other hand, there is novelty (e.g., the alternative novel challenge to the conventional wisdom about reason by William James to "defend...the right to violate the principle of evidentialism in order to justify hypothesis venturing," in his Will-to-Believe Doctrine, in *Sec. 2.2.1*; the alternative novel challenge to the conventional wisdom about the differences between magic and religion by way of combining the two into "religious magic," in *Sec. 2.2.2*; the alternative novel challenge to the conventinal wisdom about "a powerful intelligent designer" by David Hume, in that there may be "several deities combine in contriving and framing the world" instead, in *Sec. 2.3.1*; the alternative novel challenge to the conventional wisdom about religion as necessary, by Gould and Lewontin for the "by-product" view of the evolutionary origin of religions, in *Sec. 2.3.2*; the alternative novel challenge to the established views of "mainstream" religious traditions by the rise of "new religious movements" after WWII, in *Sec. 2.4.1*; the alternative novel challenge to conventional wisdom about spirituality by NRMs, which often offer something "different" from the "mainstream" views, in *Sec. 2.4.2*; the alternative novel challenge to the conventional wisdom about "core shamanism" by Hamer by way of his original attempt to "reinvent shamanism in a modern form, drawing from core shamanism," in *Sec.*

2.5.1; the alternative novel challenge to this ancient animistic conventional wisdom by the followers of the New Age Movement in our time who reconstruct ancient animism by believing "in spirits that are, or live in...technology" too, not just in nature, in *Sec. 2.5.2*; the alternative novel challenge to the conventional wisdom about the validity of the belief in God by those in the psychobiology of religion, in that "God is in the brain," in *Sec. 3.2.1*; the alternative novel challenge to this conventional wisdom about God by a "new idea that people have evolved by natural selection" in modern times, as pointed out by Adler, in *Sec. 3.2.2*; the alternative novel challenge to the conventional wisdom about creationism by Darwin and Mendel for the modern evolutionary theory, in *Sec. 3.3.1*; the alternative novel challenge to the conventional wisdom about the ancient Greek claim of the circular motions of the planets by a more modern view in Western culture in the 17th century and beyond, that the motions of the planets are elliptical, in *Sec. 3.3.2*; the alternative novel challenge to the pre-modern conventional wisdom about the fusion of church and state by the secularists in modern times for the separation of church and state, in *Sec. 3.4.1*; the alternative novel challenge to the conventional wisdom about the importance of religious faith by Marx and other state atheists, in that religion is instead "the opium of the people," in *Sec. 3.4.2*; the alternative novel challenge to this conventional wisdom about Christianity by Nietzsche with his critique of the "decadent" values and holy falsehood in Christianity, in *Sec. 3.5.1*; and the alternative novel challenge to the conventional wisdom about defending religion in religious philosohy by the philosophers of religion who examine religious issues "dispassionately by what are thought of as those in two 'camps': adherents or believers, and non-believers," in *Sec. 3.5.2*).

And the reverse direction also holds true.

Again, it should be stressed, however, that there are different shades of gray (or different degrees of truth) in the two opposites, and the classification is not necessarily mutually exclusive either. In fact, even when some combinations of the two occur, they only end up sharing the same dialectic relationship, but in a different degree.

Also, there are some other relationships (as a kind of family resemblance) which have something in common with the principle, but they are not exactly the same but only more or less comparable, which varies from case to case.

Good examples of family resemblance in relation to the principle are convergence-divergence (or convergent thinking vs. divergent thinking), normalness-nonnormalness, conformity-nonconformity, and so on.

11th Thesis: The Evolution-Transformation Principle

The eleventh thesis refers to the evolution-transformation principle (on the multiple kinds of agency). in the category of "agency" in existential dialectics (which was first worked out in *FAE* and then in other books of mine).

This principle—and the symmetry-asymmetry principle, for instance—are both about agency. More precisely, the word "agency," in a formal definition, refers to "a person or thing through which power is exerted or an end is achieved." (MWD 2007) It therefore does not have to necessarily involve an intelligent lifeform.

Because of this dual meaning in agency, the evolution-transformation principle is more concerned with *the kind of agency*, that is, both about the *evolution* in the state of nature (e.g., an object of natural beauty) and the *transformation* in the world of intelligent lifeforms (e.g., a work of art). There is no evolution without transformation—and vice versa.

In classical Darwinian evolutionary theory (as more detailedly analyzed in *BNN*), evolution is "blind." But in the human world, change often takes place because of the conscious intervention of humans in transforming society and culture, just to cite two instances.

And the transformative part of the principle precisely refers to the other dimension in the dual meaning of agency, in giving technology (as invented by intelligent lifeforms like humans and, soon, post-humans) a major role to play in the change of the world, which is something that I extensively analyzed in *FHC* in the context of the technophilic lifeworld, espeically though not exclusively since modern times.

For instance, on the one hand, there is evolution (e.g., the natural evolution of humans to use reason, emotions, and other faculties for survival in the state of nature, in *Sec. 2.2.1*; the natural evolution of humans to live and encounter many seemingly inexplicable natural phenomena in the state of nature, in *Sec. 2.2.2*; the natural evolution of humans to live in the state of nature, with no systematic cosmologies, in *Sec. 2.3.1*; the natural evolution of humans to use tools and live together in the state of nature, in *Sec. 2.3.2*; the natural evolution of humans to live in the state of nature without any knowledge of "human rights," in *Sec. 2.4.1*; the natural evolution of humans to live in the state of nature, in *Sec. 2.4.2*; the natural evolution of humans to live in the state of nature, with such hazards as illness, injury, death, etc., in *Sec. 2.5.1*; the natural evolution of humans to live with nature in the state of nature, in *Sec. 2.5.2*; the natural evolution of humans to live in the state of nature with their fear of, or awe toward, the powerful forces of nature, at times with some mental delusion about them, in *Sec. 3.2.1*; the natural evolution of humans to live in the state of nature, with a sense of awe towards natural forces, in *Sec. 3.2.2*; the natural evolution of lifeforms like plants and animals on Earth as depicted in "the tree of life," according to evolutionary biology, in *Sec. 3.3.1*; the natural evolution of humans to live in the state of nature with a primitive understanding of the working of the universe, in *Sec. 3.3.2*; the natural evolution of humans to live in the state of nature in a group like a clan, a tribe, etc., in *Sec. 3.4.1*; the natural evolution of humans to live in awe towards nature in the state of nature, with their superstitious beliefs, in *Sec. 3.4.2*; the natural evolution of humans to live in the state of nature, with their "natural" values, which also allow violence, war, etc., for Nietzsche, in *Sec. 3.5.1*; and the natural evolution of humans to live in the state of awe towards nature, in the pre-historical days, in *Sec. 3.5.2*).

On the other hand, there is transformation (e.g., the technical transformation of human life by way of the invention of the epistemological theory known as fideism, in *Sec. 2.2.1*; the technical transformation of human relationship with nature by way of the invention of religious magic, together with its different stories for different adherents, in *Sec. 2.2.2*; the technical transformation of human thought by way of the invention of religious cosmology in a systematic way, as shown in the intellectual tradition of the teleological argument, in *Sec. 2.3.1*; the technical transformation of human life by way of the invention of systematic religions in the evolution of civilization, in *Sec. 2.3.2*; the technical transformation of human living together by way of the invention of the philosophy of "human rights," in *Sec. 2.4.1*; the technical transformation of human living by way of the invention of NRMs for a different quest for community and spirituality, in *Sec. 2.4.2*; the technical transformation of human life by way of the invention of religions, such as shamanism and later more organized religions, for a systematic systems of ideas for the explanation and even treatment of these hazards, in *Sec. 2.5.1*; the technical transformation of human living with nature by the invention of a religion along the animistic way for ancestor worship, rituals to honor animals, etc., in *Sec. 2.5.2*; the technical tranfromation of human relation with nature by the invention of the psychobiology of religion, for a deeper understanding of the relationship between "disinhibited temporal lobes" and the experiences of "psychic" or "spiritual" phenemena, or of mental delusion like that, in *Sec. 3.2.1*; the technical transformation of human awe towards nature by the invention of the idea of power drive in faith development, such that "we compensate for our imperfections and feelings of inferiority" to "become one with God," in *Sec. 3.2.2*; the technical transformation of lifeforms like those of humans by way of the invention of new technologies for humans to master nature, in *Sec. 3.3.1*; the technical transformation of human understanding of the universe by the invention of heliocentrism by Copernicus, Galileo, and other thinkers, in *Sec. 3.3.2*; the technical transformation of human grouping by way of the invention of a political system based on the separation of church and state in a large community, in *Sec. 3.4.1*; the technical transformation of human view about the world by the invention of state atheism to eradicate all such superstitious beliefs, especially in regard to religion, in *Sec. 3.4.2*; the technical transformation of human values in the state of nature by the invention of the theologies of Judaism and Christianity, such that, for Nietzsche, "[n]atural values become utterly valueless. The priest sanctifies and bestows all value. Disobedience of God...is 'sin.' Subjection to God...is redemption," in *Sec. 3.5.1*; and the technical transformation of human view towards nature by the invention of systematic religious philosophies like Christianity, Islam, Hinduism, etc., in *Sec. 3.5.2*).

And the reverse direction also holds true.

Again, it should be stressed, however, that there are different shades of gray (or different degrees of truth) in the two opposites, and the classification is not necessarily mutually exclusive either. In fact, even when some combinations of the two occur, they only end up sharing the same dialectic relationship, but in a different degree.

Also, there are some other relationships (as a kind of family resemblance) which have something in common with the principle, but they are not exactly the same but only more or less comparable, which varies from case to case.

Good examples of family resemblance in relation to the principle are inorganicness-volition, nonwillingness-willingness, naturalness-technologicalness, naturalness-nonnaturalness, and so on.

12th Thesis: The Symmetry-Asymmetry Principle

The twelveth thesis is labeled as the symmetry-asymmetry principle (on the relationships among existents) in the category of "agency" in existential dialectics (which was also already worked out in my previous books), in that there is no asymmetry without symmetry—and vice versa.

For instance, the Same can be symmetric and asymmetric towards the Others. But in case of asymmetry (as analyzed in *BDPD*), oppression and self-oppression can occur. So, when the Same is asymmetric towards the

Others, the Same can also be relatively asymmetric towards itself in self-oppression, just as the Others can be likewise towards themselves. The subsequent oppressiveness is dualistic, as much by the Same against the Others and itself, as by the Others against the Same and themselves. Both oppression and self-oppression can be achieved by way of downgrading differences between the Same and the Others and of accentuating them.

This is true, even though not all forms of asymmetry have to be about oppression and self-oppression.

In addition, from Chapter Three of *FPHG*, symmetry is not perfect, to be understood in an approximate sense under many life circumstances. With this clarification in mind, hereafter are some empirical examples.

For instance, on the one hand, there is symmetry (e.g., the co-existence of different views concerning the epistemological validity of faith in intellectual history, be they fideist, scientific, or else, in *Sec. 2.2.1*; the co-existence of different forms of rationality in human history, regardless of whether they are about magic, religion, or science, in *Sec. 2.2.2*; the co-existence of different ways to think about the cosmos, regardless of whether this is by way of the teleological argument, the Big Bang theory, or else, in *Sec. 2.3.1*; the co-existence of different schools of thought about religion through the ages, be they creation theory, the exaptative view of religion, etc., in *Sec. 2.3.2*; the co-existence of different views on religious conversion in the world, in *Sec. 2.4.1*; the co-existence of "mainstream" and "new" religions after WWII, in *Sec. 2.4.2*; the co-existence of different religions throughout the ages, in *Sec. 2.5.1*; the co-existence of different versions of religion in history, in *Sec. 2.5.2*; the co-existence of different views about the validity of the beliefs in God, regardless of whether they are religious or scientific, in *Sec. 3.2.1*; the co-existence of different schools of thought about God throughout the ages, in *Sec. 3.2.2*; the co-existence of different schools of thought about the emergence of lifeforms, in *Sec. 3.3.1*; the co-existence of different sides in the debate about the Galileo affair, in *Sec. 3.3.2*; the co-existence of different political systems in human history, in *Sec. 3.4.1*; the co-existence of different views about religion throughout human history, in *Sec. 3.4.2*; the co-existence of different ways of life in human history, in *Sec. 3.5.1*; and the co-existence of different philosophical views about religion throughout the ages, in *Sec. 3.5.2*).

On the other hand, there is also asymmetry (e.g., the acceptance of fideism among those in the tradition of Pascal, Kierkegaard, Wittgenstein, and James—but the popularity of the scientific spirit among those in the tradition of Sagan and his follow scientists, in *Sec. 2.2.1*; the more influence of science in our time—but the popularity of magic in antiquity, in *Sec. 2.2.2*; the popularity of the teleological argument in antiquity—but the influential rise of the Big Bang theory in our times, in *Sec. 2.3.1*; the popularity of creation theory in medieval times—but the rise of the evolutionary view of religion in our times, in *Sec. 2.3.2*; the rise of th discourse on religious conversion as a "human right" after WWII—but the disagreements about religious conversion as a "human right" among countries, since some Islamic countries "carry imprisonment or the death penalty for those leaving Islam and those enticing Muslims to leave Islam," in *Sec. 2.4.1*; the larger number of NRMs, when compared with the number of "mainstream" world religions, after WWII—but the greater number of followers of "mainstream" world religions, when compared with the number of followers of NRMs, after WWII, in *Sec. 2.4.2*; the popularity of shamanism in Paleolithic times—but the popularity of medical science in our times, in *Sec. 2.5.1*; the greater influence of animism in hunting-gathering societies—but the rise of organized religions in agricultural and industrial societies, in *Sec. 2.5.2*; the popularity of the theistic argument for the validity of the beliefs in God among those who are deeply religious—but the skepticism towards the validity of the belief in God among those like the new atheists in the 21st century, namely, Richard Dawkins, Daniel Dennett, Sam Harris and Christopher Hitchens, for instance, in *Sec. 3.2.1*; the popularity in the older days of "the traditional belief that people were placed deliberately on earth as God's ultimate creation"—but the rise in our times of the evolutionary "idea that people have evolved by natural selection," in *Sec. 3.2.2*; the popularity of creationism in medieval Europe—but the rise of evolutionary theory in modern Europe, in *Sec. 3.3.1*; the formal apology by Pope John Paul II in 2000 in regard to the Galileo affair—but the criticism of Galileo by Cardinal Ratzinger in 1990, who later became Pope Benedict XVI in 2005, in *Sec. 3.3.2*; the pervasiveness of the fusion of church and state in pre-modern states—but the rise of the secular states in modern times, in *Sec. 3.4.1*; the dominance of religion in the medieval era—but the dominance of state atheism in the modern Communist Bloc, in *Sec. 3.4.2*; the acceptance of the Jewish way of life among the Jews in antiquity—but the rise of the Christian way of life among the Christians later, as the rebellious child "within Judaism," in *Sec. 3.5.1*; and the prevalence of religious philosophy in the older days—but the rise of the philosophy of religion as a separate field of study in the modern days, in *Sec. 3.5.2*).

And the reverse direction also holds true.

Again, for the last time, it should be stressed, however, that there are different shades of gray (or different degrees of truth) in the two opposites, and the classification is not necessarily mutually exclusive either. In fact, even when some combinations of the two occur, they only end up sharing the same dialectic relationship, but in a different degree.

Also, there are some other relationships (as a kind of family resemblance) which have something in common with the principle, but they are not exactly the same but only more or less comparable, which varies from case to case.

Good examples of family resemblance in relation to the principle are strength-weakness, balance-extremity, harmoniousness-unharrmoniousness, potence-impotence, reflexiveness-unreflexiveness, equality-inequality, and something like that.

13th Thesis: The Softness-Hardness Principle

The thirteenth thesis refers to the softness-hardness principle (on the force of change) in the category of "agency" in existential dialectics, in that any change by an agent, be it organic (like humans) or non-organic (like natural objects), can occur in a forceful (aggressive) or gentle (pacific) way, which can come in all shapes and sizes, of course. There is no softness without hardness—and vice versa.

For instance, on the one hand, there is softness (e.g., the praise of those who appeal to faith for the defense of religious experience, especially by those in the tradition of fideism, in *Sec. 2.2.1*; the use of magic to improve life, like its use "in healing to numb the sensation of pain, allowing healing to take place more easily," even if only perceptually, in *Sec. 2.2.2*; the use of cooperation in religious living, in *Sec. 2.3.2*; the existence of voluntary or "active" conversion, in *Sec. 2.4.1*; the joining of a NRM by an enthusiastic new member, in *Sec. 2.4.2*; the spirits in the world of shamanism can help the cure of ailments, in *Sec. 2.5.1*; the egalitarian view of humans "on a roughly equal footing with other animals, plants, and natural forces," as taught in animism, in *Sec. 2.5.2*; to treat those who conform in relation to one's ideology as "good," in stage 3 of Fowler's stage model, in *Sec. 3.2.2*; the practice of cooperation among social insects "such as bees, termites and ants," in *Sec. 3.3.1*; the acceptance of those in defense of geocentrism by the Catholic Church in the time of Galileo, in *Sec. 3.3.2*; the welcome to the secularists in power in modern Turkey, in *Sec. 3.4.1*; the praise of those who accepted state atheism in the Soviet Union, in *Sec. 3.4.2*; the promise of "redemption" to those who accept the "subjection to God [the priest]," in *Sec. 3.5.1*; and the polytheistic tolerance towards the existence of different gods in Hinduism, in *Sec. 3.5.2*).

On the other hand, there is hardness (e.g., the punishment of those who use reason for the defense of science, with negative implications for religion, as shown in the Galileo affair, in *Sec. 2.2.1*; the punishment by "stoning" against those who do not practice religious magic correctly in "ancient Judaism," as in "Saying the name of God without good reason," in *Sec. 2.2.2*; the use of competition for "the survival of the fittest," in *Sec. 2.3.2*; the existence of coerced or "forced" conversion, in *Sec. 2.4.1*; the leaving of a NRM by a disaffected member, in *Sec. 2.4.2*; the spirits in the world shamanism can inflict harm too, in *Sec. 2.5.1*; the hunting and killing of animals by humans for their consumption, as permitted in animism, in *Sec. 2.5.2*; to treat those who do not conform in relation to one's ideology as "bad," since they are seen as "the Other," in stage 3 of Fowler's stage model, in *Sec. 3.2.2*; the practice of competition, like a predator killing its prey, in *Sec. 3.3.1*; the house arrest of those like Galileio by the Catholic Church for his belief in heliocenrism, in *Sec. 3.3.2*; the discrimination against the Islamic fundamentalists who do not accept secularism in modern Turkish politics, in *Sec. 3.4.1*; the punishment of those who accepted Russian Orthodox Christianity in the Soviet Union, in *Sec. 3.4.2*; the punishment of those who dare the "disobedience of God [the priest]," which is cursed as a "sin," in *Sec. 3.5.1*; and the monotheistic exclusiveness in accepting only one god among the Christians, in *Sec. 3.5.2*).

And the reverse direction also holds true.

Again, it should be stressed, however, that there are different shades of gray (or different degrees of truth) in the two opposites, and the classification is not necessarily mutually exclusive either. In fact, even when some combinations of the two occur, they only end up sharing the same dialectic relationship, but in a different degree.

Also, there are some other relationships (as a kind of family resemblance) which have something in common with the principle, but they are not exactly the same but only more or less comparable, which varies from case to case.

Good examples of family resemblance in relation to the principle are peacefulness-violence, cooperation-competition, pacificity-aggression, dovishness-hawkishness, reward-punishment, peace-war, and the like.

14th Thesis: The Regression-Progression Principle

The fourteenth thesis is called the regression-progression princple (on the direction of history) in the category of "outcome" in existential dialectics (which was also already worked out in my previous books), in that neither the cyclical nor the linear views are adequate for explaining many phenomena at all levels. There is no regression without progression—and vice versa.

History progresses to more advanced forms, but with a regressive touch. Examples include no freedom without unfreedom, no equality without inequality, and no civilization without barbarity. This is not an inevitable law, but merely a highly likely empirical trend.

For instance, on the one hand, there is regression (e.g., the regression made by fideism, as shown in the problems pointed out by the critics, in *Sec. 2.2.1*; the regression made in religious magic as shown in the problems pointed out by the critics, in *Sec. 2.2.2*; the regression made by the teleological argument, as shown in the unresolved problems pointed out by the critics, in *Sec. 2.3.1*; the regression made in the history of religion, as shown in holy crusades where countless individuals were killed, in *Sec. 2.3.2*; the regression made by the politics of religious conversion, as shown by the disagreements among different countries and individuals about the legal rights of religious conversion and its limits, in *Sec. 2.4.1*; the regression made by NRMs as revealed by the criticisms from disaffected ex-members who "seek…redress for perceived wrongs or look…to expose perceived wrongdoings," in *Sec. 2.4.2*; the regression made by shamanism, as shown by the phenomenon of "fraudulent shamans" in different cultures and the "shamanic mass movement, the Ghost Dance, [which] swept through many tribes of Native Americans" to unsuccessfully get rid of the white invaders in the late 19th century, in *Sec. 2.5.1*; the regression made by animism, as shown by the problems pointed out by the critics, in *Sec. 2.5.2*; the regression made in the experiences of "psychic" or "spiritual" phenemena by those individuals who, afterwards, "had completely lost their ability to pray, others suffered continuous severe psychosomatic physical pains and illnesses and endured periods of painful alienation from God," in *Sec. 3.2.1*; the regression made in stage 1 of Fowler's stage model, in that "the child's imagination can be 'possessed' by unrestrained images of terror and destruction from the unconscious, and the exploitation of the fertile imagination by enforced taboos and indoctrination," in *Sec. 3.2.2*; the regression made by evolutionary theory, as revealed in the criticisms by the critics, in *Sec. 3.3.1*; the regression made by the heliocentric model, as shown in the failure of Galileo's theory of tides in his attempt to defend heliocentrism, in *Sec. 3.3.2*; the regression made in the secular order, as shown in the four failures as analyzed in *FHC*, in *Sec. 3.4.1*; the regression made in antireligion, as revealed in the failures of state atheism as pointed out by the critics, in *Sec. 3.4.2*; the regression made in religions like Judaism and Christianity as shown in the criticisms by Nietzsche in regard to their "decadence" and "lies," in *Sec. 3.5.1*; and the regression made in the philosophy of religion, in that it is unable to provide answers to the critical questions to religion that can satisfy everyone or at least most people, in *Sec. 3.5.2*).

On the other hand, there is progress (e.g., the progress made by fideism in exploring the relationship between faith and its contribution "to live fuller and better lives," in *Sec. 2.2.1*; the progress made in religious magic for healing and other tangible results, under certain circumstances, in *Sec. 2.2.2*; the progress made by the teleological argument in helping us be more aware of the possible existence of an intelligent designer in the metaphysical realm beyond the reach of science, in *Sec. 2.3.1*; the progress made in the history of religion, as shown in cooperative living, in *Sec. 2.3.2*; the progress made by the United Nations Universal Declaration of Human Rights to encourage religious conversion as a human right, in *Sec. 2.4.1*; the progress made by NRMs as shown by satisfied members who stay, in *Sec. 2.4.2*; the progress made by shamanism, as shown by the history of healing, etc. by shamans, in *Sec. 2.5.1*; the progress made by animism to help us understand the close relationship between humans and others in nature, in *Sec. 2.5.2*; the progress made in the experiences of "psychic" or "spiritual" phenemena by those individuals who, afterwards, "may acquire moral consciences" as "magnanimity replaces self-centeredness," and "the changes they perceive in themselves are…rewarding, undoubtedly, both to themselves and to their families," in *Sec. 3.2.1*; the progress made in stage 1 of Fowler's stage model, in that "the advantages of this stage are the birth of imagination and the growing ability to grasp and unify one's perception of reality," in *Sec. 3.2.2*; the progress made by evolutionary theory, for a better understanding of the evolution of life on Earth, in *Sec. 3.3.1*; the progress made by the heliocentric model in helping us understand why the sun is the center of the solar system, in *Sec. 3.3.2*; the progress made in secularism for the separation of church and state, in *Sec. 3.4.1*; the progress made in antireligion to help us understand the dark sides of religion, as pointed out by various notable individuals on antireligion, in *Sec. 3.4.2*; the progress made in religious like Judaism and Christianity for the better understanding of the need to search for spirituality in human life, in *Sec. 3.5.1*; and the progress made in the philosophy of religion to clarify the usage of such words like "God," etc., in *Sec. 3.5.2*).

And the reverse direction also holds true.

Again, it should be stressed, however, that there are different shades of gray (or different degrees of truth) in the two opposites, and the classification is not necessarily mutually exclusive either. In fact, even when some combinations of the two occur, they only end up sharing the same dialectic relationship, but in a different degree.

Also, there are some other relationships (as a kind of family resemblance) which have something in common with the principle, but they are not exactly the same but only more or less comparable, which varies from case to case.

Good examples of family resemblance in relation to the principle are cost-benefit, undesirability-desirability, badness-goodness, risk-opportunity, and so forth.

15th Thesis: The Same-Difference Principle

The fifteen thesis refers to the same-difference principle (on the metamorphosis of change) in the category of "outcome" in existential dialectics (which was worked out in *ALD* and other books of mine), in that an entity, as it evolves over time, can be both different from and similar to its opposing alternatives and does not have to be solely more different from them over time. There is no similarity without difference—and vice versa.

Opposites are not absolute in a black-or-white fashion; so, an entity can become relatively more similar to (or more different from) its opposite over time.

This is further constrained by another principle, that is, the symmetry-asymmetry principle about the relationships among existents under the category about agency in existential dialectics, in that if there is symmetry (equality) between two entities, there is likewise asymmetry (inequality) emerging in a different way.

For instance, on the one hand, there is similarity in outcome (e.g., the contribution to the varieties of life experience, regardless of whether this is done with the use of reason or the appeal to faith, in *Sec. 2.2.1*; the contribution to life improvement and transformation, regardless of whether this is done by magic, religion, or science, in *Sec. 2.2.2*; the contribution to the understanding of the universe, regardless of whether this is achieved by way of the teleological argument, the Big Bang theory, or else, in *Sec. 2.3.1*; the contribution to the regulation and control of members in societies, regardless of whether this is true for primate societies or human societies, in *Sec. 2.3.2*; the contribution to the molding of human behaviors and beliefs, regardless of whether this be done by lax legal rights for religious conversion or strict limits on its exercise, in *Sec. 2.4.1*; the contribution to the regulation and control of behaviors and beliefs, regardless of whether this be done in "mainstream" religious organizations or in NRMs, in *Sec. 2.4.2*; the contribution to the curing of ailments in human life, regardless of whether this be done by shamanism or by modern science, in *Sec. 2.5.1*; the contribution to the regulation and control of human beliefs and behaviors, regardless of whether this be done by way of animism or of organized religions like Christianity, in *Sec. 2.5.2*; the contribution to the molding of beliefs and behaviors, regardless of whether this be done by way of "psychic" or "spiritual" experiences or by way of rational conversion, in *Sec. 3.2.1*; the contribution to the motivation of people to act, regardless of whether this be done by science or by religion, in *Sec. 3.2.2*; the contribution to the understanding of how lifeforms come into existence over time on Earth, regardless of whether it is shown by creationism or by evolutionary theory, in *Sec. 3.3.1*; the contribution to the prediction of "various celestial motions" of the planets, regardless of whether this be achieved by way of the Ptolemaic model or the heliocentric model, in *Sec. 3.3.2*; the contribution to law and order in political society, be this done by the secular state or the religious state, in *Sec. 3.4.1*; the contribution to the molding and control of human beliefs and behaviors, regardless of whether this be achieved by way of state atheism or by way of organized religion, in *Sec. 3.4.2*; the contribution to the molding of human beliefs and values, regardless of whether this be done by way of Judaism, Christanity, and Nazism, for instance, in *Sec. 3.5.1*; and the contribution to the molding of different beliefs about the larger universe, regardless of whether this be accomplished by way of theism, agnostism, atheism, etc., in *Sec. 3.5.2*).

On the other hand, there is difference in outcome (e.g., the contribution to the enrichment of life experience in a more emotional way with the appeal to faith—but the contribution to the enrichment of life experience in a more sober way with the use of reason, in *Sec. 2.2.1*; the contribution to life improvement and transformation by religious magic in terms of the practice of religious artifacts, sacrifice, etc.—but the contribution to life improvement and transformation by science in terms of medications, physical therapy, etc., in *Sec. 2.2.2*; the contribution to the understanding of the universe by way of the teleological argument for the possible existence of an intelligent designer in the metaphysical realm—but the contribution to the understanding of the universe by way of the Big Bang theory for a beginning without an intelligent designer, in *Sec. 2.3.1*; the contribution to the regulation and control of members in primate societies by way of social norms in group living—but the contribution to the regulation and control of members in human societies by way of "two extra levels of sophistication," namely, "much more rigorous" moral codes, and "a degree of judgment and reason, not seen in the animal kingdom," as shown by de Waal, in *Sec. 2.3.2*; the contribution to the molding of human behaviors and beliefs by way of lax legal rights for religious conversion to encourage ideational individualism—but the contribution to the molding of human behaviors and beliefs by way of strict limits on religious conversion to encourage ideational collectivism, in *Sec. 2.4.1*; the contribution to the regulation and control of behaviors and beliefs by way of the teaching of "mainstream" religious organizations, for instance, in regard to the existence of a monolithic deity in Christianity—but the contribution to the regulation and control of behaviors and beliefs by way of the teaching of NRMs, for instance, in regard to the view of "God" only as a "metaphor" by some "naturalistic" new religious groups, in *Sec. 2.4.2*; the contribution to the curing of ailments in human life by way of shamanism, especially with more success in psychosomatic cases—but the contribution to the curing of ailments in human life by way of modern science, with more success in physical cases, in *Sec. 2.5.1*; the contribution to the regulation and control of human beliefs and behaviors by way of animism for a more egalitarian treatment of nature—but the contribution to the regulation and control of human beliefs and behaviors by way of organized religions like Christianity for humans to play the role of stewardship of nature in an inegalitarian way, in *Sec. 2.5.2*; the contribution to the molding of beliefs and behaviors by way of "psychic" or "spiritual" experiences with their consequent traumatic "consciousness shifts"—but the contribution to the molding of beliefs and behaviors by way of rational conversion with their consequent ability to "produce a reasonable and coherent defense of their beliefs" in God," especially among those of "the most able philosophers and scientists in the world today," in *Sec. 3.2.1*; the contribution to the motivation of people to act by way of religion with its "religious fervour" for "perfection" and "superiority"—but the contribution to the motivation of people to act by way of science with its "scientific" spirit for the discovery of "truth" in the physical world, in *Sec. 3.2.2*; the contribution to the understanding of how lifeforms come into existence over time on Earth by way of creationism on the basis of a supernatural being—but the contribution to the understanding of how lifeforms come into existence over time on Earth by way of evolutionary theory on the basis of such processes like variation, mutation, inheritance, adapation, and selection, together with chance, in *Sec. 3.3.1*; the contribution to the prediction of "various celestial motions" of the planets by way of the Ptolemaic model, if needed on a "fairly well" basis, by pre-modern standards—but the contribution to the prediction of "various celestial motions" of the planets by way of the heliocentric model, if needed on a more accurate basis, by modern standards, in *Sec. 3.3.2*; the contribution to law and order in political society by the secular state for the separation of church and state—but the contribution to law and order in political society by the religious state for the fusion of religion and state, in *Sec. 3.4.1*; the contribution to the molding and control of human beliefs and behaviors by way of state atheism for the suppression of all religious beliefs and practices—but the contribution to the molding and control of human beliefs and behaviors by way of organized religion for the glorification of religious beliefs and practices, in *Sec. 3.4.2*; the contribution to the molding of human beliefs and values by way of Judaism and Christanity for "peace," "love," etc.—but the contribution to the molding of human beliefs and values by way of Nazism for "war," "power," etc., in *Sec. 3.5.1*; and the contribution to the molding of different beliefs about the larger universe by way of theism for the existence of a supernatural reality—but the contribution to the molding of different beliefs about the larger universe by way of atheism for the non-existence of a supernatural reality, in *Sec. 3.5.2*).

And the reverse direction also holds true.

Again, it should be stressed, however, that there are different shades of gray (or different degrees of truth) in the two opposites, and the classification is not necessarily mutually exclusive either. In fact, even when some combinations of the two occur, they only end up sharing the same dialectic relationship, but in a different degree.

Also, there are some other relationships (as a kind of family resemblance) which have something in common with the principle, but they are not exactly the same but only more or less comparable, which varies from case to case.

Good examples of family resemblance in relation to the principle are homogeneity-heterogeneity, we-they, and so forth.

16th Thesis: The Post-Human Substitution

And the sixteenth thesis is about the role of "post-humans," which I originally proposed in my previous books, starting with the first book titled *The Future of Human Civilization* in 2000 and all others afterwards.

As already pointed out in *Sec. 1.8*, I need to emphasize, as this is something that I used to repeat (*almost verbatim*) from my previous books, two clarifications here about the term "post-human" as a neologism in my works.

Firstly, the word "post-human" here should *not* be confused with another term which looks similar but has a totally different meaning in the literature of postmodernism, namely, "post-humanism"—which constitutes a critique of "humanism" as tradionally understood (especially, though not exclusively, in relation to the idea of progress in science and reason in the Enlightenment project). (WK 2008)

My works reject the project of "postmodernism" and propose the future world of what I orignally called "after-postmodernity" in *FHC* and *FCD*, for instance.

And secondly, the word "post-human" here should also *not* be confused with a similar term which is used to champion the ideology of technology for the future co-existence between humans and cyborgs in "trans-humanism." (WK 2008a)

Instead, my term "post-human" in relation to "posthuman-ism" also rejects "transhumanism" (especially, though not exclusively, in relation to the promises of technology) and refers to something else altogether, that is, the future extinction of humans and its post-human successors in deep space and beyond unto multiverses.

My critique of "transhumanism" was more extensively elabroated in *Sec. 2.4.1* of *BEPE*.

With these two clarifications in mind (as summarized in *Table 1.31*)—the post-human substitution in religion can be addressed in relation to five main directions, based on the comparative-substitutive theory of religion as analysed in this book (together with my visions as already worked out in my previous books).

Firstly, the "post-human" substitution in religion will learn from the comparative-substitutive theory of religion in relation to the dialectic context of sacredness and secularness—especially in the larger dialectic context of no sacredness without secularness (and vice versa).

Secondly, the "post-human" substitution in religion will also learn from the comparative-substitutive theory of religion in relation to the four perspectives of the mind, nature, society, and culture.

Thirdly, the "post-human" substitution in religion will also learn from the comparative-substitutive theory of religion in relation to the non-privilege of any specific theory over others in the literature and the non-integration of them all (as they are not necessarily compatible with each other).

Fourthly, the "post-human" substitution in religion will have to confront the new challenges as posed by the long-term civilizational development of intelligent life in the distant future, both here on this planet Earth and elsewhere in deep space until multiverses.

As this is something that I regularly pointed out in my previous books for background information (and summarize here, *almost verbatim*), I already worked out, in my numerous books, what these new challenges will be and provide different original visions to meet them—especially, in regard to the future evolutions of the mind (e.g., "the contrarian personality," "the hyper-martial body," "the hyper-sexual body," "floating consciousness," "hyper-spatial consciousness," "unfolding unconsciousness," "thinking machines," "thinking robots," "genetically altered superior beings," "cyborgs," and others), of nature (e.g., "post-Earth geology," "post-cosmology," "the alteration of space-time," "the creation of new matter-energy," "selective geometry," and the like), of society (e.g., "multifaceted war and peace," virtual organizations, different versions of "post-capitalism" and "post-democracy," the movement of "cyclical progression" at both structural and systemic levels, "ambivalent technology," and so forth), and of culture (e.g., "post-human mind games," the rise of "post-civilization," "transformative aesthetic experience," "contrastive mathematical-logic," and the whatnot) in history (e.g., the age of "after-postmodernity"), in the context of my approaches in relation to methodology (e.g., "sophisticated methodologial holism," "critical-dialectic formal science," etc,) and ontology (e.g., "existential dialectics," "contrastive rationality").

Of course, the examples (as listed above) are not exhaustive but illustrative, since my numerous books have worked out many other visions (as already roughly summarized in *Sec.1.8* and *Sec. 1.9*). Many, though not all, of my visions on the mind, nature, society, culture, history, methodology, and ontology (as cited above) are summarized in the tables as shown in Chapter One and Chapter Four (especially in *Table 4.43* about my original theories on numerous topics).

And finally, or fifthly, the "post-human" substitution in religion will also learn from the comparative-substitutive theory of religion in regard to the need to move towards the higher spirituality (as further elaborated in the next section).

Towards the Higher Spirituality

This "post-human" substitution in religion from the comparative-substitutive theory of religion to transcend both sacredness and secularness towards the higher spirituality has path-breaking implications for some soul-searching questions which have exhausted many of the best and the brightest minds in history—What is the meaning of life? What is God? Does God exist? Is there heaven or hell after death? And….?

Questions like this have continued their relevance in our time, as shown in the controversy concerning the secular underestimation of religion, on the one hand, and its opposing view, on the other hand (as already introduced in *Sec. 1.1*)—which have much distracted the mind from seeing the other (different) sides of both sacredness and secularness, with the impoverishing consequence on our understanding of religion and its future.

Contrary to the opposing views in the debate, the promise of secularness (on one side of the fence, as already discussed in Chapter Three) and the importance of sacredness (on the other side of the fence, as already analyzed in Chapter Two) are neither possible nor desirable to the extent that their respective ideologues would like us to believe.

If sacredness has its importance, it has its limitation too, as the other side of the same coin. This view that sacredness can be good (from the perspective of sacredness) is something that those on the side of secularness often do not take seriously.

Conversely, if secularness has its promise, it likewise has its pitfall, as the other side of the same mirror. This view that secularness can also be good (from the perspective of secularness) is something that those on the side of sacredness often do not endorse.

This conclusion can be carried out to its logical endpoint, in two major ways.

Firstly, sacredness and secularness cannot exist without each other, in a dialectic manner as revealed by the twenty-one principles in existential dialectics (which are summarized in this concluding chapter). There is no sacredness without secularness—just as there is no secularness without sacredness.

And secondly, in the long run of civilizational development for intelligent life, both on earth and, later, even more importantly, in deep space unto multiverses—both sacredness and secularness are to be transcended into different spiritual concerns that our world in this relativley primitive historical era has never known.

Religion then will still be needed in the post-human future, just as it has existed for much of human history. Each age has its own versions of religion, to the extent that what constitutes a religion varies from one age to another—as shown in the changes from shamanism (in *Sec. 2.5.1*) and animism (in *Sec. 2.5.2*) in the Paleolithic period (and afterwards) into systematic organized religions in different human cultures in later times (like Christianity, Islam, Hinduism, and Buddhism).

The awe of religion will not disappear (contrary to what some secular ideologues would like us to believe), although it will take new (different) forms in each new historical era. There are plenty of good reasons for this, as already explained in this book from the perspectives of the mind, nature, society, and culture.

Consider the essential question of faith (as already addressed in *Sec. 2.2.1*), as an example here (for a recap).

Faith will still be needed in the post-human future for three rationales (as explained below, for illustration).

The first ratonale is that reason and experience alone cannot answer all the profound questions in life. This is true for humans as much as for post-humans. Even should post-humans have more amazing cognitive abilities that humans in our time could not even imagine, they would confront more insurmountably complex problems that humans in our time do not. When reason and experience do not provide compelling answers to profound life problems, faith will continue to have a role to play.

The second rationale is that there are some life predicaments which invoke intense emotions. If humans confront some life predicaments like the didactic of Abraham's act to sacrifice Isaac in Kieerkegaard's fiction, post-humans will likewise have their own versions of life predicaments on Earth and later in deep space until multiverses, in a way that humans in their entire history hitherto existing have never known. Faith will continue to have a role to play insofar as intense emotions are needed in certain life predicaments.

And the third rationale is that, in situations when reason and experience are not sufficient to resolve profound life problems and emotions can give intelligent life the much needed solace and enrichment for life, faith will continue to have a role to play.

These three rationales for the future relevance of religion (with the issue of faith as an example here) are only illustrative, as they are concerned only with the mind, but there are other perspectives (of nature, society, and culture) to be considered too. In fact, they were already addressed in this book (and other previous ones of mine).

In this way, those secular ideologues who would like to see the disappearance of religion in future times may have confused it with magic. Unlike religion, magic has been increasingly (though not completely) fused with science and technology, to the extent that, as Arthur C. Clarke (1962) once aptly observed, "any sufficiently advanced technology is indistinguishable from magic." Even then, magic can still have another future role insofar as it is linked with religion in religious magic, as opposed to non-religious magic (as already addressed in *Sec. 2.2.2*).

In any event, the next question is, What distinctive forms of religion will the post-humans take? Surely, they will not literally continue the human religions hitherto existing in human history; rather, they will substitute them with their own post-human versions which are more suitable to their histories and the environments in deep space until multiverses.

We already know, from the history of human religions, that the earliest forms like shamanism and animism were later superseded by some more systematic ones like organized religions in different cultures over time. For instance, Christianity, as an organized religion, has two advantages over shamanism, in that, firstly, it distances itself from magic by delegating it into the mundane realm and focusing on the sacred realm instead and, secondly, it provides a systematic analysis of its own alternative religion in an extensively elaborated text (like the Bible) for its members.

By the same logic, human religions will likewise be superseded by post-human forms of religion for future spirituality in deep space until multiverses. In the process, elaborated systems of religion for post-humans which are more suitable for those in deep space and beyond will emerge.

I already provided some visions towards this future spiritual direction for post-humans in my previous books. One of my favorite examples, as this is something that I often did in my previous books, is what I already explained in Chapter 10 of *The Future of Capitalism and Democracy* (2002), concerning why and how there will be more spiritual transformations to come, especially in relation to the two value ideals of (i) transcending freedom in floating existence and (ii) transcending equality in the rivalry of cosmic hegemony.

Even then, these two value ideals constitute only a small fraction of other future transformations of the mind, nature, society, and culture (as already addressed in my other books on my other different visions of the future).

In the end, what is understood as "God" (or "gods") for the ultimate truth and power in the human versions of religion may well be substituted into different cosmic variants of what I already visioned as "floating consciousness," "hyper-spatial consciousness," "unfolding unconsciousness," and other tremendous transformations in the post-human future at its peak in the entire universe or, alternatively, multiverses.

But this post-human future of religion will be neither "heaven" nor "hell," as it will instead be contextualized within the constraints of existential dialectics.

Welcome to this future post-human world of religion, beyond sacralness and secularness (towards the higher spirituality), for better and for worse—not to be judged by the wishes and concerns of present humans but by the contingent values and beliefs of future post-humans in a way that all human history hitherto existing has never known.

Table 4.1. Sophisticated Methodological Holism (Part I)

• "My methodological holism implies the partiality-totality principle in the ontology of existential dialectics (see the table on the partiality-totality principle for summary), which is against the varieties of (a) reductionism and (b) reverse-reductionism, in relation to (i) concept, (ii) theory, (iii) methodology, and (iv) ontology." (*FC*)

• "[M]y methodological holism here is not opposed to methodological individualism but includes it (and, for that matter, other methodologies too)…." (*FPHC*) For this reason (and others too, as summarized hereafter), my version of methodological holism is sophisticated—not vulgar as sometimes used by inapt scholars using the same term. (*FC*)

• "[M]y methodological holism does not democratically presume that all levels are equally valid, as all levels are not created equal. In other words, in relation to issue X, level A may be more relevant than level B, but in relation to Y, level B can be more relevant than level A instead." (*FPHC*) One excellent example of this vulgar democratic presumption is what I called in *BNN* "the compromise fallacy." (*FC*)

• My methodological holism does not presume that a lower level of analysis is more important than a higher level, solely because the former serves as the foundation for the latter—and vice versa, for that matter. One excellent example of this reductionistic presumption is what I called in *FPHST* "the foundation fallacy." (*FPHST, FC*)

(continued on next page)

Table 4.1. Sophisticated Methodological Holism (Part II)

• "[M]y methodological holism does not make any a-priori postulation that there must be a definite (and, for that matter, indefinite) number of levels" in any analysis. (*FPHC*) Nor does it dogmatically require that there must be a certain combination of levels of analysis in a given inquiry. (*FC*)

• "[M]ethodological holism, in my usage, does not assume that all levels…can necessarily be integrated, since methodological holism is not aimed to search for the holy grail of 'an integral theory…' (as is the case for Wilber). In other words, it allows that sometimes some levels may experience irreducible gaps between them, to be understood, at best, as empirical correlations, not as causal relations…." (*FPHC*)

• "[D]ifferent levels may overlap and even interact with each other in a given context (but sometimes may not), and the fact that I even proposed different ways of re-classifying the levels (whenever needed) in *FDC* reinforces this point….The dual danger here is either forcefully making different levels interact when they are just different (or, metaphorically speaking, apples and oranges) or inappropriately ignoring their interactions when some situations instead require them." (*FPHC*)

• "[T]o understand different levels from their own (unique) perspectives (as required by my methodological holism) is not the same as trying to reduce them to a preferred level in the process of learning from other levels. This second kind of multidisciplinary work is not genuine and does no justice to the unique complexities and merits inherent at each level." (*FPHC*)

(continued on next page)

Table 4.1. Sophisticated Methodological Holism (Part III)

• "[My] methodological holism walks a fine line between the artificial classification (separation) of levels and the simultaneous incorporation of them, if only for the sake of human scholarly endeavor. It should be reminded that nature does not impose upon itself the academic classification of the levels of analysis as humans have. The enterprise of classification is therefore anthropocentric." (*FPHC*)

• "[M]y methodological holism advocates neither epistemic subjectivism nor epistemic non-subjectivism (e.g., realism, idealism, and historicism), neither epistemic relativism (e.g., subjectivism, historicism) nor epistemic absolutism (e.g., realism, positivism), neither epistemic reductionism nor epistemic emergencism, and neither epistemic objectivism (e.g., realism, idealism) nor epistemic historicism....Neither does methodological holism, in my usage, accept the false meta-conceptual dichotomy between nominalism and realism....These false dichotomies...are to be transcended. In other words, methodological holism does not fully accept epistemic realism, positivism (a form of epistemic idealism), historicism, subjectivism, and reductionism in epistemology and philosophy of science but learns from the strengths and weaknesses of all of the opposing approaches without siding with any of them...." (*FPHC*)

• "Sophisticated methodological holism is subject to the constraints as imposed by the syntax of existential dialectics (e.g., the partiality-totality principle and the predictability-unpredictability principle). Even in predictability, outcomes are subject to uncertainty, the degree of which varies from case to case." (*FC*)

(continued on next page)

Table 4.1. Sophisticated Methodological Holism (Part IV)

• "Sophisticated methodological holism—when applied, especially though not exclusively, as illustrated in my numerous works—can enrich the understanding of reality in some distinctive ways. Here are three examples (as revealed in each of my books)." (*FPHCT*; *FPHL*)

—"Firstly, it provides a comprehensive analysis of a subject matter, from which much can be learned about reality," "both in relation to the perspectives of the mind, nature, society, and culture and also in relation to a new classification of the subject matter."

—"Secondly, it suggests some visions of the future in relation to the subject matter in question."

—"And thirdly, it proposes some insights on meta-theory (e.g., methodology and ontology) in general—with the clear understanding, however, of the dilemma of specific vs. general ontology (as shown in the table on the syntax of existential dialectics in the context of the dilemma of ontology). For this very reason, all of these ways are important, without reducing one into the analysis of another."

• "In the end, my meta-theory (both sophisticated methodological holism and existential dialectics) serves as a foundation to unify all domains of knowledge into *an unified theory of everything* (by way of some ontological principles and the comprehensive perspectives of the mind, nature, society, and culture). This is so, without commiting the sins of reductionism and reverse-reductionism (as often seen in many holistic approaches, with the fad of sysems approach—be it about systems theory, chaos theory, complexity theory, or else—as a most recent notorious example, which I debunked in *The Future of Complexity* and also in *The Future of Post-Human Formal Science*). My distinctive approach makes good use of different schools of thought without favoring any of them nor trying to integrate them (as they are not necessarily compatible with each other), so as to adjust for subjectivity, diversity, conflict, and complexity, for example. In this sense, the word "unified" does not have to mean integrative approach, in a narrow sense, nor systems approach, in a broad one, both of which I reject while learning from them." (*FPHFS*; *FPHS*)

Sources: A summary of *Sec.1.2* in *FPHC*—and also from *BNN*, *FPHST*, *ALD*, *FC*, *FPHCT*, and the rest of all other books of mine. See the books for more detail.

Table 4.2. On Reductionism and Reverse-Reductionism (Part I)

- **The Partiality-Totality Principle**
  —The partiality-totality principle in the ontology of existential dialectics targets against the varieties of reductionism and reverse-reductionism (as already worked out in my previous books).

- **Against the Varieties of Reductionism**
  —*Conceptual Reductionism*
    - Some illustrative instances involve myriad dualities like mind vs. body, self vs. world, democracy vs. non-democracy, and the like (as already addressed in *FHC*, *FPHC*, and *BDPD*, for instance).

  —*Theoretical Reductionism*
    - A fascinating case study concerns what I originally called "the foundation fallacy" in *FPHST*, in any attempt to naively understand space-time from the physical perspective as the foundation and, consequently, to dangerously dismiss other perspectives.
    - In *FAE*, I elaborated further these versions of reductionism in the literature on aesthetics (e.g., form vs. content, representation vs. expression, critics vs. artists, and externalism vs. internalism).
    - In *FIA*, I revealed other forms of reductionism in the literature on information architecture (e.g., the constructivist argument).
    - In *FPHU*, I showed the persistent legacy of reductionism, this time, in the literature on anomalous experience (e.g., the obsession with physics, chemistry, and biology for explaining anomalous experience).
    - In *FPHE*, I examined another case of reductionism in action, in the context of engineering (e.g., technical constraints vs. normative constraints).
    - In *FPHMM*, I elaborated one more version of reductionism, in relation to the three domains of communication (e.g., the competing views on sending, connecting, and receiving).
    - In *FPHCT*, I explored another version of reductionism, in relation to invention and innovation (e.g., the bio-psychological argument vs. the socio-cultural arguments).

(continued on next page)

Table 4.2. On Reductionism and Reverse-Reductionism (Part II)

- **Against the Varieties of Reductionism *(cont'd)***
  —*Theoretical Reductionism (cont'd)*
  - In *FPHG*, I identify another version of reductionism, in relation to infinity, symmetry, and dimensionality (e.g., the Euclidean argument vs. the non-Euclidean arguments).
  - In *FPHUP*, I analyzed another version of reductionism, in relation to density and void (e.g., the engineering argument and the ecology argument).
  - In *FPHL*, I examined another version of reductionism, in relation to structure and context (e.g., the structuralist argument and the contextualist argument).
  - In *PFHO*, I explored another version of reductionism, in relation to communcation, decision-making, and leadership (e.g., the rational-system argument vs. the natural-system argument).
  - In *PFHMA*, I revealed another version of reductionism, in relation to the martial body and spirit (e.g., the spiritual argument vs. the materialist argument vs. the defensive argument).
  - In *PFHS*, I analyzed another version of reductionism, in relation to the sexual body and spirit (e.g., the naturalist argument vs. the constructivist argument).
  - In *PFHLAW*, I examined another version of reductionism, in relation to law (e.g., the necessity argument vs. the contengency argument).
  - In *FPHWP*, I showed another version of reductionism, in relation to war and peace (e.g., the aggressivist argument vs. the pacifist argument).
  - In *BEPE*, I analyzed another version of reductionism, in relation to morality and immorality (e.g., the objectivist argument vs. the non-objectivist argument vs. the skeptical argument).
  - In *BCOS*, I examined another version of reductionism, in relation to the contested beginnings and speculative ends of the universe (e.g., the scientific argument vs. the religious argument vs. the esoteric argument vs. the metaphysical argument).
  - In *FPHP*, I show another version of reductionism, in relation to normality and abnormality (e.g., the natural argument vs. the social argument vs. the cultural argument vs. the mental argument).

(continued on next page)

Table 4.2. On Reductionism and Reverse-Reductionism (Part III)

- **Against the Varieties of Reductionism *(cont'd)***
  —*Theoretical Reductionism (cont'd)*
  - In *FPHGEOL*, I scrutinized another version of reductionism, in relation to statics and dynamics (e.g., the catastrophe argument vs. the uniformity argument vs. the revision argument).
  - In *FPHCHESS*, I showed another version of reductionism, in relation to tactics and strategy (e.g., the natural argument vs. the social argument vs. the cultural argument vs. the mental argument).
  - And in *FPHR*, I reveal another version of reductionism, in relation to secularness and sacredness (e.g., the critical argument vs. the skeptical argument vs. the theist argument).

  —*Methodological Reductionism*
  - A good instance concerns the debate between different versions of qualitative and quantitative methods (as already analyzed in *FC* and also *FHC*). In *FPHML*, I examined similar reductionism, this time, in the literature on mathematical logic (e.g., the obsession with consistency, soundness, and completeness). And in *FPHFS*, I also explored the problems of reductionism in the context of formal science (e.g., the analytical argument).

  —*Ontological Reductionism*
  - An excellent example is the debate between emergentism and reductionism in complexity theory and also in psychology (as elaborated in *FPHC*, in the context of Being and Becoming).

- **Against the Varieties of Reverse-Reductionism**
  —*Conceptual Reverse-Reductionism*
  - Any concept of "art" (e.g., fine art, cave art, outsider art, junk art) is deemed acceptable in postmodernism (as already addressed in Ch.4 of *FHC*).

(continued on next page)

Table 4.2. On Reductionism and Reverse-Reductionism (Part IV)

- **Against the Varieties of Reverse-Reductionism** ***(cont'd)***
  —*Theoretical Reverse-Reductionism*
    - There are numerous art and literary theories co-exist. Take the case of literary studies, as there are now Literary Structuralism, Marxist Literary Criticism, New Criticism, Phenomenology, Hermeneutics, Language-Game Literary Criticism, Feminist Literary Criticism, Reception Theory, Reader Response Criticism, Poststructuralism, Semiotics, Pyschoanalytic Literary Criticism, just to cite some well-known ones, with no one being said to be better than any others (as detailedly analyzed in Ch.4 of *FHC*). (S. Raman 1997) In *BNN*, I even introduced "the compromise fallacy" as another good illustration of theoretical reverse-reductionism, in misleadingly treating both genetic and environmental approaches as equally valid.

  —*Methodological Reverse-Reductionism*
    - There is the "anything-goes" mentality in postmodernism (e.g., doing art without praxis, doing art with praxis, and doing art by sublation), as analyzed in Ch.4 of *FHC*. And in *FPHFS*, I also exposed the problems of reverse-reductionism in the context of formal science in relation to systems theory.

  —*Ontological Reverse-Reductionism*
    - There are likewise no privileged ontology, and the door is open for anything in postmodernism (e.g., the equal status of the ontology of Being vs. that of Becoming, as already addressed in Ch.4 of *FHC*—and also in *FPHC).* In *FAE*, I also introduced another version of reverse-reductionism, that is, "the pluralist fallacy," in the context of understanding aesthetic experience, for instance—although this fallacy has been committed not exclusively in relation to the ontological level (but also at the conceptual, theoretical, and methodological ones).

Sources: From my previous books.

Table 4.3. The Concepton of Existential Dialectics (Part I)

- **Sets and Elements**
  - —Sets
    - Ex: the Same
    - Ex: the Others
  - —Elements
    - Ex: whites in 20th century America (in the set of "the Same")
    - Ex: Iraq during the U.S. invasion in 2003 (in the set of "the Others")

- **Relations, Operations, Functions**
  - —Relations (e.g., "belongs," "equals to," "is greater than")
    - Ex: symmetric interactions within the Same (or the Others)
    - Ex: asymmetric interactions between the Same and the Others
  - —Operations (e.g., "and," "or," "not," "if…then")
    - Ex: if the Same oppresses the Others, it will also oppress itself.
    - Ex: the Same is not the Others.
  - —Functions (e.g., goals)
    - Ex: the Same is hegemonic in relation to the Others.

- **Truth Values**
  - —"1" if True (in Symbolic Logic)
    - Ex: the proposition that imperial Japan was hegemonic to China during WWII
  - —"0" if False (in Symbolic Logic)
    - Ex: the proposition that Grenada invaded France in 2003
  - —"1" & "0" if Both True and False (in Dialectic Logic)
    - Ex: the proposition that the rabbit-duck picture refers to a duck
  - —"~1" & "~0" if Neither True Nor False (or N/A, in Dialectic Logic)
    - Ex: the proposition that God really exists

(continued on next page)

Table 4.3. The Conception of Existential Dialectics (Part II)

- **Axioms, Postulates, Theorems, Principles**
  - —Axioms
    - Ex: the reflexive axiom—"any quantity is equal to itself"
  - —Postulates
    - Ex: the SSS postulate—"if the three sides of a triangle are congruent to their corresponding parts, then the triangles are congruent"
  - —Theorems (and Principles) in Existential Dialectics
    - In Relation to Method
      - –#1: The formalness-informalness principle
      - –#2: The absoluteness-relativeness principle
      - –#3: The partiality-totality principle
      - –#4: The predictability-unpredictability principle
      - –#5: The explicability-inexplicability principle
    - In Relation to Structure
      - –#6: The finiteness-transfiniteness principle
      - –#7: The preciseness-vagueness principle
      - –#8: The simpleness-complicatedness principle
      - –#9: The openness-hiddenness principle
      - –#10: The denseness-emptiness principle
    - In Relation to Process
      - –#11: The change-constancy principle
      - –#12: The order-chaos principle
      - –#13: The slowness-quickness principle
      - –#14: The expansion-contraction principle
    - In Relation to Agency
      - –#15: The theory-praxis principle
      - –#16: The convention-novelty principle
      - –#17: The evolution-transformation principle
      - –#18: The symmetry-asymmetry principle
      - –#19: The softness-hardness principle
    - In Relation to Outcome
      - –#20: The regression-progression principle
      - –#21: The same-difference principle

(continued on next page)

Table 4.3. The Conception of Existential Dialectics (Part III)

Notes: The categories and examples in each are solely illustrative (not exhaustive). The comparison is also relative (not absolute), nor are they mutually exclusive. As generalities, they allow exceptions.
Sources: Starting from Ch.6 of *BCPC* and also from other books of mine

Table 4.4. The Syntax of Existential Dialectics I: The Principles (Part I)

- **In Relation to Method**

—*The Formalness-Informalness Principle*
(On the Formal Requirements of Logical Systems)

- The formal requirements of a logical system (e.g., consistency, soundness, and completeness) have both usefulness and non-usefulness, to the extent that, if there are formal systems requiring them, there are alternative ones which do not. Thus, it does *not* exclude classical logics but simply goes beyond both classical and non-classical logics, while learning something from each. There is no formalness without informalness—and vice versa.
- For instance, existential dialectics can make use of both classical logics under certain conditions (e.g., especially, though not exclusively, when they are clear-cut, etc.) and non-classical logics under alternative conditions (especially, though not exclusively, when they are "unknown," "irrelevant," "ambiguous," "possible," with "different degrees of truth," empirically inconsistent in a desirable way, etc.). (WK 2008u)
- Family resemblance: e.g., logicalness-nonlogicalness, rationality-nonrationality, etc.
- Sources: From *FPHML*. See also my later books.

—*The Explicability-Inexplicability Principle*
(On the Underlying Mechanisms of Things)

- Both explicability and inexplicability are part of the understanding of things. There is no explicability without inexplicability—and vice versa.
- This principle tells us the duality of the research dilemma, in that, if reality can be explained in some ways, it also has its other ways which are not quite explainable, at a given point in time.
- Family resemblance: e.g., underlyingness-regularness, causation-regularness, causation-correlation, etc.
- Sources: Especially from *FPHU*—and also *FPHC*. See also my later books.

(continued on next page)

Table 4.4. The Syntax of Existential Dialectics I: The Principles (Part II)

- **In Relation to Method *(cont'd)***
  - *—The Predictability-Unpredictability Principle (On the Occurrence of Events)*
    - Both predictability and unpredictability have a major role to play in the occurrence of things, so that neither determinism nor indeterminism wins the centuries-old fight. There is no predictability without unpredictability—and vice versa.
    - There are events which are predictable, just as there are those which are not. Or what is regarded as unpredictable at one point in time may turn out to be predictable later, and, conversely, what is deemed as predictable may turn out to not be so predictable. Even in predictability, outcomes are subject to uncertainty, the degree of which varies from case to case.
    - Family resemblance: e.g., sureness-arbitrariness, etc.
    - Sources: Especially from *FC*. See also my later books.
  - *—The Partiality-Totality Principle (On the Relationships between Whole and Parts)*
    - The whole is not the sum of the parts. There is no partiality without totality—and vice versa.
    - Any inquiry about a phenomenon in the work is to guard against the varieties of (a) reductionism and (b) reverse-reductionism.
    - Reductionism and reverse-reductionism can be (i) conceptual, (ii) theoretical, (iii) methodological, and (iv) ontological.
    - Family resemblance: e.g., individualisticness-holisticness, partness-wholeness, analysis-synthesis, etc.
    - Sources: Especially from *FC*. See also my later books.

(continued on next page)

Table 4.4. The Syntax of Existential Dialectics I: The Principles (Part III)

• **In Relation to Method** ***(cont'd)***

—The Absoluteness-Relativeness Principle

(On the Multiplicity of Things)

- There is the multiplicity of things in reality, be they about entities, qualities (or properties), and relationships, such that what is acceptable from one standpoint may not be so from another. For instance, if there is something absolute, there is likewise something relative. There is no absoluteness without relativeness—and vice versa.
- Both absoluteness and relativeness here are also relevant to different modalities often cited in the literature on ontology, such as possibility (e.g., something "can" happen) and its opposite (e.g., impossibility), probability (e.g., something "will" happen) and its opposite (e.g., improbability), and necessity (e.g., something "should" happen) and its opposite (e.g., contingency).
- Family resemblance: e.g., uniformity-diversity, internalness-externalness, immanence-transcendence, etc.
- Sources: From *FPHK*. See also my later books.

(continued on next page)

Table 4.4. The Syntax of Existential Dialectics I: The Principles (Part IV)

- **In Relation to Structure**

  —*The Finiteness-Transfiniteness Principle*

  (On the Nature of Numbers)

  - If there are finite things, there are likewise transfinite ones. There is no finiteness without transfiniteness—and vice versa.
  - To avoid confusion, my usage of the word "transfinite" here differs radically from the one used by Cantor (and other mathematicians) for "relative" infinity—and is more limited, in light of the problems confronting any attempt to understand the idea of infinity, be it by intuition, imagination, and conception (as detailedly analyzed in *Sec. 2.2.3* of *FPHG*).
  - Instead, by "transfinity," I allow numbers which can be many times larger—or smaller, for that matter—than the finite things that we encounter in daily life, but they do not have to be related to the idea of infinity at all (which may not exist).
  - Of course, there may be some *borderline* cases, in which it is not clear whether the number in question is transfinite (in my usage) or simply a mathematical convenience. A good example of a borderline case is the Planck unit of length for "the smallest space possibly measured in nature," which is "less than billionths of trillionths of trillionths of an inch" (or something like 1.6×10^{-35} meters).
  - That said—my usage of "transfinity" can also resolve (or better, dissolve) an age-old problem in philosophy known as "Zeno's paradoxes" (as already explained in *Sec. 2.2.3* of *FPHG*).
  - Family resemblance: e.g., boundedness-quasiunboundedness, smallness-largeness, microness-macroness, etc.
  - Source: From *FPHG*. See also my later books.

(continued on next page)

Table 4.4. The Syntax of Existential Dialectics I: The Principles (Part V)

- **In Relation to Structure** ***(cont'd)***

  —*The Simpleness-Complicatedness Principle*
  (On the Interconnection among Things)
  - Both simpleness and complicatedness are vital, without favoring one over the other, in that each is utilized, depending on the basis of the perspectives of nature, the mind, culture, and society. And even when a combination of them is preferred, the dilemma is only shifted to a combinational degree of concern. There is no simpleness without complicatedness—and vice versa.
  - In relation to taxonomy, simpleness has its heuristic usefulness, just as complicatedness has its realistic representation, for instance. And in relation to network, simpleness has its economical attractiveness, just as complicatedness has its practical reliability, for instance.
  - Family resemblance: e.g., inflexibility-flexibility, standardization-specialization, imperfectness-perfectness, superficiality-depth, shallowness-deepness, economicalness-elaboratedness, plainness-circumspection, onesidedness-multisidedness, etc.
  - Sources: Especially from *FIA*. See also my later books.

  —*The Denseness-Emptiness Principle*
  (On the Distribution of Entities in Space)
  - Both density and void are needed, in relation to the mind, nature, culture, and society, albeit in different ways. There is no denseness without emptiness—and vice versa.
  - For clarity, the term "void" is used here only as an approximation of emptiness (depending on the degree of the lack of density), since, in physics, it is well known that "empty" space is not really empty all the way, because it can be full of energy (e.g., random quantum fluctuations at the sub-atomic level, and, for that matter, dark energy in the universe) and matter (e.g., different versions of sub-atomic particles, and, for that matter, dark matter in the universe).
  - Family resemblance: e.g., fullness-voidness, nearness-farness, concentration-dispersion, etc.
  - Sources: First worked out in *FPHUP*. See also my later books.

(continued on next page)

Table 4.4. The Syntax of Existential Dialectics I: The Principles (Part VI)

- **In Relation to Structure *(cont'd)***
  —*The Preciseness-Vagueness Principle*
  (On the Refinement of Things)
  - Both preciseness and vagueness are important, not that one is better than the other, but that both are used, in different degrees of preference, in accordance to the contextual application from the perspectives of nature, the mind, culture, and society. Even when both are used in a combination, the dilemma is shifted instead to one of combinational concern. There is no preciseness without vagueness—and vice versa.
  - In relation to taxonomy, preciseness has its taxonomic clarity, just as vagueness has its classificatory flexibility, for instance. And in relation to network, vagueness has its explorative liberty, just as preciseness has its conceptual definitiveness, for instance.
  - Family resemblance: e.g., clarity-ambiguity, directness-indirectness, quantitativeness-qualitativeness, describability-nondescribability, specificity-obscurity, specificity-generality, thickness-thinness, concretness-abstractness, etc.
  - Sources: Especially from *FIA*. See also my later books.

(continued on next page)

Table 4.4. The Syntax of Existential Dialectics I: The Principles (Part VII)

• **In Relation to Structure** ***(cont'd)***
—*The Openness-Hiddenness Principle*
(On the Detection of Things)
- Reality has its hidden face, just as it is open to outside view in some other ways. There is no openness without hiddenness—and vice versa.
- For instance, in the context of anomalous experience, certain aspects of reality can be open for examination (e.g., the experiment with SPECT images, the transmission of telepathemic bit, and the use of metonymies and metaphors). Other aspects, however, remain hidden, and examples include the elusive deeper nature of spiritual reality in the intangible realm, the undetectability of different branched universes, the underlying mechanisms of signals traveling between different folds of physical space-time, and the dependence on language and the bias for science and logic).
- Family resemblance: e.g., overtness-covertness, publicness-privateness, openness-closedness, transparency-secrecy, openness-biasedness, etc.
- Sources: Especially from *FPHU*. See also my later books.

• **In Relation to Process**
—*The Change-Constancy Principle*
(On the Alteration of Things)
- Change occurs over time, although constancy is also allowed. There is no change without constancy—and vice versa.
- Asymmetry undergoes changes over time, so does symmetry.
- Old players fade away, and new ones emerges, with ever new causes and ever new forms.
- Family resemblance: e.g., dynamicness-staticness, instability-stability, etc.
- Sources: First named in *BCPC*. Especially from *FHC*, *FCD*, and *FPHC*. See also other books of mine (from that point on).

(continued on next page)

Table 4.4. The Syntax of Existential Dialectics I: The Principles (Part VIII)

- **In Relation to Process *(cont'd)***

  —*The Expansion-Contraction Principle*
  (On the Growth of Things)

  - Entities in the world can both expand in some ways and contract in other ones, as part of their nature. There is no expansion without contraction—and vice versa.
  - For instance, in the context of anomalous experience, one of its most fascinating expressions is none other than the analysis of different causes of the slow but steady expansion (and, furthermore, if put in a different way, unfolding) of unconsciousness.
  - Family resemblance: e.g., conquest-autarky, rise-fall (or up-down), spread-shrink, extendingness-shorteningness, etc.
  - Sources: Especially from *FPHU*. See also my later books.

  —*The Slowness-Quickness Principle*
  (On the Speed of Change)

  - Both slowness and quickness co-exist, with their own internal tension, to the extent that each fights for its own relevance with the other, in accordance to the perspectives of nature, the mind, culture, and society, without one being the victor and the other being the vanquished in the long haul. Even when both are chosen in other cases, this dilemma is only transferred into something else with a combinational character. There is no slowness without quickness—and vice versa.
  - In relation to taxonomy, quickness has its efficient usability, just as slowness has its aesthetic appeal, for instance. And in relation to network, quickness has its adventurous readiness, just as slowness has its risk-adverse convenience, for instance.
  - Family resemblance: e.g., inconvenience-convenience, passiveness-activenessness, gradualness-abruptness, deceleration-acceleration, etc.
  - Sources: Especially from *FIA*. See also my later books.

(continued on next page)

Table 4.4. The Syntax of Existential Dialectics I: The Principles (Part IX)

• **In Relation to Process** ***(cont'd)***

—*The Order-Chaos Principle*

(On the Pattern of Things)

- Both order and chaos are vital in the process of change in the world. The preference for order is biased, since it does not give sufficient attention to the vital role of chaos in the transformation of the world (without somehow reducing it for the understanding of order). There is no order without chaos—and vice versa.
- The scientific search for order in the world is often a hidden bias in its ontological obsession with order, since chaos is often treated as the "bad" guy, with order as the "good" guy (for the end goal of science).
- Neither order nor chaos is the final end of the world, and one is not to be treated as the means for the other in the transformation of things. Both are fundamental in their recurrent dialectical interactions with each other over time, without reducing one for the other.
- Family resemblance: e.g., lawfulness-disorder, order-disorder, etc.
- Sources: Especially from *FC*. See also my later books.

• **In Relation to Agency**

—*The Softness-Hardness Principle*

(On the Force of Change)

- This has to do with *the force of change* under the category about agency in existential dialectics, in that any change by an agent, be it organic (like humans) or non-organic (like natural objects), can occur in a forceful (aggressive) or gentle (pacific) way, which can come in all shapes and sizes, of course. There is no softness without hardness—and vice versa.
- Family resemblance: e.g., peacefulness-violence, cooperation-competition, pacificity-aggression, dovishness-hawkishness, reward-punishment, peace-war, etc.
- Sources: Especially from *ALD*. See also my later books.

(continued on next page)

Table 4.4. The Syntax of Existential Dialectics I: The Principles (Part X)

- **In Relation to Agency** ***(cont'd)***
  —*The Symmetry-Asymmetry Principle*
  (On the Relationships among Existents)
  - There is no symmetry without asymmetry—and vice versa.
  - For instance, the Same can be symmetric and asymmetric towards the Others. But in case of asymmetry, oppression and self-oppression can occur. So, when the Same is asymmetric towards the Others, the Same can also be relatively asymmetric towards itself in self-oppression, just as the Others can be likewise towards themselves.
  - The subsequent oppressiveness is dualistic, as much by the Same against the Others and itself, as by the Others against the Same and themselves.
  - Both oppression and self-oppression can be achieved by way of downgrading differences between the Same and the Others and of accentuating them.
  - This is true, even though not all forms of asymmetry have to be about oppression and self-oppression.
  - In addition, from Chapter Three of *FPHG*, symmetry is not perfect, to be understood in an approximate sense under many life circumstances.
  - Family resemblance: e.g., strength-weakness, balance-extremity, harmoniousness-unharrmoniousness, potence-impotence, reflexiveness-unreflexiveness, equality-inequality, etc.
  - Sources: From all my books, starting with *FHC*. First named in *BCPC*. See, for instance, *FCD* for more details on the Same and the Others.

(*continued on next page*)

Table 4.4. The Syntax of Existential Dialectics I: The Principles (Part XI)

- **In Relation to Agency *(cont'd)***

  —*The Theory-Praxis Principle*
  (On the Duality of Knowledge))

  - This has to do with the duality of knowledge in existential dialectics, in that, if there is theoretical construction, there is likewise its practical application, both technical and normative. There is no theory without praxis—and vice versa.
  - Family resemblance: e.g., discovery-application, knowledge-action, invention-innovation, etc.
  - Source: Especially from *FPHE*. See also my later books.

  —*The Evolution-Transformation Principle*
  (On the Multiple Kinds of Agency)

  - This principle (and the symmetry-asymmetry principle) are both about *the agency of change*. The word "agency," in a formal definition, refers to "a person or thing through which power is exerted or an end is achieved." (MWD 2007b) It therefore does not have to necessarily involve an intelligent lifeform.
  - Because of this dual meaning in agency, the evolution-transformation principle is more concerned with *the multiple kinds of agency*, that is, both about the *evolution* in the state of nature (e.g., an object of natural beauty) and the *transformation* in the world of intelligent lifeforms (e.g., a work of art, an air-conditioner, etc.). There is no evolution without transformation—and vice versa.
  - And the transformative part of the principle precisely refers to the other dimension in the dual meaning of agency, in giving technology a major role to play in the change of the world, which is something that I extensively analyzed in *FHC* in the context of the technophilic lifeworld, espeically though not exclusively since modern times.
  - Family resemblance: e.g., inorganicness-volition, nonwillingness-willingness, naturalness-technologicalness, naturalness-nonnaturalness, etc.
  - Sources: Especially from *FAE*. See also other books of mine.

(*continued on next page*)

Table 4.4. The Syntax of Existential Dialectics I: The Principles (Part XII)

- **In Relation to Agency** ***(cont'd)***
  - —*The Convention-Novelty Principle*
    (On the Nature of Creative Thinking)
    - If there is conventional wisdom, there is likewise novel challenge, to the extent that both convergent and divergent thinking are part of life. There is no convention without novelty—and vice versa.
    - In addition, in this context of the convention-novelty principle, there are, in the absence of better words, what I want to call (a) *creative techniques* and (b) *creative traits*, which, when satisfied—in relation to the larger context of the mind, nature, society, and culture—can be used to enhance creative works. The list of creative techniques and traits (as summarized in *Table 4.1* of *FPHCT*) are not exhaustive, of course, but the examples here constitute a great beginning of understanding the structure of creative thinking.
    - Yet, lest the reader gets carried away by the euphoria about creative thinking in our time, it should be reminded that creative thinking has its own possibilities and limits (as shown in *Table 2.1* of *FPHCT* on invention), just as it has its own promises and pitfalls (as shown in *Table 3.1* of *FPHCT* on innovation). In the end, it should also be stressed that creative thinking has its own desirability and dark sides (as shown in *Table 4.2* of *FPHCT*).
    - This has important daily implications for an average individual, and the word "average" here allows different degrees of variation from one individual to another in a population, at any given point in history.
    - Family resemblance: e.g., convergence-divergence, normalness-nonnormalness, conformity-nonconformity, etc.
    - Sources: First from *FPHCT*. See also my later books.

(*continued on next page*)

Table 4.4. The Syntax of Existential Dialectics I: The Principles (Part XIII)

- **In Relation to Outcome**

  —*The Regression-Progression Principle*
  (On the Direction of History)

  - Neither the cyclical nor the linear views are adequate for explaining many phenomena at all levels. There is regression without progression—and vice versa.
  - History progresses to more advanced forms, but with a regressive touch. Examples include no freedom without unfreedom, no equality without inequality, and no civilization without barbarity.
  - This is not an inevitable law, but merely a highly likely empirical trend.
  - Family resemblance: e.g., cost-benefit, undesirability-desirability, badness-goodness, risk-opportunity, etc.
  - Sources: From all my books, starting with *FHC*. First named in *BCPC*.

  —*The Same-Difference Principle*
  (On the Metamorphosis of Change)

  - An entity, as it evolves over time, can be both different from and similar to its opposing alternatives and does not have to be solely more different from them over time. There is no similarity without difference—and vice versa.
  - Opposites are not absolute in a black-or-white fashion; so, an entity can become relatively more similar to (or more different from) its opposite over time.
  - Family resemblance: e.g., homogeneity-heterogeneity, we-they, etc.
  - Sources: Especially from ALD. See also my later books.

Notes: The features in each principle are solely illustrative (not exhaustive). The comparison is also relative (not absolute), nor are they mutually exclusive. As generalities, they allow exceptions.

Table 4.5. The Syntax of Existential Dialectics II: The Principles as Short Cuts (Part I)

• The principles should be treated with caution, lest misunderstanding occurs, since they do not constitute rigid dualities (or dichotomies).

• The reason is that each pair in an ontological principle consists of two opposites, which are, however, merely short cuts both for multiple variations and degrees, as well as for different interactions with multiple other entities unlike them. In this light, each pair can end up having hundred (or even thousand, if not more) different versions, which interact with hundred (or even thousand, if not more) other entities. There are two clarifications here.

• Firstly, this conception of shortcuts is not mutually exclusive nor absolute, in that the opposites can come in all shapes and sizes, with different degrees. For instance, by analogy, just as there are different degrees of the two colors "white" and "black"—there are likewise different degrees of the opposites in each ontological pair, to the extent that there can be multiple entities (not only two) interacting with each other in each pair.

• And secondly, this conception of shortcuts do not ignore other possible entities in interacting with the two opposites (with their different versions) in each pair. For instance, by analogy, there are not only the two colors "white" and "black" as opposites, since there are other colors too besides them like "yellow," "green," "purple," or else. The same logic can be applied to each ontological pair, in that they also interact with other entities, not with only two of them (with their different versions).

• Therefore, with these two clarifications in mind—each pair in an ontological principle serves only as an abbreviation for something more complicated and, therefore, although it contains two opposites, it should not be confused as a duality (dualism).

(continued on next page)

Table 4.5. The Syntax of Existential Dialectics II:
The Principles as Short Cuts
(Part II)

• Existential dialectics rejects any dualism (or dichotomy) as too rigid and instead allows the multiplicity of entities, to the extent that between the two opposites in each pair exist many other alternatives to choose from. They are named in that short form for aesthetic elegance, instead of listing all possible entities between the two opposites in the title.

• To be dialectic is to go beyond any rigid dichotomy and transcend into something different altogether in the long haul. One may be tempted to call the dialectic logic here with a different name like existential "multilectics" (instead of "dialectics"), but this naming is incorrect (or even misleading), for the two reasons aforestated.

• After all, each ontological pair come in all shapes and sizes (with different degrees) and do not exist by themselves but also interact with other entities unlike them. The virtue of revealing an ontological pair is to show how they relate within themselves (in multiple versions) and also interact with others unlike them (also in multiple versions).

• This will be clear in the table on "the dialectic constraints imposed by the principles."

Source: From Ch.1 of *FPHK*

Table 4.6. The Syntax of Existential Dialectics III: The Principles as Family Resemblances

• Each ontological principle is generic, with some other comparable ontological pairs to be put in the same family (like a *family resemblance*). Ludwig Wittgenstein (1953) once suggested the idea of "family resemblance" in explaining different games classified under the same family called *games*.

• Why should, for instance, playing football and chess as playing "games," when it is well understood that football is not the same as chess? The answer is that, although each game is different and has different rules, many of them (though not all) share, more or less, some commonalites (e.g., scoring as necessary for winning).

• And this is so, even though some games share more than some others in any given selection of critieria, and no two games are exactly identical. So, his point here is that there is no essential core which is common to all games, and the best that one can look for is some characteristics which are common to many (but not all) games. (A. Biletzki 2006)

• By the same logic—in the previous section on selection criteria, the flexibility-inflexibility pair can be put in the family resemblance of the simpleness-complicatedness principle, although the two pairs are not exactly identical. Likewise, the directness-indirectness pair can be put in the family resemblance of the preciseness-vagueness principle, although, again, the two pairs are not exactly identical.

• In this sense, which specific pair in a family should be used to designate the name of the family can be at times a bit arbitrary, but with good reason.

• For illustration, in the context of method, the partiality-totality principle can take the different form like individualisticness-holisticness, just as the explicability-inexplicability principle can take the different form like underlyingness-regularness—although each two pairs are not exactly identical and have slightly different meanings and usages. A more comprehensive listing of this family resemblance for all other principles is shown in the table on the syntax of existential dialectics.

Source: From Ch.1 of *FPHK*

Table 4.7. The Syntax of Existential Dialectics IV: The Dialectic Constraints Imposed by the Principles (Part I)

• **Co-Existent and Asymmetric**

—The principles, as they constitute the syntax of existential dialectics, are dialectic in character, such that, when they are applied, they impose dialectic constraints on how reality is to be understood. Consider, say, the symmetry-asymmetry principle as an illustration here, in order to summarize two main characters of the dialectic constraints in question.

—Firstly, to be dialectic here is to go beyond the narrow dichotomies (and, for that matter, any rigid multi-dimensional classificatory scheme), be they about "self" vs. "world," "freedom" vs. "unfreedom," "barbarity" vs. "civilization," "individuality" vs. "communality," and so on.

—One way to do so (to go beyond) is to consider them all in terms of co-existence (without favoring one over the rest). For instance, my theory of "post-civilization" (to be summarized later in the section on the pragmatics of existential dialectics) is to go beyond barbarity and civilization in terms of understanding barbarity and civilization as being co-existent. And the same logic can be said in relation to my theories of "post-democracy," "post-capitalsm," and others (also to be introduced later in the section on the pragmatics of existential dialectics), in regard to freedom vs. unfreedom, equality vs. inequality, communality vs. individuality, spirituality vs. materiality, and so on.

—But to consider them all (in the dichotomies—and, for that matter, in any rigid multi-dimensional classifactory schme) as co-existent is not the same as to imply that the opposites in any classificatory scheme are all equal, since, in accordance to the symmetry-asymmetry principle (as an illustration here), if they are equal in terms of being considered as co-existent, they are asymmetric in terms of being unequal in dialectic interaction (e.g., X can be more dominant than Y in case A, or Y is more dominant than X in case B).

(continued on next page)

Table 4.7. The Syntax of Existential Dialectics IV: The Dialectic Constraints Imposed by the Principles (Part II)

—For this reason, there are different versions of "post-democracy" and "post-capitalism" in my theories. As an illustration, in version I of the theory of post-democracy, freedom is more dominant than equality, whereas in version II of the theory of post-democracy, equality is more so than freedom.

—But this "X more than Y" has to be understood in the context of dialectic logic (not in conventional logic), in that both "X" and "Y" are important in post-democracy (in the context of dialectic logic), but in an asymmetry way. By contrast, in conventional logic, it often favors one over the other—be it in regard to privileging freedom over equality in Fascism, favoring freedom relatively more than equality in Liberal Democracy, or favoring equality relatively more than freedom in Socialist Democracy. In the latter two cases (about Liberal Democracy and Socialist Democracy), the difference between dialectic logic and conventional logic can be one in degree, not in kind—in this sense, albeit not in other senses.

—The same logic can be said about the relatonships between individuality and communality, between spirituality and materiality, and between formal legalism and informal legalism in the different versions of my theory of post-capitalism.

• **Transcendent**

—Secondly, to be dialectic is to go beyond the narrow dichotomies (and, for that matter, any rigid multi-dimensional classificatory scheme) in another way, this time, in a transcendent way, that is, in exploring other possibilities or even other issues not considered within the narrow confines of narrow dichotomies (and, for that matter, any rigid multi-dimensional classificatory scheme).

(continued on next page)

Table 4.7. The Syntax of Existential Dialectics IV: The Dialectic Constraints Imposed by the Principles (Part III)

—As an analogy, to go beyond the narrow color dichotomy of "black" and "white" is not just to choose both "black" and "white" (as in the first meaning) but also to explore other color options (e.g., "green," "purple," "blue," etc.—and, alternatively, "shade," "line," "curve," etc.). By the same logic, to go beyond "democracy" is to transcend democracy (as in version III of the theory of "post-democracy") and to explore other possibilties of lifeforms (e.g., floating consciousness, hyper-spatial consciousness, etc., to live beyond the narrow obsession with freedom and equality).

—This dialectic character of the principles in existential dialectics has important implications for the pragmatics of existential dialectics (as will be clear shortly, in the section on the pragmatics of existential dialectics).

Notes: The examples here are solely illustrative (not exhaustive). The comparison is also relative (not absolute), nor are they mutually exclusive. As generalities, they allow exceptions.

Sources: First explicitly stated in *ALD*. Also from all other books of mine.

Table 4.8. The Syntax of Existential Dialectics V: Further Clarifications (Part I)

• **Pioneering**
—Firstly, the total number of ontological principles is unknown, to be discovered later, as our knowledge of the world becomes more advanced.
—Consequently, the principles as introduced in my books are not exhaustive, with new ones being added, whenever more of them are discovered in later research.
—At least, future generations can pick up where I leave off and continue the discovery.
—In this sense, my work should be treated as a pioneering effort for the development of a systematic, comprehensive analysis of a new general ontology for the future of knowledge.

• **Flexible**
—Secondly, the principles are not rigidly classified, as they can be reclassified in a different way.
—For instance, the preciseness-vagueness principle is classified under the category of "structure" but can be reclassified under the category of "method," although in so doing, it has a different meaning in the context of method.
—The same logic applies to the same-difference principle under the category of "outcome," which can be reclassified under the category of "structure," although in so doing, once more, it has a different meaning in the context of structure.

• **Mutually Constraining**
—Thirdly, the principles are to be understood together, not that each prinicple is to be analyzed independently of others. After all, the principles are mutually constraining, in that they work together as a whole.

(continued on next page)

Table 4.8. The Syntax of Existential Dialectics V: Further Clarifications (Part II)

- **Selectively Useful**
  —Fourthly, the principles are relevant to all subject matters, but some principles are more useful to some subject matters than others—as implied in the symmetry-asymmetry principle. This is true, even if different studies of the same kind can yield different views about the degree of relevance for each ontological principle, depending on the specific nature of a research in question, needless to say.

- **Anti-Reductionistic**
  —And fifthly, the principles constitute only two levels of analysis, this time, at the ontological and methodological levels—while other levels of analysis (from the perspectives of the mind, nature, society, and culture) are also needed, in order to understand reality in its totality (as explained in the section on "sophisticated methodological holism," so as to avoid the dual dangers of reductionism and reverse-reductionism).

Notes: The examples here are solely illustrative (not exhaustive). The comparison is also relative (not absolute), nor are they mutually exclusive. As generalities, they allow exceptions.
Sources: From my previous books like *FHC*, *FCD*, *FPHC*, *BDPD*, *BCPC*, *BNN*, *FC*, *FAE*, and so on.

Table 4.9. The Syntax of Existential Dialectics VI: The Dilemma of Specific vs. General Ontology (Part I)

• Ontology is often more complicated and imposes some seemingly insurmountable difficulties concerning what constitutes a kind of ontology which can be valid enough to be accepted by the wider intellectual community in question. An excellent example concerns what I want to call *the dilemma of ontology* in relation to the relationship between "specific ontology" and "general ontology." (M. Bunge 1999; R. Corazzon 2007)

• On the one hand, "general ontology," as Mario Bunge (1999) put it, "studies all existents." But, on the other hand, "special ontology studies one genus of thing or process—physical, chemical, biological, social, etc." (M. Bunge 1999; R. Corazzon 2007)

• Consequently, the relationship between the former and the latter is that, as an illustration, "whereas general ontology studies the concepts of space, time, and event, the ontology of the social investigates such general sociological concepts as those of social system, social structure, and social change." (M. Bunge 1999; R. Corazzon 2007)

• With this formal definition in mind, the relationship between the two forms of ontology only poses *the dilemma of ontology*, in that general ontology is possible to the extent that its general contructs must be broad enough to serve as the "lowest common denominator" for all disciplines, but this character of the lowest common denominator is not only hard to find but also its usefulness is limited. (WK 2008b)

• But specific ontology fares no better either, in that its specific constructs primarily serve a specific discipline in question, although other disciplines can appropriate them for their own purposes, but in a different context (especially, though not exclusively, when used as a metaphor from one field to another). For instance, the Kantian category of understanding under the heading of "quantity" constitutes a type of specific ontology, which is specific to the discipline of mathematics, although other disciplines can make use of the categories in their own context.

(continued on next page)

Table 4.9. The Syntax of Existential Dialectics VI: The Dilemma of Specific vs. General Ontology (Part II)

• A solution lies in my proposal of "sophisticated methodological holism," which requires all levels of analysis in any subject matter. See the tables on sophisticated methodological holism, and on reductionism and reverse-reductionism, for more details.

Source: From *Sec. 1.4* of *FPHK*

Table 4.10. The Syntax of Existential Dialectics VII: Types of Inappropriate Family Resemblances

- **Inadequate Family Resemblances**
  —Ex: consistency-inconsistency: the formalness-informalenss principle
  —Ex: cognition-noncognition: the formalness-informalness principle

- **Compound Family Resemblances**
  —Ex: reality-nonreality: the formalness-informalness principles, the absoluteness-relativeness principle
  —Ex: normality-abnormality: the symmetry-asymmetry principle, the density-emptiness principle, the convention-novelty principle, the same-difference principle
  —Ex: structure-context: the simpleness-complicatedness principle, the theory-praxis principle
  —Ex: freedom-unfreedom: the symmetry-asymmetry principle, the expansion-contraction principle
  —Ex: morality-immorality: the denseness-emptiness principle, the symmetry-asymmetry, the same-difference principle
  —Ex: particularness-universalness: the preciseness-vagueness principle, the simpleness-complicatedness principle
  —Ex: pureness-mixedness: the absoluteness-relativeness principle, the simpleness-complicatedness principle, the same-difference principle
  —Ex: shortsightedness-foresightedness: the partiality-totality principle, the simpleness-complicatedness principle
  —Ex: shorttermness-longtermness: the partiality-totality principle, the simpleness-complicatedness principle, the slowness-quickness principle

Notes: The examples here are solely illustrative (not exhaustive). The comparison is also relative (not absolute), nor are they mutually exclusive. As generalities, they allow exceptions.
Source: First summarized in *BEPE* (and updated in later books)

Table 4.11. The Semantics of Existential Dialectics

- **Abstract Structure vs. Specific Meanings**
  - —The syntax of existential dialectics so understood in terms of ontological principles only gives us the structure of ontology in the world, in an abstract (general) sense. These principles by themselves do not tell us the specific meanings in a given context.
  - —In order to grasp the specific meanings of the principles in a given context, it is necessary to study the semantics of existential dialectics. And the analysis of the ontological principles as family resemblances in the section on syntax is only a starting point (and thus overlaps a bit with the semantics of existential dialectics here).
  - —With this caveat in mind, the reason that I have often gone in great lengths in my previous books on different subjects is to explain the specific meanings of the principles when applied in different contexts.

- **Specific Meanings in Specific Fields**
  - —For instance, in *FPHST*, I used the first three principles (i.e., the change-constancy principle, the regression-progression principle, and the symmetry-asymmetry principle) to propose "the perspectival theory of space-time," for a better way to understand space and time—especially, though not exclusively, in relation to future post-human history (as summarized in *Table 3.6*, *Table 3.7*, *Table 3.8*, and *Table 3.9*). In so doing, I had to introduce concepts and theories specific to the field of physics and other related fields (e.g., "absolute space" and "absolute time" in "classical mechanics" and "relative space-time" in "the theory of relativity").
  - —In *BNN*, I also exploited the three principles to propose the "transcendent" approach to the study of genes and memes as a new way to understand the interaction between nature and nurture. In so doing, I had to explore concepts and theories in the world of evolutionary theory (e.g., "mutation," "variation," "adaptation," "selection," and "inheritance" in Darwinian evolutionary theory) and neural biology (e.g., "chromosome," "gene," "DNA," "RNA," "protein," "neuron," "neural network," and "behavior").

Notes: The categories and examples in each are solely illustrative (not exhaustive). The comparison is also relative (not absolute), nor are they mutually exclusive. As generalities, they allow exceptions.
Sources: First explicitly stated in *ALD*. Also from all other books of mine.

Table 4.12. The Pragmatics of Existential Dialectics (Part I)

• **The Two-Way Street Connecting Theory and Meta-Theory**

—The pragmatics of existential dialectics is not a one-way street (that is, using the ontological principles for theoretical insights in praxis) but a two-way one, that is, (a) from meta-theory to theory, and (b) from theory to meta-theory.

—(a) On one side of the street, the ontological principles can inspire some theoretical insights in praxis, that is, in relation to some specific fields.

—(b) On the other (opposing) side of the street, however, the study of a subject matter in the specific fields in turn reveals some more hitherto unknown ontological principles to be discovered and identified. For this reason, three new principles were added in *FC*, one in *FAE*, and two in *ALD*, on top of the original three in *BCPC*—after some research on the specific subject matters.

• **Direct and Indirect Applications**

—*Direct*

- The logic of existential dialectics can shed some theoretical insights on diverse phenomena in the world, and good instances are the pertinent use of the principles of existential dialectics for the theoretical insights on the freedom/unfreedom dialectics, the equality/inequality dialectics, and the wealth/poverty dialectics in my previous works.
- My latest books like *FPHST* and *BNN* also use the principles to reveal some theoretical insights on the perspectives of space and time (as in *FPHST*) and of nature and nurture (as in *BNN*).

—*Indirect*

- The theoretical insights can further be used to reveal other phenomena directly from them (viz., the theoretical insights) and therefore indirectly from the principles themselves. A good instance is the use of the theoretical insights on the freedom/unfreedom and equality/inequality dialectics for the understanding of the civilization/barbarity dialectics.

(continued on next page)

Table 4.12. The Pragmatics of Existential Dialectics (Part II)

- **Direct and Indirect Applications (*cont'd*)**
    - Even in indirect applications, however, a phenomenon under study can still be directly related back to the principles themselves. In the example as cited above, the civilization/barbarity dialectics can be directly related to the principles of existential dialectics without the intermediate role of the freedom/unfreedom and equality/inequality dialectics.

- **Multiple Levels of Application**

—The theoretical insights can be applied to different levels of analysis, even though in a given example, it may refer to one level only. For instance, in the example concerning the freedom/unfreedom dialectics, it can be used at the structural level (e.g., in relation to the theory of cyclical progression of hegemony), but it can be exploited as well for other levels (e.g., the theory of post-capitalism at the institutional level).

Notes: The categories and examples in each are solely illustrative (not exhaustive). The comparison is also relative (not absolute), nor are they mutually exclusive. As generalities, they allow exceptions.
Sources: From Ch.6 of *BCPC*. See also other books of mine.

Table 4.13. The Freedom-Unfreedom Dialectics (Part I)

• **On Having**

—*In Relation to the Technological*

(1) if freer from submission to Nature, then less free from ecological degradation (Deep and Social Ecology), even if in a hi-tech form

(2) if freer from technological inconvenience / backwardness, then less free from technological control and the loss of privacy

(3) if freer from technological (material) backwardness, then less free from the abusive (barbaric) maltreatment of the primitive Others

—*In Relation to the Everyday*

(1) if freer from abject poverty, then less free from artificial needs/discontents (Frankfurt School)

(2) if freer from sensual suppression, then less free from violent sublimation (Freud)

(3) if freer from the snobbishness of high culture, then less free from the shabbiness (leveling-off effect) of mass culture (Tocqueville)

(4) if freer from the inefficiency of traditional "compassionate economy," then less free from the bondage of a "ruthless [competitive] economy" (Keynes)

(5) if freer from anarchy in the state of nature (system fragmentation), then less free from government regulations and controls in system integration

(continued on next page)

Table 4.13. The Freedom-Unfreedom Dialectics (Part II)

• **On Belonging**

—In Relation to the Good and the Just

(1) if freer from disciplinary society, then less free from society of control (Foucault)

(2) if freer from the tyranny of one or a few, then less free from the tyranny of the majority (or sometimes, minority veto)

(3) if freer from elitist decision making, then less free from political gridlock/cleavage

(4) if freer from arbitrary (discretionary) administration, then less free from bureaucratic irrationality (Weber) and legal trickery (loopholes)

• **On Being**

—In Relation to the True

(1) if freer from unscientific dogmas, then less free from instrumental abyss (nihilism). Or conversely, if freer from meaninglessness, then less free from dogmas.

(2) if freer from the bondage of partiality/partisanship (e.g., prejudice, discrimination), then less free from the danger of impartiality and neutrality (e.g., opportunism, unrealisticness, lack of compassion, inaction)

(3) if freer from making generalizations, then less free from being unable to understand much of anything

—In Relation to the Holy

(1) if freer from collective conscience, then less free from social loneliness

(2) if freer from religious absoluteness, then less free from spiritual emptiness

—In Relation to the Beautiful/Sublime

(1) if freer from artistic non-autonomy, then less free from aesthetic disillusion (deconstruction)

(continued on next page)

Table 4.13. The Freedom-Unfreedom Dialectics (Part III)

Notes: The examples in each category are solely illustrative (not exhaustive), and the comparison is relative (not absolute), nor are they necessarily mutually exclusive. And some can be easily re-classified elsewhere. As generalities, they allow exceptions.
Sources: A reconstruction from Ch.10 of *FCD*, based on *FHC*

Table 4.14. The Equality-Inequality Dialectics (Part I)

• **On Having**

—*In Relation to the Technological*

(1) if more equal in treating Nature with spiritual unity, then less equal in suppressing the dominant drive to transcend it altogether

—*In Relation to the Everyday*

(1) if more equal in building social plurality, then less equal in leveling-off effects (e.g., the subsequent relative intolerance of high/intellectual ethos in mass culture industry)

(2) if more equal in socioeconomic distribution beyond a certain point, then less equal in efficiency (e.g. resentment, the erosion of work ethics)

(3) if more equal in urging an affirmative action program, then less equal in creating victim mentality (in oneself), stigma (from others), reverse discrimination (against the once privileged), and mediocracy (against the more able)

• **On Belonging**

—*In Relation to the Good and the Just*

(1) if more equal in banning monarchic/oligarchic exclusion, then less equal in producing "the tyranny of the majority" or of "minority veto"

(2) if more equal in encouraging participatory decision making, then less equal in inducing political divisiveness (gridlock/cleavage in power blocs) and organizational oligarchy

(3) if more equal in institutionalizing a decentralized bureaucracy, then less equal in falling into more territorial/turf politics (intrigues)

(continued on next page)

Table 4.14. The Equality-Inequality Dialectics (Part II)

- **On Being**
  - —In Relation to the Beautiful / Sublime
    - (1) if more equal in accepting diverse styles ("anything goes" mentality), then less equal in artistic good quality (in leveling-off effects against the best)
  - —In Relation to the True
    - (1) if more equal in tolerating multiple viewpoints (no matter how extreme), then less equal in epistemic standards
  - —In Relation to the Holy
    - (1) if more equal in celebrating any cults and sects (no matter how questionable), then less equal in spiritual depth and authenticity

Notes: The examples in each category are solely illustrative (not exhaustive), and the comparison is relative (not absolute), nor are they mutually exclusive. And some can be easily reclassified elsewhere. As generalities, they allow exceptions.
Sources: A reconstruction from Ch.10 of *FCD*, based on *FHC*

Table 4.15. The Duality of Oppression in Existential Dialectics: Oppression and Self-Oppression (Part I)

- **From the Same to the Others and Itself**
  - —The Oppression by the Same against the Others
    - • *By way of downgrading differences*
      - –Ex: on judiciary caprice for corporate crimes (*Sec.2.2.1.2.1*)
      - –Ex: on the deceptive politics of liberation (*Sec.3.5*)
      - –Ex: on the humanitarian mystique (*Sec.4.4*)
      - –Ex: on the fad of emotional intelligence (*Sec.5.3*)
    - • *By way of accentuating differences*
      - –Ex: on the legal sophistry of self-defense (*Sec.2.3*)
      - –Ex: on the legal semantics of proportionality (*Sec.2.4*)
      - –Ex: on the tricky politics of external threat (*Sec.3.4*)
      - –Ex: on the appeal of the Far Right for democracy (*Sec.5.4*)
      - –Ex: on the democratic axis of evil (*Sec.5.5*)
      - –Ex: on the democratic way of brutality and revenge (*Sec.5.6*)
      - –Ex: on democratic autocracy (*Sec.6.4*)
  - —The Oppression by the Same against Itself
    - • *By way of downgrading differences*
      - –Ex: on the politics of fear (*Sec.2.2*)
      - –Ex: on the trickery of compassionate conservatism (*Sec.3.2*)
      - –Ex: on the deceptive politics of patriotism (*Sec.3.3*)
    - • *By way of accentuating differences*
      - –Ex: on the caprice of due process on domestic suspects (*Sec.2.2*)
      - –Ex: on the false security/freedom dilemma (*Sec.6.5.2*)

(continued on next page)

Table 4.15. The Duality of Oppression in Existential Dialectics: Oppression and Self-Oppression (Part II)

- **From the Others to the Same and Themselves**
  —The Oppression by the Others against the Same
  - *By way of downgrading differences*
    –Ex: on judiciary caprice in the reverse direction (*Sec.2.2.1.2.2*)
    –Ex: on equal pay (*Sec.6.2.1.1*)
    –Ex: on equal representation (*Sec.6.2.1.2*)
    –Ex: on affirmative action program (*Sec.6.3.1.1*)
    –Ex: on same-sex marriage (*Sec.6.3.1.2*)
  - *By way of accentuating differences*
    –Ex: on sexual harassment (*Sec.6.2.2.1*)
    –Ex: on physical violence (*Sec.6.2.2.2*)
    –Ex: on sexual exploitation (*Sec.6.2.2.3*)

  —The Oppression by the Others against Themselves
  - *By way of downgrading differences*
    –Ex: on the reverse-class mystique (*Sec.4.2*)
    –Ex: on the reverse-black mystique (*Sec.4.3*)
    –Ex: on self-discrimination by downgrading (*Sec.6.3.2.2*)
  - *By way of accentuating differences*
    –Ex: on self-discrimination by accentuating (*Sec.6.3.2.1*)

Notes: The examples are solely illustrative (not exhaustive), nor are they mutually exclusive. As generalities, they allow exceptions. Also, both forms of oppression co-exist in all of the examples, so the listing of them are only meant in a relative, not absolute, sense.
Source: A summary of the sections (as cited) in Chs.2-6 of *BDPD*. See text for more info and references.

Table 4.16. The Structure of Existential Dialectics I: The Freedom/Unfreedom and Equality/Inequality Dialectics

• Each freedom and equality produces its own unfreedom and inequality, regardless of whether the pair occurs in political society (with the nation-state), in civil society (with some autonomy from the state), or elsewhere (e.g., in the private sphere of individual homes)—and regardless of whether freedom and equality are understood as "negative" or "positive."

• Oppression is dualistic, as much by the Same against the Others and itself, as by the Others against the Same and themselves.

• Both forms of oppression and self-oppression can be achieved by way of downgrading differences (between the Same and the Others) and of accentuating them.

• The relationships are relatively asymmetric between the Same and the Others and relatively symmetric within them. This is true, even when the Same can be relatively asymmetric towards itself in self-oppression, just as the Others can be likewise towards themselves.

• Symmetry and asymmetry change over time, with ever new players, new causes, and new forms.

Notes: The examples in each category are solely illustrative (not exhaustive) nor necessarily mutually exclusive, and the comparison is relative (not absolute). As generalities, they allow exceptions. "Negative" freedom is freedom "from" (e.g., freedom from poverty), whereas "positive" freedom is freedom "to" (e.g., freedom to the state of enlightenment). "Negative" equality is "procedural" equality (e.g., equality of opportunity), while "positive" equality is "substantive" equality (e.g., equality of outcome). Existential dialectics impose constraints on freedom and equality in democracy, non-democracy, and post-democracy. There is no utopia, in the end; even should there be one, dystopia would exist within it.
Sources: From *Table 1.5* of *BDPD*—and also from *FHC*, *FCD*, and *FPHC*

Table 4.17. The Structure of Existential Dialectics II: The Wealth/Poverty Dialectics

• There is no wealth without poverty, just as there is no poverty without wealth.

• The wealth/poverty dialectics occurs in the realms of having, belonging, and being, in relation to the material, relational, and spiritual.

• The wealth/poverty dialectics also expresses itself at the multiple levels of analysis in accordance to methodological holism, be they about the micro-physical, the chemical, the biological, the psychological, the organizational, the institutional, the structural, the systemic, the cultural, and the cosmological.

• The wealth/poverty dialectics is a different manifestation of existential dialectics in general, subject to the principles in its logic of ontology—just as the freedom/unfreedom and equality/inequality dialectics are likewise.

• There is no economic utopia, in the end; even should there be one, dystopia would exist within it.

Notes: The main points here are solely illustrative (not exhaustive) nor necessarily mutually exclusive, and the comparison is relative (not absolute). As generalities, they allow exceptions.
Sources: From *BCPC*. See also *FCD* and *FHC*.

Table 4.18. The Structure of Existential Dialectics III: The Civilization/Barbarity Dialectics

• There is no civilization without barbarity.

• The civilization/barbarity dialectics applies in the four civilizing processes (e.g., the rationalizing process, the pacifying process, the stewardizing process, and the subliming process).

• The civilization/barbarity dialectics is another (different) manifestation of existential dialectics in general, subject to the principles in its logic of ontology—just as the freedom/unfreedom and equality/inequality dialectics and the wealth/poverty dialectics are likewise.

• There is no utopia, in the end; even should there be one, dystopia would exist within it.

Notes: The main points here are solely illustrative (not exhaustive) nor necessarily mutually exclusive, and the comparison is relative (not absolute). As generalities, they allow exceptions.
Sources: From *BCIV*. See also *FCD*, *FHC*, and *BDPD*.

Table 4.19. The Double Sides of Virtual Organizations (Part I)

- **Psychological**
  —Ex: virtual psychosis
  —Ex: impersonality and loneliness in quaternary social relations

- **Organizational**
  —Ex: the race for power and interests
  —Ex: the world of unequal successes
  —Ex: the bureaucratic life of its own
  —Ex: lesser accountability and transparency

- **Economic**
  —Ex: the economic divides
  —Ex: the erosive impact of commercialization

- **Political**
  —Ex: the anti-authoritarian myth
  —Ex: different power struggles among groups (e.g., Conservative, Reformist, Radical)

- **Structural**
  —Ex: different localities (e.g., climates, scenery)
  —Ex: divided domains (e.g., core, peripheral, sub-peripheral)
  —Ex: substitution effect of social capital

- **Systemic**
  —Ex: uneven advances in transportation and communications, and geographical migration

- **Cultural**
  —Ex: conflicting civilizational fabrics (e.g., Confucian, Islamic, Western)
  —Ex: the bias of the Liberal Democratic agenda
  —Ex: the addiction to moral fanaticism

(continued on next page)

Table 4.19. The Double Sides of Virtual Organizations (Part II)

Notes: These categories and examples are solely illustrative (not exhaustive), and some of the items can be reclassified somewhere else. Nor are they mutually exclusive. Since they are generalities, exceptions are expected.
Source: From Ch.7 of *FCD*

Table 4.20. Beyond the World of Titans, and the Remaking of the World Order

- **Hyper-Empires**
  —Ex: The Chinese Union
  —Ex: The Indian Union

- **Meso-Empires**
  —Ex: The European Union
  —Ex: The North American Union

- **Micro-Empires**
  —Ex: The Latin American Union
  —Ex: The Middle Eastern Union

- **The Rest of the World**
  —<u>Odd Powers</u>
    - Ex: Japan
    - Ex: Russia

  —<u>The Poor Club</u>
    - Ex: The African Union

  —<u>Ambivalent Regions</u>
    - Ex: Southeast Asia
    - Ex: Oceania
    - Ex: South Asia
    - Ex: Central Asia
    - Ex: Southern/Eastern Europe
    - Ex: North Africa
    - Ex: Central America
    - Ex: Others (e.g., the Korean peninsula)

Source: A summary of Chs.2-5 (of *BWT*)

Table 4.21. The Origins of Authoritarian Liberal Democracy

- **The Geopower of Nature (Ch.4 of *ALD*)**
  —Ex: Power Character and Geographical Strategy
  —Ex: Living Space and Territorial Expansion
  —Ex: Strategic Heartland and Containment

- **The Biopsychology of the Mind (Ch.5 of *ALD*)**
  —Ex: The Bell Curve and Mass Intelligence
  —Ex: Group Analysis and Mass Knowledge
  —Ex: Groupthink and Elite (Mis)calculation

- **The Disciplinary Control of Society (Ch.6 of *ALD*)**
  —Ex: Social Organizations of Ruthlessness
  —Ex: Social Institutions of Greed
  —Ex: Social Structure of Exclusion
  —Ex: Social Systems of Violence

- **The Molding Force of Culture (Ch.7 of *ALD*)**
  —Ex: The Tradition of Conquest
  —Ex: The Rationalization of Unreason

Notes: The examples in each category are solely illustrative (not exhaustive), and they are also relative (not absolute), nor are they mutually exclusive. As generalities, they allow exceptions.
Source: A summary of Chs.4-7 of *ALD*

Table 4.22. The Theory of Post-Democracy I: The Priority of Freedom over Equality (Part I)

- **Differences**
  - —*For the aggressive Lions (the strong Elitists)*
    - •Setting up rank distinctions among unequals (e.g., between inferior humans and superior post-humans, or later among inferior post-humans and superior ones, relatively speaking)
    - •Yearning for being not only distinguished from unequals, but also the first among equals (the best of the very best)
    - •Soul-searching for a high spiritual culture (not the trashy one for the masses). Mass culture is a dirty joke for them.
  - —*For the manipulative Foxes (the weak Counter-Elitists)*
    - •Seeking a gentle hegemony by way of more communitarian concerns (for inferior humans and, later, inferior post-humans)
    - •Being more sympathetic to less formal-legalistic institutions and values

- **Similarities**
  - —*For both Lions and Foxes*
    - •Exploring different spheres of non-human consciousness in the cosmos (something vastly superior than the human one)
    - •Recognizing the democratic illusions (e.g., no freedom without unfreedom, no equality without inequality, or simply no justice without injustice, and vice versa)

(continued on next page)

Table 4.22. The Theory of Post-Democracy I: The Priority of Freedom over Equality (Part II)

Notes: The two callings and examples in each category are solely illustrative (not exhaustive), since there will be many different post-human value ideals in the distant future of post-human civilization. The comparison is also relative (not absolute) towards post-democracy, so this is not just a version of free-market democracy (nor Fascism/Nazism, as shown in the table later on democracy, non-democracy, and post-democracy). Nor are they mutually exclusive. As generalities, they allow exceptions. And the specific forms of post-human post-democratic ideals need to be further developed in future after-postmodern history, as they will be different from the ones we now know. The point here is to solely give an extremely rough picture of a small part of the world to come that we have never known.
Source: From Ch.10 of *FCD*. Refer to text for more info and references.

Table 4.23. The Theory of Post-Democracy II: The Priority of Equality over Freedom

- **Hybrid Versions of**
  —Ex: the Trans-Feminine Calling
  —Ex: the Trans-Sinitic Calling
  —Ex: the Trans-Islamic Calling
  —Ex: the Trans-Outerspace Calling

- **Qualifications**
  —These four versions of post-capitalist value ideals need not automatically be post-democratic, just as capitalism does not necessarily mean democracy. They are two different entities—though closely related.
  —But up to a certain threshold of elevating equality at the farther expense of freedom, the democratic ideals will be overcome and cease to exist.
  —The overcome will not be socialist or communist, but post-democratic with no freedom without unfreedom and no equality without inequality, subject to the constraints of existential dialectics.

Notes: The callings are solely illustrative (not exhaustive), since there will be many different post-human value ideals in the distant future of post-human lifeforms. The comparison is also relative (not absolute), nor are they mutually exclusive. As generalities, they allow exceptions. And the specific forms of post-human post-democratic ideals need to be further developed in future after-postmodern history, as they will be different from the ones we now know. The point here is to solely give an extremely rough picture of a small part of the world to come that we have never known.
Source: From Ch.10 of *FCD*. Refer to text for more info and references.

Table 4.24. The Theory of Post-Democracy III: The Transcendence of Freedom and Equality (Part I)

- **Transcending Freedom in Floating Existence**
  —*Freedom*: seeking an ultimate elimination of the body. Being without the body. The aim is to transcend freedom in the end into a metaphysical state (i.e., beyond the physique).
  —*Unfreedom*: yet facing difficult trade-offs. The sacrifice of bodily existence and its joyfulness. An eternal boredom in floating existence in dark deep space, though with alternative pleasures. There is no free lunch even in the state of transcending freedom.

- **Transcending Equality in the Rivalry of Cosmic Hegemony**
  —*Inequality*: competing to outlast other lifeforms in floating existence, or just marginalizing them for one's hegemonic expansiveness in the rest of the cosmos (and even beyond). Universalism is only for the mediocre.
  —*Equality*: accepting only those of one's rank as equal partners in the vast spacetime for cosmic supremacy. Even here, the aim is to transcend equality into a metaphysical state.

(continued on next page)

Table 4.24. The Theory of Post-Democracy III: The Transcendence of Freedom and Equality (Part II)

Notes: Do not confuse this transcendence of freedom and equality (as one version of post-democracy) with the naïve temptation to transcend the freedom/unfreedom and equality/inequality dialectics. Existential dialectics hold true for freedom and equality in all cultures and societies—past, present, or future (i.e., democracy, non-democracy, and post-democracy), regardless of whether freedom and equality are conventionally understood as "negative" or "positive."
Also, the two features and examples in each are solely illustrative (not exhaustive), since there will be many different post-human value ideals in the distant future of post-human lifeforms. The comparison is also relative (not absolute), nor are they mutually exclusive. As generalities, they allow exceptions. And the specific forms of post-human ideals even for these radically alien floating lifeforms (and others unknown to us) need to be further developed in future after-postmodern history, as they will likely be different from the ones herein illustrated. The point here is to solely give a very rough picture of a small part of the extremely alien world to come that we have never known.
Source: From Ch.10 of *FCD*. Refer to text for more info and references.

Table 4.25. Democracy, Non-Democracy, and Post-Democracy (Part I)

- **Democracy**

—*Theoretical Constructs*

•The pursuit of freedom and equality (in various degrees), regardless of whether freedom and equality can be understood as "negative" or "positive"

(1) more equality than freedom: The relative priority of the good over the right

(2) more freedom than equality: The relative priority of the right over the good

—*Types*

•Only (1): Different versions of communitarian moral universalism

•Only (2): Different versions of liberal moral universalism

•(1) or (2): Different versions of anarchic (non-nation-state) moral universalism

•(1) or (2): Different versions of postmodern moral localism

- **Non-Democracy**

—*Theoretical Constructs*

•The focus on (1') equality or (2') freedom, but not both, regardless of whether freedom and equality can be understood as "negative" or "positive"

—*Types*

•Only (1'): Different versions on the Far Left (e.g., Stalinism, Robespierrianism)

•Only (2'): Different versions on the Far Right (e.g., Nazism, absolute monarchism)

(continued on next page)

Table 4.25. Democracy, Non-Democracy, and Post-Democracy (Part II)

• **Post-Democracy**
—*Theoretical Constructs*
•The priority of (1'') equality over freedom, or (2'') freedom over equality, or (3'') the transcendence of freedom and equality, regardless of whether freedom and equality are "negative" or "positive." In degree, (1'') or (2'') is less than (1') or (2') but more than (1) or (2)—respectively.
•Like democracy and non-democracy, post-democracy is also subject to the freedom/unfreedom and equality/inequality dialectics (or existential dialectics in general). Unlike them, post-democracy acknowledges the constraints of existential dialectics and no longer value freedom and equality as sacred virtues. There is no utopia, in the end; even were there one, dystopia would exist within it.
—*Types*
•(1''): Different versions of trans-Sinitic value ideals
•(1''): Different versions of trans-feminine value ideals
•(1''): Different versions of trans-Islamic value ideals
•(1''): Different versions of trans-outerspace value ideals
•(2''): Different versions of post-human elitist value ideals
•(3''): Different versions of the value ideals of floating consciousness (etc.)

(continued on next page)

Table 4.25. Democracy, Non-Democracy, and Post-Democracy (Part III)

Notes: The examples are solely illustrative (not exhaustive), nor are they mutually exclusive. As generalities, they allow exceptions. "Negative" freedom is freedom "from" (e.g., freedom from poverty), whereas "positive" freedom is freedom "to" (e.g., freedom to the state of enlightenment). "Negative" equality is "procedural" equality (e.g., equality of opportunity), while "positive" equality is "substantive" equality (e.g., equality of outcome). Existential dialectics impose constraints on freedom and equality in democracy, non-democracy, and post-democracy, regardless of whether freedom and equality can be understood as "negative" or "positive" in conventional discourse. Therefore, do not confuse the transcendence of freedom and equality in (3'') with the naïve temptation to transcend existential dialectics. There is no utopia, in the end; even should there be one, it would not exist without dystopia embedded within it.
Sources: A summary, based on my previous works, especially Ch.5 of *FHC*, Chs.5-10 of *FCD*, Chs.2-4 of *FPHC*, and Chs.1 & 7 of *BDPD*. The reader should consult the books for more analysis, as this is only a summary here.

Table 4.26. Multiple Causes of the Emergence of Post-Democracy (Part I)

- **At the Micro-Physical Level**
  —Ex: intelligent life without the human physical-chemical system
  —Sources: Ch.7 of *FHC*; Chs.9-10 of *FCD*; Ch.1 of *FPHC*

- **At the Chemical Level**
  —Ex: space radiation and toxins
  —Sources: Ch.7 of *FHC*; Chs.9-10 of *FCD*

- **At the Bio-Psychological Level**
  —Ex: exo-biological evolution in deep space
  —Ex: genetic engineering of new beings
  —Ex: limits of cognitive partiality
  —Ex: illusions of emotional neutrality
  —Ex: human biological inequality
  —Ex: the rise of unfolding unconsciousness
  —Sources: Ch.2 & Chs.9-10 of *FCD*; Ch.7 of *FHC*; Ch.4 of *BCPC*; *FPHU*

- **At the Institutional Level**
  —Ex: the flawed logic of equality
  —Ex: the conflicting nature of governance
  —Sources: Ch. 5 of *FHC*; Chs. 6 & 10 of *FCD*; Ch. 3 of *FPHC*; Chs.2-5 of *BDPD*

- **At the Organizational Level**
  —Ex: e-civic alienation
  —Ex: the dark sides of formal-legalistic routines
  —Sources: Ch.3 of *FHC*; Ch.7 of *FCD*; Ch.3 of *FPHC*

- **At the Structural Level**
  —Ex: ever new forms of inequities, at home and abroad
  —Ex: the emergence of China, women, and Islam as major actors
  —Sources: Chs.5-6 of *FHC*; Chs.7, 9 & 10 of *FCD*; Chs.4-5 of *BDPD*

(continued on next page)

Table 4.26. Multiple Causes of the Emergence of Post-Democracy (Part II)

- **At the Cultural Level**
  —Ex: freedom/unfreedom dialectics
  —Ex: equality/inequality dialectics
  —Ex: system fragmentation and integration
  —Sources: Ch.5 of *FHC*; Chs. 3, 9 & 10 of *FCD*; Ch.4 of *FPHC*; Ch.1 of *BDPD*; Ch.4 of *BCPC*

- **At the Systemic Level**
  —Ex: space habitats (in zero-gravity) and colonization
  —Ex: ultra advanced future info systems
  —Ex: qualitative demography
  —Sources: Ch.7 of *FHC*; Chs.9 &10 of *FCD*

- **At the Cosmological Level**
  —Ex: the colonization of multiverses
  —Ex: the alteration of space-time and the creation of new matter-energy
  —Ex: the expansion of floating consciousness
  —Ex: the spread of hyper-spatial consciousness
  —Sources: Ch.7 of *FHC*; Chs.9 &10 of *FCD*; Ch.4 of *FPHC*; *FPHST*

Notes: The examples in each category are solely illustrative (not exhaustive), and some of the items can be reclassified somewhere else. Nor are they always mutually exclusive. Since they are generalities, exceptions are expected.
Sources: Especially from *FHC*, *FCD*, *FPHC*, *BCPC*, *BDPD*, *FPHST*, and *FPHU*. See also other books and my perspectives on civilizational holism.

Table 4.27. Some Clarifications about Post-Capitalism and Post-Democracy (Part I)

• The prefix "trans-" in the first category of post-capitalism (with its four versions) refers to something "going beyond" (not "uniting" or "combining"). Ex: *Sec.10.3.3* of *FCD*; *Sec.2.4* & *Sec.4.4* of *FPHC*; *Sec.7.2* of *BCPC*

• Such terms like "post-democracy," "post-capitalism," "post-human elitist," "trans-feminine calling," and the like as used in my works are more for our current intellectual convenience than to the liking of future humans and post-humans, who will surely invent more tasteful neologisms to call their own eras, entities, and everything else, for that matter. But the didactic point here is to use the terms to foretell what the future might be like, not that its eras and entities must be called so exactly and permanently.
Ex: *Sec.11.1* of *FCD*; *Sec.7.2* of *BCPC*

• The four versions in the first category of post-capitalist value ideals need not automatically be post-democratic, just as capitalism does not necessarily mean democracy. They are two different entities—though closely related. But up to a certain threshold of elevating equality at the farther expense of freedom, the democratic ideals will be overcome and cease to exist. The same is true for the post-human elitist calling in the second category of post-capitalism in relation to post-democracy, depending on the extent to which freedom is elevated at the expense of equality.
Ex: *Sec.10.4.3.3* of *FCD*; *Table 3.9* of *FPHC*; *Table 7.6* of *BDPD*

• The comparison in each of the three realms of existence in all forms of post-capitalism is not absolute, but relative. Examples include "communal" vs. "individualistic," and the like.
Ex: Notes in *Table 10.8*, *Table 10.9*, *Table 10.10*, & *Table 10.11* of *FCD*; Chs.2-4 of *FPHC*; *Sec.7.2* of *BCPC*

(continued on next page)

Table 4.27. Some Clarifications about Post-Capitalism and Post-Democracy (Part II)

• The emergence of post-capitalism (and post-democracy, for that matter) has multiple causes (to not be reduced to one or only a few).
Ex: Ch.10 of *FCD*, Chs.2-4 of *FPHC*; *Sec.1.3* & *Sec.7.2* of *BCPC* (or *Table 1.8* & *Table 7.11*)

• The specific forms of post-capitalism (and post-democracy, for that matter) need to be further developed in future after-postmodern history, as they will be different from the ones we now know. The point here is to solely give an extremely rough sketch of a world to come that we have never known.
Ex: *Sec.10.3.3* & *Sec.10.4.3.3* of *FCD*; *Table 10.14* & *Table 10.15* of *FCD*; *Sec.7.2* of *BCPC*

• All forms of post-capitalism are not part of a "teleological law," but of "historical trends" only. The same is also true for all forms of post-democracy.
Ex: *Sec.7.1* of *FHC*; *Sec.9.5.3.2* & *Sec.10.3.4.2* of *FCD*; *Sec.7.2* of *BCPC*

• Post-capitalism is not better than capitalism in an "absolute" sense but only fits in better, on the basis of the historical contingency of culture, society, nature, and the mind in some future eras. The same is true for post-democracy in relation to democracy. The term "better" is historically relative.
Ex: *Sec.10.3.3* of *FCD*; *Sec.1.7* of *BDPD*; *Sec.1.5* of *BCPC*

(continued on next page)

Table 4.27. Some Clarifications about Post-Capitalism and Post-Democracy (Part III)

• All forms of post-capitalism and post-democracy are subject to the constraints of existential dialectics. In the process, the dialectic direction is to go beyond the conventional "either-or" dichotomies (e.g., freedom vs. unfreedom, equality vs. inequality, freedom vs. equality, individuality vs. communality, spirituality vs. materiality, formal legalism vs. informal legalism, etc.). As is true in post-civilization, to go beyond the dichotomies is to acknowledge the co-existence of both in each dichotomy, although the degree of scaling one over the over varies from case to case (e.g., the theory of post-capitalism I, the theory of post-capitalism II, the theory of post-democracy I, the theory of post-democracy II, etc.)—but is not to be extreme in largely favoring one over the other, *on average* (all things considered). There is no utopia to be had in the end; even should there be one, dystopia would exist within it.
Ex: Ch.5 of *FHC*; *Sec.10.4.4.2* of *FCD*; *Sec.1.5* of *BDPD*; *Sec.1.3* of *BCPC*; *BCIV*

• All forms of post-capitalism, however different from each other though they are, share one common feature, in that they all inspire for a higher spiritual culture. The same is also true for post-democracy.
Ex: *Sec.10.3*, *Sec.10.4* & *Sec.10.5* of *FCD*; *Chs.2-4* of *FPHC*; *Sec.7.2* of *BCPC*

• All forms of post-capitalism try to avoid the excess in capitalist consumerism by favoring more basic than artificial needs in having, but the quality and quantity of these "basic" needs will be measured by future standards, not by our current ones. Standards are historically relative.
Ex: *Sec.10.3*, *Sec.10.4* & *Sec.10.5* of *FCD*; Ch.2 of *FPHC*; *Sec.7.2* of *BCPC*

(continued on next page)

Table 4.27. Some Clarifications about Post-Capitalism and Post-Democracy (Part IV)

• All forms of post-capitalism make use of a different degree of political authority with advanced info systems in future history and strives for higher spiritual cultures (especially in the post-human age), while acknowledging the constraints of existential dialectics and no longer valuing free market (as in capitalism) and economic control (as in non-capitalism) as sacred virtues.
Ex: *Sec.10.3.4.2*, *Sec.10.3*, *Sec.10.4* & *Sec.10.5* of *FCD*; Chs.2-4 of *FPHC*; *Sec.1.5* of *BDPD*; *Sec.7.2* of *BCPC*

Notes:: The main points here are solely illustrative (not exhaustive) nor necessarily mutually exclusive, and the comparison is relative (not absolute). As generalities, they allow exceptions. The sections as cited are only illustrative (not exhaustive).
Sources: From *FHC*, *FCD*, *FPHC*, and *BDPD*

Table 4.28. The Theory of Post-Capitalism I.1: By Group— Ex: Spiritual/Communal in the Trans-Feminine Calling

• **More Communal Than Individual**
—*Sharing*: learning from others, as different ideas mutually enrich
—*Cooperative*: encouraging a sense of shared leadership and teamwork

• **More Informal-Legalistic Than Formal-Legalistic**
—*Specific*: listening more from the heart than from the head, to know a person as a concrete, not as an abstract, unit
—*Affective*: thinking and acting with others on a more affective tone. Business can mix with an emotional touch.
—*Ascriptive*: hiring (or firing) can be done on the basis of merit (or lack of it), but deep solidarity (sisterhood) is important too.
—*Particularistic*: making decisions on the basis of cost-benefit analysis, but a given group relationship is vital

• **More Spiritual Than Secular**
—*Long-Term Looking*: sharing for a long-term relationship (e.g., love, friendship), not just for a short-term gain
—*Loving/Caring*: showing compassion for the sufferings of others, without quickly blaming and pre-judging
—*Respectful*: showing acceptance about others' feelings (and thoughts)

Notes: The categories and examples are solely illustrative, since there can be different versions, and the comparison is relative (not absolute), nor are they mutually exclusive. As generalities, they allow exceptions. The specific forms of the trans-feminine version need to be further developed in future after-postmodern history, as they will be different from the ones we now know, since the prefix "trans-" here means going beyond or deconstructing the feminine values, while using them as the inspirational point at the beginning.
Source: From Ch.10 of *FCD*. Refer to text for more info and references.

Table 4.29. The Theory of Post-Capitalism I.2: By Nation-State— Ex: Spiritual/Communal in the Trans-Sinitic Calling

---

• **More Communal Than Individualistic**
—*Centralized*: being more top-down in management
—*Collective*: encouraging more group cooperation
—*Social*: investing in trust and connection

• **More Informal-Legalistic Than Formal-Legalistic**
—*Specific*: knowing more of those related or connected
—*Affective*: behaving in a paternalistic, hierarchical way
—*Ascriptive*: favoring family members and those related
—*Particularistic*: building connection (guanxi) as imperative

• **More Spiritual Than Secular**
—*Expansionist*: diffusing civilizational values (e.g., the superiority complex of civilizationalism)
—*Holistic*: synthesizing things into a panoramic horizon
—*Historical*: learning from the lessons of the ancient past
—*Respectful*: deferential to elders and superiors

Notes: The categories and examples are solely illustrative, since there can be different versions, and the comparison is relative (not absolute), nor are they mutually exclusive. As generalities, they allow exceptions. The specific forms of the trans-Sinitic version need to be further developed in future after-postmodern history, as they will be different from the ones we now know, since the prefix "trans-" here means going beyond or deconstructing the Sinitic values, while using them as the inspirational point at the beginning.
Source: From Ch.10 of *FCD*. Refer to text for more info and references.

Table 4.30. The Theory of Post-Capitalism I.3: By Region— Ex: Spiritual/Communal in the Trans-Islamic Calling

- **More Communal Than Individualistic**
  —*Collective*: building the webs of relationships to bind individuals
  —*Sharing*: cultivating the established "wisdom" through common experience
  —*Cooperative*: stressing harmony, solidarity, and commonality

- **More Informal-Legalistic Than Formal-Legalistic**
  —*Specific*: making efforts to know well the participants (family and larger community) in matters of common concern
  —*Affective*: mixing work with language and ritual on explicit religious (Islamic) ideals, texts, stories, and examples
  —*Ascriptive*: privileging local history and custom on relationships among kinship groups
  —*Particularistic*: preferring an unbiased insider with ongoing connections to all parties

- **More Spiritual Than Secular**
  —*Historical*: learning from the lessons of the past as a source of stability and guidance
  —*Deferential*: showing respect for age, experience, status, and leadership in communal affairs
  —*Honorable*: emphasizing face, dignity, prestige, and fairness
  —*Compassionate*: giving mercy and charity ("Zahah") to others

Notes: The categories and examples are solely illustrative (not exhaustive), and the comparison is relative (not absolute), nor are they mutually exclusive. As generalities, they allow exceptions. The specific forms of the trans-Islamic version need to be further developed in future after-postmodern history, as they will be different from the ones we now know, since the prefix "trans-" here means going beyond or deconstructing the Islamic values, while using them as the inspirational point at the beginning.
Sources: From Ch.10 of *FCD*. Refer to text for more info and references, especially from the works by George Irani (2000) and C. Murphy (September 19, 2001).

Table 4.31. The Theory of Post-Capitalism I.4: By Universe— Ex: Spiritual/Communal in the Trans-Outerspace Calling

- **More Communal Than Individual**
  —*Cooperative*: requiring teamwork in small space habitats
  —*Sharing*: learning from, and enjoying being with, each other in a small group in outer space

- **More Informal-Legalistic Than Formal-Legalistic**
  —*Specific*: knowing more about each other to facilitate living and working together in space, both as fellow astronauts and space-mates
  —*Affective*: being friendly and social to each other as vital to working and living in small space quarters
  —*Ascriptive*: nurturing comaraderie among fellow astronauts as if they are family members over time
  —*Particularistic*: building work relationship with enduring memory in a space mission

- **More Spiritual Than Secular**
  —*Long-Term*: looking beyond selfish materialistic concerns in a precarious space environment with potential life or death
  —*Loving/Caring*: cultivating deep bondage for the success of a long term space mission
  —*Transcendent*: searching for life meaning in outer space

Notes: The calling and examples in each category are solely illustrative (not exhaustive), since there will be many different outer-space value ideals in the distant future of space colonization. The comparison is also relative (not absolute), nor are they mutually exclusive. As generalities, they allow exceptions. And the specific forms of trans-outer-space calling need to be further developed in future after-postmodern history, as they will be different from the ones we now know, since the prefix "trans-" here means going beyond or deconstructing the current outer-space values, while using them as the inspirational point at the beginning. The point here is to solely give an extremely rough picture of a small part of the world to come that we still do not know much about.
Source: From Ch.10 of *FCD*. Refer to text for more info and references.

Table 4.32. The Theory of Post-Capitalism II: Spiritual/Individualistic in the Post-Human Elitist Calling (Part I)

- **More Individualistic Than Communal**
  —Setting up rank distinctions among unequals (e.g., between inferior humans and superior post-humans, or later among inferior post-humans and superior ones, relatively speaking)
  —Yearning for being not only distinguished from unequals, but also the first among equals (the best of the very best)
  —Recognizing the constraints of equality/inequality dialectics (or existential dialectics in general)

- **More Spiritual Than Secular**
  —Soul-searching for a high spiritual culture (not the trashy one for the masses). Mass culture is a dirty joke for them.
  —Exploring different spheres of non-human consciousness in the cosmos (something vastly superior than the human one)
  —Recognizing the constraints of freedom/unfreedom dialectics (or existential dialectics in general)

- **Qualifications**
  —Although post-human elitist post-democracy is comparable to post-human elitist post-capitalism in some respects, the former does not necessarily imply the latter (post-human elitist post-capitalism), just as democracy does not have to entail capitalism. They are two different (though related) entities.
  —But up to a certain threshold of incorporating government intervention with advanced info systems in future civilizations for higher spiritual concerns at the expense of the free market and materialist pursuit, the capitalist ideal will be overcome.
  —The overcome will not be Fascist or feudalistic, but post-capitalist, subject to the constraints of existential dialectics.

(continued on next page)

Table 4.32. The Theory of Post-Capitalism II: Spiritual/Individualistic in the Post-Human Elitist Calling (Part II)

Notes: The calling and examples in each category are solely illustrative (not exhaustive). The comparison is also relative (not absolute), nor are they mutually exclusive. As generalities, they allow exceptions. And the specific forms of post-human elitist post-capitalism need to be further developed in future after-postmodern history, as they will be different from the ones we now know, while using them as the inspirational point at the beginning. The point here is to solely give an extremely rough picture of a small part of the world to come that we still do not know much about.
Sources: From Ch.10 of *FCD* (and also *FPHC*, *BDPD*, and *BCPC*). Refer to the text for more info and references.

Table 4.33. Capitalism, Non-Capitalism, and Post-Capitalism (Part I)

- **Capitalism**
  - *Theoretical Constructs*
    - Allocation of scarce resources among alternative wants largely by free market for competition (whose characteristics in its ideal form include, for instance, no barrier to entry or exit, homogeneity, perfect information, a large number of buyers/sellers, and perfect factor mobility)
    - More formal-legalistic than informal-legalistic, more individualistic than communal, and more material (secular) than spiritual
    - Either (1) minimal government or (2) relatively active government
  - *Types*
    - Only (1): Different versions of market capitalism (e.g., the U.S.)
    - Only (2): Different versions of welfare capitalism (e.g., Sweden)

- **Non-Capitalism**
  - *Theoretical Constructs*
    - Allocation of scarce resources among alternative wants mainly by political authority for policies (which can be regulative, redistributive, symbolic, and participatory)
    - More informal-legalistic than formal-legalistic
    - Either (1') more individualistic (for the elites), often (though not always) for material (secular) concerns, or (2') more communal (for the masses), often (though not always) for spiritual concerns
  - *Types*
    - Only (1'): Different versions on the Right (e.g., Fascist corporate-state economy for the glory of the new Rome, medieval lord-vassal-serf economy for the power of the feudalistic order)
    - Only (2'): Different versions on the Left (e.g., Soviet command economy for the creation of the New Socialist Man)

(continued on next page)

Table 4.33. Capitalism, Non-Capitalism, and Post-Capitalism (Part II)

• **Post-Capitalism**

—*Theoretical Constructs*

•Allocation of scarce resources among alternative wants largely by political authority with advanced info systems in future civilizations, subject to existential dialectics. In degree of allocating by authority, post-capitalism is more than capitalism but less than non-capitalism.

•More spiritual than secular (material)

•Either (1'') more individualistic or (2") more communal

•Like capitalism and non-capitalism, post-capitalism is also subject to the freedom/unfreedom and equality/inequality dialectics (or existential dialectics in general). There is no utopia, in the end; even were there one, dystopia would exist within it.

•Unlike capitalism and non-capitalism, post-capitalism makes use of a different degree of political authority with advanced info systems in future civilizations and strives for higher-spiritual cultures (especially in the post-human age), while acknowledging the constraints of existential dialectics and no longer valuing free market (as in capitalism) and economic control (as in non-capitalism) as sacred virtues.

—*Types*

•Only (1"): Different versions of post-human elitist value ideals

•Only (2''): Different versions of trans-Sinitic value ideals

•Only (2''): Different versions of trans-feminine value ideals

•Only (2''): Different versions of trans-Islamic value ideals

•Only (2''): Different versions of trans-outerspace value ideals

---

(continued on next page)

Table 4.33. Capitalism, Non-Capitalism, and Post-Capitalism (Part III)

Notes: The calling and examples in each category are solely illustrative (not exhaustive). The comparison is also relative (not absolute), nor are they mutually exclusive. As generalities, they allow exceptions. And the specific forms of each calling need to be further developed in future after-postmodern history, as they will be different from the ones we now know, while using them as the inspirational point at the beginning. The point here is to solely give an extremely rough picture of a small part of the world to come that we still do not know much about.
Source: From Ch.10 of *FCD*. Refer to the text for more info and references.

Table 4.34. Multiple Causes of the Emergence of Post-Capitalism (Part I)

- **At the Micro-Physical Level**
  —Ex: intelligent life without the human physical-chemical system
  —Ex: mastering of quantum mechanics, electromagnetism, and other fields for the understanding of a broad range of anomalous experiences and the application for artificial intelligence for spiritual quest
  —Sources: Ch.7 of *FHC*; Chs.9-10 of *FCD*; Ch.1 of *FPHC*

- **At the Chemical Level**
  —Ex: space radiation and toxins
  —Sources: Ch.7 of *FHC*; Chs.9-10 of *FCD*

- **At the Bio-Psychological Level**
  —Ex: exo-biological evolution in deep space
  —Ex: genetic engineering of new beings
  —Ex: limits of human cognition
  —Ex: the rise of unfolding unconsciousness
  —Sources: Ch.2 & Chs.9-10 of *FCD*; Ch.7 of *FHC*; *FPHU*

- **At the Institutional Level**
  —Ex: the flawed logic of the free market
  —Ex: the need of a post-autistic economics
  —Sources: Ch.10 of *FCD*

- **At the Organizational Level**
  —Ex: the dark sides of formal-legalistic routines
  —Sources: Ch.3 of *FHC*; Ch.7 of *FCD*; Ch.3 of *FPHC*

- **At the Structural Level**
  —Ex: ever new forms of inequities, at home and abroad
  —Ex: the emergence of China, women, and Islam as major actors
  —Sources: Chs.5-6 of *FHC*; Chs.7, 9 & 10 of *FCD*; Chs.4-5 of *BDPD*

(continued on next page)

Table 4.34. Multiple Causes of the Emergence of Post-Capitalism (Part II)

• **At the Cultural Level**
—Ex: freedom/unfreedom dialectics
—Ex: equality/inequality dialectics
—Sources: Ch.5 of *FHC*; Chs.3 & 10 of *FCD*; Ch.4 of *FPHC*; Ch.1 of *BDPD*

• **At the Systemic Level**
—Ex: space habitats (in zero-gravity) and colonization
—Ex: ultra advanced future info systems
—Ex: qualitative demography
—Sources: Ch.7 of *FHC*; Chs. 9 & 10 of *FCD*

• **At the Cosmological Level**
—Ex: the colonization of multiverses
—Ex: the alteration of space-time and the creation of new matter-energy
—Ex: the expansion of floating consciousness
—Ex: the spread of hyper-spatial consciousness
—Sources: Ch.7 of *FHC*; Chs. 9 & 10 of *FCD*; Ch.4 of *FPHC*; *FPHST*

Notes: The examples in each category are solely illustrative (not exhaustive), and some of the items can be reclassified somewhere else. Nor are they always mutually exclusive. Since they are generalities, exceptions are expected.
Sources: Especially from *FHC*, *FCD*, *FPHC*, *BCPC*, *BDPD*, *FPHST*, and *FPHU*. See also other books and my perspectives on civilizational holism.

Table 4.35. The Theoretical Debate on Civilization

- **The Progressive Theory of Civilization**
  —*Thesis*: The "civilizing" process is "good," as opposed to the "barbarizing" process as something "bad," relatively speaking.
  —*Discourse*: Especially, though not exclusively, in the Enlightenment era and a bit before. Example: Thomas Hobbes—in that the tribes in primitive societies were "savages."

- **The Romantic Theory of Barbarity**
  —*Thesis*: The "civilizing" process is "bad," as opposed to the "barbarizing" process as something "good," relatively speaking.
  —*Discourse*: Especially, though not exclusively, in the Counter-Enlightenment circle. Example: Jean-Jacques Rousseau—in that civilization "corrupts" men, and the "savages" are in fact "noble."

- **The Moderate Theory of Civilization**
  —*Thesis*: The "civilizing" process is "good," but there is a price to pay, especially in systematic (compulsive) self-control.
  —*Discourse*: Especially, though not exclusively, in some late modern and postmodern circles. Example: Norbert Elias—in that social manners become more refined in the civilizing process, but self-control also becomes more systematic.

- **The Theory of Post-Civilization**
  —*Thesis*: The civilizing process is as evil and good as barbarity, and each cannot exist without the other, to be eventually superseded by post-civilization unto the post-human age.
  —*Discourse*: Proposed by Peter Baofu. See the rest of *BCIV* for more analysis.

Source: From *BCIV* on the theoretical debate

Table 4.36. No Freedom Without Unfreedom in the Civilizing Processes (Part I)

- **The Rationalizing Process (at the Level of Culture)**
  —if freer from the dominance of unreason (as in barbarism) in the civilizing process, then less free from the rationalizing process (be it in the form of the principle of either transcendence or immanence)
  —if freer from the principle of immanence in the rationalizing process, then less free from the inclination to commit terror in the name of reason and the relative underdevelopment of non-reason (e.g., in relation to yoga and meditation)
  —if freer from the principle of transcendence in the rationalizing process, then less free from the relative underdevelopment of reason (e.g., in relation to systematic methodology) and the occurrence of oppression in the name of non-reason

- **The Pacifying Process (at the Level of Society)**
  —if freer from the dominance of pillage (as in savagery) in the civilizing process, then less free from the pacifying process (be it in the form of external control or self-control)
  —if freer from self-control in the pacifying process, then less free from the temptation of expansionist oppression and rebellious mindset in external control
  —if freer from external control in the pacifying process, then less free from the gruesome psychological self-torture and conformism in self-control

- **The Stewardizing Process (at the Level of Nature)**
  —if freer from the dominance of nature (as in the state of nature) in the civilizing process, then less free from the stewardizing process (be it in the form of the stewardship of creation or the covenant with nature)
  —if freer from the stewardship of creation in the stewardizing process, then less free from material underdevelopment, relatively speaking, and spiritual exclusion in the covenant with nature
  —if freer from the covenant with nature in the stewardizing process, then less free from ecological degradation and spiritual disconnection from nature in the stewardship of creation

(continued on next page)

Table 4.36. No Freedom Without Unfreedom in the Civilizing Processes (Part II)

- **The Subliming Process (at the Level of the Mind)**
  —if freer from the dominance of spontaneity (as in the wild state of the mind) in the civilizing process, then less free from the subliming process, be it in the form of (cyclical-centric) self-refinement or (linear-centric) self-discipline
  —if freer from (cyclical-centric) self-refinement in the subliming process, then less free from the (linear-centric) self-regimen (as a form of neurosis)
  —if freer from (linear-centric) self-discipline in the subliming process, then less free from the (cyclical-centric) self-torture (equally as a form of neurosis)

Notes: The examples in each category are solely illustrative (not exhaustive), and the comparison is relative (not absolute), nor are they necessarily mutually exclusive. And some can be easily re-classified elsewhere. As generalities, they allow exceptions.
Sources: From *BCIV*. See also *FHC*, *FCD*, *FPHC*, *BDPD*, and *BCPC*.

Table 4.37. No Equality Without Inequality in the Civilizing Processes (Part I)

- **The Rationalizing Process (at the Level of Culture)**
  —if more equal for the role of rationalization in the rationalizing process (of civilizational making), then less equal for that of mythicization (as in barbarism)
  —if more equal for the principle of transcendence in (linear-centric) rationalizing process, then less equal for the principle of immanence
  —if more equal for the principle of immanence in (cyclical-centric) rationalizing process, then less equal for the principle of transcendence

- **The Pacifying Process (at the Level of Society)**
  —if more equal for pacification in civilizational making, then less equal for the institution of pillaging and others (as in savagery)
  —if more equal for external control, relatively speaking, in pacifying process, then less equal for self-control
  —if more equal for self-control, relatively speaking, in pacifying process, then less equal for external-control

- **The Stewardizing Process (at the Level of Nature)**
  —if more equal for stewardship in the stewardizing process (of civilizational making), then less equal for reverent (submissive) existence (as in barbarism)
  —if more equal for the stewardship of creation in (linear- centric) stewardizing process, then less equal for the (cyclical-centric) covenant with nature for harmonious co-existence
  —if more equal for the (cyclical-centric) covenant with nature in the stewardizing process, then less equal for the (linear-centric) stewardship of nature for domination

(continued on next page)

Table 4.37. No Equality Without Inequality in the Civilizing Processes (Part II)

- **The Subliming Process (at the Level of the Mind)**
  —if more equal for the role of reason in the subliming process, then less equal for that of unreason (as in the natural state of wildness)
  —if more equal for the primacy of reason in (linear-centric) subliming process, then less equal for other faculties (e.g., intuition, existential feelings, and analogous thinking) in cyclical-centric one
  —if more equal for the exercise of other faculties (e.g., intuition, existential feelings, and analogous thinking) in cyclical-centric subliming process, then less equal for the role of reason in linear-centric counterpart

Notes: The examples in each category are solely illustrative (not exhaustive), and the comparison is relative (not absolute), nor are they mutually exclusive. And some can be easily reclassified else-where. As generalities, they allow exceptions.
Sources: From *BCIV*. See also *FHC*, *FCD*, *FPHC*, *BDPD*, and *BCPC*.

Table 4.38. Five Theses on Post-Civilization

• Post-civilization no longer treats civilization as good and barbarity as evil (relatively speaking), nor does it nostalgically regard barbarity as good and civilization as evil (relatively speaking again). Civilization is as evil and good as barbarity.

• Post-civilization also no longer accepts the dichotomy between civilization and barbarity. Civilization cannot exist without barbarity. It is no longer necessary to preserve civilization, any more than it is imperative to destroy barbarity. To go beyond civilization and barbarity is to acknowledge the co-existence of both, although the degree of scaling one over the over varies from case to case—but is not to be extreme in largely favoring one over the other, *on average* (subject to the constraints of existential dialectics).

• Post-civilization is thus subject to the constraints of existential dialectics. There is no freedom without unfreedom, and no equality without inequality, for instance. There will be no utopia; even should there be one, there would be dystopia embedded within it.

• Post-civilization will eventually replace civilization (as a form of life settlement), to be dominated by post-capitalist and post-democratic lifeforms here on earth and in deep space (besides other alien lifeforms that we have never known), unto the post-human age in multiverses. Those few post-humans who keep civilization will live in a "post-human civilization," while the rest (the majority), who choose post-civilization, will evolve towards the state of "post-human post-civilization." One therefore should not confuse "post-human civilization" with "post-human post-civilization," as the two are not the same.

• Post-civilization will confront psychosis as a primary problem in the culture of virtuality unto the post-human age, just as civilization has neurosis as a primary one of its own (although both neurosis and psychosis are major problems in both).

Notes: The comparison in each category is relative (not absolute), nor are they necessarily mutually exclusive. And some can be easily re-classified elsewhere. As generalities, they allow exceptions.
Sources: From *BCIV*. See also *FHC*, *FCD*, *FPHC*, *BDPD*, and *BCPC*.

Table 4.39. Barbarity, Civilization, and Post-Civilization

- **The Rationalizing Process (at the Level of Culture)**
  —*Barbarity*
    - More mythicizing than rationalizing, relatively speaking
  —*Civilization*
    - More rationalizing than mythicizing, relatively speaking
  —*Post-Civilization*
    - Beyond the dichotomy, subject to existential dialectics

- **The Pacifying Process (at the Level of Society)**
  —*Barbarity*
    - More pillaging than pacifying, relatively speaking
  —*Civilization*
    - More pacifying than pillaging, relatively speaking
  —*Post-Civilization*
    - Beyond the dichotomy, subject to existential dialectics

- **The Stewardizing Process (at the Level of Nature)**
  —*Barbarity*
    - More revering than stewardizing, relatively speaking
  —*Civilization*
    - More stewardizing than revering, relatively speaking
  —*Post-Civilization*
    - Beyond the dichotomy, subject to existential dialectics

- **The Subliming Process (at the Level of the Mind)**
  —*Barbarity*
    - More impulsing than subliming, relatively speaking
  —*Civilization*
    - More subliming than impulsing, relatively speaking
  —*Post-Civilization*
    - Beyond the dichotomy, subject to existential dialectics

Notes: The comparison in each category is relative (not absolute), nor are they necessarily mutually exclusive. And some can be easily re-classified elsewhere. As generalities, they allow exceptions.
Sources: From *BCIV*. See also *FHC*, *FCD*, *FPHC*, *BDPD*, and *BCPC*.

Table 4.40. Types of Super Civilization in the Cosmos (Part I)

- **Type I**
  —a civilization which gains control of and uses the total energy output "falling on its planet from its sun for interstellar communication" (or, in general, space colonization). For N. Kardashev, who proposed the first three types, human civilization is currently Type Zero (Type O), which is below even Type I, since its present energy consumption for all purposes, let alone for interstellar communication, is still 10,000 times less.

- **Type II**
  —a civilization which gains control of and uses directly the total energy output of its sun for interstellar communication (or, in general, space colonization).

- **Type III**
  —a civilization which gains control of and uses the total energy output of its galaxy for interstellar communication (or, in general, space colonization).

- **Type IV**
  —a civilization which gains control of and uses the total energy output of its cluster of galaxies for interstellar communication (or, in general, space colonization).

- **Type V**
  —a civilization which gains control of and uses the total energy output of its supercluster of galaxies for interstellar communica-tion (or, in general, space colonization).

(continued on next page)

Table 4.40. Types of Super Civilization in the Cosmos (Part II)

- **Type…n**
  —So continues the series in what I call the cyclical progression of hegemony in the cosmos and beyond.

Notes: The Russian astrophysicist Nikolai Kardashev proposed the first three types of super civilization in terms of total energy out-put for interstellar communication. (CSM 1979) I extend his argument further to propose Type IV, Type V, Type VI, and Type…n, in the context of my claim about the cyclical progression of he-gemony in the cosmos and beyond.
Sources: From *Table 9.4* of *FCD*. See *FHC*, *FCD*, and *FPHC* for more info.

Table 4.41. The Civilizational Project from Pre-Modernity to After-Postmodernity (Part I)

	Pre-Modern	*Modern*	*Postmodern*	*After-Postmodern*
Main narratives	•Sacralness •Courtliness •Vitalism •Animism	•Freedom •Equality •Fraternity	•Multiplicity •Hybridization	•Naked contingency •Cyclical progression of hegemony
Main institutions	•Monarchy •Aristocracy •Feudalism •Holy order •Primitivism	•Capitalism •Liberalism •Socialism •Nazism •Fascism	•Capitalism •Liberalism •Postmodern politics of difference	•Post-Capitalism •Post-Democracy •Others
Main technological and economic revolutions	•Agricultural	•Service •Industrial	•Informational	•Biological •Material •Energy •Space •Others

(continued on next page)

Table 4.41. The Civilizational Project from Pre-Modernity to After-Postmodernity (Part II)

	Pre-Modern	*Modern*	*Postmodern*	*After-Postmodern*
Main agents	•Males •Upper strata •Mini-states	•Males •Upper strata •Whites •Empires	•Males •Upper strata •Whites •Others •Supra-states •IO's	•Post-humans •Humans •Others
Main impacts	•Local	•Inter-national	•Global	•Outer-space •Multiverse
Main outcomes	•Towards moderntiy •Rise of linear- & cyclical-centric civiliza-tions	•Towards post-modernity •Dominance of linear-centric civilization	•Towards after-post-moderntiy •Linear-centric civiliza-tion in crisis	•Towards human (& maybe post-human) extinction •Rise of post-civiliza-tion, especially in post-human forms of space-time

Notes: The examples in each category are solely illustrative (not exhaustive) nor necessarily mutually exclusive, and the comparison is relative (not absolute). As generalities, they allow exceptions.

Sources: From *Table 10.16* of *FCD*—and also from *BCIV* on post-civilization (and *FPHST*)

Table 4.42. Civilizational Holism (Part I)

• **At the Micro-Physical Theoretical Level**
—Ex: Mastering of quantum mechanics, electromagnetism, and other fields for the understanding of a broad range of anomalous experiences and theapplication for artificial intelligence (*Sec.1.4.1* of *FPHC*)

• **At the Chemical Theoretical Level**
—Ex: Unprecedented expansion of (and violence to) the mind through ever new forms of drugs (and virtual technologies, for that matter) (Ch.9 of *FCD*)

• **At the Biological Theoretical Level**
—Ex: Humans are not biologically equal, on the basis of race, gender, ethnicity, age, and whatnot. (*Sec.2.6* & Ch.10 of *FCD*; *BNN*) And post-humans will experience the same fate, in an even more amazing way.

• **At the Psychological Theoretical Level**
—Ex: Human cognitive impartiality and emotional neutrality are quite limited. (*Secs.2.4-2.5* of *FCD*)
—Ex: Rise of Floating Consciousness (Ch.10 of *FCD*; Chs.1 & 4 of *FPHC*) and Unfolding Unconsciousness (*FPHU*)

• **At the Organizational Theoretical Level**
—Ex: Administrative colonization of deep space, with less legal-formalism in some corners. (Chs.9-10 of *FCD*)

• **At the Institutional Theoretical Level**
—Ex: Both capitalism and democracy will not last, to be superseded by different versions of post-capitalism and post-democracy in after-postmodernity. (Ch.10 of *FCD*)

(continued on next page)

Table 4.42. Civilizational Holism (Part II)

- **At the Structural Theoretical Level**
  —Ex: Social stratification reappears in ever new forms, also with new causes and new players in the cyclical progression of hegemony. (Chs.8-10 of *FCD*)
  —Ex: The world of hyper-empires, and the union of the unions (*BWT*)

- **At the Systemic Theoretical Level**
  —Ex: Outerspace expansion: local → regional → global → solar → galactic → clustery → multiversal (Ch.9 of *FCD*)
  —Ex: Demographic transition: human extinction, and the rise of post-humans (e.g., cyborgs, thinking machines, thinking robots, genetically altered superior beings, floating consciousness, hyper-spatial consciousness) (Ch.4 of *FPHC*; Ch.10 of *FCD*; & Ch.7 of *FHC*)
  —Ex: New technological forces in material sciences, electronic and communication sciences, energy sciences, biosciences, manufacturing and engineering sciences, and space sciences (Ch.10 of *FCD* & Ch.7 of *FHC*)
  —Ex: Systematic dominance towards nature for space colonization (Chs.9-10 of *FCD*; Chs.2 & 7 of *FHC*)

- **At the Cultural Theoretical Level**
  —Ex: The post-human transcendence of freedom and equality (Ch.10 of *FCD*)
  —Ex: Methodological Holism (Ch.1 of *FCD*; Ch.1 of *FPHC*; *Sec.2.1* & *Sec.2.5* of *BCPC*)
  —Ex: The Evolution from Barbarity to Post-Civilization (*BCIV*)

- **At the Cosmological Theoretical Level**
  —Ex: Mastering of dark matter and dark energy, and the exploration of multiverses (Ch.4 of *FPHC*; Ch.10 of *FCD*; & Ch.7 of *FHC*)
  —Ex: Alternation of space-time (*FPHST*)
  —Ex: The emergence of hyper-spatial consciousness (*FPHC*)

(continued on next page)

Table 4.42. Civilizational Holism (Part III)

- **At Other Levels**
  —Ex: Historical: pre-modernity → modernity → postmodernity → after-postmodernity (human distinction, and the rise of post-humans, including floating consciousness, hyper-spatial consciousness, and unfolding unconsciousness) (Ch.7 of *FHC*; Ch.10 of *FCD*; *FPHC*; *FPHU*)

Notes: These examples are solely illustrative (not exhaustive), and some of the items can be reclassified somewhere else. Nor are they always mutually exclusive. Since they are generalities, exceptions are expected. And the comparison is relative, not absolute.
Sources: From *Table 5.1* of *FPHC*—with details from *FHC*, *FCD*, and the rest of my books. Not every aspect in each category as discussed in all my books are presented here, since there are too many issues. For more info, also consult the table on theories on civilizational holism and, of course, the books themselves.

Table 4.43. Theories on Civilizational Holism (Part I)

I. Theories in Relation to Nature

—*At the Macro-Physical (Cosmological) Theoretical Level*

- 45. Resettlement Theory of Geology (Peter Baofu) (*FPHGEOL*)
- 44. Theory of Post-Cosmology (Peter Baofu) (*BCOS*)
- 43. Theory of Hyper-Spatial Consciousness (Peter Baofu) (Ch.4 of *FPHC*; *FPHG*)
- (• 41). Selective Theory of Geometry (Peter Baofu) (*FPHG*)
- (• 40). Perspectival Theory of Space-Time (Peter Baofu) (*FPHST*)
- (• 39). Dialectic Theory of Complexity (Peter Baofu) (*FC*)
- (• 9). Theory of Floating Consciousness (Peter Baofu) (Ch.10 of *FCD*; Chs.1 & 4 of *FPHC*)
- 42. Theory of the Geopower of Nature (Peter Baofu) (Ch.4 of *ALD*)

—*At the Micro-Physical Theoretical Leve*

- 41. Selective Theory of Geometry (Peter Baofu) (*FPHG*)
- 40. Perspectival Theory of Space-Time (Peter Baofu) (*FPHST*)
- 39. Dialectic Theory of Complexity (Peter Baofu) (*FC*)

(continued on next page)

Table 4.43. Theories on Civilizational Holism (Part II)

II. Theories in Relation to Culture

—At the Cultural Theoretical Level

- • 38. Mediative-Variative Theory of Chess (Peter Baofu) (*FPHCHESS*)
- • 37. Theory of Post-Ethics (Peter Baofu) (*BEPE*)
- • 36. Dualistic Theory of Mass Culture (Peter Baofu) (Ch.2 of *FHC*)
- • 35. Comparative Theory of Religion—also known as the Comparative-Substitutive Theory of Religion (Peter Baofu) (Ch.3 of *FHC*; Ch.9 of *FCD*; Ch.1 of *FPHK*; *FPHR*)
- • 34. Theory of Post-Civilization (Peter Baofu) (*BCIV*)
- • 33. Theory of the Trinity of Modernity to Its After-Postmodern Counterpart (Peter Baofu) (*FHC*; Ch.10 of *FCD*)
- • 32. Transformative Theory of Aesthetic Experience (Peter Baofu) (*FAE*)
- (• 17). Theory of Post-Capitalism (Peter Baofu) (Ch.10 of *FCD*; Chs.2 & 4 of *FPHC*; *BCPC*)
- (• 16). Theory of Post-Democracy (Peter Baofu) (Ch.10 of *FCD*; Chs.3 & 4 of *FPHC*; *BDPD*)
- (• 5). Theory of Existential Dialectics, or the Holistic Theory of Knowledge (Peter Baofu) (*FHC*; *FCD*; *FPHC*; *BDPD*; *FC*; *FAE*; *ALD; FIA; FPHK*; etc,)
- (• 4). Contrastive Theory of Rationality (Peter Baofu) (*FPHML*)
- (• 2). Theory of Methodological Holism (Peter Baofu) (Ch.1 of *FCD*; Ch.1of *FPHC*; *Sec.2.1* & *Sec.2.5* of *BCPC*; *FC*; *FPHK*; etc.)

(continued on next page)

Table 4.43. Theories on Civilizational Holism (Part III)

III. Theories in Relation to the Mind

—*At the Biological Theoretical Level*

- 31. Theory of Contrastive Advantages (Peter Baofu) (*Sec.2.6* & Ch.10 of *FCD; BNN*)
- (• 24). Theory of Floating Consciousness (Peter Baofu) (Ch.10 of *FCD*; Chs.1 & 4 of *FPHC*)

—*At the Psychological Theoretical Level*

- 30. Contrarian Theory of Personality (Peter Baofu) (*FPHP*)
- 29. Theory of Virtual Sexuality (Peter Baofu) (*FPHS*)
- 28. Expansive-Contractive Theory of Martial Arts (Peter Baofu) (*FPHMA*)
- 27. Multilogical Theory of Learning (Peter Baofu) (*FPHL*)
- 26. Comprehensive Theory of Creative Thinking (Peter Baofu) (*FPHCT*)
- 25. Theory of Unfolding Unconsciousness—also known as the Unfolding Theory of Anomalous Experience (Peter Baofu) (*FPHU*)
- 24. Theory of Floating Consciousness (Peter Baofu) (Ch.10 of *FCD*; Chs.1 & 4 of *FPHC*)
- 23. Theory of Cognitive Partiality (Peter Baofu) (*Sec.2.4* of *FCD*; *Sec.4.5.1.1* of *BCPC*)
- 22. Theory of Emotional Non-Neutrality (Peter Baofu) (*Sec.2.5* of *FCD*; *Sec.4.5.2* of of *BCPC*)
- 21. Theory of Behavioral Alteration (Peter Baofu) (*Sec.4.5.3* of *BCPC*)

Table 4.43. Theories on Civilizational Holism (Part IV)

IV. Theories in Relation to Society

—*At the Organizational Theoretical Level*

- 20. Theory of E-Civic Alienation (Peter Baofu) (Ch.7 of *FCD*)
- 19. Combinational Theory of Organization (Peter Baofu) (*FPHO*; Ch.6 of *ALD*)

—*At the Institutional Theoretical Level*

- 18. Reconstruction of Theory of Law (Peter Baofu) (*FPHLAW*)
- 17. Theory of Post-Capitalism (Peter Baofu) (Ch.10 of *FCD*; Chs.2 & 4 of *FPHC*; *BCPC*)
- 16. Theory of Post-Democracy (Peter Baofu) (Ch.10 of *FCD*; Chs.3 & 4 of *FPHC*; *BDPD*)
- 15. Dynamic Theory of Comparative Political Systems (Peter Baofu) (*ALD*)

—*At the Systemic Theoretical Level*

- 14. Contingent Theory of Urban Planning (Peter Baofu) (*FPHUP*)
- 13. Totalistic Theory of Communication (Peter Baofu) (*FPHMM*; *FCD*; *FHC*)
- 12. Ambivalent Theory of Technology (Peter Baofu) (*FPHE*; *FCD*; *FHC*)
- 11. Multifaceted Theory of War and Peace (Peter Baofu) (Ch.9 of *FCD*; Ch.1 of *FPHK*)
- 10. Theory of Post-Humanity (Peter Baofu) (Ch.7 of *FHC*; Chs.3, & 10 of *FCD*; Chs.1, 3 & 4 of *FPHC*; and other books of mine)
- 9. Theory of the Cyclical Progression of System Integration and Fragmentation (Peter Baofu) (Chs.9-10 of *FCD*)
- 8. Synthetic Theory of Information Architecture (Peter Baofu) (*FIA*)

(continued on next page)

Table 4.43. Theories on Civilizational Holism (Part V)

IV. Theories in Relation to Society (*cont'd*)
—At the Structural Theoretical Level
- 7. Theory of the Cyclical Progression of Hegemony (Peter Baofu) (Chs.9-10 of *FCD*; Chs.1, 3 & 4 of *FPHC*; *BDPD*)
- 6. Theory of the Cyclical Progression of Empire-Building (Peter Baofu) (*BWT*)

V. Meta-Theories (in Relation to Theories)
—At the Ontological Meta-Theoretical Level
- 5. Theory of Existential Dialectics, or the Holistic Theory of Knowledge (Peter Baofu) (*FHC*; *FCD*; *FPHC*; *BDPD*; *FC*; *FAE*; *ALD; FIA; FPHK*; etc,)
- 4. Contrastive Theory of Rationality (Peter Baofu) (*FPHML*)

—At the Methodological Meta-Theoretical Level
- 3. Critical-Dialectic Theory of Formal Science (Peter Baofu) (*FPHFS*)
- 2. Theory of Methodological Holism (Peter Baofu) (Ch.1 of *FCD*; Ch.1of *FPHC*; *Sec.2.1* & *Sec.2.5* of *BCPC*; *FC*; *FPHK*; etc.)

VI. Theories in Relation to the Rest
—At Other Levels (Historical)
- 1. Theory of the Evolution from Pre-Modernity to After-Postmodernity (Peter Baofu) (*FHC*; Ch.9-10 of *FCD*; *FPHC*)

Notes: All these theories are my constructions, as some of the main contributions of my grant project on civilization and its future. These examples are solely illustrative (not exhaustive), and some of the items can be reclassified somewhere else. Nor are they always mutually exclusive. Since they are generalities, exceptions are expected.
Sources: From my previous books.

Table 4.44. Three Great Future Transformations of Mind Games

- **Virtual Games**
  —Ex: online chess
  —Ex: virtual experience

- **Novel Games**
  —Ex: new chess variants
  —Ex: new chess engines

- **Post-Human Mind Games**
  —Ex: the quest for broader/deeper mental benefits of chess playing
  —Ex: games designed for the evolution of the mind into different body-less forms (e.g., "floating consciousness," "hyper-spatial consciousness," "unfolding unconsciousness")

Notes: The examples in the categories are solely illustrative (not exhaustive), and the comparison is relative (not absolute), nor are they necessarily mutually exclusive. And some can be easily re-classified elsewhere. As generalities, they allow exceptions.
Sources: From *Sec. 4.16* of *FPHCHESS*. See text for more info. Also, consult *FCD* for strategy and tactics in warfare and *FPHO* for strategy and tactics in organization.

BIBLIOGRAPHY

Adler, Alfred. 1956. *The Individual Psychology of Alfred Adler*. H. L. Ansbacher and R. R. Ansbacher, eds. New York: Harper Torchbooks.

Adler, Margot. 2006. *Drawing Down the Moon: Witches, Druids, Goddess-Worshippers, and Other Pagans in America*. New York: Penguin.

Adrian, William. 2005. "Truth, Freedom, and (Dis)order in the American University" (April 02). *Christian Higher Education*, 4: 2, 145-154.

Allen, Richard. 2001. "Psuedo Shamans Cherokee Statement." <http://www.thepeoplespaths.net/Articles2001/RLAllen-CherokeeStatement-Shamans.htm>.

Altermann, W.; & J. Kazmierczak. 2003. "Archean Microfossils: A Reappraisal of Early Life on Earth." *Research in Microbiology*, 154 (9): 611–17.

American Association for the Advancement of Science (AAAS). 2006. "Statement on the Teaching of Evolution" (February 16). <http://www.aaas.org/news/releases/2006/pdf/0219boardstatement.pdf>.

_____.1922. "AAAS Resolution: Present Scientific Status of the Theory of Evolution" (December 26). <http://archives.aaas.org/docs/resolutions.php?doc_id=450>.

American Heritage Dictionary of the English Language (AHDEL). 2006. "Animism." Boston, MA: Houghton Mifflin.

American Indian Cultural Support (AICS). 2010. "Declaration of War Against Exploiters of Lakota Spirituality" (May 16). <http://www.aics.org/war.html>.

Amesbury, Richard. 2005. "Fideism." *Stanford Encyclopedia of Philosophy*. <http://plato.stanford.edu/entries/fideism/>.

Aschheim, Steven E. 2000. *Nietzsche Legacy in Germany, 1890-1990*. Stuttgart: J.B. Metzler.

Bache, Christopher. 1996. "A Perinatal Interpretation of Frightening Near-Death Experiences: A Dialogue with Kenneth Ring." *Journal of Near-Death Studies*, 15(2). <http://primal-page.com/bache4.htm#ceb>.

_____.1991. "Mysticism and Psychedelics: The Case of the Dark Night." <http://primal-page.com/night.htm>.

_____.1985. "A Reappraisal of Teresa of Avila's Supposed Hysteria." *Journal of Religion and Health,* 24 (4). <http://primal-page.com/bache3.htm>.

Baggini, Julian. 2003. *Atheism: A Very Short Introduction.* Oxford: Oxford University Press.

Bainbridge, William Sims; & Rodney Stark. 1987. *A Theory of Religion.* New York: P. Lang.

Barker, E. 1983. "The Ones Who Got Away: People Who Attend Unification Church Workshops and Do Not Become Moonies." *Of Gods and Men: New Religious Movements in the West.* E. Barker, ed. Macon, GA: Mercer University Press.

Baofu, Peter. 2010. *The Future of Post-Human Chess: A Preface to a New Theory of Tactics and Strategy.* Cambridge, England: Cambridge International Science Publishing, Ltd.

______.2010a. *The Future of Post-Human Geology: A Preface to a New Theory of Statics and Dynamics.* Cambridge, England: Cambridge International Science Publishing, Ltd.

______.2010b. *Beyond Ethics to Post-Ethics: A Preface to a New Theory of Morality and Immorality.* Charlotte, NC: Information Age Publishing.

______.2010c. *Beyond Cosmology to Post-Cosmology: A Preface to a New Theory of Different Worlds.* Cambridge, England: Cambridge International Science Publishing, Ltd.

______.2010d. *The Future of Post-Human Personaltiy: A Preface to a New Theory of Normality and Abnormality.* Cambridge, England: Cambridge International Science Publishing, Ltd.

______.2010e. *The Future of Post-Human War and Peace: A Preface to a New Theory of Aggression and Pacificity.* Cambridge, England: Cambridge Scholars Publishing.

______.2010f. *The Future of Post-Human Formal Science: A Preface to a New Theory of Abstraction and Application.* Cambridge, England: Cambridge Scholars Publishing.

______.2010g. *The Future of Post-Human Law: A Preface to a New Theory of Necessity, Contingency, and Justice.* Cambridge, England: Cambridge Scholars Publishing.

______.2010h. *The Future of Post-Human Sexuality: A Preface to a New Theory of the Body and Spirit of Love Makers.* Cambridge, England: Cambridge Scholars Publishing.

______,2009. *The Future of Post-Human Martial Arts: A Preface to a New Theory of the Body and Spirit of Warriors.* Cambridge, England: Cambridge Scholars Publishing.

______.2009a. *The Future of Post-Human Organization: A Preface to a New Theory of Communication, Decision-Making, and Leadership.* Cambridge, England: Cambridge Scholars Publishing.

______.2009b. *The Future of Post-Human Language: A Preface to a New Theory of Structure, Context, and Learning*. Cambridge, England: Cambridge Scholars Publishing.

______.2009c. *The Future of Post-Human Urban Planning: A Preface to a New Theory of Density, Void, and Sustainability*. Cambridge, England: Cambridge Scholars Publishing.

______.2009d. *The Future of Post-Human Geometry: A Preface to a New Theory of Infinity, Symmetry, and Dimensionality*. Cambridge, England: Cambridge Scholars Publishing.

______.2009e. *The Future of Post-Human Creative Thinking: A Preface to a New Theory of Invention and Innovation*. Cambridge, England: Cambridge Scholars Publishing.

______.2009f. *The Future of Post-Human Mass Media: A Preface to a New Theory of Communication*. Cambridge, England: Cambridge Scholars Publishing.

______.2009g. *The Future of Post-Human Engineering: A Preface to a New Theory of Technology*. Cambridge, England: Cambridge Scholars Publishing.

______.2008. *The Future of Post-Human Mathematical Logic: A Preface to a New Theory of Rationality*. Cambridge, England: Cambridge Scholars Publishing.

______.2008a. *The Future of Post-Human Knowledge: A Preface to a New Theory of Methodology and Ontology*. Oxford, United Kingdom: Chandos Publishing (Oxford) Ltd.

______.2008b. *The Future of Post-Human Unconsciousness: A Preface to a New Theory of Anomalous Experience*. Cambridge, England: Cambridge Scholars Publishing.

______.2008c. *The Future of Information Architecture: Conceiving a New Way to Understand Taxonomy, Network, and Intelligence*. Oxford, United Kingdom: Chandos Publishing (Oxford) Ltd.

______.2007. *The Rise of Authoritarian Liberal Democracy: A Preface to a New Theory of Comparative Political Systems*. Cambridge, England: Cambridge Scholars Publishing.

______.2007a. *The Future of Aesthetic Experience: Conceiving a Better Way to Beauty, Ugliness, and the Rest*. Cambridge, England: Cambridge Scholars Publishing.

______.2007b. *The Future of Complexity: Conceiving a Better Way to Understand Order and Chaos*. London, United Kingdom: World Scientific Publishing Co.

______.2007c. *Beyond the World of Titans, and the Remaking of World Order: A Preface to a New Logic of Empire-Building*. Cambridge, England: Cambridge Scholars Publishing.

______.2006. *Beyond Nature and Nurture: Conceiving a Better Way to Understand*

Genes and Memes. Cambridge, England: Cambridge Scholars Publishing.

______.2006a. *The Future of Post-Human Space-Time: Conceiving a Better Way to Understand Space and Time*. New York: Peter Lang Publishing, Inc.

______.2006b. *Beyond Civilization to Post-Civilization: Conceiving a Better Model of Life Settlement to Supersede Civilization*. New York: Peter Lang Publishing, Inc.

______.2005. *Beyond Capitalism to Post-Capitalism: Conceiving a Better Model of Wealth Acquisition to Supersede Capitalism*. New York: The Edwin Mellen Press.

______.2004. *The Future of Post-Human Consciousness*. New York: The Edwin Mellen Press.

______.2004a. *Beyond Democracy to Post-Democracy: Conceiving a Better Model of Governance to Supersede Democracy*. Volume 1. New York: The Edwin Mellen Press.

______.2004b. *Beyond Democracy to Post-Democracy: Conceiving a Better Model of Governance to Supersede Democracy*. Volume 2. New York: The Edwin Mellen Press.

______.2002. *The Future of Capitalism and Democracy*. Maryland: The University Press of America.

______.2000. *The Future of Human Civilization*. Volume 1. New York: The Edwin Mellen Press.

______.2000a. *The Future of Human Civilization*. Volume 2. New York: The Edwin Mellen Press.

Barbour, Ian G. 1968. "Science and Religion Today." *Science and Religion: New Perspectives on the Dialogue*. Ian G. Barbour, ed. New York: Harper & Row.

Barrow, John D. 1998. *Impossibility: The Limits of Science and the Science of Limits*. Oxford: Oxford University Press.

BBC News 24 (BBC). 2007. Interview with Richard Dawkins conducted by Stephen Sackur for the HardTalk programme (July 24).

Behe, M.J. 1996 "Darwin under the Microscope" (October 29). *New York Times*. <http://www.arn.org/docs/behe/mb_dm11496.htm>.

Berlin, Isaiah. 1969. *Four Essays on Liberty*. London: Oxford University Press.

Biletzki, Anat; & Anat Matar. 2006. "Ludwig Wittgenstein" (Nov. 17). *Stanford Encyclopedia of Philosophy*. <http://plato.stanford.edu/entries/wittgenstein/>.

Bird-David, Nurit. 1999. "'Animism' Revisited: Personhood, Environment and Relational Epistemology." *Current Anthropology*, 40: S67.

Blancarte, Roberto. 2006. "Religion, Church, and State in contemporary Mexico." *Changing Structure of Mexico: Political, Social, and Economic Prospects*. Laura Randall, ed. New York: M.E. Sharpe.

Bonting, Sjoerd Lieuwe. 2005. *Creation and Double Chaos: Science and Theology in Discussion*. Minneapolis: Fortress Press.

Boston Globe, the (BG). 2008. "Pope Cancels Speech at University in Rome" (Janaury 16). <http://www.boston.com/news/world/europe/articles/2008/01/16/pope_cancels_speech_at_university_in_rome/>.

Bowler, Peter J. 2003. *Evolution: The History of an Idea*. Berkeley, CA: University of California Press.

Burkhardt, Margaret; & Mary Gail Nagai-Jacobson. 2002. *Spirituality: Living Our Connectedness*. Abany, NY: Delmar/Thomson Learning.

Bunge, Mario. 1999. *Dictionary of philosophy*. Amherst, MA: Prometheus Books.

Bunting, Madeleine. 2007. "The New Atheists Loathe Religion Far Too Much to Plausibly Challenge It" (May 07). *The Guardian*. <http://www.guardian.co.uk/commentisfree/2007/may/07/comment.religion>.

Campbell, Joseph & Bill Moyers. 1991. *The Power of Myth*. Betty Sue Flowers, ed. New York, New York: Anchor Books.

Caplan, Bryan. 2010. "Why Religious Beliefs Are Irrational, and Why Economists Should Care" (May 09). <http://econfaculty.gmu.edu/bcaplan/ldebate.htm>.

Carroll, Robert. 2009. "Agnosticism" (February 22). *The Skeptic's Dictionary*. <http://skepdic.com/agnosticism.html>.

Carroll, Rory. 2000. "Pope Says Sorry for Sins of Church" (March 13). *The Guardian*. <http://www.guardian.co.uk/world/2000/mar/13/catholicism.religion>.

Catholic Encyclopedia (CE). 2007. "Secularization." <http://www.newadvent.org/cathen/13677a.htm>.

Catholic News Agency (CAN). 2008. "Rejection of Pope's Speech is Fear of Dialogue between Faith and Reason, Professor Says" (January 15). <http://www.catholicnewsagency.com/new.php?n=11454>.

Cavalier-Smith, T. 2006. "Cell Evolution and Earth History: Stasis and Revolution." *Philosophical Transactions of the Royal Society B Biological Sciences*, 361 (1470): 969–1006. <http://www.ncbi.nlm.nih.gov/pmc/articles/PMC1578732/?tool=pmcentrez>.

Center for Inquiry (CI). 2010. "Declaration in Defense of Science and Secularism." <http://www.centerforinquiry.net/dc/>.

Chase, Scott. 1993. "Tachyons" (March). *Physics FAQ*. <http://math.ucr.edu/home/baez/physics/ParticleAndNuclear/tachyons.html>.

Clarke, Arthur C. 1962. *Profiles of the Future; An Inquiry into the Limits of the Possible*. New York, Harper & Row.

Cline, Austin. 2010. "Agnosticism & Thomas Henry: Huxley How Did Huxley Understand Being an Agnostic?" (May 09). <http://atheism.about.com/od/aboutagnosticism/a/huxley.htm>.

Clottes, Jean. 2010. "Paleolithic Cave Art in France" (May 16). <http://www.bradshawfoundation.com/clottes/page7.php>.

Corazzon, Raul. 2007. "Definitions of Ontology: From Nicolai Hartmann to the Present Time." <http://www.formalontology.it/section_4_two.htm>.

Corbett, Dan. 2008. "Introduction to String Theory" (November 23). *ThinkQuest.* <http://library.thinkquest.org/27930/stringtheory1.htm>.

Cousins, Ewert. 1992. "Preface." *Modern esoteric spirituality.* Antoine Faivre, Jacob Needleman, Karen Voss, eds. New York: Crossroad.

Croucher, Rowland, et al. 2003. "Fowler's Stages of Faith in Profile" (January 4). John Mark Ministries. <http://jmm.aaa.net.au/articles/2219.htm>.

Czaplicka, M. A. 1914. *Shamanism in Siberia.* <http://www.sacred-texts.com/sha/sis/sis05.htm>.

Darwin, Charles. 1859. *On the Origin of Species.* London: John Murray.

Davis, Coloquially. 1996. "Joing a 'Cult': Religious Choice or Psychological Aberration?" *Journal of Law and* Health. <http://www.religioustolerance.org/cult_art.htm>.

Dawkins, Richard. 2006. *The God Delusion.* Boston, MA: Houghton Mifflin Co.

DeLong, E.; & N. Pace. 2001. "Environmental Diversity of Bacteria and Archaea." *Systematic Biology*, 50 (4): 470–8.

Dennett, Daniel C. 2007. "The Evaporation of the Powerful Mystique of Religion." Edge: World Question Center. <http://edge.org/q2007/q07_1.html#dennett>.

_____.1995. *Darwin's Dangerous Idea: Evolution and the Meanings of Life.* New York: Simon & Schuster.

Derrida, Jacques. 1984. *The Ear of the Other: Otobiography, Transference, Translation.* Claude Levesque and Christie McDonald, eds. Peggy Kamuf, tr. NY: Schocker Books.

Dimond, Peter. 2010. "Examining the Theological Status of Geocentrism and Heliocentrism and the Devastating Problems This Creates for Baptism of Desire Arguments" (May 09). <http://www.mostholyfamilymonastery.com/Geocentrism.pdf>.

Doolittle, W. F., & E. Bapteste. 2007. "Pattern Pluralism and the Tree of Life Hypothesis" (February). *Proceedings of the National Academy of Sciences of the U.S.A.* 104 (7): 2043–9. <http://www.pnas.org/cgi/pmidlookup?view=long&pmid=17261804>.

Dubuisson, Daniel. 2007. "Exporting the Local: Recent Perspectives on 'Religion' as a Cultural Category." *Religion Compass*: 1.6.

_____.2003. *The Western Construction of Religion: Myths, Knowledge, and Ideology.* William Sayers, tr. Baltimore, MD: Johns Hopkins University Press.

Duenwald, Mary. 2002. "Religion and Health: New Research Revives an Old Debate" (May 07). *New York Times.* <http://query.nytimes.com/gst/fullpage.html?res=9E04E0DE1730F934A35756C0A9649C8B63>.

Duhaime, Jean. 2003. "Les Témoigagnes de Convertis et d'ex-Adeptes (English: The Testimonies of Converts and Former Followers." *New Religions in a*

Postmodern World. Mikael Rothstein and Reender Kranenborg, eds. Aarhus: Aarhus University Press.

Dyall S.; M. Brown; & P. Johnson. 2004. "Ancient Invasions: From Endosymbionts to Organelles." *Science*, 304 (5668): 253–57. <http://www.sciencemag.org/cgi/content/abstract/304/5668/253>.

Dzuback, Mary Ann. 1990. *Hutchins, Adler, and the University of Chicago: A Critical Juncture.* Chicago, Il: The University of Chicago Press.

Edwards, Paul. 2005. "Atheism." *The Encyclopedia of Philosophy*, 1: 359. Donald M. Borchert, ed.

Ehrlich, Paul. 2000. *Human Natures: Genes, Cultures, and the Human Prospect.* Washington, D.C.: Island Press.

Encyclopedia Britannica (EB). 2007. "Atheism" (June 07). <http://www.1911encyclopedia.org/Atheism>.

Everett, Hugh. 1957. "'Relative State' Formulation of Quantum Mechanics" (July). *Reviews of Modern Physics*, vol. 29, no.3. <http://www.univer.omsk.su/omsk/Sci/Everett/paper1957.html>.

Eskow, R. J. 2006. "Reject Arguments For Intolerance—Even From Atheists" (January 04). *The Huffington Post.* <http://www.huffingtonpost.com/rj-eskow/reject-arguments-for-into_b_13240.html>.

______.2005. "Blind Faith: Sam Harris Attacks Islam" (October 11). *The Huffington Post.* <http://www.huffingtonpost.com/rj-eskow/blind-faith-sam-harris-at_b_8686.html>.

Evans, C. Stephen. 1985. *Philosophy of Religion: Thinking about Faith.* Downers Grove, IL: InterVarsity Press.

Evans-Pritchard, E.E. 1976. *Witchcraft, Magic, and Oracles Among the Azande.* England: Oxford University Press.

Fahlbusch, Erwin; & Geoffrey William Bromiley. 1999. "Panentheism." *The Encyclopedia of Christianity*, 4: 21. <http://books.google.com/books?id=sCY4sAjTGIYC&pg=PA21>.

Falasca-Zamponi, Simonetta. 2000. *Fascist Spectacle: The Aesthetics of Power in Mussolini's Italy.* Berkeley: University of California Press.

Fales, Evan. 2007. "Naturalism and Physicalism." *The Cambridge Companion to Atheism*: 122–131. Michael Martin, ed. England: Cambridge University Press.

Falwell, Jerry. 2001. "Jerry Falwell—Quotations—Seventh quotation" (September 15). <http://www.positiveatheism.org/hist/quotes/foulwell.htm>.

Feldman, Noah. 2005. *Divided by God.* New York: Farrar, Straus and Giroux.

Fernandez-Armesto, Felipe. 2003. *Ideas that Changed the World.* Dorling Kindersley Publishers Ltd.

Finocchiaro, Maurice A. 1989. *The Galileo Affair: A Documentary History.* Berkeley, CA: University of California Press.

Firehammer, Reginald. 2005. "Basic Principles of Ontology" (January 05).

<http://usabig.com/autonomist/philosophy/ontology2.html>.

Fitzgerald, Timothy. 2000. *The Ideology of Religious Studies*. Oxford: Oxford University Press.

Ford, David. 2009. "Theology and Religious Studies for a Multifaith and Secular Society." *Theology and Religious Studies in Higher Education*. D. L. Bird and Simon G. Smith, eds, London: Continuum.

Forterre, P.; N. Benachenhou-Lahfa; F. Confalonieri; M. Duguet; C. Elie; B. Labedan. 1992. "The Nature of the Last Universal Ancestor and the Root of the Tree of Life, Still Open Questions." *BioSystems*, 28 (1–3): 15–32.

Fowler, James W. 1981. *Stages of Faith: The Psychology of Human Development and the Quest for Meaning*. San Francisco, CA: Harper & Row.

Franklin, James. 2001. *The Science of Conjecture: Evidence and Probability Before Pascal*. Baltimore, MD: Johns Hopkins University Press.

Fremont-Barnes, Gregory. 2007. *Encyclopedia of the Age of Political Revolutions and New Ideologies, 1760-1815*. Westport, CT: Greenwood Publishing Group.

Freud, Sigmund. 1950. *Totem and Taboo: Some Points of Agreement between the Mental Lives of Savages and Neurotics*. James Strachey, tr. New York: W. W. Norton & Company.

Futuyma, Douglas J. 2005. *Evolution*. Sunderland, MA: Sinauer Associates, Inc.

Galanter, Marc, ed. 1989. *Cults and New Religious Movements: A Report of the Committee on Psychiatry and Religion of the American Psychiatric Association*. Washington, DC: The Association.

_____.1983. "Unification Church ('Moonie') Dropouts: Psychological Readjustment after Leaving a Charismatic Religious Group." *American Journal of Psychiatry*.

Geisler, Norman. 1999. "Panentheism—Part Two." *Baker Encyclopedia of Christian Apologetics*. <http://www.johnankerberg.org/Articles/_PDF Archives/theological-dictionary/TD1W1001.pdf>.

Giambalvo, Carol, 1993. "Post-Cult Problems: An Exit Counselor's Perspective." *Recovery from Cults: Help for Victims of Psychological and Spiritual Abuse*, Michael D. Langone, ed. New York: W.W. Norton & Company. <http://www.icsahome.com/infoserv_articles/giambalvo_carol_postcult_problems.htm>.

Gledhill, Ruth. 2009. "Archbishop of Westminster Attacks Atheism but Says Nothing on Child Abuse" (May 22). *The Times*. <http://www.timesonline.co.uk/tol/comment/faith/article6334837.ece>.

Gonick, Larry. 1990. *The Cartoon History of the Universe*. New York: Doubleday.

Gott, J. Richard. 2002. *Time Travel in Einstein's Universe*. Boston : Houghton Mifflin.

Gould, S. J. 1991. "Exaptation: A Crucial Tool for an Evolutionary Psychology." *Journal of Social Issues*, 47: 43–65.

Guardian, the (GR). 2001. "Has the World Changed?" (October 11). <http://www.guardian.co.uk/world/2001/oct/11/afghanistan.terrorism2>.

Guth, Alan. 1997. *The Inflationary Universe: The Quest for a New Theory Of Cosmic Origins*. New York: Helix Books.

Habgood, John Stapylton. 1964. *Religion and Science*. London, England: Mills & Boon.

Hadden, J.; & D. Bromley, eds. 1993, *The Handbook of Cults and Sects in America*. Greenwich, CT: JAI Press, Inc.

Harpur, Tom. 2004. *The Pagan Christ: Recovering the Lost Light*. Toronto, Canada: Thomas Allen Publishers.

Harris, Sam. 2006. *Letter to a Christian Nation*. New York: Knopf.

Harrison, Paul A. 1999. *The Elements of Pantheism: Understanding the Divinity in Nature and the Universe*. Boston, MA: Element.

Harrison, Peter. 1998. *The Bible, Protestantism, and the Rise of Natural Science*. Cambridge, England: Cambridge University Press.

Haynes, Jeff. 2009. *Routledge Handbook of Religion & Politics*. New York: Taylor and Francis.

Higginbotham, Joyce. 2002. *Paganism: An Introduction to Earth-Centered Religions*. St. Paul, MN: Llewellyn.

Himma, Kenneth Einar. 2006. "Design Arguments for the Existence of God." The *Internet Encyclopedia of Philosophy*. James Fieser and Bradley Dowden, eds. <http://www.iep.utm.edu/design/#SH1b>.

Hitchens, Christopher. 2007. *God Is Not Great: How Religion Poisons Everything*. New York : Twelve (Hachette, Warner).

Holyoake, G. J. 1896. *The Origin and Nature of Secularism*. London, England: Watts and Co.

Hume, David. 1956. *The Natural History of Religion*. H. E. Root, ed. London: A. & C. Black.

_____.1779. *Dialogues concerning Natural Religion*. London: M.DCC.LXXIX.

Ingold, Tim. 2000. *Totemism, Animism and the Depiction of Animals in The Perception of the Environment: Essays on Livelihood, Dwelling and Skill*. London, England: Routledge.

Internet Encyclopedia of Philosophy, the (IEP). 2006. "English Deism." <http://www.utm.edu/research/iep/d/deismeng.htm#Hume%27s%20Influence>.

Interacademy Panel on International Issues (IAP). 2006. "IAP Statement on the Teaching of Evolution." <http://www.interacademies.net/Object.File/Master/6/150/Evolution%20statement.pdf>.

Introvigne, Massimo. 2001. "The Future of Religion and the Future of New Religions" (June 15). <http://www.cesnur.org/2001/mi_june03.htm>.

_____.1999. "'So Many Evil Things': Anti-Cult Terrorism via the Internet." <http://www.cesnur.org/testi/anticult_terror.htm>.

Isaak, Mark. 2005. "Claim CB090: Evolution without Abiogenesis." TalkOrigins Archive. <http://www.talkorigins.org/indexcc/CB/CB090.html>.

_____.2004. "Index to Creationist Claims, Claim CC363: Requirements for fossilization." The TalkOrigins Archive. <http://www.talkorigins.org/indexcc/CC/CC363.html>.

Johnston, Ian. 1999. "History of Science: Early Modern Geology." Malaspina University-College. <http://records.viu.ca/~johnstoi/darwin/sect2.htm>.

Johnson, P. 1990. "Evolution as Dogma: The Establishment of Naturalism." <http://www.arn.org/docs/johnson/pjdogma1.htm>.

Joyce, Gerald F. 2002. "The Antiquity of RNA-Based Evolution." *Nature*, 418 (6894): 214–21. <http://www.nature.com/nature/journal/v418/n6894/full/418214a.html>.

Kahn, Michael. 2008. "Earliest Known Shaman Grave Site Found: Study" (November 3). *Reuters*. <http://www.reuters.com/article/idUSL3146544>.

Kaiser, D. 2001. "Building a Multicellular Organism." *Annual Review of Genetics,* 35: 103–23. <http://arjournals.annualreviews.org/doi/abs/10.1146/annurev.genet.35.102401.090145>.

Kaku, Michio. 1994. *Hyperspace: A Scientific Odyssey Through Parallel Universes, Time Warps, and The Tenth Dimension.* Illustrations by Robert O'Keefe. Oxford: Oxford University Press.

Kalupahana, David J. 1975. *Causality—The Central Philosophy of Buddhism.* Honolulu: University Press of Hawaii.

Kamiya, Gary. 2007. "Bush's Favorite Historian" (May 08). <http://www.salon.com/news/opinion/kamiya/2007/05/08/alistair_horne/index.html>.

Kaufman, Marc. 2006. "Think Tank Will Promote Thinking" (November 15). *The Washington Post.* <http://www.washingtonpost.com/wp-dyn/content/article/2006/11/14/AR2006111401176.html>.

Kenny, Anthony John Patrick. 2006. *What I believe*. New York: Continuum.

Kehoe, Alice Beck. 2000. *Shamans and Religion: An Anthropological Exploration in Critical Thinking*. Prospect Heights, IL: Waveland Press.

King, Barbara. 2007. *Evolving God: A Provocative View on the Origins of Religion*. New York: Doubleday Publishing.

Knoll, K. L. 2009. "'The Ethics of Being a Theologian" (July 27). *Chronicle of Higher Education*.

Koenig, Harold G.; & Harvey Cohen. 2001. *The Link between Religion and Health: Psychoneuroimmunology and the Faith Factor*. Oxford: Oxford University Press.

Koestler, Arthur. 1959. *The Sleepwalkers: A History of Man's Changing Vision of the Universe*. Middlesex, England: Penguin Books.

Kosmin, Barry. 2007. "Contemporary Secularity and Secularism." *Secularism & Secularity: Contemporary International Perspectives*. Barry A. Kosmin and Ariela Keysar, eds. Hartford, CT: Institute for the Study of Secularism in Society and Culture.

Kottak, Conrad Phillip. 2005. *Window on Humanity: A Concise Introduction to Anthropology*. New York: The McGraw–Hill Companies, Inc.

Kowalewski, David. 1980. "Protest for Religious Rights in the USSR: Characteristics and Consequences." *Russian Review*, 39 (4): 426-441.

Kress, Howard; R. Sosis; & J. S. Boster. 2007. "Scars for War: Evaluating Alternative Signaling Explanations for Cross-Cultural Variance in Ritual Costs." *Evolution and Human Behavior*, 28: 234–247.

Kuhn, Thomas S. 1957. *The Copernican Revolution*. Cambridge: Harvard University Press.

Kunin, V.; L. Goldovsky; N. Darzentas; C. Ouzounis. 2005. "The Net of Life: Reconstructing the Microbial Phylogenetic Network." *Genome Research*, 15 (7): 954–9. <http://www.genome.org/cgi/pmidlookup?view=long&pmid=15965028>.

Kusukawa, Sachiko. 1999. "Starry Messenger. The Telescope." Department of History and Philosophy of Science of the University of Cambridge. <http://www.hps.cam.ac.uk/starry/galtele.html>.

Kutschera, U.; & K. Niklas. 2004. "The Modern Theory of Biological Evolution: An Expanded Synthesis." *Naturwissenschaften*, 91 (6): 255–76. <http://springerlink.metapress.com/content/grn8g0cmyya3jb69/>.

Lang, B.; M. Gray; & G. Burger. 1999. "Mitochondrial Genome Evolution and the Origin of Eukaryotes." *Annual Review of Genetics*, 33: 351–97. <http://arjournals.annualreviews.org/doi/abs/10.1146/annurev.genet.33.1.351>.

Lapidus, Ira M. 1975. "The Separation of State and Religion in the Development of Early Islamic Society." *International Journal of Middle East Studies*, 6 (4): 363-385.

Larson, E. J; & L. Witham, 1997. "Scientists Are Still Keeping the Faith." *Nature*, 386: 435–436. <http://www.nature.com/doifinder/10.1038/386435a0>.

_____.1997a. "Many Scientists See God's Hand in Evolution." *Reports of the National Center for Science Education*, 17 (6): 33. <http://ncse.com/rncse/17/6/many-scientists-see-gods-hand-evolution>.

Latreille, A. 2002. "French Revolution." *New Catholic Encyclopedia*, 5: 972-973.

Lewis, Bob. 2007. "'Jerry's Kids' Urged to Challenge 'Radical Secularism'" (May 19). *The Christian Post*. <http://www.christianpost.com/article/20070519/27517_'Jerry's_Kids'_Urged_to_Challenge_'Radical_Secularism'.htm>.

Lewontin, R.; & S. Gould. 1979. "The Spandrels of San Marco and the Panglossian Paradigm: A Critique of the Adaptationist Programme."

Proceedings of the Royal Society B, 305: 581–598.

Lieberman, Philip. 1991. *Uniquely Human*. Cambridge, MA: Harvard University Press.

Lienard, Pascal; & P. Boyer. 2006. "Whence Collective rituals? A Cultural Selection Model of Ritualized Behavior." *American Anthropologist*, 108): 824–827.

Lindberg, David; & Ronald L. Numbers. 2010. "Beyond War and Peace: A Reappraisal of the Encounter between Christianity and Science" (May 09) <http://www.asa3.org/ASA/PSCF/1987/PSCF9-87Lindberg.html>.

Luisi, P.L; F. Ferri; P. Stano. 2006. "Approaches to Semi-Synthetic Minimal Cells: A Review." *Naturwissenschaften*, 93 (1): 1–13. <http://www.springerlink.com/content/y218jk71n1k40785/>.

Luper, Steven. 1999. *Existing: An Introduction to Existential Thought*. Europe: McGraw-Hill Education.

Maier, Hans. 2004. *Totalitarianism and Political Religions*. Jodi Bruhn, tr. New York: Routledge.

Maliowski, Bronisław. 1954. *Magic, Science and Religion and Other Essays*. USA: Anchor Books.

Mandell, Arnold. 1980. "The Psychobiology of Transcendence: God in the Brain." *The Psychobiology of Consciousness*. Richard J. Davidson and Julian M. Davidson, eds. New York: Plenum Publishing.

Martin, W. 2005. "The Missing Link between Hydrogenosomes and Mitochondria." *Trends in Microbiology*, 13 (10): 457–59.

Martinez-Torron, Javier. 2001. "Freedom of Religion in the Case Law of the Spanish Constitutional Court." *Brigham Young University Law Review*.

Marx, Karl. 1844. *A Contribution to the Critique of Hegel's Philosophy of Right*. Paris: Deutsch-Französische Jahrbücher. <http://www.marxists.org/archive/marx/works/1843/critique-hpr/intro.htm>.

Mauss, Marcel. 1972. *A General Theory of Magic*. R. Brain, tr. New York: Norton Library.

Mayhew, P.J. 2007. "Why Are There So Many Insect Species? Perspectives from Fossils and Phylogenies." *Biological Reviews, Cambridge Philosophical Society*, 82 (3): 425–54. <http://www3.interscience.wiley.com/journal/117981242/abstract>.

McAleer, Neil. 1987. *The Mind-Boggling Universe*. New York: Doubleday & Co.

McFadden, G. 1999. "Endosymbiosis and Evolution of the Plant Cell." *Current Opinion in Plant Biology*, 2 (6): 513–19.

McGrath, Alister E. 2006. *The Twilight of Atheism*, New York: Random House.

Merriam-Webster's Collegiate Dictionary Online (MWD). 2010. "Sacred" (May 10). <http://www.m-w.com/dictionary/sacred>.

_____.2007. "Agency" (March 20). <http://www.m-w.com/dictionary/agency>.

Morgan, Philip. 2003. *Fascism in Europe, 1919-1945*, New York: Routledge.

Mossner, Ernest Campbell. 1967. "Deism." *The Encyclopedia of Philosophy*, 2: 326-336.

Munby, D. L. 1963. *The Idea of a Secular Society*. London, England: Oxford University Press.

Murphy, Todd. 2010. "Spiritual Aptitude Test" (May 18). <http://www.shaktitechnology.com/anchored_TL_test.htm>.

Narr, Karl. 2008. "Prehistoric Religion." *Britannica Online Encyclopedia*. <http://concise.britannica.com/oscar/print?articleId=109434&fullArticle=true&tocId=52333>.

NationMaster.com (NM). 2010. "Europe>Belarus>Religion" (May 23). <http://www.nationmaster.com/country/bo-belarus/rel-religion>.

______.2010a. "Europe>Moldova>Religion" (May 23). <http://www.nationmaster.com/country/md-moldova/rel-religion>.

______.2010b. "Asia>Georgia>Religion" (May 23). <http://www.nationmaster.com/country/gg-georgia/rel-religion>.

New Scientist (NS). 2008. "Special Report on Evolution" (January 19). <http://www.newscientist.com/topic/evolution>.

NewsHour (NH). 2000. "A Papal Apology" (March 13). <http://www.pbs.org/newshour/bb/religion/jan-june00/apology_3-13.html>.

Niebuhr, Reinhold. 2010. "Secularized Civilization" (May 22). <http://www.religion-online.org/showarticle.asp?title=472>.

Nielsen, Kai. 2010. "Atheism." *Encyclopædia Britannica*. <http://www.britannica.com/EBchecked/topic/40634/atheism>.

______.& D. Z. Phillips. 2005. *Wittgensteinian Fideism?* London, England: SCM.

Nietzsche, Friedrich. 1990. *The Anti–Christ*. Michael Tanner, intr. R. J. Hollingdale, tr. Penguin Books.

Norris, Pippa; & Ronald Inglehart. 2004. *Sacred and Secular. Religion and Politics Worldwide*. Cambridge, MA: Cambridge University Press.

Nova Online (NO). 2000. "Time Can Vary." <http://www.pbs.org/wgbh/nova/time/thinktime.html>.

O' Leary, Don. 2006. Roman *Catholicism and Modern Science: A History*. New York: Continuum Books.

Ohno, S. 1997. "The Reason for as well as the Consequence of the Cambrian Explosion in Animal Evolution." *Journal of Molecular Evolution*, 44 (1): S23–7.

Owen, H. P. 1971. *Concepts of Deity*. London: Macmillan.

Owen, Richard. 2009. "Pope Says Condoms Are Not the Solution to Aids—They Make it Worse" (March 17). *Times Online*. <http://www.timesonline.co.uk/tol/comment/faith/article5923927.ece>.

Oxford Companion to Philosophy (OCP). 1995. "Humanism." Ted Honderich, ed.

England: Oxford University Press.

Page, Jeremy. 2005. "The Rise of Russian Muslims Worries Orthodox Church" (August 05). *The Times*. <http://www.timesonline.co.uk/tol/news/world/article551693.ece>.

Patri, Umesh; & Prativa Devi. 1990. "Progress of Atheism in India: A Historical Perspective" (February). Atheist Centre 1940-1990 Golden Jubilee. <http://www.positiveatheism.org/india/s1990a22.htm>.

Penfield, Wilder. 1955. "The Role of the Temporal Cortex in Certain Psychical Phenomena." *The Journal of Mental Science*, 424.

Persinger, Michael. 1983. "Mystical Experiences as Artifacts of Temporal Lobe Function: A General Hypothesis." *Perceptual and Motor Skills*, 57: 1255-1262.

Peretó, J. 2005. "Controversies on the Origin of Life." International Microbiology, 8 (1): 23–31. <http://www.im.microbios.org/0801/0801023.pdf>.

Polkinghorne, John. 1998. *Science and Theology: An Introduction*. Minneapolis, MN: Fortress Press.

Pollard, William Grosvenor. 1961. *Physicist and Christian: A Dialogue between the Communities*. Greenwich, CT: Seabury Press.

Poole, A.; & D. Penny. 2007. "Evaluating Hypotheses for the Origin of Eukaryotes." *Bioessays*, 29 (1): 74–84. <http://www3.interscience.wiley.com/journal/114030360/abstract>.

Poster, Carol. 2005. "Protagoras (c.490–c.420 BCE)" (April 27). *The Internet Encyclopedia of Philosophy*. <http://www.iep.utm.edu/p/protagor.htm>.

Psenner, R.; & J. T. Trevors. 2001. "From Self-Assembly of Life to Present-Day Bacteria: A Possible Role for Nanocells." *FEMS Microbiology Reviews*. <http://www3.interscience.wiley.com/journal/118975234/abstract?CRETRY=1&SRETRY=0>.

Raman, Shankar. 1997. Lectures on Literary Theory. Cambridge, MA: MIT (spring).

Ratzsch, Del. 2009. "Teleological Arguments for God's Existence." *The Stanford Encyclopedia of Philosophy* (Winter). Edward N. Zalta, ed. <http://plato.stanford.edu/archives/win2009/entries/teleological-arguments/>.

Rocco, Alyce. 2007. "25 Quotes About God" (November 29). <http://www.associatedcontent.com/article/463839/does_god_exist.html>.

Rossano, Matt. 2007. *Supernaturalizing Social Life: Religion and the Evolution of Human Cooperation*. <http://www2.selu.edu/Academics/Faculty/mrossano/recentpubs/Supernaturalizing.pdf>.

Rose, Charlie. 1996. "Carl Sagan's Last Interview" (Part 1 of 3). <http://www.youtube.com/watch?v=jod7v-m573k>.

Rowe, William L. 1998. "Atheism." *Routledge Encyclopedia of Philosophy*, 10.

Edward Craig, ed.

Russell, Bertrand. 2004. *History of Western Philosophy*. New York: Routledge.

Russell, Jeffrey. 1997. *Inventing the Flat Earth: Columbus and Modern Historians*. New York : Praeger.

Rutherford, Matthew. 2008. "The Evolution of Morality." <http://eprints.gla.ac.uk/3723/1/rutherford3723.pdf>.

Salak, Kira. 2010. ""Lost Souls of the Peyote Trail" (May 16). National Geographic Adventure. <http://www.kirasalak.com/Peyote.html>.

_____.2010a. "Hell and Back" (May 16). National Geographic Adventure. <http://www.kirasalak.com/Peru.html>.

Schloss, P.; J. Handelsman. 2004. "Status of the Microbial Census." *Microbiology and Molecular Biology Reviews,* 68 (4): 686–91. <http://www.ncbi.nlm.nih.gov/pubmed/15590780>.

Schopf, J. 2006. "Fossil Evidence of Archaean Life." *Philosophical Transactions of the Royal Society: B Biological Sciences*, 361 (1470): 869–85. <http://www.ncbi.nlm.nih.gov/pmc/articles/PMC1578735/?tool=pmcentrez>.

_____.1994. "Disparate Rates, Differing Fates: Tempo and Mode of Evolution Changed from the Precambrian to the Phanerozoic." *Proceedings of the National Academy of the Sciences of the USA*, 91 (15): 6735–42. <http://www.ncbi.nlm.nih.gov/pmc/articles/PMC44277/?tool=pmcentrez>.

Schmitt, Karl M. 1962. "Catholic Adjustment to the Secular State: the Case of Mexico, 1867-1911." *Catholic Historical Review,* 48 (2): 182–204. <http://www.jstor.org/pss/25017032?cookieSet=1>.

Segal, Robert. 2004. *Myth: A Very Short Introduction.* Oxford: Oxford University Press.

Sem, Tatyana. 2010. "Shamanic Healing Rituals" (May 16). Russian Museum of Ethnography. <http://www.museum.state.il.us/exhibits/changing/journey/healing.html>.

Sharratt, Michael. 1994. *Galileo: Decisive Innovator*. Cambridge, MA: Cambridge University Press.

Sheldrake, Philip. 2007. *A Brief History of Spirituality*. Malden, MA: Blackwell Pub.

Shermer, Michael. 2004. "Why Are We Moral: The Evolutionary Origins of Morality." *The Science of Good and Evil.* New York: Times Books.

_____.1999. *How We Believe: Science, Skepticism, and the Search for God.* New York: William H Freeman.

_____.1999a. "Why People Believe in God: An Empirical Study on a Deep Question." *American Humanist Association.* <http://www.findarticles.com/p/articles/mi_m1374/is_6_59/ai_57800244>.

Shirer, William. 1960. *The Rise and Fall of the Third Reich, a History of Nazi*

Germany. New York, Simon and Schuster.

Shlain, Leonard. 1991. *Art and Physics: Parallel Visions in Space,Time, and Light*. New York: William Morrow and Co., Inc.

Smith, George H. 1989. *Atheism: The Case against God*. Amherst, New York: Prometheus Books.

Sosis, Richard; & Candace Alcorta. 2003. "Signaling, Solidarity, and the Sacred: The Evolution of Religious Behavior." *Evolutionary Anthropology*, (12): 264–274.

Speyrer, John. 2010. "Mysticism and Psychopathology" (May 18). <http://primal-page.com/templobe.htm>.

Spielvogel, Jackson. 2005. *Western Civilization: Combined Volume*. Stamford, CT: Thomson Wadsworth.

Stanford Encyclopedia of Philosophy (SEP). 2007. "Pantheism" (May 17). <http://plato.stanford.edu/entries/pantheism/#Ath>.

Stark, Rodney; & Roger Finke. 2000. *Acts of Faith: Explaning the Human Side of Religion*. Berkeley, CA: University of California Press.

Tallet, Frank. 1991. *Religion, Society and Politics in France Since 1789*. New York: Continuum International Publishing.

Tambiah, S. J. 1990. *Magic, Science, Religion, and the Scope of Rationality*. Cambridge: Cambridge University Press.

Time Magazine (TIME). 1931. "Staggerers Unstaggered" (December 07). <http://www.time.com/time/magazine/article/0,9171,930406,00.html>.

Tipler, Frank J.; & John Barrow. 1986. *The Anthropic Cosmological Principle*. John A. Wheeler, foreword. Oxford, England: Oxford University Press.

Toner, P. 1909. "The Existence of God: The argument from Design." *The Catholic Encyclopedia*. New York: Robert Appleton Company. <http://www.newadvent.org/cathen/06608b.htm#IBc>.

Trevors, J.T., & D. Abel. 2004. "Chance and Necessity Do not Explain the Origin of Life." *Cell Biology International*, 28 (11): 729–39. <http://www.cellbiolint.org/cbi/028/cbi0280729.htm>.

U.S. Department of State (USDS). 2009. "Kazakhstan: International Religious Freedom Report 2007." <http://www.state.gov/g/drl/rls/irf/2009/127366.htm>.

_____.2007. "Russia: International Religious Freedom Report 2007." <http://www.state.gov/g/drl/rls/irf/2007/90196.htm>.

Valentine. J.W.; & D. Jablonski. 2003. "Morphological and Developmental Macroevolution: A Paleontological Perspective." *International Journal of Developmental Biology*, 47 (7–8): 517–22. <http://www.ijdb.ehu.es/web/paper.php?doi=14756327>.

_____.D. Jablonski; & D. Erwin. 1999. "Fossils, Molecules and Embryos: New

Perspectives on the Cambrian Explosion" (March 01). *Development*, 126 (5): 851–9. <http://dev.biologists.org/cgi/reprint/126/5/ 851>.

Voltaire, Francois-Marie Arouet. 1901. "On the Existence of God." *The Works of Voltaire.* William F. Fleming. Werner, tr.

Wade, Nicholas. 2007. "Scientist Finds the Beginnings of Morality in Primate Behavior" (March 20). *New York Times.* <http://www.nytimes.com/2007/03/20/science/20moral.html?_r=2&pagewanted=all&oref=slogin>.

_____.2006. *Before The Dawn, Discovering the Lost History of Our Ancestors.* London: Penguin Books.

Wallace, B. Alan, ed. 2003. *Buddhism & Science: Breaking New Ground.* New York: Columbia University Press.

Walsh, T. 2006. "Combinatorial Genetic Evolution of Multiresistance." *Current Opinion in Microbiology*, 9 (5): 476–82.

Ward, Keith. 2006. *Is Religion Dangerous?* London: Lion.

Waters, E. R. 2003. "Molecular Adaptation and the Origin of Land Plants." *Molecular Phylogenetics and Evolution*, 29 (3): 456–63.

Weber, Max. 1930. *The Protestant Ethic and the Spirit of Capitalism.* Talcott Parsons, tr. New York: Scribner.

Whitlock, G. 1996. "Roger Boscovich, Benedict de Spinoza and Friedrich Nietzsche: The Untold Story." *Nietzsche-Studien*, 25.

Wiebe, Donald. 2000. *The Politics of Religious Studies: The Continuing Conflict with Theology in the Academy.* New York: Palgrave Macmillian.

Wikipedia (WK). 2010. "Religious Studies" (May 08). <http://en.wikipedia.org/ wiki/Religious_studies>.

_____.2010a. "Theology" (May 08). <http://en.wikipedia.org/wiki/Theology>.

_____.2010b. "Religion" (May 08). <http://en.wikipedia.org/wiki/Religion>.

_____.2010c. "Spirituality" (May 08). <http://en.wikipedia.org/wiki/Spirituality>.

_____.2010d. "Philosophy of Religion" (May 08). <http://en.wikipedia.org/ wiki/Philosophy_of_religion>.

_____.2010e. "Pantheism" (May 08). <http://en.wikipedia.org/wiki/Pantheism>.

_____.2010f. "Panentheism" (May 08). <http://en.wikipedia.org/wiki/ Panentheism>.

_____.2010g. "Deism" (May 08). <http://en.wikipedia.org/wiki/Deism>.

_____.2010h. "Theism" (May 09). <http://en.wikipedia.org/wiki/Theism>.

_____.2010i. "Agnosticism" (May 09). <http://en.wikipedia.org/wiki/ Agnosticism>.

_____.2010j. "Atheism" (May 09). <http://en.wikipedia.org/wiki/Atheism>.

_____.2010k. "Criticism of Atheism" (May 09). <http://en.wikipedia.org/wiki/

Criticism_of_atheism>.

_____.2010l. "Relationship between Religion and science" (May 09). <http://en.wikipedia.org/wiki/Science_and_religion>.

_____.2010m. "Secularism" (May 09). <http://en.wikipedia.org/wiki/Secularism>.

_____.2010n. "Separation of Church and State" (May 09). <http://en.wikipedia.org/wiki/Separation_of_church_and_state>.

_____.2010o. "Faith" (May 10). <http://en.wikipedia.org/wiki/Faith>.

_____.2010p. "Fideism" (May 10). <http://en.wikipedia.org/wiki/Fideism>.

_____.2010q. "William James" (May 10). <http://en.wikipedia.org/wiki/William_James>.

_____.2010r. "Magic (Paranormal)" (May 11). <http://en.wikipedia.org/wiki/Magic_(paranormal)>.

_____.2010s. "Magic and Religion" (May 11). <http://en.wikipedia.org/wiki/Magic_and_religion>.

_____.2010t. "Magical Thinking" (May 11). <http://en.wikipedia.org/wiki/Magical_thinking>.

_____.2010u. "Teleological Argument" (May 12). <http://en.wikipedia.org/wiki/Teleological_argument>.

_____.2010v. "Evolutionary Origins of Religion" (May 13). <http://en.wikipedia.org/wiki/Evolutionary_origin_of_religions>.

_____.2010w. "Evolutionary Psychology of Religion" (May 13). <http://en.wikipedia.org/wiki/Evolutionary_psychology_of_religion>.

_____.2010x. "Religious Conversion" (May 14). <http://en.wikipedia.org/wiki/Religion_conversion>.

_____.2010y. "Proselytism" (May 14). <http://en.wikipedia.org/wiki/Proselytism>.

_____.2010z. "New Religious Movement" (May 15). <http://en.wikipedia.org/wiki/New_religious_movements>.

_____.2010aa. "Opposition to Cults and New Religious Movements" (May 15). <http://en.wikipedia.org/wiki/Opposition_to_cults_and_new_religious_movements>.

_____.2010bb. "Shamanism" (May 16). <http://en.wikipedia.org/wiki/Shamanism>.

_____.2010cc. "Anthropology of Religion" (May 16). <http://en.wikipedia.org/wiki/Anthropology_of_religion>.

_____.2010dd. "Animism" (May 17). <http://en.wikipedia.org/wiki/Animism>.

_____.2010ee. "Criticism of Religion" (May 18). <http://en.wikipedia.org/wiki/Criticism_of_religion>.

_____.2010ff. "New Atheists" (May 18). <http://en.wikipedia.org/wiki/New_

atheists>.

_____.2010gg. "Psychology of Religion" (May 19). <http://en.wikipedia.org/wiki/Psychology_of_religion>.

_____.2010hh. "Stages of Faith Development" (May 19). <http://en.wikipedia.org/wiki/Stages_of_faith_development>.

_____.2010ii. "Evolution" (May 20). <http://en.wikipedia.org/wiki/Evolution>.

_____.2010jj. "Objections to Evolution" (May 20). <http://en.wikipedia.org/wiki/Objections_to_evolution>.

_____.2010kk. "Heliocentrism" (May 21). <http://en.wikipedia.org/wiki/Heliocentrism>.

_____.2010ll. "Geocentrism" (May 21). <http://en.wikipedia.org/wiki/Geoocentrism>.

_____.2010mm. "Equaint" (May 21). <http://en.wikipedia.org/wiki/Equaint>.

_____.2010nn. "Galileo Affair" (May 21). <http://en.wikipedia.org/wiki/Galileo_affair>.

_____.2010oo. "Galileo Galilei" (May 21). <http://en.wikipedia.org/wiki/Galileo_Galilei>.

_____.2010pp. "Secularization" (May 22). <http://en.wikipedia.org/wiki/Secularization>.

_____.2010qq. "Secularism" (May 22). <http://en.wikipedia.org/wiki/Secularism>.

_____.2010rr. "Sociology of Religion" (May 22). <http://en.wikipedia.org/wiki/Sociology_of_religion>.

_____.2010ss. "Antireligion" (May 23). <http://en.wikipedia.org/wiki/Antireligion>.

_____.2010tt. "Religious Persecution" (May 23). <http://en.wikipedia.org/wiki/Religious_persecution>.

_____.2010uu. "State Atheism" (May 23). <http://en.wikipedia.org/wiki/State_atheism>.

_____.2010vv. "The Philosophy of Nietzsche" (May 24). <http://en.wikipedia.org/wiki/Philosophy_of_Nietzsche>.

_____.2010ww. "The Antichrist (Book)" (May 24). <http://en.wikipedia.org/wiki/The_Antichrist_(book)>.

_____.2010xx. "Friedrich Nietzsche" (May 24). <http://en.wikipedia.org/wiki/Friedrich_Nietzsche>.

_____.2010yy. "The Will to Power" (February 12). <http://en.wikipedia.org/wiki/Will_to_power>.

_____.2010zz. "The Philosophy of Religion" (March 25). <http://en.wikipedia.org/wiki/Philosophy_of_religion>.

_____.2008. "Posthumanism" (October 20). <http://en.wikipedia.org/wiki/

Posthumanism>.

_____.2008a. "Transhumanism" (October 20). <http://en.wikipedia.org/wiki/Transhumanism>.

_____.2008b. "Lowest Common Denominator" (March 26). <http://en.wikipedia.org/ wiki/Least_common_denominator>.

_____.2008c. "Infinity" (November 11). <http://en.wikipedia.org/wiki/Infinity>.

_____.2008d. "Transfinite Number" (November 10). <http://en.wikipedia.org/wiki/Transfinite_ number>.

_____.2008e. "Quantum Mechanics" (November 26). <http://en.wikipedia.org/wiki/Quantum_mechanics>.

_____.2008f. "Copenhagen Interpretation" (November 26). <http://en.wikipedia.org/wiki/Copenhagen_interpretation >.

_____.2008g. "Many Worlds Interpretation" (November 26). <http://en.wikipedia.org/wiki/Many_Worlds_Interpretation>.

_____.2008h. "Hyperspace (Science Fiction)" (November 23). <http://en.wikipedia.org/wiki/Hyperspace_(science_fiction)>.

_____.2008i. "Time Travel" (November 26). <http://en.wikipedia.org/wiki/Time_travel#Time_dilation>.

_____.2008j. "Wormhole" (November 25). <http://en.wikipedia.org/wiki/Wormhole>.

_____.2007. "Linguistics" (March 04). <http://en.wikipedia.org/wiki/Linguistics>.

Wikiversity (WKV). 2008. "Why 10 Dimensions" (November 23). <ttp://en.wikiversity.org/wiki/Why_10_dimensions>

Wittgenstein, Ludwig.1953. *Philosophical Investigations*. G. E. M. Anscombe and R. Rhees, eds. G.E.M. Anscombe, tr. Oxford: Blackwell.

Wolpert, Lewis. 2006. *Six Impossible Things before Breakfast, The Evolutionary Origins of Belief.* New York: Norton.

Yong, Amos. 2005. "Buddhism and Science: Breaking New Ground (review)." *Buddhist-Christian Studies*, 25: 176-180.

INDEX

•A•

•B•

•D•

•E•

•F•

•G•

•H•